The Basics of Western Philosophy

THE BASICS OF WESTERN PHILOSOPHY

Eugene Kelly

Basics of the Social Sciences

GREENWOOD PRESS

Library of Congress Cataloging-in-Publication Data

Kelly, Eugene, 1941–
    The basics of western philosophy / Eugene Kelly.
      p. cm.
    Includes bibliographical references and index.
    ISBN 0–313–32352–6 (alk. paper)
    1. Philosophy—History. I. Title II. Series.
    B72.K43   2004
    190—dc22   2003061613

British Library Cataloguing in Publication Data is available.

Library of Congress Catalog Card Number: 2003061613
ISBN: 0–313–32352–6

First published in 2004

Greenwood Press, 88 Post Road West, Westport, CT 06881
An imprint of Greenwood Publishing Group, Inc.
www.greenwood.com

Printed in the United States of America

The paper used in this book complies with the
Permanent Paper Standard issued by the National
Information Standards Organization (Z39.48–1984).

10 9 8 7 6 5 4 3 2 1

In memory of my brother, Walter D. Kelly (1927–1996)

CONTENTS

Preface   xi

PART I: THE ACTIVITY OF PHILOSOPHY   **1**

Chapter 1: The Nature of Philosophy   **3**
Philosophy As Theory of Theories   5
Philosophy As the Search for Conceptual Clarity   6
Philosophy As the Search for a Better Way of Living   7
Philosophy in Education: The Allegory of the Cave   8

Chapter 2: Logic and Language   **13**
The Ideal of Reason   13
Formal Logic   14
Statements and Arguments   14
Truth-Functional Logic   17
Informal Logic   21
Criticizing Informal Arguments: The Premisses   22
Criticizing Informal Arguments: The Language   23
Criticizing Informal Arguments: The Warrant   24
Linguistic Analysis   27
The Technique of Analysis   27
Ethics and Linguistic Analysis: An Application   28

Chapter 3: A Sketch of the History of Philosophy   **31**
Why Philosophers Study the History of Philosophy   31
Ancient Philosophy   32
Before Philosophy   32
Pre-Socratic Philosophy   33

Contents

The Golden Age of Greek Philosophy 35
Greco-Roman Philosophy 37
Medieval Philosophy 41
Christian Philosophy at the Close of the Roman Empire 41
The High Middle Ages 44
The Modern World 45
The Early Modern Period 45
The Enlightenment 50
Rationalists and Empiricists 52
The Nineteenth Century 56
The Contemporary World 59
General Characteristics 59
Pragmatism 62
Logic and Language in the English-Speaking World 63
Philosophy on the European Continent 64

PART II: THE PROBLEMS OF PHILOSOPHY 67

Chapter 4: Metaphysics 69
Aristotle and the Problem of Being 69
The Early Greek Cosmologists 70
Plato and the Origin of Metaphysics 73
Aristotle 79
The Physical Make-up of a Substance 79
The Dynamics of Change 80
The Fixity of Things 82
Early Modern Metaphysics 84
Descartes 85
Dualism, Materialism, and Idealism 87
Metaphysics in Early Modern Great Britain 89
Locke 90
Hume 91
Kant and the Critique of Metaphysics 93
Hegel 96
Metaphysics in the Twentieth Century 98
The European Continent 98
Metaphysics in Great Britain and the United States 103
History and Metaphysics in the Twentieth Century 103

Chapter 5: Epistemology 105
The Problem of Knowledge in the Ancient World 105
The Challenge of Skepticism 108
The Tree in the Forest 108
Illusions 109
The Problem of Universals in the Middle Ages 110
The Modern Formulation of the Problem of Knowledge 112

Descartes: Rational Knowledge 112
Primary and Secondary Qualities 113
Locke: Empirical Knowledge 114
Hume and the Problem of Induction 115
Kant and Transcendental Idealism 118
Hegel and Absolute Idealism 121
Twentieth-Century Epistemology on the
European Continent 121
Hermeneutics and Historicism 122
Phenomenology 124
Contemporary Epistemology in the English-
Speaking World 125
Russell 125
The Influence of the Vienna Circle 127
Wittgenstein 127
Pragmatism 128
Metaphysics and Epistemology 131

Chapter 6: Ethics **133**
Moral Experience 134
The Subject Matter of Ethics 135
Choice 135
Freedom 135
Moral Relativism 137
Normative Ethics 139
Theories of Virtue 139
Rule-Based Ethics 145
Contemporary Issues in Ethics 165
Moral Skepticism 165
New Efforts in Moral Theory 166

Chapter 7: Social and Political Philosophy **177**
Theory of Justice: Characteristics 177
Plato: Justice As Harmony 179
Aristotle: The State and the Individual 184
Social and Political Philosophy in the Middle Ages 186
Saint Augustine 186
Saint Thomas Aquinas 187
Idealism and Realism: The Early Modern World 189
Thomas Hobbes 189
John Locke 193
Jean-Jacques Rousseau 197
The Nineteenth Century: Radicalism and Liberalism 204
Karl Marx 204
John Stuart Mill 210

Contents

Social and Political Philosophy in the
Twentieth Century   213
    Critical Theory   213
    Recent Social and Political Philosophy in
    the United States   217

Chapter 8: Philosophy of Religion   **225**
God and Philosophy   225
Defining the Concept of God   227
    The Uniqueness of God   227
    God's Omnipotence   227
    God's Eternity   228
    God As a Person   230
    God's Moral Nature   231
    The Euthyphro Question   231
    God's Purposes   233
    Divine Love   233
Arguments for God's Existence   234
    The Ontological Argument   235
    The Cosmological Argument   238
    The Teleological Argument   239
An Argument against God's Existence:
The Argument from Evil   241
God and Linguistic Philosophy   243

Chapter 9: Science and Human Nature   **247**
The Problem of Human Nature   247
    Evolution and Human Nature   248
    The Conflict between Science and Religion   250
The Scientific Approach to Human Nature   250
    Psychoanalysis   251
    Behaviorism   254
    The Problem of Free Will   256
    Genetics and Human Nature   258
    Neurophysiology and the Philosophy of Mind   260
A Humanist Approach to Human Nature: Existentialism   265
    The Absurdity of Human Existence   266
    Consciousness   267
    Freedom   270
    "Existence Precedes Essence"   271
    Dread, the Other, and Bad Faith   272
Postscript   274
Timeline   275
Bibliography   281
Index   289

PREFACE

The Basics of Western Philosophy is an introduction to Western philosophy. By *Western* we refer to the tradition of abstract or theoretical reasoning that began among the Greeks of Ionia after 585 B.C.E. and brought to a high level of sophistication by Plato and Aristotle in the fourth century B.C.E. Philosophers today trace the history of their subject, and the fundamental questions it raises, to those thinkers. The Western philosophical tradition can be contrasted with such systems of thought as that of Buddhism in East Asia, Confucianism in China, or Vedantic Hinduism in India.

This basic introduction to Western philosophy provides an easy access to the nature, processes, traditions, and problems of philosophy. It may be used by high-school students, undergraduates in colleges and universities, and by the general public. The book is divided in two parts. Part I is an overview of the activity of philosophy. The first chapter is an essay on the spirit of philosophy. Philosophy originally understood itself (1) as an effort to solve broad problems of human life, and (2) as a life of virtue, contemplation, analysis, and teaching. Its tradition of encouraging an exploration of unsolved intellectual problems has played a unique role in teaching and learning in the Western world. Chapter 2 studies the method of logical analysis invented by the Ancient Greeks and modified in the modern world. Chapter 3 concerns the philosophical traditions and offers a sketch of the history of philosophy from the earliest Greek thinkers in the sixth century B.C.E. to the philosophers working today.

Part II explores the problems of philosophy. Each of its chapters analyzes a central concept of philosophy: Being, Knowledge, Moral Goodness, Justice, God, and the Human Being. Chapter 4, on metaphysics, studies the problem of Being, whose origin is in the thought of Aristotle. Chapter 5 discusses epistemology, the theory of knowledge. Chapter 6, on ethics, discusses theories of right and wrong action, and describes some central problems of ethics today.

Chapter 7, on social and political philosophy, is concerned with the nature of justice and its applications to an understanding and criticism of existing forms of government. Chapter 8 discusses the philosophy of religion and considers arguments concerning the nature and existence of God. Chapter 9, on science and human nature, or philosophical anthropology, considers the phenomenon of the human being and the insights into our nature offered by recent biological, psychological, physiological, and philosophical theories. The individual chapters stand alone and can be read profitably without reference to the others.

The Basics of Western Philosophy contains many sidebars offering background material to the discussions in the text and capsule biographies of some of the philosophers studied. Words in bold in the text refer the reader to nearby sidebar topics. The book is illustrated by approximately fifteen photographs and sketches.

The book contains a timeline incorporating most of the greatest individual contributors to philosophy and schools of philosophy. The life spans of each contributor are coordinated with the watershed events in Western history. An extended bibliography is found at the end of the work. It lists easily available editions of works by the primary sources of philosophy, the philosophers themselves. Secondary works on the nature, problems, major figures, history of philosophy, and scholarly contributions to each of the six problems of philosophy discussed in this book are also listed in the bibliography. A star indicates those works that are accessible to introductory students.

The author wishes to thank the Perry-Casteñeda Library, Thoemmes Press, and the Library of Congress for permission to use its copies of the photographs. He also wishes to thank his students, friends, and colleagues at the New York Institute of Technology, where he has taught for the past twenty-six years, for their continuing support and encouragement of his teaching and research. Special thanks go also to his wife, Zuzana Kelly, who was always ready to help in the shaping and production of this work.

PART I

The Activity of Philosophy

CHAPTER 1

The Nature of Philosophy

This chapter discusses some characteristics of philosophy. The following topics will be considered:

- Philosophy As Theory of Theories
- Philosophy As the Search for Conceptual Clarity
- Philosophy As the Search for a Better Way of Living
- Philosophy in Education: Plato's Allegory of the Cave

The question of the nature of philosophy is itself a philosophical question. This truism does not mean that philosophy is an undefinable mystery, or that the definition of its nature "is up for grabs by anyone who wishes to call himself a philosopher. "What is philosophy?" is a philosophical question just because philosophy attempts to answer questions about the nature or **essence** of a thing or the meaning of a word. The meaning of the word *philosophy* has varied during the centuries, and yet its nature presents itself in the practices of those who exercise it. A theory of philosophy must account for as many different historical activities as possible that call themselves philosophical.

> **ESSENCE:** The nature or substance of a thing; what makes it what it is. Essence is opposed to *accident,* which describes what qualities a thing happens to possess. For example, the Greeks thought the essence of the human being was his reason. "Walks upright" or "has an opposable thumb" were considered accidents.

The derivation of the word *philosophy* reveals something of its nature. The term is said to have been coined by Pythagoras (582?–500? B.C.E.) from the word *philo,* that is love for or yearning for and *sophia,* that is, wisdom. To

René Descartes. © *National Library of Medicine.*

call yourself a "Sophist" implies that you think yourself wise. Now a person may be uncertain whether she truly possesses wisdom and correctly understands the nature of things, but she may be certain that she wishes to be wise. Perhaps for that reason Pythagoras and later Greeks called themselves lovers of wisdom. This key idea is that philosophy is not just the possession of understanding, but the loving search for it. Philosophy is different from the practical desire for knowledge, that is, knowledge that gives us power over nature and over other people. The impulse to philosophy comes from a desire to make the world a part of yourself, by grasping the whole of things, or even specific things, as they truly are. It may begin with a sense of vulnerability: a sense that *I may not be wise, may not know what I think I know.* With that uncertainty and that inspiration, the philosophical adventure begins. The philosophical spirit rejects the opinions of the crowd and begins its quest for knowledge by itself. It is always willing to learn from the past, but it judges for itself. It balances conflicting opinions if it cannot resolve them. It looks for new ways to express the nature of things as they present themselves to the mind's eye. The philosopher is willing to stand on his own feet intellectually and to scrutinize critically what he had up to then taken for granted, or accepted because everyone else does, or because they come with the authority of some book in the library. Philosophy is a quest that appears whenever people can liberate themselves from the pressure of tradition, and from authorities who suspect any new ideas of heresy.

The story of René Descartes (1596–1650) is inspiring in this regard. Descartes had gone to one of the best schools in France and had learned a lot about history and philosophy and law and the sciences of his times. Yet upon his graduation, he felt he had no guarantee that anything of what he had been taught was true. He had not examined things himself but simply taken what he was told about them on the authority of his teachers and their books. He resolved, therefore, to doubt everything that could be doubted until he arrived at rock-bottom truths that he could perceive clearly and distinctly, much as we perceive truths of mathematics. Only then could he hope to rebuild knowledge upon a firm foundation. What a liberating idea—to throw away one's books after college and *learn to see* for oneself!

Descartes's voyage of discovery was a very personal adventure. To characterize philosophy more generally, one can look at the kind of activities and their purposes in which philosophers have engaged. Five kinds of activities and purposes that are central to philosophy can be distinguished.

PHILOSOPHY AS THEORY OF THEORIES

Just because philosophy asks about the nature of things, it must ask about its own nature. In the so-called "hard" sciences, like physics or biology, or even mathematics, philosophy has attempted to play a regulating role by asking questions about the nature of mathematical objects, such as numbers, or causal laws, or the proper methods of inquiry in the sciences. Philosophers of science may ask questions about what kind of evidence is required to support adequately a thesis in the sciences, so that the thesis may lay claim to being true. Science cannot be concerned with evaluating the assumptions that it makes about the nature of the objects it probes, the nature of the inquiry itself, and the reasons a person may have for accepting the assertions of scientists as true. It is the task of philosophers of science to assess critically the strength and the logical coherence of these assumptions. This theorizing about theory is sometimes called *meta*science, a term that conveys the idea of being above or beyond science. Some philosophers have held that an analysis of these questions must take place *before* all science. How, they ask, can we expect the work of scientists to be intellectually acceptable if it lacks a secure philosophical foundation? Other thinkers have been willing to accept the work of scientists as independent of philosophy, and as advancing through the exercise of practically effective methods. These thinkers have confined themselves to the philosophical exploration of the scientific method and the activity of scientists in their laboratories and classrooms. Their intent is not metascientific, but *descriptive,* for they try to describe what scientists do, while the intent of critical metaphysics-science is *prescriptive,* for these philosophers set rules for scientists.

A similar situation is found in the branch of philosophy known as *ethics;* it too may be critical or descriptive, or both. Let us assume that the moral beliefs that most people accept as properly regulating their behavior toward other people—rules such as the Ten Commandments, which prohibit lying, stealing, murder, selfishness, and the like, or the requirements of virtue, such as courage, generosity, or love of one's neighbor—are generally valid. Philosophical ethics attempts to specify the *content* and the *foundations* of these moral systems. It seeks out possible conflicts in the rules, their application to concrete situations, and their justification as moral commands. Ethics may ask such questions as these: What should one do if telling lies in some situations could save a human life? Does capital punishment conflict with our sense of the sacredness of human life? What is the commandment "Do not commit adultery" based upon? The variety of possible answers to this last question is well-known. Some will say that adultery is wrong because it is against the will of God. Others will say that adultery is wrong if, and only if, it has harmful consequences. Still others will claim that the wrongness of adultery consists in the evil will of the adulterer, his or her selfishness, or lack of concern for obligations to others. Some may argue that adultery is not evil, but marriage is, or that adultery is not evil if both partners agree to it. From these activities and questions we see that it is the nature of philosophy to explore critically the foundations of human practices, such as science, politics, religion, or morality.

PHILOSOPHY AS THE SEARCH FOR CONCEPTUAL CLARITY

We can think of this first activity of philosophy, its description or critique of the assumptions of the sciences or morals, in a more general way. Philosophy is the search for conceptual clarity in all areas of life. The great example of this search is the life and activity of Socrates. Believing he had been charged by the god Apollo to examine his fellow Athenians to see if he were wiser than they, Socrates asked men with a reputation for wisdom about the concepts that were basic in the subject of their wisdom. It became apparent in each case that the wisdom and knowledge that these men claimed to possess came to nothing, for they were not able even to clarify the meanings of the terms they used. This requirement of conceptual clarity for what we today call professional expertise makes sense. A teacher, after all, should be able to give an account not just of what she teaches, but what it is to learn, and what things are worth teaching. Thus, in the early writings of Socrates's student, Plato, we read about how Socrates challenged a general to explain the notion of courage (*Laches*); challenged his friends about the nature of friendship (*Lysis*); asked a religious man about the nature of piety (*Euthyphro*); asked an actor about how he is able to move an audience (*Ion*). These dialogues are called *aporetic,* because they do not end with a satisfactory definition of the concept in question. The disputants eventually give up the search, and the dialogue ends with a sense of confusion and uncertainty. Plato leaves the reader with the sense that she has a lot of work to do to make sure that she has not allowed her own mind to be filled with the same sort of confusions to which Socrates's expert friends were subject.

Conceptual analysis has a practical import. Our minds are full of ideas, many of which we use in practical life to justify some course of action. Thus, Socrates's friend, General Laches, believes himself to be qualified to be a general. Moreover, he leads men into battle, tries to inspire them with courage, and is courageous himself. Yet he cannot state clearly just what courage is. Now if our ideas are not clear, then the practices we justify by means of them may be unsound. A scientist may refer to causal laws to explain phenomena but be unable to give a clear account of the notion of *cause,* or a psychologist may treat patients for some mental illness without being able to define thoroughly the nature of illness, or even of mind. A small child, on being told to go to his room as a punishment for some misbehavior may shout, "That's not fair!" without being able to give an adequate account of fairness. And, if he can't say what fairness is, how can he know that he is being treated unfairly? Similarly, a person may know many facts about the history of democracy in America, may know how democracy works (how we enact laws, for example); he may know how to live in a democracy (how to vote, how to find a lawyer). Yet that person may never have reflected upon what democracy is essentially, that is, upon the theory of democracy. That is a philosophical question. When we begin to reflect upon how complex familiar things really are, we are struck with wonder and curiosity, for, Aristotle once said, all philosophy begins in wonder.

PHILOSOPHY AS THE SEARCH FOR A BETTER WAY OF LIVING

Philosophy, like science, requires determination, intelligence, and the love of inquiry, and not just of learning. It also requires courage, for we have to rely upon the clarity of our own minds. Our minds are fallible, and prone to error. We often jump to conclusions without having examined the evidence, for example. We have all accepted many ideas as true that have turned out instead to be false, or confused, or we find ourselves unable to give an adequate account of them. The ancient Greeks noticed this component of courage in the philosophical life, and they tied it to another function of philosophy: the philosopher as the person trying to achieve the Good Life, a life of the kind of virtue and moral excellence that makes human flourishing possible. To achieve these ends, one must make philosophical practice a lifetime endeavor. One's efforts at conceptual analysis must have relevance to one's efforts to live well and happily. There is no virtue without knowledge, said Socrates, as he tried to convince his fellow Athenians that since their minds are demonstrably full of confusions and half-truths, their personal lives, lacking the guidance of knowledge, must also lack moral excellence. At his trial, Socrates made this point in a negative way. Whatever the outcome of the trial, he said, he will go on asking questions and practicing philosophy with each person he meets. "'My friend,' I will go on asking in my usual way, 'you are an Athenian, and belong to the city that is the greatest and most famous in the world for its wisdom and strength. Are you not ashamed that you spend your time pursuing such trivialities as acquiring as much wealth and reputation and honor as possible, and give no thought at all to knowledge, and understanding, and the perfection of your soul?'"

Today's philosophers may wonder whether "moral excellence" is a chimerical notion, or part of an unjustified political claim to privilege the authority of those said to possess it. Professional philosophers, it seems obvious, are not morally better men and women, in the main, than other people are. Perhaps we can say at least this much: philosophy is *intended* to have moral influence on its practitioners. It is pedagogical in its purpose, wherever it appears, for it requires persons desiring to be philosophers to have the courage and determination to think, and to think for themselves. That is the assumption behind requiring students to study philosophy at college; it is not simply another subject to learn but is a way of life that opens the mind and prepares it for the reception of ideals: the life of the mind, the life of reason, the lifetime of inquiry.

PHILOSOPHY IN EDUCATION: THE ALLEGORY OF THE CAVE

It is relatively easy to define any of the other subjects people learn at college—physics, say, or medicine, or criminal justice—in terms of its focus on *subject matter,* some consistent if evolving *methodology,* and some *practical purpose.* The practical purposes of the subjects mentioned might be flying to Mars, curing diseases, or establishing a reasonable and just means of dealing with crime. Philosophy, however, has no specific subject matter but ranges over conceptual problems in all fields. It has no consistent methodology but has developed many. Moreover, philosophy is not a *logy,* that is, a study of some phenomena (biology = study of *bios,* or life), but rather a love of understanding in general. Like all love it is impelled toward what it loves and tries to understand what it loves, so to possess it more firmly. And this passionate and tenacious desire for understanding may be turned upon the persons trying to understand the world. The Oracle at Delphi commanded, "Know thyself!" If knowledge is inspired by love, through philosophy we may come to know ourselves better, and if virtue is inspired by knowledge, then the study of philosophy may make us better persons, also.

Education, the training of young people in the accumulated knowledge of a culture, is said to have been made possible by the *discovery of the future.* Imagine the first human being who did not throw away a tool he had fashioned once had used it but saved it for some future occasion that he could visualize, although it was not then present to him. Eventually he would teach others how to make and use the tool he had created. The skill of toolmaking would become part of the cultural heritage of his tribe and could be passed on to the next generation. Civilizations require education to insure that each new person does not have to rediscover the techniques and inventions of a previous generation. In early antiquity, even at the highest levels of education, the teaching of literacy to scribes and priests was intended to meet the practical needs of the community for skilled workers; scribes could keep accounts and publish the king's orders, and priests could recite the prayers and rituals that the culture believed necessary for its continuing prosperity. The Greeks were the first people in history to have conceived of education as empowering the individual person, that is, as making him effective mentally, politically, and morally. To them, education had to provide for all of the earlier functions; they too needed competent scribes, priests, artisans, and farmers. However, their notion of education had two additional social purposes.

First, the Greeks were the first known people to practice democracy. This form of government, unlike all others, requires the participation of responsible citizens in government. These citizens must make and understand the laws. They must be made responsible to other citizens and be able to defend themselves in courts of law against accusations of having broken the laws and damaging civil society. Citizens must be able to develop and express opinions about the policies of the *polis*, the city-state, and its policies and activities. The practice of democracy is an education in itself. In debating public policy with other citizens, each citizen learns to think, to inquire, and to know. The first Greek private professional teachers were called *Sophists*. They trained young men in what we would today call language skills and trained minds for the effective participation in the give-and-take of democratic life.

POLIS: The Greeks, unlike most other people, were not subjects of a single king, or subject to the same form of government in each of their cities. The Greek-speaking people were divided politically. Each city was sovereign over its own territory and had a form of government peculiarly its own.

Second, at least since the time of the pre-Socratic philosophers, the Greeks speculated upon the human soul. Most early civilizations possessed an idea of a soul, which they usually conceived as a kind of breath of life that survived death and met a fate that varied widely in the beliefs of different cultures. The afterlife of the soul was at times thought of as a shadowlike existence in Hades, or as a return to a place where the deceased would meet members of his family who had already passed on, or as a kind of holding-pen where souls were kept while awaiting their rebirth in a new body. The Greeks made a decisive addition to these notions. They came to think of the soul as the principle of the unique individual. It is at the seat of human character, and the ground of the possibility of our awareness of our own existence. This soul became the object of higher education. Education released a person's soul from its immersion in the physical and mental environment into which it had been born and prepared the person to think in a new way about a new kind of object. Socrates told his fellow Athenians to "care for their souls." They should turn their thoughts away from the changing individual things of this world and look into the nature of things. From this new standpoint the soul can examine the nature of things rather than study their practical uses, and obtain the knowledge that perfects the soul. The Greeks called the state of cultivation of the soul that is fostered by education *paideia*. A society needs doctors, engineers, lawyers, and barbers, no doubt, but it also needs men and women who will bring the force of their unique personalities to these practical tasks: They must not simply be trained but cultivated, not simply educated but enlightened, not simply doctors or lawyers, but individuals.

The idea that education can and must produce enlightened individuals for the sake of the *polis* was expressed by Plato in his Allegory of the Cave,

Plato. © *Library of Congress.*

which appears in his great work, *The Republic.* The Allegory expresses in symbolic form many of Plato's views on metaphysics and epistemology. Its primary purpose is to make visible the difference between the philosophically educated person and the person who is not so enlightened and has not come to understand the nature of the objects and events that he sees with his senses. Plato's Socrates tells his friends to imagine men in an underground cave. They have been chained to a wall in this cave since birth and can look only in one direction, straight before them. Unknown to them, above and behind them is a walkway upon which men walk carrying objects of all kinds. Behind these bearers is a fire, and the light of the fire casts shadows of the objects carried by the men upon the far wall. These shadows are the only things the prisoners can see; the shadows are their world, and when they speak to each other, they speak about the shadows and give them names.

If one of them should be released from his chains and forced to stand up and gaze at the bearers of objects and at the fire behind them, he would feel pain in his long-unused legs. The light of the fire would blind his eyes. If he were forced to make the long, arduous climb out of the cave, he would go unwillingly. When he arrived outside the cave, he would again be able to see nothing, so blinded would he be by the light of the sun. Yet in time, his eyes would grow accustomed to the light. He would first be able to see the shape of objects in the moonlight, then their colors in the reflections in the lake or under the shade of a tree. Finally, he would be able to see the objects themselves, of which before he had seen only the shadows, in the full light of the sun. Perhaps someday, Socrates adds, he would be able to gaze upwards toward the sun itself, which Plato calls the image of all being and the source of all knowledge. If this man were to return to the cave and attempt to enlighten his fellow prisoners about the world outside the cave, they would think him mad. If he persisted in his efforts to enlighten them, then, if they could get their hands on him, they would surely kill him.

This is a very pessimistic conclusion. It expresses Plato's conviction that most men and women will never escape their prejudices and blindness and become philosophers. The chains of darkness and, perhaps, simple intellectual laziness and dishonesty tie them to the current opinions of their fellows as to what is true and false, and what is worthy of esteem and what not. Yet Plato believed in higher education, at least for the few people who show a capacity for it. They are the people who possess not just what we today call intelligence, but possess the emotional attitude we spoke of earlier: the love of knowledge for its own sake, and the desire to take part in the world by understanding, through inquiry, as much of it as one can.

All higher education today is based on Plato's idea that some of us can pass from *seeing* to *understanding,* from a *practical* grasp of how things work to a *theoretical* understanding of their nature. There is nothing terribly complex or mysterious about this idea. A person knows in a certain sense that a cup is on the table next to him as he writes; he knows what it is for, where you purchase such things, why you should choose it and not a glass tumbler to hold coffee. Yet his training may fail him in his efforts to understand it. It has a cylindrical shape, but unless he has studied solid geometry, he would not be able to grasp its structure; he may think it is made of ceramic, but, unless he has studied pot-making, he could not say much about how it was shaped, fired, glazed, or how the handle was attached to it. He knows, if only because he has heard people say so, that the material it is made of can be resolved into molecules, and those into atoms, and those into still finer stuff; but if he has not studied chemistry and atomic physics, he could not say much at all about those matters. It seems that this person is in a rather deep cave of ignorance even for such an everyday object as a cup! But if he has both aptitude and desire, he could make the long arduous climb out of the cave of ignorance about geometric shapes, ceramic materials and techniques, and physical matter, and understand the theories governing these things.

This philosophical education that leads from appearance to reality is essentially different from elementary and secondary education. Children are given skills and knowledge, but are not considered to be sufficiently mature and autonomous to interpret the meaning of their new knowledge and to apply their new skills on their own. Philosophy, which is rarely taught before college, takes us to a new standpoint for inquiry. It demands autonomy of us, for each of us is to defend his or her opinions. Success in this great adventure of autonomous inquiry does not require so much the transmission of facts, but moral and mental discipline, or the determination to inquire into what is yet unseen: the nature, the structure, and the principles of things. The students in this way make new use of the skills of careful reading, rational thinking, and clear writing that they learned as children in school, and learn to inquire by themselves.

There is a course in college, usually taught by philosophers, that comes before a serious intellectual encounter with philosophy, its problems, and its history. That course is called logic. In the following chapter, we will consider some principles and techniques of logical analysis, the justification of claims to knowledge, and the analysis of the language we use to make those claims. Many educators think that logic is the most important course offered at college, indeed, the presupposition of all independent theoretical work. A brief study of logic will prepare the reader for the analysis of philosophical theories in Part II of this book.

CHAPTER 2

Logic and Language

THE IDEAL OF REASON

Would anyone think of a scientist in her laboratory and an economics professor writing a book about business cycles as idealists? Of course, in their personal conduct, such people may be far from idealistic, and they may believe that no matter how hard they work, success is a matter of luck or of unfair advantages. But in one way they are idealists: They believe that if they keep at their research, they will be rewarded by understanding something about the world. This ideal assumes that the world is knowable, either as a whole, or at least in part. It holds that persons are not doomed to total ignorance about the world, although parts of it may be forever beyond their grasp. Those parts that are knowable, these idealists believe, are not a hopeless jumble of unrelated facts possessing no order or structure. One fact may relate to another fact, and one event in the world may be logically or causally connected to others. To know is to have evidence for claims about these structures and interconnections. Surely, the idealist believes, some parts of the world can be adequately known, if only we are diligent and logical in the pursuit of knowledge.

Science is not as generous to its practitioners as it may seem. Often a bit of insight is the reward of a lifetime of labor in the service of the Ideal of Reason, and thinking is hard work. Moreover, the pursuit of this ideal goes against the natural inclination to accept the beliefs that we have learned at school or in our daily newspaper. Many of the greatest thinkers have experienced moments when they despaired of ever truly knowing anything at all, when the world seemed to them to have no rational order at all, and when all their learning and supposed wisdom appeared to be only foolishness. No doubt the denial of a rational order to things may be partial. A person may claim that we have genuine knowledge of the physical world in physics, but that, for example, a rational theology or a thoroughgoing rational psychology is impossible, because, in the first case, the human mind is not equipped to penetrate the mysteries of God, if such a being exists, or, in the second case, human behavior is caused in part by human beings' free and unpredictable will.

Wherever the Ideal of Reason is practiced, however, it is assumed that the world possesses a rational order and the mind can know something about it. The desire for knowledge leads these idealists on. They argue in favor of the theories and beliefs that they have developed through thought and research. They give reasons for their beliefs, and they expect others to do the same. They are willing to listen to counterarguments and to reasons for beliefs different from their own. They try to judge, given opposing arguments about the same subject matter, which of many arguments is the stronger, or the truer. This concern with the question of whether any given argument can be shown to be *conclusive,* or at least stronger than any known counterargument, gave rise to the science of logic.

The chapter is divided in three parts:

- Formal Logic
- Informal Logic
- Linguistic Analysis

FORMAL LOGIC

Statements and Arguments

Logic is the study of arguments. An *argument* is a set of statements, one of which is asserted to be true *because* the others are true. The statement whose truth follows from the truth of the others is called the *conclusion* of the argument. The other statements are its *premisses. Statements* are sentences that have the capacity of being either true or false. Some sentences do not have that capacity. For example, "Please close the door" is neither true nor false and hence is not a statement. The kinds of statement first analyzed by logicians were *categorical* statements, where a **class** of properties is predicated of a substance or class of substances. Statements can be about a particular thing or a single member of a class, as in "George W. Bush is a president of the United States." This proposition asserts that a specific man is a member of the class of American presidents. Statements can also be about all members of a class, such as "All dogs are mammals," where the class of dogs is the subject, and the class of mammals the predicate. "All objects in free fall near the surface of the Earth accelerate uniformly at the rate of $32f/s^2$" predicates the quality of accelerating uniformly at the rate of $32f/s^2$ of the class of bodies in free fall near the surface of the Earth.

CLASSES: The imaginary collection of objects that possess some common property, such as the class of shoes or the class of red things. General terms denote classes of objects.

Aristotle. © *National Library of Medicine.*

An argument is required whenever a person is asked, "Why do you believe that statement A is true?" The conclusion of the argument—the statement asserted to be true because the other statements are true—is statement A; the premisses of the argument are the reasons given for the belief that the conclusion is true. A *deductive* argument is one in which the conclusion follows necessarily from the premisses (if the premisses are true, then the conclusion must be true). Something about the way the premisses are related to each other and to the conclusion necessitates the truth of the conclusion if the premisses are true. An *inductive* argument asserts that the conclusion is probably true if the premisses are. That is, in an inductive argument the premisses give the reasons why one may believe that the conclusion is likely to be true, perhaps more likely than any other available conclusion.

Aristotle (384–322 B.C.E.) was the first to describe the typical structures of arguments. His set of treatises on this subject, *The Organon,* begins with a description of categories, or the kinds of predicates the subject of a statement may have. He discovered that there are ten categories, that is, ten different kinds of things about a subject or class of subjects: It may possess substance (Socrates), quantity (5′ 8″ tall), relation (taller than Plato), quality (just, healthy), activity (is speaking), passivity (is being spoken to), position (sitting), temporality (at noon), place (in the agora), and state (wearing shoes). Through the act of predication, we assert something: We say about Socrates that he is wearing shoes, for example. In this way, one of the phenomena in which is the idea of truth appears, for it is either true or false to say of Socrates that he is shod. This statement is true, Aristotle believed, if Socrates is wearing shoes. Aristotle then distinguished four ways in which a category can be predicated of another; we can predicate mortality (a quality) of humankind (a class of substances) *universally* or *particularly, positively* or *negatively:* "All men are mortal"; "No men are mortal"; "Some men are mortal"; "Some men are not mortal." Clearly there are logical implications discoverable among such statements. For example, if "All men are mortal" is true, then "Some men are not mortal" must be false; if "No men are mortal" is false, then "No mortals are men" must also be false, and the like. Such relations are called *immediate* implications. Where two categorical statements function as the premises of an argument, and the conclusion is a categorical statement, we have what is called a *categorical syllogism.* Such syllogisms are said to be *valid* if it is not possible for the premises to be true and the conclusion false. The most famous example of a categorical syllogism is

	All men are mortal	(Premiss 1)
	Socrates is a man	(Premiss 2)
Therefore,	Socrates is mortal	(Conclusion)

Something about the structure of this argument or the way it is put together makes it impossible for the premises to be true and the conclusion false. In the *Organon,* Aristotle undertakes a formal analysis of the structures of all such arguments without regard for their content. *Syllogistic logic* provides us with a set of standards of validity for arguments having this form, and a set of techniques for deciding, given any argument in the form, whether those standards have been met. In the past two centuries, these ideas have been developed under the title of *truth-functional logic.*

Any statement is either true or false. Some statements are simple, that is, they describe some aspect of the world either correctly or incorrectly.

Jack went up the hill

describes a state of affairs. We may not know whether in fact the statement is true—whether this Jack did in fact go up the hill at some given time, but we do know that our simple statement is either true *or* false—there is no other possibility.

Again, some statements are complex, that is, they contain more than one simple statement:

Jack went up the hill and Jill went up the hill

Of course, this statement is either true or false also. But note that its truth or falsity will be a function of the truth or falsity of the simple statements that make it up. Only *if* "Jack went up the hill" is true, *and* if "Jill went up the hill" is true, will "Jack went up the hill and Jill went up the hill" be true. Now since "Jack went up the hill" may be true or false, and "Jill went up the hill" may also be true or false, there are exactly four possibilities of the truth and falsity of both simple statements with respect to one another. If we abbreviate, we can easily show these four possibilities in a table. "A" will stand for the simple statement "Jack went up the hill" and "B" for the simple statement "Jill went up the hill." Then

(1)   either   A is true and B is true
(2)   or   A is true and B is false
(3)   or   A is false and B is true
(4)   or   A is false and B is false.

According to the usual meaning of *and,* only in the first case (1) will A and B be true; in the other cases it is false.

Truth-Functional Logic

Truth-functional logic begins with a definition of such *operators* as *and.* It defines their meaning in terms of how they determine the **truth** or falsity of the complex statements in which they appear. The definitions state the way in which the *truth* of a complex statement is a function of the simple statements that make it up. We can simplify the above table, which defines the meaning of "and" by substituting "T" for "true" and "F" for "false," and further by substituting the dot "·" for "and." The result, in table form, will be as follows:

Figure 2.1

	A	B	A · B
(1)	T	T	T
(2)	T	F	F
(3)	F	F	F
(4)	F	F	F

Such a table is called a *truth-table* definition of (A · B). It will enable us to see more clearly the structure of truth-functional arguments in which such complex statements as "A · B" appear. For example, it follows from the above definition of the operator *and* that the truth of "Jack went up the hill" follows from the truth of "Jack went up the hill and Jill went up the hill." If the compound "A · B" is true, then the atomic statement "A" must be true.

TRUTH: "What is truth?" is often given as an example of a question in philosophy. Philosophy is thought of by many people as a futile subject, for it asks unanswerable questions, as this one is assumed to be. Although the concept of truth has never been given an entirely satisfactory analysis, philosophers have made some progress in clarifying it. An example of such attempts is the *correspondence theory of truth* (and its variant, the *semantic* theory of truth, developed in this century by Russell, Carnap, Tarski, and others). It holds that truth consists in the *relationship* between language (some statement) and the world (some state of affairs that the statement is about). There is truth when some statement corresponds to some state of affairs. Of course, philosophers must clarify what is meant by a *state of affairs* and how it is possible for a linguistic entity to *correspond* to something *in the world*. But this theory gives us some understanding of why we say "Jack went up the hill" and is true if and only if our Jack did go up the hill we have in mind.

Some complex statements are of the following kind:

If Harry Truman is president of the United States, then he is commander in chief of the armed forces of the United States.

These complex statements are called hypotheticals. There are many kinds of **hypothetical statements**. In logic, the kind known as *material implication* is studied. Material implications assert that the truth of the simple statement, "Truman is President of the United States" (let us call that statement C), is a sufficient condition of the truth of the simple statement, "Truman is commander in chief of the armed forces in the United States" (let us call that statement D).

Again, there are four possibilities:

(1)   either   C is true and D is true
(2)   or   C is true and D is false
(3)   or   C is false and D is true
(4)   or   C is false and D is false.

Logicians normally substitute the horseshoe ⊃ for the operation involved in material implication. The operation is defined, then, in the following truth-table

Figure 2.2

	A	B	A ⊃ B
(1)	T	T	T
(2)	T	F	F
(3)	F	T	T
(4)	F	F	T

HYPOTHETICAL STATEMENTS: Note that not all statements of the form "if . . . then . . . " are *hypothetical* statements. If one says, "if you have a headache, then you ought to take an aspirin," one is not asserting that the truth of your having a headache is a condition of the truth of the statement, "you ought to take an aspirin." Rather, one is suggesting what you ought to do. Hypotheticals are always *truth-functional:* the truth of the if-statement (called the *antecedent*) is a sufficient condition of the truth of the then-statement (called the *consequent*). A hypothetical does not assert that if the if-statement is false, then the then-statement must be false: take for example the hypothetical statement, "if this dog is a horse, then this dog has four legs." The antecedent may be false (the dog is not a horse) and yet the consequent may be true (this dog has four legs). The hypothetical statement asserts only that if the antecedent is true, then the consequent is true.

This is, of course, simply a definition; it is stipulated by logicians and does not conform to our everyday sense of hypothetical statements. It does seem strange that a hypothetical statement is considered true even if the C statement is false. Causal statements are an obvious example of this problem.

If blue litmus paper is put in an acid, it will turn red

would not be considered true if no one ever put blue litmus paper in acid. But the hypothetical statement asserts only what will happen if blue litmus paper is put in acid; it does not refer to cases in which no blue litmus paper is added to acid. And so the logician considers cases 3 and 4 to be true cases of C ⊂ D. In fact, our above hypothetical about Truman is true, even though Truman is not president at this time, and it would still be true if we substituted John Doe for Truman.

Negation is another typical operation in formal logic and in everyday language. We remember that "Jack went up the hill" is a statement, that is, a sentence that is either true or false. If the statement is true, then

Jack did not go up the hill, or It is not the case that Jack went up the hill

is false, and if

Jack went up the hill

is false, then

It is not the case that Jack went up the hill

is true.

Substituting, again, "A" for "Jack went up the hill, and using the tilde "~" for its negation, "~A," we get the truth-table

Figure 2.3

	A	~A
(1)	T	F
(2)	F	T

This truth-table definition is of the operation of negation, and, as in the earlier cases, it displays how the truth or falsity of the statement "~A" is a function of the truth or falsity of the statement "A."

Here is a simple syllogism in truth-functional form:

$A \supset B$
A
Therefore B

Some logic textbooks refer to any argument having this form as an example of a rule or axiom of truth-functional logic. The rule has the name *modus ponens,* and it serves to justify any specific argument having this form. We can see from the truth-table for the operator "⊂" that this argument-form is valid. For there is no case in which both "A ⊂ B" and "A" are true and "B" is false. That is all an argument requires for it to be valid: It is not possible for the premisses to be true and the conclusion false. The argument may nonetheless be *unsound* if in fact one of the premisses is false. Thus the argument, "If a person is a Frenchman, then that person is an Asian; Jean is a Frenchman, therefore Jean is an Asian," is a substitution-instance of the valid argument-form called *modus ponens,* but it is unsound because at least one of its premisses, "If a person is a Frenchman, then that person is an Asian," is false.

This section has given us the beginnings of a logical language from which all material content has been abstracted. Instead of considering particular simple and complex statements and their truth-functional relations, we are able to consider truth-functional relations alone, by substituting "A," "B," and "C" for specific statements, or even more abstractly, symbols such as "p," "q," and "r" for any statements whatever. These latter symbols are called *sentential variables.* Such a language has the purpose of allowing us to see logical relations more clearly and thus to analyze and evaluate the thinking that underlies specific arguments. Moreover, truth-functional logic is capable of great extension and can be made into a very flexible instrument for the analysis of arguments or conceptual relationships in most fields by the addition of definitions of further operations and by what are called axioms, or the grammatical rules of a logical language.

INFORMAL LOGIC

The goal of the science of logic is to distinguish a good argument from a bad argument. It describes neither how people think in fact (that would be the subject matter of psychology), nor how people must think (there are no laws of thought; if there were, people could not reason poorly), but rather how people *ought* to think for the Ideal of Reason to have a chance of success.

The techniques of deductive analysis are useful when one attempts to evaluate the arguments in the natural sciences and in mathematics. Yet not all arguments possess a deductive structure and can be given a truth-functional form. Some arguments are not deductive but **inductive**, that is, they provide grounds for their conclusions that are only probable. To evaluate an inductive argument is to give reasons for judging the argument to be plausible or implausible, rather than valid or invalid by virtue of its structure, as with deductive arguments. The logician will have to provide us with different techniques for analyzing and criticizing arguments of a more informal or inductive type.

INDUCTION: Some logicians define induction more narrowly than is done here. They may identify it with (1) the process of hypothesis-formation in scientific discovery, where the scientist goes from an observation of disparate facts to a tentative solution to some perplexing problem, or (2) with a type of inference in which conclusions are drawn about a class of entities on the basis of a set of observations of members of the class—as when we make claims about the properties common to all stars on the basis of a close study of limited numbers of them. This latter process is called *inductive generalization*. Induction is defined here so as to include not only arguments typical of the sciences, but of everyday life—indeed we characterize as inductive any argument whose warrant is not of the deductive type.

Analysis begins by breaking arguments into their component elements. The components we will be most interested in are those that are vulnerable to controversy. These are the critical points where it is most easy for errors and confusion to conceal themselves. We can distinguish three such critical points in an argument, whether deductive or inductive.

The first is the truth or falsity of the premises: If it can be shown that any of the premises are false, the plausibility of the argument is decreased. In valid deductive arguments, the falsity of the premises renders the argument unsound.

Second, the language used in the argument may be vague or ambiguous: If it can be shown that there is a shift in meaning of any of the terms used in the argument, the entire argument will have to be reassessed. Until the vagueness or the ambiguity can be eliminated or resolved, the argument must be considered implausible.

Third, the warrant for the conclusion may be inadequate. In deductive logic, the "warrant" is the formal rule intended to justify the claim that the premisses support the conclusion. The argument-form identified as *modus ponens* is an example of such a warrant. In informal logic, the warrant may be more nebulous and difficult to identify. The warrants of these informal arguments do not depend on a purely formal structure.

Criticizing Informal Arguments: The Premisses

Logic, as such, is not concerned with the truth or falsity of premisses. Questions of fact must be resolved by observation, and the logician has to concern himself only with the extent to which the premisses, if true, support their conclusion. Logic is not science. When a historian attempts to draw conclusions as to the levels of agriculture in ancient Carthage, he may include in his premisses the claim that the level of rainfall in antiquity in North Africa was 30 percent higher than at the present time. The logician cannot argue this point; she simply assumes it to be true and then examines the degree to which it supports the conclusion.

Still, a logician must be concerned for the quality of the evidence provided for the truth of the premisses. A premiss may be thought true because it is warranted by another argument, of which it is the conclusion. But then the logician must ask what is the warrant for the previous argument and its premisses, and so on. We can be confident that an argument is sound only if the premisses stand on a firm foundation. Today it seems clear that the hypotheses of the empirical sciences admit to no deductive proof and hence are always open to new challenges. Caution is called for and there is no guarantee of certainty. But it is always reasonable in an inquiry to ask the author of an argument upon what he bases his confidence in his premisses.

A further philosophical question that appears here is that of legitimate sources of knowledge. Many claimants to the title of a legitimate source of knowledge can be named. They include *common sense, clear and evident insight, experience, sensory perception, intuition, expert authority, testimony of eyewitnesses,* or *established tradition.* Those who pursue the Ideal of Reason frequently endeavor to establish an order among these modes of knowledge, such that, in case of a disagreement as to fact, the evidence obtained by means of the higher mode would be granted greater plausibility. What does one believe, if one's experience contradicts the authority of one's tradition, or if the purported discoveries of science (the paradoxes generated by relativity theory, for instance) contradict the testimony of one's senses?

Consider the following argument:

It is by no means surprising that higher forms of civilization should have developed later in sub-Saharan Africa than elsewhere. For the conditions of trade and commerce, two of the most effective spurs to the growth of civilization were absent there. Southern Africa has no navigable rivers that might afford an easy means of shipping goods from tribe to tribe, and pack animals could not be used due to the presence of the tsetse fly, which is debilitating to both man and beast.

The conclusion of this argument is: "It is not surprising that higher forms of civilization appeared later in sub-Saharan Africa than elsewhere." There are three major factual considerations advanced as premisses. The first premiss is, "Commerce and trade are spurs to the development of civilization." This appears to be claimed as a universal truth about human history, for the writer does not say that trade and commerce are usually or "most often" or "sometimes" spurs to civilization. However, his use of the word *spurs* is considerably less forceful than "cause" or "sufficient condition." It leaves open the possibility that civilization could rise without these spurs and suggests only that its development would not be as rapid. The evidence in favor of this relation between trade and commerce and the rise of civilization is, of course, nowhere stated; the author apparently assumes that common sense coupled with a minimum of knowledge of human history will serve to convince his reader of the truth of his claim.

The second premiss is: "Commerce and trade were inhibited by the absence of navigable rivers." The third premiss is: Commerce and trade were inhibited by the presence of the tsetse fly." The first premiss describes a universal state of affairs; no reference is made to Africa in it. The second and third premisses are descriptive of conditions obtaining specifically in sub-Saharan Africa, that part of the world mentioned in the conclusion. But what do the third and the second premisses have to do with the first? They describe the conditions that make sub-Saharan Africa a case of the universal state of affairs described in the first premiss; they support the conclusion by giving particular facts about a situation, which qualifies it to be considered a case of a more general fact. Now the particular facts mentioned in the second and third premisses are themselves supported by evidence mentioned in the argument. The second premiss is given support by the further assertion that navigable rivers provide an easy means of transporting goods, and the third premiss by the further assertion that the tsetse fly is debilitating to pack animals. Such facts give the conclusion indirect support; they support it insofar as they support the premisses.

In sum, several questions may be asked about the facts cited by the premisses. What is the evidence in their favor? And what is the relation each fact has to the others? Is evidence given in support of the premisses, and what is the nature of that evidence? Are any of the premisses more general than others? Is the conclusion given indirect support by considerations advanced in support of the premisses?

Criticizing Informal Arguments: The Language

The second mode of criticizing informal arguments concerns the clarity of the language used in the argument. No general rules enable us to judge upon the truth or falsity of premisses, and no general rules allow us to decide when the language used in the argument is misleading. Yet the logician can make some distinctions that will help us in deciding some cases. A *substantive* concept is one referring to or denoting classes of properties common to some objects.

"Cup" refers to the class of things that are cups; "young" refers to the class of things that are young. In the case of those concepts that are vague, we find ourselves unable to be certain as to which objects make up the class. For example, it is very difficult to decide which governments belong to the class of "democracy." An ambiguous term, on the other hand, refers to more than one class of objects, such as the terms *spirits* (= ghosts *or* distilled beverages) or *record* (= a collection of data *or* analog recording for a phonograph).

Most terms that are vague or ambiguous are obviously so, and it is easy to guard against the confusions they inject into arguments. But this is not always the case. Where there is uncertainty, the person who wrote the argument may be called upon to give a *precising definition,* that is, a definition of the disputed term as he intends to use it in the context of his argument. Thus a person may define *democracy* as the term was used in ancient Athens, or as it does in fact or ought to define the political practices in our own society. In this way, many disputes about words may be ended.

But not all such disputes are simply about words. Some arguments involve terms that are more systematically ambiguous, that is, that vary with the traditions and beliefs of the speaker. A precising definition will not resolve many disputes about words, for what is at stake is not simply the legitimate *uses* of the term, but the nature of the entity designated by it—and this may not be easily determinable. Such disputes are thus not merely verbal, they are substantive, and resist clarification by merely linguistic means.

The most frequently encountered logical error arising out of the misuse of words is that of composition, or its counterpart, division. This error involves the uncritical assumption that terms properly referring to a member of a class must also refer to the class itself (composition), or the reverse (division). For example, it does not follow from the fact that each member of an all-star baseball team is an excellent player that the team as a whole is an excellent one. Teams are not just aggregates of players, they are made up of players who have learned to play together. To argue otherwise would be as absurd as to assume that because each part of a machine is light in weight, the machine as a whole must be light in weight. The rule here is that *aggregates may have different properties from the sum of the properties of their parts.* Of course they may have the same properties: if each part of a machine is green, the machine as a whole will be green. The point is that we cannot assume that to be so in all cases. Logic does not provide us with a warrant for inferring properties pertaining to the whole from properties pertaining to the part, or vice versa. If it is shown that a term has shifted in meaning or reference as one goes from the premisses to the conclusion, the argument will lose its initial plausibility.

Criticizing Informal Arguments: The Warrant

The third and last means of criticizing an informal argument concerns the nature of the warrant. An argument, as defined earlier, is a group of statements about which it is claimed that one of them is true because the others are true. It is the varying nature of this *because* that must now be considered. Why should one accept a given statement as true because one accepts certain other statements as true? In the case of deductive arguments the warrant is a rule (such as *modus ponens*) or set of rules of an accepted logical language that justify the transition from one set of statements to another. In informal logic it is impossible to specify a unique set of rules that warrant the conclusion of an argument. Yet two important criteria of successful warrants can be specified: the *relevance* of the premisses to the conclusion, and the *degree of sufficiency* of the premisses.

The general form of all rules concerning relevance is *nothing must appear in the conclusion that is not contained in the premisses.* If a person argues that there should be some form of national health insurance in the United States because such programs have always proven beneficial in other countries, she must also establish that conditions in the United States relevant to health care are similar to conditions in those countries where systems of national health insurance are already found. Otherwise, she cannot claim that her general premiss (health care has always proven beneficial in other countries) is relevant to this new case, that of the United States. In order to judge the plausibility of the argument, therefore, it must also be considered how similar the conditions in the United States are to conditions in those countries in which national health insurance has been instituted; and that is to raise the question of sufficiency. When the evidence supporting the conclusion seems insufficient, we can choose to suspend judgment, or to seek out a better argument. Yet the more that the person who argues in support of national health insurance for Americans can show relevant similarities between conditions in the United States and conditions in countries where systems of national health insurance are already established, the stronger the argument becomes.

How strong might she make her argument? Or, to put the question in the language of the law court, when, if ever, is the truth of a conclusion established beyond a reasonable doubt? No matter how many relevant similarities between the United States and other nations that have health insurance, our health-care advocate could never be sure that she has not overlooked some relevant dissimilarity—that is, one that would cause national health insurance to have disastrous, rather than beneficial, consequences in this country.

The argument about civilization in sub-Saharan Africa can also be studied for its sufficiency. The relevance of the premisses to the conclusion can again be established by reference to the parallel deductive argument form, *modus ponens:* We are given a general fact, and an effort is made to show that the conditions in sub-Saharan Africa justify the conclusion that those conditions are an example of the generalization. Even if it could be shown that the generalization is universally true, it could nonetheless be true either that trade and commerce were not absent in sub-Saharan Africa (the premisses do not assert that they were absent, just that there could have been no trade and commerce via rivers or beasts of burden), or that higher civilization did not develop for some other reasons, such that even if navigable rivers and healthy beasts of burden had been available, trade and commerce and thus higher civilization would not have developed. Again, the premises do not exclude that possibility, nor is it possible to exclude all alternative possibilities.

Nonetheless, the argument as stated has a certain **plausibility**. Its author might respond to the above objections by asking: "All right, if there was trade and commerce in sub-Saharan Africa throughout history, how would goods have been transported? Or if there are causes for the failure of civilization to take off that are more important, because they encompass and imply the absence of trade and commerce, what are they? And why should I believe (= what are your reasons for asserting) that claims about such matters are true?" In this way, the person defending the argument turns his efforts from amassing facts in support of his view to an attack upon alternative explanatory arguments, which he attempts to reject as irrelevant or as insufficient. The argument then takes an adversarial form, where each side tries to give the strongest support to the conclusion it favors. As in a court of law, the truth must be arrived at by considering the relative merits of conflicting claims, but, unlike the law court, the argument need not be restricted to two opposing possibilities, as in criminal or civil cases. For there may be any number of ways of accounting for the failure of civilization to take off in sub-Saharan Africa.

PLAUSIBILITY: Some philosophers and logicians have suggested that it ought to be possible to assign numerical values to the probabilities asserted by inductive arguments, such that the probability of the truth of a deductive argument, given the truth of the premises, is 1. Thus we would be able to state, "The probability of the truth of claim A given the truth of the evidence claims P, Q, R . . . is x.." In some cases such clear-cut evaluations might be possible; however, it appears that a certain subjective component in the evaluation of informal arguments is unavoidable. Some persons are convinced by an argument, while others are not. Even where it can be shown that the probability of a given conclusion relative to a certain body of evidence is, say, 0.8, some persons will be ready to accept the conclusion as a basis for action, whereas others will not. We all know that people will go on picnics even if the weatherman says the probability of rain is 80 percent. On such occasions the logician can do little more than point out the strengths and weaknesses of the argument and the likelihood of the conclusion, and leave conviction or disbelief, action or inaction, to the individual.

Logicians apply the following four criteria to the assessment of kinds of informal argument. They may help one judge whether a given informal argument is sufficient to command belief.

First, in the case of conclusions asserting *causal* claims: Does the claim *allow us to predict events of a different type than those referred to in the premisses?* Does it suggest further investigations that would bear upon the truth or falsity of the conclusion? Clearly, the more such predictions hold true, the more plausible is the causal claim made in the conclusions.

Second, *how many factual claims are made in the premises, and how well established are they?* The plausibility of a universal claim will vary with the amount of information given in the premises. If you wish to claim that black cats bring bad luck, you had better support your claim with as many specific instances of black-cat induced bad luck as possible, and they ought to involve different cats, different people, and different sorts of bad luck!

Third, *how well does the conclusion cohere with what we already know about the subject?* Coherence refers to the degree to which the claim made by the conclusion is supported (or fails to find support) by other, related facts. Our claim about black cats does not cohere well with what we think we know about the causes of bad luck (carelessness, drunkenness, defective implements) and is for that reason rendered less plausible.

Fourth, in the cases of arguments given in explanation of some phenomenon: *Does the argument account for the phenomenon in the most simple way?* In general, the strength of an inductive generalization or a causal claim increases with the simplicity with which it allows one to account for phenomena. The heliocentric theory, first proposed in modern times by Copernicus (1473–1543), won acceptance because of the greater simplicity with which it accounted for the known facts than the earlier geocentric theory. The clarity and simplicity of the argument about civilization in Africa surely point in its favor.

LINGUISTIC ANALYSIS

The twentieth century has been justly called the century of analysis. Mainstream philosophy in the English-speaking world today takes the form of language analysis. The languages analyzed may be artificial logical languages, whose creation traces to nineteenth-century efforts to formalize logical and mathematical relationships. Or logicians may study the ordinary language spoken by the linguistic community to which they belong. Very broadly, ordinary-language analysis can be traced to Ludwig Wittgenstein's lectures at Cambridge in the 1930s and 1940s. Linguistic analysis attempts to clarify and sometimes solve the perennial questions of philosophy by examining the ordinary uses of the terms with which those problems had been stated. Two examples of procedures typical of linguistic analysis will be developed briefly here.

The Technique of Analysis

The problem of the nature of knowledge has been discussed since the time of Plato's dialogue *Theaetetus*. What is knowledge? How do we know if what we call knowledge really is true? What is it that makes certain statements true and others false? A language philosopher might proceed by asking how the term *knowledge* or *to know* functions in everyday language. If a person says, "Johnny knows that smoking is bad for you," she is laying claim to at least three pieces of information. First, that Johnny *believes* that smoking is bad for you (otherwise she would not say he knew it, even if she thought he had reason to believe it). Second, that she believes that smoking is bad for you (otherwise, she would not say Johnny knew it, but only that he believed it. Would an adult ever say that Johnny knows that Santa Claus comes at Christmas time?). Third, that Johnny has *reason to believe* that smoking is bad for you (otherwise she wouldn't say that he knew it, only that he believes it). The point is that whether knowledge exists or not in fact, we may at least try to show what we mean by knowledge. We see by this procedure that philosophers reflect intuitively upon what we already have in our minds, however vaguely. In this case the object of the reflection is the verb "to know," and the ways we use it.

Ethics and Linguistic Analysis: An Application

Philosophers have also studied the structure of the language of morals in an effort to achieve a coherent account of what is meant by the terms people **use** in moral discussions. They wish to show just what we mean by the words we use to express our sense of values. Take, for example, a phrase that we often hear used today: We must respect "the value of life." Almost everyone would see something positive in that phrase. But what does "valuing life" commit the speaker to? Is he talking about life in general, that is, is he including such living things as bugs, or leaves on trees, or amoebas, or fetuses, in his list of things that deserve respect? And what is he committing himself to when he says people must "respect" them? Does the phrase imply that people must seek to preserve their lives, or simply regard them with admiration, or grant them the same right of pursuing their own good that we grant to human beings?

USE AND MENTION: In logic, a distinction is made between the *use* and the *mention* of a term, and between the *meaning* and the *reference* of a term. A person uses a term when it appears in a sentence to refer to something, as the use of "cat" in the sentence, "The cat is asleep," or "A cat is a housepet." One mentions a term in a sentence such as, "The word 'cat' has three letters." The distinction is important, because language can be used to speak about something or other, but in analysis we frequently wish to speak of the elements of language themselves. The meaning of a term (what it *connotes*) is the set of notions associated with it. The reference of a term (its *denotation*) is the class of things it refers to. "Cat" means "a feline housepet"; "Cat" refers to the class of things that are cats, that is, to the object, and not to the word.

Other terms in the English language, which might be thought of as essentially vague, or as having only emotional or rhetorical value, have become the focus of interest of some moral philosophers. Think of such a concept as *trust*. The term is vague, no doubt. When acquaintances or associates ask to be trusted, and someone agrees to do so, they are usually uncertain about a variety of things: Is he implying that he is going to act in their interests? Does he really intend to do so? How far are they to trust him, or how far is it reasonable for them to do so? He may at times seem untrustworthy, in that he does not always keep his promises to other persons and is concerned excessively for his own interest. Should that be cause for them to limit the trust they have in him? Does trusting him mean never asking, either him or other persons who know him, whether he is being faithful to their trust? It is impossible to answer those questions with any generality; each new situation of that kind would have to be judged on its own merits, and on the merits of the persons involved.

But the term *trust,* though it may be dismissed as insignificant just because of its inherent vagueness, is still an enormously significant concept in our everyday life. Trust is in some measure the unfelt support under our feet that enables us to go about our daily business. We trust in the police to do their jobs. We trust that the persons we encounter along our way will not assault us or steal our property. We trust that the bus will come along more or less as scheduled, and that the elevator will not strand us between floors. When that trust is broken— when we are robbed, or we read that the police take bribes, or when the bus drivers suddenly go on strike—we feel insecure; our ability to go about our business, our concern for the welfare of others, and our ability and willingness to pursue our own happiness and to do our bit for the rest of humankind—is impaired. Therefore, philosophers ask questions like these: What is trust? In what ways does it function in the ways we come to agreements with others, or have expectations about their future behavior? What are the implications of a clear understanding of the mutuality of trust for our notions of social justice, love, or even the value of human life? Clearly, attempts to formulate policy on issues like these can be assisted fundamentally by the efforts to analyze clearly and coherently the underlying values of life and respect that they each involve.

Some work in linguistic analysis attempts to draw inferences from our uses of language to the political and social practices of human beings. Since at least the appearance of Thomas Nagel's 1973 watershed paper, "Sexual Perversion," a study of the moral dimensions of homosexuality, a large philosophical literature has been produced on topics that were usually treated by journalists, clergy persons, politicians, and self-styled moralists. Capital punishment, abortion, suicide, the citizens' rights to privacy, the rights of children and the institutionalized (the insane, retarded, or comatose), and the rights of nonhuman animals have all come under logical scrutiny in the last 30 years. Philosophers have relied in these efforts upon the analysis of the linguistic structures that presumably embody the moral experiences of the speakers of that language, and they have appealed to standards of logical consistency and to a real, if not a universal, consensus in arguing for specific normative positions. The analysis of the structures of a language is assumed to give the speaker of that language an understanding of the way her speech expresses even the simplest ethos of her community and even determines her practical behavior. For example, the concept of "perversion" when modified by the adjective "sexual," in Nagel's article, demonstrates a kind of moral connection between the two: Nagel noted that the very fact that sexuality could be spoken of as a thing that can be perverted tells us something about the moral perspectives and practical attitudes of the speakers of the language. This perspective, he hopes, will be amenable to change, given a proper philosophical analysis of the phenomena in question.

CHAPTER 3

A Sketch of the History of Philosophy

WHY PHILOSOPHERS STUDY THE HISTORY OF PHILOSOPHY

All students of philosophy must undertake a study of the subject's history. This necessity is greater in philosophy than in most of the other systematic sciences. There are three fundamental reasons for the engagement of philosophers in the history of philosophy.

First, *earlier thinkers formulated the problems analyzed today.* Philosophy is the analysis of ideas and beliefs that persons conducted in dialogue with each other. This dialogue has a history, and the history conditions in some measure discussions in philosophy today. Philosophy does not attempt to read the book of nature, as do physics and biology; philosophy's book is the collection of theory and opinion about phenomena and experience that has formed, during philosophy's long history, about its central areas of concern. It must enter, therefore, into dialogue with thinkers in the past who have contributed ideas of value to that collection.

Second, *all human dialogue is affected by the historical conditions in which it takes place.* The questions people ask and the answers that appear reasonable to them are related in some unclear way to the specific historical situation they live in. Questions about social justice, for example, will have a different import and reference in medieval aristocracies and feudal economies than in today's technology-driven capitalist democracies. Yet human beings who lived in those earlier social and economic systems had the same intellects, the same fundamental needs, the same passions and fears. Those living today can learn from those living in earlier times how their questions came to be formulated, and how earlier answers can inform our search for clarity today.

Third, *philosophy is part of a long tradition of inquiry.* That tradition extends to the ancient world of Greece and Rome and is distinct from the traditions of thought of other cultures, which also trace their intellectual heritage to ancient times. The meaning and the point of the inquiries undertaken by philosophers today are derived from their understanding of that tradition.

No single chapter of a book can do justice to the immense and complex history of the Western philosophical tradition. This chapter will confine itself to a description of its chief figures and intellectual characteristics. Most textbooks classify that history under the following four rubrics:

- Ancient Philosophy
- Medieval Philosophy
- The Modern World
- The Contemporary World

The bibliography of primary sources will offer a list of easily available editions, in English, of the major works of the thinkers discussed here.

ANCIENT PHILOSOPHY

Before Philosophy

Greek thought, like most thought in the cultures of the Bronze Age, was originally poetic, religious, and dramatic. Most early written explanations of natural phenomena, or of the fundamental features of human life, were based upon what we generally call myth. Myths are narrative representations of the actions of gods, of early heroes, of monsters, and of demonic or benevolent humanized forces, such as Fate or Necessity. Intelligent and curious people of antiquity required some sort of explanation of familiar natural phenomena: Why do people use fire? Why do they live in houses, instead of caves or trees, as the other animals do? What brings the rain? Why do we have kings? Who gave humankind the art of writing, or of making other kinds of tools? Direct observation cannot answer such questions. Yet if people can tie fanciful explanations of these things to the wonderful stories told by poets and grandmothers about the gods and about ancient times, they may feel, perhaps, that they understand them. What was initially strange will become familiar and natural.

So, for example, the Greeks answered the question of why and how men use fire to cook and heat their homes by the tale of the rebellion of the god Prometheus against Zeus, king of the gods. Having pity upon the humans living beneath Olympus, abode of the gods, Prometheus decided to give them fire in defiance of Zeus's orders, who feared that men would become too powerful if they possessed it. For this gift, and for his stubborn refusal to obey Zeus, the Greeks revered Prometheus, and some people even today look to him for inspiration when they dare to go against what the preachers have told them about God's will. But Prometheus was punished dreadfully for his rebellion; he was chained to a rock, and a huge bird was sent to him each evening to devour his liver, which was regenerated the next morning.

Such a story works on many levels: It explains our possession of fire, it warns us against going beyond human limits and defying the gods, and it encourages, in a way, those who would try. Yet one feature of this story is clear: if people believe that humans received fire from the gods, they will never attempt to discover the facts of the case: how primitive humans slowly learned the art of making, using, and controlling fire. Myth inhibits science, or makes it unnecessary.

Pre-Socratic Philosophy

The first person to break with ancient myth and set the Greeks on a new way of understanding the world was Thales. His dates are uncertain, but historians place him at the beginning of the sixth century B.C.E. He lived on the eastern coast of the Aegean, and the school he founded is called "Milesian," after the name of the city in which he and two of his younger friends, Anaximander and Anaximenes, lived. Thales's great breakthrough was to imagine that the world had a rational order. When he famously declared, against the evidence of the senses, that all things are made of water, he opened his fellows to the possibility that the order of visible phenomena could be explained by invisible but impersonal structures that human reason can make visible. Things do not happen a certain way because the gods are angry or glad, but because things manifest an underlying lawful order. And with this thought, no doubt, most people today would agree.

Thales was the first in a line of thinkers who collectively are called the pre-Socratics. They formed schools in various cities of Greece, where they debated issues of *cosmology,* the theory of how the physical world is put together in time and space. They speculated on the substance of which things are made, on the forces that cause things to happen and the principles that determine how phenomena unfold, and on the natures of space and time themselves. They often understood the forces that determine the changes in the underlying substance as spiritual in nature. However, they did not return to the position before Thales appeared and take these spiritual forces as the idiosyncratic activity of gods. Rather, the forces they invoked manifested consistency and regularity, not arbitrary will. They seemed to be founded in principles, rather than in the fickle desires of the gods, and could be the objects of science rather than of religious reverence. Some, such as Anaximenes, thought that we could understand all change as the action of familiar processes in nature, such as evaporation and condensation. Others imagined that nature's operations are similar to processes typical of human crafts, such as felting, and that events in nature could be thought of as resulting from more or less of these processes. This notion suggests an idea that would later become crucial to science: that people can trace what appears to them as *qualitative* changes to *quantitative* changes. For example, instead of saying, "today is (qualitatively) warmer than yesterday," we can say, "today the high was (quantitatively) 6° Celsius warmer than yesterday."

Empedocles (490?–430 B.C.E.), a philosopher of Sicily, conceived of the sources of change more spiritually, on analogy with Love and Hate (or Strife). He appears to have believed that the cosmos is subject to cycles of birth and death and rebirth, in which the fundamental stuff of the universe, Earth, Air, Fire, and Water, were progressively separated out from each other and recombined by love and strife, thereby producing the myriad appearances of things.

These efforts to discover the nature of the forces that produce change assume that change is a fundamental characteristic of the cosmos. However, Heraclitus (540?–475? B.C.E.), a philosopher of Ephesus, appears to have been struck by a fatal flaw in the philosophy of Thales and his immediate followers. All of the Milesians thought that the cosmos was reducible to some one original stuff, such as Thales's water. Heraclitus's objection might be rewritten in the following manner: If there is some one original material stuff, then how is it possible for that stuff to become what it is not, namely the appearances? How can, for example, water change from water to what it was not, namely to an acorn, or the air, or a mountain? One solution to this problem is associated with Heraclitus's famous remark, "You cannot step into the same river twice, for the water (of the river) is constantly new."

Yet Heraclitus, like most Greeks, believed in the solidity and reality of the things of this world. Despite his affirmation of the transient nature of all things, he appears to have believed that although the river itself may change, the riverbed remains relatively stable. Accordingly, Heraclitus taught that all changing things, all novelty in the world, occurs under the governance of laws, the *logos,* the objective principle of order in the cosmos. If there has to be an original substance out of which all things come, even in the face of the problem of explaining how "what is not" (the appearances) comes to be out of "what is" (the substantial original reality), we must choose the most malleable and changeable thing of all for that substance—and Heraclitus chose *fire.* The *logos* orders fire into the stable/unstable features of things in the cosmos. In Heraclitus, things easily turn into their opposites—cold into hot or dry into wet. This makes sense, for if fire is the primordial substance, then strife and the clash of opposites should be the key metaphor that expresses the character of this universe.

Heraclitus's ideas were criticized by a thinker named Parmenides, who was from the Greek colony of Elea, an area on the southwest coast of Italy. We possess fragments of a poem in which Parmenides describes a mysterious journey with a goddess who teaches him to distinguish between the way of truth and the way of error. Heraclitus's way, Parmenides teaches, is that of error: he makes flux the essence of reality. The way of truth, which the reason alone can understand, is that "the nothing" cannot be conceived or spoken of; only that which is, being itself, exists. Change or becoming is impossible, because it requires that "what is" emerges from something that "is not," or being from nonbeing. Yet it is characteristic of the world of appearance that things come into existence that were not there a moment ago. The idea does violence to our reason, which tells us that nothing can come to be out of nothing. Parmenides's doctrine thus has the unsettling consequence that the entire changing world of appearance must be an illusion to which we all are subject.

If philosophy tells us that our common sense view of the world is an illusion, then philosophy cannot hope to understand the very features of the world that we want to understand. It is not at all surprising that at the end of the pre-Socratic period there arose professional teachers of wisdom called **Sophists,** many of whom abandoned serious philosophy and maintained an attitude of skepticism in matters of knowledge and cynicism in morals. Some maintained that both knowledge and moral culture are artificial and based in prejudice. A famous remark of this kind was attributed to the Sophist Protagoras (480?–411? B.C.E.): "Man is the measure of all things, of those that are, that they are, of those that are not, that they are not." This profound but science-weary statement seems to argue that a view of reality that goes beyond appearances to some objective truth about the world is not possible for a human being. Things move, he might have thought, as far as we perceive them to move, and things remain the same so long as we hold on to them.

SOPHISM: The Sophists were men well versed in pre-Socratic philosophy and in the practical sciences. In a time before the development of universities or institutes for advanced studies, they offered themselves as teachers, for a fee, to young men of wealth. Many of the Sophists trained their pupils in rhetoric, or public speaking, which at the time was an important skill for persons who wished to make a name for themselves in Greek political life. Socrates famously accused them of teaching how to make the true appear to be false and the false to be true, rather than how to know and speak the truth, and how to make oneself appear to be just, rather than how to be truly just.

The Golden Age of Greek Philosophy

Socrates

The lives of Socrates (469–399 B.C.E.), Plato (427–347 B.C.E.), and Aristotle (384–322 B.C.E.) are intertwined. Plato, a wealthy young man with strong affinities for politics, became the student of Socrates, who turned him toward the life of the mind, and Plato became in turn the teacher of Aristotle. Socrates had little interest in cosmological questions and turned instead the skills of analysis of the cosmologists to questions of a moral and social nature. He is said to have "called philosophy down from heaven," and brought it into the daily concerns of people for achieving order, harmony, and happiness in their lives and in their social and political world. He never wrote any treatises, preferring the "living speech" of intellectual discussion with others to writing. He argued with Sophists, for example, attempting to show them that their pretended knowledge of the nature of the virtues—of courage, wisdom, justice, temperance, and piety—was bogus. He maintained against many of them, however, that some genuine knowledge of values and of the nature of things was available to human beings, and that nothing is as important for human happiness as the pursuit of knowledge. The unexamined life, he said, is not worth living.

Plato

Plato's surviving work, with the exception of some letters, consists of dialogues in which men are depicted discussing a variety of intellectual problems. The earlier dialogues show Socrates in intense discussions with friends and Sophists, usually about some disputed concept. These early dialogues are immensely alive, for the discussions take place on the background of daily life in Athens. We see Socrates prodding men from all walks of that life to "give birth" to whatever wisdom they have about some issue that arises out of the practical problems of everyday life, but which leads into the highly abstract questions of philosophy. Plato most likely intended these dialogues as teaching instruments, and perhaps also as showing to his fellow Athenians what a great mistake they had made in prosecuting Socrates. Most of Plato's life was spent in Athens, except for three brief adventures in the Greek colony of Syracuse in what is now Sicily. He was called there by a relative of the tyrant who ruled the city to assist in the education of the tyrant's son. Hoping to influence the young man in a positive direction and perhaps to make of him or his uncle a philosopher-king like the one he had written of in *The Republic,* Plato answered the call. He eventually became embroiled in palace intrigues, the details of which are unknown, and he barely escaped with his life. Plato's last years were spent teaching at the Academy, where he wrote dialogues that explore cosmological issues (for example, the *Timaeus*) and modified somewhat the political philosophy developed in *The Republic* (*Statesman* and *Laws*). He died at the age of eighty, his pen still in his hand, so the legend tells us.

Aristotle

Aristotle was the son of a physician attached to the royal family of Macedonia, in northern Greece. He came to Athens as a young man, presumably because of the great reputation of Plato, and studied and worked at the Academy for twenty years. We have no clear idea what Aristotle's studies with Plato involved, or whether the younger philosopher disagreed profoundly with his teacher while he was still the older man's student. In works written after leaving Plato's Academy, Aristotle refers with respect to Plato and the Academics still at Plato's school, but he rejects many of their key concepts, and especially their daring speculations about the Forms. Plato had asserted the existence of a realm of ideas, the Forms, in addition to the intelligible features of the things we see. For Plato, there are desks, the idea of a desk embodied in the word *desk,* and deskness itself, the Form of Desk. Such an enlargement of what the world contains was unnecessary, Aristotle believed, to account for things that we experience. He explains the primary features of the world, being and change, by a close observation of the intelligible features of the physical world, rather than by intuitive *reflection on abstract ideas.* This difference in the starting-point of all inquiry—the rationalism of Plato and the empiricism of Aristotle—pervades all subsequent Western philosophy. The famous painting by Raphael, *The School of*

Raphael's *The School of Athens.* © *The Art Archive / Vatican Museum Rome / Album/Joseph Martin.*

Athens, expresses nicely the spiritual distance between the two men. It shows Plato, an old man, gesturing upward, suggesting, perhaps, that all metaphysics must begin with celestial and spiritual things. Meanwhile Aristotle gestures vigorously toward the ground, suggesting, perhaps, that all metaphysics must begin with the contemplation of the world given to the senses.

When Aristotle died, he left behind some friends and students who continued the school he had founded, and an enormous body of work on almost every area of ancient science. His studies on the weather, on the parts of animals, on politics, poetry, the theater, and the soul go in depth and detail far beyond any known work of his time. Some of this work may have been done by students on his instructions, and most of it seems to be intended as lecture notes rather than as finished treatises. Yet for almost two thousand years after his death, Aristotle was known as "the master of them that know," and, except for a few areas of science—anatomy and medicine, for example—Europe was not able to go beyond his achievements until the scientific revolution that began after 1500 C.E.

Greco-Roman Philosophy

The period in Western history between the conquests of Alexander (who became King of Macedonia in 330 B.C.E.) and the collapse of the Western Roman Empire (fifth and sixth centuries C.E.) is called Greco-Roman. The initial period, up to the beginning of the Roman Empire (Octavian, first Emperor of Rome, after 27 B.C.E.) is called the Hellenistic Age. Its greatest intellectual achievements took place in the cities founded by Alexander's successors, Pella in Macedonia, Antioch in Syria, and, especially, Alexandria in Egypt. Men of learning and achievement flocked to this city, for it had the greatest library in the ancient Western world, and a great museum dedicated to scientific studies. Many of the achievements of the Hellenistic Age were in applied science and technology, and the Roman Empire was known more for its feats of engineering than for pure science and philosophy. The situation is slightly different in the case of social and political philosophy. The Romans and the peoples who lived under their sway did not produce large theoretical works about the proper ends of government, the relation of the individual to society, the nature of a perfect or utopian state, or even the art of politics. They did produce, however, a great body of laws. Even more than a cosmopolitan *polis* like Athens, the Romans required a system of law that could be practiced by all the different peoples living in their vast empire, and that would be recognized by the many different peoples they ruled over as both rational and fair. They needed a common law that supplemented local traditional and religious laws and provided a kind of legal common currency for the magistrates—such, for example, as Pontius Pilate—whom the Roman authorities sent out from Rome into the provinces. The *Corpus Juris Civilis,* a large compilation of Roman law compiled under the rule of Justinian I, became the basis of much subsequent European law. Some of the great jurists that Rome produced, such as Ulpian or Paulus, are important sources of the conflicting concepts of common and natural law that figures so prominently in early modern European political theory.

"Schools" of Philosophy

Yet there were schools of philosophy during those centuries, the influence of which spread throughout the empire, and which continued until the final closing of the Academy in Athens by Justinian (529 C.E.), and the final destruction of the great library in Alexandria by the Muslim invaders in the seventh century C.E. Plotinus (205–270), the originator of what is called Neo-Platonism, studied in Alexandria, and the school he founded in Rome flourished for more than three hundred years. Neo-Platonism teaches that all reality emanates in stages from the "One." The One was thought of in terms of Plato's notion of the Form of Forms, the Form of the Good. This philosophy was mystical in tone, and the Neo-Platonists were sympathetic to the mystical elements in early Christianity, which began to win large numbers of converts outside of the Jewish people among whom it originated by the end of the second century C.E. Christianity spread through the eastern part of the Roman empire the century after the death of Christ and was eventually adopted by the entire Greco-Roman world. Alexandrian civilization provided Christianity with some of its Greek-speaking Church Fathers.

The secular and nonmystical schools that dominated the Greco-Roman world until its collapse were of a moral and social kind. The major schools were

Skepticism, Cynicism, Epicureanism, and *Stoicism.* Cynicism, which traces its roots to Socrates's student Antisthenes, will be mentioned in the chapter on ethics. Skepticism will be discussed in the chapter on epistemology. The schools of Epicureanism and Stoicism were not defined by their approach to knowledge, as were the schools founded by Plato and Aristotle. Rather, they taught people to practice the life of virtue and wisdom that was embodied by some founding teacher. Their purpose was not simply the discovery and transmission of knowledge, as schools and colleges do today, but the achievement of freedom and virtue and happiness. The moral discourse of the teachers who led these schools, the examples they set, and the practices they demanded of their students were intended to mold the behavior of students. They all borrowed from the example of Socrates, whose life was a model of commitment to inquiry, to moderation, and to virtue, while bearing up, not proudly, but with the fortitude and inner strength that is the source of true happiness, to the uncomprehending opposition of small and vindictive men. Stoics and Epicureans taught the science of cosmology, however, for their adherents wished to show that the style of life they thought to be conducive to human happiness was in conformity with a philosophically founded concept of nature.

Epicureanism

Epicureanism and Stoicism are *perennial philosophies*, that is, they have arisen in different forms in many times and places. They respond to the difficulties of *living well* and *being happy.* Life is hard: pleasures are few and often destructive, and success in politics, business, or war is uncertain. A human life is always threatened with disaster. How to live in such a world? One answer to these questions was given by Epicurus (341–270 B.C.E.), who lived in Athens. Most of what we have of his thought was preserved by the historian Diogenes Laërtius (third century C.E.), and by descriptions of this thought written by his students and opponents. The word *Epicurean* suggests today a life of luxurious pleasures, of fancy food and wine, and frivolous but sophisticated entertainment. This is true of Epicurus only insofar as he was a *hedonist,* believing that the Good Life is the life of pleasure. He argued, however, that the pleasures a wise person should enjoy are not the beastly pleasures of drunkenness, lust, and gluttony, but the more refined pleasures that appeal to the practiced tastes of a person of leisure. But here too, Epicurus asserts an important proviso to his hedonism: refined pleasures are only possible for a person who has put his entire being in a state of *ataraxia,* that is, of quiet and harmony, of peace of mind devoid of fear or selfish desire. Such a state is immune to all disturbances of the mind or the flesh, whereas the habitual enjoyment of physical pleasure only increases our capacity for pain. Indeed, the desire for pleasure itself perturbs the mind; we must learn to take pleasure in the mere fact of our existence, which is possible only when the body is at ease, suffering from no lack of what is necessary for its well-being. This hard-won tranquility of mind and body makes it possible for a person to enjoy the pleasures of knowledge, of gardening, of peaceful music, simple food, and the taste of pure water. The highest pleasure lies in the contemplation of the happiness and majesty of the gods. Epicurus's recipe for the good life understandably led him to recommend a disengagement from political activity and even a refusal to marry and have children, for such things are disruptive of one's tranquility. He denied that the gods take notice of us, for engagement in human struggles and folly would disturb their tranquility. We have therefore nothing to fear from the gods, he taught. Death is nothingness, and therefore it too cannot harm us. Thus, the truth or falsity of philosophical doctrines is measured in terms of its contribution to our tranquility.

The Stoics

Stoicism, to modern ears, is the doctrine that teaches people to "keep a stiff upper lip" in the face of adversity, and even to prepare for and expect the worst in life. In the ancient world, Epictetus (55–c.135) taught a more subtle version of this perennial wisdom. Fortune may decree that a person will suffer poverty, disease, or death; no one is able to protect oneself securely from such terrible things. However, we are able to control our attitude toward death and disease and poverty. We can learn, with proper guidance, to love whatever fortune may decree. First we must realize that life does not guarantee to anyone that he will live in prosperous circumstances. The things that people possess are not theirs by any right of nature, nor do they come with any guarantee that they are theirs to keep. People desirous of being happy must learn, therefore, to look upon all things as merely given to them for a time, and to be ready to give them up when the time comes. Fall in love with nothing! for the object of your love is doomed to pass on. "Is your wife dead?" says Epictetus in the *Enchiridion,* a notebook of his sayings compiled by his students. "She has been given back. Is your child dead? He too has been given back. Has your fortune been taken from you? Has not that then also been given back? You say, 'But he who has taken it [the fortune] from me has done so wrongly!' Yet what difference does it make by whose hand the fortune was given back? Enjoy what you have as long as you possess it, as a traveler does with his inn." Learn to love your fate, whatever it may be, says this tired but noble wisdom, and you will enjoy a tranquil flow of life. We cannot recover what we lose, but we can cure the sorrow of loss. If we desire nothing, then any attainment or loss will not affect us; we will become masters of our existence.

The greatest representatives of Stoicism in the Roman Empire were the Roman dramatist and statesman Seneca (4? B.C.E.–65 C.E.), and the Emperor Marcus Aurelius (121–180 C.E.). Marcus Aurelius is remembered as the most virtuous of Roman emperors. Concerned for the poor, he sold many of his own possessions to alleviate poverty, and his love of learning led him to found chairs of philosophy in Athens. The threat to the empire posed by barbarians in the northeast called him away from Rome more often than he desired, and his reflections on his education in Stoicism, and his efforts to develop sufficient strength of mind to bear the trials that fortune had thrust upon him, are contained in his *Meditations*. This great work has given solace and comfort to men and women facing the hardships of living and acting in difficult times and has restored their will to push on, to strive to accomplish the duties that they have freely undertaken.

MEDIEVAL PHILOSOPHY

Christian Philosophy at the Close of the Roman Empire

The collapse of the political institutions that had sustained European civilization upon the fall of Rome caused sea changes in humankind's self-awareness, just as the enormous changes in the structures of political and economic power during the last century have had their effects upon humankind's philosophical outlook. The governments under which we live today, our social structures, our deepest views about humankind and its world, the self-awareness we possess, are of a far different sort than in the medieval world that followed upon the fall of Rome. Indeed, most people in the Western world today feel a greater affinity with the beliefs and conditions of fifth-century B.C.E. Athens or even imperial Rome than with those of the Middle Ages. Yet the medieval philosophers had their spiritual roots in Christianity and their intellectual roots in Plato and Aristotle. Christianity, which had begun as a small mystical sect dedicated to the figure of Jesus and the coming of His Kingdom, became, after twelve centuries of reflection, a universal philosophy of great depth and power.

The early phase of this development was dominated by the first great Christian philosopher, St. Augustine (354–430) and the later by that of St. Thomas Aquinas (c. 1225–1274). With the Christianization of the Roman Empire, and its eventual collapse under the invasions of Germanic barbarians, philosophy was shaken to its foundations and forced to reconsider its presuppositions. The concept of state and society, and humankind in its relationship to God, were especially affected. The Greeks and the Romans never doubted that social life under some form of government was the natural state of humankind, and, if the government is just, it served the highest human good, the happiness and virtue of its citizens. Christianity, however, had a different sense of man's highest good. Its beliefs concerning humankind's origins, its obligations to a higher power, and the moral governance of the cosmos by God, were foreign to both Plato and Aristotle and, of course, to the Greco-Roman schools. A few general and perhaps obvious contrasts between the tenor of Christian beliefs and the ancient secular philosophies may be offered.

First, Christianity looked upon humankind as having a supernatural vocation. We are all destined to eternal life after our sojourn in this world is over. True, the ancients generally believed in some continuation of the person after the death of the body—the belief was necessitated by the nearly universal belief in ghosts and spirits. The denial of an afterlife by the Stoics and Epicureans seems to have been motivated more by a desire to be free of the fear of death and a horrible afterlife than by a philosophical conviction. A few of the ancients, such as

Plato, believed in the possibility of reincarnation. But the picture of the afterlife was never conceived of as eternal, and it was not portrayed, as it was in Christianity, as a place either of everlasting joy in the presence of God, or of eternal torment in hellfire. The Christian idea required that people, whatever their vocation here on Earth, prepare themselves for Judgment Day, when God will separate the saved from the damned. Since civil society was obviously incapable of performing such a task, people turned instead to the only institution that appeared ready and able to lead believers to salvation, the Christian church. This shift forced thinkers to examine the proper relationship between the growing civil authority of bishops and popes and the secular lords and kings.

Second, Christianity thought of the world as *fallen.* The disobedience of God by Eve and Adam were believed to have tainted the human race with original sin. Christians have struggled with this fantastic doctrine, inherited from *Genesis,* the first book of the *Tanach*, or Hebrew Bible, across the centuries. At its most negative, it is thought to imply the corruption of human nature and our need of grace from God as the only hope for our salvation or even for our goodness here on Earth. If so, we cannot think of ourselves as autonomous and self-sufficient, as Aristotle believed. The secular state was thought to share in this inherent wickedness, and the Roman Empire, even despite its acceptance of Christianity, was thought to be the equivalent of the ancient city of Babylon, depicted in the Bible as the seat of moral depravity. God may call some of humankind to salvation, but a government cannot be saved. The Socratic question of the Good Life had therefore to be reformulated. The Good Life, for these thinkers, became the Christian life of prayer and devotion, not the life of happiness through virtuous activity, and not by participation in the state and in the civil society of which they were citizens and members.

A third change in thinking about humankind and society prompted by Christianity can be discerned in Augustine's works. The concept of *history* took on new significance for Christians, and it continued its influence even in the modern secular world. When thinkers in antiquity turned to history, not just to understand past events and the forces that brought them about, but to question the inner meaning and direction of human history in general, they saw it as a cyclical waxing and waning of kingdoms and empires. Like individual human lives, empires were thought to be born, grow to maturity, lapse into senility, and die. No doubt the empires and the ways of life they fostered were part of a larger evolution toward the eventual extinction of humankind. The human race had passed through successive ages in the minds of the ancients. It began with a supposed prehistoric Golden Age, then, in order, had passed to the Silver, Bronze, and Iron Ages—a passage downward to ever more feeble and unhappy states. But the cycle of empires could, in principle, be endless, and life and its history had no significance beyond themselves.

These notions of human history were unacceptable to Christian thinkers like Augustine, who saw history as a kind of progress, by God's grace, from an original Fall through successive stages of redemption, to a final cataclysm called Armageddon. Then there will be the Second Coming of Christ, and, at last, the

St. Augustine. © *Thoemmes.*

end of the world, when the angel Gabriel will blow his horn, the Earth will fall into ashes, and the gates of Heaven and Hell will close forever. Consequently, it became important for Christians to understand the inner meaning of such great historical events as the fall of the Roman Empire. The Roman state could no longer be viewed as ordained by God to create the conditions of orderly rule necessary for the redemptive process to take place, nor could Christians view Rome's fall simply as another case of one empire collapsing to make room for another. The Roman emperors were, after all, Christians, and had Christianized the Empire. Why, then, its downfall before the redemptive process was completed? Why did it not live to see Armageddon? Augustine struggled with these questions in his great work, *The City of God.*

After the collapse of the Western Roman Empire, religion and what remained of intellectual culture in Europe fell into the hands of the monastic orders. The so-called Dark Ages extend from the collapse of the empire to the slow regeneration of city life, first in Italy and then in northern Europe, after the eleventh century. There was a brief period of light at the beginning of the ninth century, when Charlemagne was crowned emperor of most of western Europe by the pope in Rome; however, the dynasty he created did not last more than a generation beyond his own. Very little literature was produced during this period, except for tales of adventure, love, and divine intercession produced or transmitted in unwritten form by bards and troubadours. Some theological and philosophical work continued in the monasteries. The most important thinker during this period was Eriugena (825–870). In his book *Periphysion,* he struggled to develop a system of negative theology, believing that since we cannot describe God in His nature, we can at least attempt to say what God is not, and so save ourselves from confusing God with things that we know. Eriugena seems to have believed that God is unknowable even to God Himself.

The High Middle Ages

In the late or high Middle Ages, a method of doing philosophy known as *scholasticism* was developed in such new universities as Oxford, Paris, Prague, and Bologna. Its initiator seems to have been **Peter Abelard** (1079–1142), who, in a book entitled *Sic et Non* (Yes and No) placed side-by-side the differing opinions about theological doctrine of various church authorities and theologians, so that readers could, as it were, enter into a debate with these authorities and attempt to develop better doctrines. When this method of comparison is practiced by groups of students and scholars in the classroom, it is a kind of renewal of Socratic dialogue in which individuals argue as acutely as they can for and against some disputed doctrine.

The greatest of the scholastics was St. Thomas Aquinas, who is today considered to have formulated the fundamental philosophical orientation and doctrine of Catholic Christianity. He was greatly influenced by Aristotle, whose philosophy had become available in Western Europe during the century before him. Convinced that the pagan Aristotle could not be ignored by Christians, but concerned that his enormous achievement could obscure the truth of Christianity, Aquinas attempted to show how Aristotle's philosophy could be put in harmony with Christian faith. Aquinas wrote voluminously. Perhaps his most important work was the *Summa Theologica,* a textbook in which doctrines concerning the world, God, and moral behavior are each presented with statements for and against them derived from Scripture and from philosophers and Christian theologians. Aquinas defends his own resolution of the controversy, showing why those who took the view opposed to his own were mistaken. Another important work by Aquinas is the *Summa contra Gentiles,* a work intended to convince others of the truth of the Christian faith.

PETER ABELARD: Abelard was an early representative of the medieval Scholastic tradition, who was born near Nantes, France, in 1079, and died near Cluny in 1142. Abelard fell in love with, had a child by, and secretly married his student Héloïse without obtaining permission of her family. When her uncle became convinced that Abelard had mistreated his daughter, abandoning her at an abbey where she had taken holy orders, he had Abelard castrated. Abelard then became a monk, and Héloïse retired to a nunnery. Their letters to each other became symbols of failed romantic love, but scholars have cast doubts on the authenticity of some of them. Very active in the theological disputes of his day, Abelard made as many enemies as friends and was once condemned for his opinions by a church council. He was the greatest thinker of his era.

Two other great Schoolmen, who were highly critical of Aquinas, were Duns Scotus (1266–1308) and William of Ockham (1280–1349). Scotus's two major works were the *Quodlibeta* and the *De Primo Principio*. He emphasized God's infinite will and opposed the intellectualism of Aquinas in favor of what is called voluntarism. For Scotus, no ideas of things to be created or rational plans for the creation of the world are in God's mind prior to the creation. Creation springs from God's infinite will; whatever God wills is good. As a result, Scotus limited far more than Aquinas what it is possible for the unaided or philosophical reason to understand of God's nature and ways. Yet Scotus believed that there are some unalterable precepts that make up the moral law, and he consequently refused to subordinate the moral will entirely to the Divine will. Ockham's greatest work is the *Commentaries* on the Sentences of Lombard and on Aristotle. He limited even more than Scotus what the unaided reason is able to know of God; even God's existence cannot be rationally proven. All theology therefore must be based upon what God has been gracious enough to reveal to us in the Holy Books. He maintained the interesting belief that one is bound to follow one's conscience in morals, even if one's conscience is erroneous, that is, not in accord with the Divine will. He is remembered for what is called Ockham's Razor, that no concepts should function in an account of things unless they are essential to the account. This notion is close to the contemporary belief in the philosophy of science that the simpler account of phenomena is to be preferred to one that is more complex.

THE MODERN WORLD

The Early Modern Period

The two centuries after Aquinas were marked by the fading of the social and political order characteristic of the Middle Ages. The economic and social system known as **feudalism** was swept away by new concentrations of power in the hands of a few, rather than many, sovereign powers, and the nation-building had begun that was eventually to result in the great nation-states of Spain, England, Holland, and France. The bubonic plague, which peaked in about 1350, killed 70 percent of the population in some parts of Europe. In those places, the recovery of economic and social stability took almost a century. The intellectual and artistic changes in Europe during these two centuries were also enormous. The period of the rediscovery of the art and literature of the Greeks and Romans that is called the *Renaissance* began in Italy after 1400 and slowly spread throughout the West. Two of its major thinkers were Marsilio Ficinio (1433–1499), a Platonist philosopher, and Pico della Mirandola (1463–1494), author of *Oration on the Dignity of Man,* who, in true Renaissance style, drew on many ancient and modern sources, including medieval Judaism, to create his metaphysical system.

FEUDALISM: *Feudalism* is the term given to the form of social organization typical of the European Middle Ages, and of many other societies at different times and places. It is characterized, first, by decentralization of government: instead of large nation-states or empires, there is local government, usually in the hands of a hereditary ruler. Second, it typically organizes individuals into estates: warrior-aristocrats and their knights and nobles, the clergy and the monastic orders, and the peasants or serfs. There are few cities; life goes on in villages, monasteries, and castles. Third, feudal government tends to be unstable, with local lords and bishops vying among themselves for power, and there is frequent warfare over territory among the nobles and their knights. Trade between regions is limited by a lack of security on the highways.

It is a platitude that humankind during this period turned from the contemplation of God to the contemplation of the human being and its world, but the signs of such a new mentality are everywhere to be found. The development of portraiture, the realistic depiction of individual persons in three-dimensional space, which was a hallmark of the Renaissance, is not found in the Middle Ages, when individual persons or things were of interest only for the spiritual lessons they could teach to persons intent upon salvation and the understanding of God's ways.

Further, by 1500, the Age of Exploration began—its first hero (or villain) was Columbus—and the enormous wealth it brought to the West helped to tip the balance of power among world civilizations in Europe's direction. Four hundred years later, most of the civilized world lived under the suzerainty of some European nation. All these events reshaping the economic and political structure of Europe had, of course, significant influence upon philosophy. The foundational features of Western civilization in the early modern world (from 1500 until the French Revolution in 1789) can be related with special force to two important developments. The first was the rise of the economic system called capitalism, and the second was the rise of physical science.

Capitalism

Without going into the heavy waters of economics, capitalism can be characterized in a way that is useful for some philosophical reflections on government and society. Capitalism arises out of what we call a market economy, forms of which existed since the Iron Age civilizations invented money. The earliest form of money were coins, whose standard value was certified by some governing authority, or the market itself determined the value of the metal of which they were made. Money is a form of exchange that makes the more difficult system of bartering unnecessary. A certain weight of gold or silver was considered equivalent in value, at some time and place, for certain commodities offered for sale. In barter, a jug of wine of a certain size might be considered equal in value to a bushel of grain of some size. But many different things may be put up for barter, and, after the exchanges agreed to by traders, the commodities are used or consumed, and nothing remains of the transaction. Money in itself is of no use for consumption, but as a medium of exchange, it survives the exchange and takes on a life of its own, independent of the commodities. Money can be bought or sold, and it can be lent out at interest.

This last idea is fundamental to capitalism, which made spectacular use of it in an institution that also existed in a rudimentary form in the ancient world, the *bank*. A bank accepts deposits of money on which it pays interest to the lender. The depositor in that way earns money without working for it. On the other hand, the bank lends out the money to persons who have deposited in it at an even higher rate of interest. Money, it is sometimes said, is the slave of its master, for it works for free. This fact, so familiar today, was once roundly criticized by the Christian churches as usury, and as contrary to God's condemnation of Adam and his descendants to "gain your bread in the sweat of your brow." And, indeed, the banking system was capable of causing great hardships. Yet when regulated by law and performed by institutions rather than by individual moneylenders, the system had a dynamic effect on society. It provided capital— cash or other means of exchange—to entrepreneurs who needed money for business enterprises. These entrepreneurs, if successful, would repay their lenders at reasonable rates of interest and use their profit for further enterprises. The bank would repay the account holders with interest, and the bank itself would profit. Eventually, a productive enterprise could raise money by selling shares in itself to persons with enough money to buy them and thereby share directly in the profits of the enterprise. These shares could themselves be bought and sold on a stock market. The result was an accumulation of capital that built up industry in Europe and eventually led to the imperial conquest of most of the world by the large ships and effective weapons that capital made possible.

This new economy affected the relationships between human beings. Persons who had no capital to invest would indeed have still to gain their bread by the sweat of their brow. If they had no marketable skills, such as a craft, they were forced to sell their muscle-power on a labor market in order to survive. The value of their work was determined by the conditions of the market, where the principle of supply and demand ruled as much in the market for labor as for commodities. A person's salary was determined by the market value of the commodities that he could produce in the course of an hour's, a week's, or a month's labor. Such a system assumes that the workers, bankers, and entrepreneurs who enter a marketplace are each of them looking out only for their own interests and, if they are smart, will maximize their income or profits even at a cost to others. Capitalism is frequently characterized as rapacious, soulless, indifferent to all human values but those of profit, and as having conjured up out of the ground, as it were, a great mass of losers in the universal animal struggle for wealth and its privileges. Yet even critics of capitalism such as Karl Marx and Friedrich Engels noted with amazement in their *Communist Manifesto* (1848) the power inherent in labor under capitalism to create whole new cities and populations, even literally to move mountains and divert rivers. For good or ill, what we call the modern world would be unthinkable without it.

Philosophy and Early Modern Science

The rise of modern science after 1500, especially the mathematical physics of **Galileo** and Newton, was the second development in the early modern world that inspired new and creative philosophical thinking. The responses of philosophers to science were ingenious and immensely complex. Science forces us to consider phenomena not only qualitatively, that is, through the forms or ideas visible on individual objects, but also quantitatively, through the physical laws that determine their working. Consider, as an example of this seminal idea, Galileo's (1564–1642) famous experiments with falling bodies. When we take an item and throw it into the air, the item rises, seems to stop, and then returns to earth. Each time we throw the object, the trajectory is somewhat different. We could never throw the object in the same way each time. To our eyes these phenomena are similar, but different. Only the mind can discern an underlying order to them. The mind that first saw this order clearly was Galileo's. By studying the rate that metal balls rolled down a carefully polished inclined plane, he determined relationships between distances, amounts of time, and rate of acceleration. Reasoning from these and other observations, he established that the distance covered by a freely falling body near the surface of the earth was one-half the rate of acceleration multiplied by the square of the time it is falling from rest. The resulting simple formula, $s = 1/2at^2$, describes the parameters of the behavior of any objects falling near the surface of the Earth. Like Thales, Galileo was seeking a way to tie together events that are similar but nonetheless different under a single theoretical structure. Thales thought that we could trace the interrelationships between items and a shared underlying substance, water, and Galileo thought that underlying mathematical laws determined disparate physical phenomena.

GALILEO GALILEI (1564–1642): Italian mathematician, physicist, and astronomer, active in Pisa, Padua, and Florence, generally considered to be the greatest of the early modern scientists. Galileo's important contributions were to astronomy and the mathematics of motion. He studied physical laws regarding falling bodies and the pendulum. His development of the telescope made possible discoveries of the moons of Jupiter and the phases of Venus. These facts supported the Copernican theory that the Earth went around the sun, an idea that was considered heretical by the Catholic Church of that time. Galileo was brought before the prelates of the Inquisition and was eventually forced to resign his professorship and placed under house arrest.

Galileo's chief concern, however, was not with philosophy. He did not think of physical laws as separate from matter, or from specific appearances. His work had clear implications for philosophy, however, for his belief that physical laws entirely determine physical events suggests a new way of interpreting things in the world and the world as a whole, namely as a mechanism of some sort.

In 1600, technology had made few of the advances that we take for granted today. Still, the craftsmanship that made the construction of ingenious devices possible, and the interest and capital people dedicated to such construction, grew rapidly after the Renaissance. The scientific revolution and the fantastic discoveries of new worlds of peoples and places around the globe, and even newer worlds of mountains on the moon, rings around Saturn, and satellites around Jupiter, were made possible by the technological developments of the time. Stronger and more seaworthy vessels made exploration across the open sea possible, and carefully crafted devices of measurement and observation made people aware of realms that had been unknown to earlier peoples. Galileo's familiar discoveries in the sky were made possible by the telescope, a simple device invented in Holland. The microscope, developed as a usable tool a half century later by Leeuwenhoek (1632–1732), revealed the inner workings of living things. The world appeared to thinkers of these early modern times as a gigantic machine, a kind of clockwork, and, many thought, if we could only understand its mechanisms, we would obtain power over things on the earth and in the heavens.

A clockwork! This metaphor, applied to the movements of the stars in the skies and even to the structure of living bodies, would have been unavailable to the Greeks and Romans, for the pendulum and weight- or spring-driven clock was an invention of the late medieval and early modern world. It has been called the parent of all mechanical devices. It works by applying a constant force, such as a spring or weight, to a system of levers, ratchets, escapements, and wheels, which transmits the force to the hands of the clock. By moving at a regular pace across a set of equidistant marks, these "hands" create, as it were, a new commodity, measurable time. And so we say, "Time is money."

The significance of the clock in the self-understanding or the world-view of early modern people is not simply that life became more regulated, and work and play could be scheduled according to the movements of the hands of the clock. It produced a new concept of cause and effect that was unknown in the ancient world. According to Aristotle, for example, there was a final or teleological cause of change. This cause was the end to which the effect is directed. The acorn, for example, unfolds toward its natural end, the oak tree, to which its nature as an acorn directs it. In this way, the future of the acorn determines its activities in the present, in the same way that a man's activity of walking along the road is determined by the destination he has in mind. For Aristotle and for most of the ancient and medieval thinkers, an element of mind, however small, is everywhere in nature. Divine love, as the final end toward which all things were believed to strive, determines the very motions of things. Dante Alighieri (1265–1321) ended his *Divine Comedy* with a reference to the "love that moves the sun and the other stars."

Now it is impossible to account for the movements of the parts of a clock in terms of its natural ends. The clock is propelled forward only by the energy of the weight or the spring. No doubt we can explain human and perhaps even animal behavior by the purposes these creatures are pursuing. But the clock is a mere mechanism; nothing determines its behavior except the measurable forces brought to bear upon it. It seems to be entirely explainable in its movements by those forces. Even the movement of the stars in the skies, if they are thought to be a kind of clockwork, must be moved by some original force or impetus that was applied to them at the creation, or, perhaps, applied at intervals by the invisible hand of God. But what moves a thing must be a kind of efficient force, not an end to which it is naturally directed or attracted, and early modern people began an effort to understand the world in which they lived in terms of the metaphor of a clockwork mechanism. The story of the abandonment of Aristotle's metaphysics of causes is the story of the banishment of mind and purpose from nature.

The Enlightenment

A further important characteristic of the modern period is the *Enlightenment*. This term usually designates the last phase of early modernism and can be dated as extending from the publication of Newton's *Principa Mathematica* (1687) until the outbreak of the French Revolution in 1789. The Enlightenment was a period of great optimism, despite the continuing warfare on the European continent and the domination of politics by an increasingly ineffectual system of monarchy and aristocracy. Some underlying reasons can be given for that optimism that have relevance to the history of philosophy.

First, the enormous success of Newtonian science in explaining large areas of physical nature, and the increasing power over nature that was being made possible by new technology, gave thoughtful people hope that science would eventually be able to solve the human puzzle as well. Since knowledge of the workings of nature had been shown to be possible, people thought we should be able, before long, to understand the working of human beings—their psychology, their politics, their social arrangements, and the like. And since scientific knowledge makes technological improvements possible, it should also be possible to apply new knowledge of human behavior to an improvement of human arrangements. Thus it was hoped that new generations would be able to create a more just society, to combat the ignorance of the peasantry, to eliminate superstition, and to increase the general prosperity.

Second, the system of capitalism discussed earlier was controlled by the middle classes. These entrepreneurs and bankers seemed to be the most dynamic part of civil society, and through their innovations and their willingness to take risks, so they believed, society was reaping great material benefits; but, they complained, they were marginalized in a society whose social, cultural, and political leaders were privileged only by their aristocratic birth, and not by their abilities or achievements. In fact, these aristocrats were a social liability. Their kings and barons were eternally engaging themselves and the people in socially useless wars fought for prestige or for the privileges of some dynasty, and the aristocratic bishops and cardinals were contributing nothing while filling the people's minds with superstitions. Complaints such as these were conducive to

Denis Diderot. © *Thoemmes.*

the growing philosophy of democracy. In the form this political doctrine took in such thinkers as Denis Diderot (1713–1784) and François Marie Arouet, known as Voltaire (1694–1778), it argued for freedom of thought and freedom from tyranny, so that individuals could make use of their intelligence and their initiative regardless of birth.

Third, the Enlightenment celebrated the use of reason above religious belief and science above superstition, or the uncritical acceptance of traditional beliefs. It demanded a different attitude toward the world and toward the human being. Kant's famous definition of enlightenment is appropriate: He called it a mental emancipation from a self-imposed immaturity by the determination to use reason in knowledge and in action. To be enlightened is to think rationally on your own. Of course such a doctrine had political consequences for its times. As much as the theory of democracy implied an attack upon the privileges of the aristocrats, so did the emphasis upon reason contain an implicit attack upon the privileges of the bishops and cardinals, which rested upon beliefs concerning their spiritual power that could not be justified by rational science. No doubt, the monopoly of spiritual power by the Catholic hierarchy had been broken in the seventeenth century by the conclusion of the Thirty Years' War, which ended by dividing Europe into Catholic and Protestant spheres. It is not surprising that the emphasis upon reason and the attack upon superstition was strongest among the Enlightenment thinkers living in the Catholic parts of Europe.

These developments did not at first affect the religious beliefs of most Europeans. Of course, the breaking of the spiritual hegemony of the Catholic

Church by the Protestant Reformation was eventually significant for the development of the new philosophies, for it permitted thinkers a greater freedom, and the Protestant lands fostered science and technology. One feature of European thought remained constant. When Europe had become Christianized during the later Roman Empire, Europeans, of course, adopted the moral beliefs developed by the ancient Jews. These beliefs differ from the teaching of Plato and Aristotle on human virtue or excellence, in that biblical teaching on morals gives a central role to moral rules, such as the Ten Commandments. However, the use of reason to criticize religion also posed a problem for ethics. Denis Diderot, who believed that religion in general was the enemy of reason and progress, raised an important objection to his own belief: If religion and God are done away with, what will motivate people to pursue goodness and refrain from evil? Does not morality depend upon the idea of a God and an afterlife in which we will be punished for our wickedness in hell and rewarded in heaven for our goodness? Some of the Enlightenment thinkers, in order to respond to this problem, attempted to put morality upon a new footing by attempting to demonstrate the rationality of moral rules.

Rationalists and Empiricists

The first of the early modern thinkers on the Continent are called *rationalists* for their belief that knowledge of the natural world could be acquired, as it is in mathematics, by thinking alone, or pure reason. The philosopher must reflect upon simple but clear and distinct ideas that can be known to be true with certainty, and to draw out the logical implications of those ideas. The model of such a procedure is again mathematics, either plane geometry, in which hundreds of theorems can be proven from a few axioms taken to be clearly and distinctly true (such as the famous Euclidean axiom that the shortest distance between two points is a straight line), or the new analytical geometry and calculus that were invented in the seventeenth century.

The first philosopher of the modern world was René Descartes (1596–1650), who attempted nothing less than a reconstruction of all knowledge by means of the methods of intuition and deduction. Believing that a reliable method of reconstruction required at least one absolutely certain starting-point to which all subsequent discoveries could be traced to as their ultimate justification, Descartes proposed to give reasons for doubting every proposition he thought true until he discovered a proposition that it was impossible to doubt. That proposition was the famous "I think, therefore I am." No reasons can be given for doubting this proposition, he thought, for whenever one attempts to do so, one runs across the fact that the very effort to doubt this proposition presupposes its truth. How can one doubt one's own existence without first existing as the subject of that doubt? This proposition, therefore, "I am a thing that thinks," must be the most certain of all beliefs, and may stand as a model of the clarity and distinctness that all knowledge must possess. Knowledge must be as intuitively clear or be deduced from propositions as clear as this one. Descartes worked out the details of his method in his autobiographical *Discourse on Method* (1637), used his method to draw conclusions about the general structure of the universe and the human being in *Meditations on First Philosophy* (1641), and applied his method to the physical sciences in *Principles of Philosophy* (1644). In mathematics, he invented what we now call analytic geometry. Descartes's method had the odd consequence of separating the human mind from the physical world, and it thereby gave to philosophy the key issue of the mind's relationship to the world, which still plagues it today.

Benedict Spinoza's (1632–1677) philosophy appears to be a radical example of Descartes's notion that philosophy should take its model of discovery and proof from mathematics and show how complex theorems about the world can be deduced from intuitively clear and distinct axioms. Although Spinoza presents his philosophy in the *Ethics* as a system of deductions from axioms and presumably uncontroversial definitions of things, his philosophy was no doubt the product of prolonged reflections to which he subsequently gave a mathematical form. As its title indicates, the *Ethics* is not simply a system of metaphysics and science, but a prescription for living well. Spinoza assumes, as we generally do not assume today, that knowledge of the nature of the physical world has moral implications for human existence and enables us to distinguish between living well and living poorly. Yet for many readers, his book has enormous spiritual force, and leaves us with what Spinoza called a joyous "intellectual love of God." God is, however, understood not as creator and lawgiver, but as the embodiment of the physical laws according to which things happen, and the power or force whereby events take place. In that sense Spinoza could write, "Everything expresses [as law and as power], in a certain and unique manner, the eternal and infinite essence of God."

Gottfried Wilhelm Leibniz (1646–1716) was born and died in Germany. Unlike Spinoza, but much like many men of the Renaissance, Leibniz's interests were very broad, and he wrote on most of the topics that were debated by philosophers and natural scientists in his day. Like Descartes, he contributed a new kind of mathematics, the calculus (whose discovery is also attributed to Newton; no doubt the discoveries were independent of each other), and was concerned to provide a basis of certainty for all science and philosophy. His contributions to logic, theory of language, and mathematics are considerable, and many commonplace distinctions and conceptualizations in philosophy, such as the Identity of Indescernables, the notion of "possible worlds," and the **Principle of Sufficient Reason** are attributed to him. His metaphysical system involves a unique notion of substance, which he called *monads*. A monad is the substance peculiar to each individual. It is absolutely simple, in that it contains no parts and cannot, therefore, be extended in space. It must therefore be spiritual. It contains every attribute correctly predicated of an individual thing or person, makes it what it is, and distinguishes it from every other thing. The monad is therefore extremely complex, although it is without parts. Each monad, although blind and aware only of itself, reflects all other monads in the universe. Leibniz's works include the *Monadology* (1714), the *Discourse on Metaphysics* (1668), and the *Theodicy* (1710).

Gottfried Wilhelm Leibniz. © *Thoemmes.*

THE PRINCIPLE OF SUFFICIENT REASON: The assertion is that for everything that happens, there must be a reason that accounts for that happening and makes it necessary. Such a notion seems obvious, as of course Leibniz thought it was; after all, if an event takes place, there must be some possible accounting for it available, even if we do not currently possess such an account. If a horse is found to be suspended in midair, all observers would immediately assume that this event has some explanation: something is holding the horse up, the law of gravity does not apply for some reason in this place, currents of air from below are forcing the horse upwards, and the like. No one would assume that the event is simply without a cause, or fundamentally random and incomprehensible. Yet the notion is not so obvious when one considers that much superstition and magic is based precisely on the notion that events can take place for no comprehensible reason. The scientific revolution was making the world a much less mysterious place, and Leibniz was one of the thinkers to try to formulate a metaphysics from which randomness, magic, and chance were banished.

The early modern thinkers who lived in Great Britain are contrasted with the continental rationalists by their almost universal emphasis upon the use of the senses, rather than pure reason, for the discovery and justification of knowledge. The tone of this philosophy, called *empiricism,* was set by Francis Bacon (1561–1626). Among his works, the *Novum Organum* (1620) seeks to establish as fundamental to method in the sciences the careful collection of empirical data and then the formulation of inductive generalizations about that data. For example, the observation of the behavior of some population of animals would allow us to draw true conclusions regarding their mating and eating habits, the length of their life span, their relationships with each other, and the like. Such a procedure is, of course, fundamental to many of the empirical sciences, but most observers today believe that the process of scientific discovery is far more complex than Bacon realized.

The other British empiricists, who will be discussed at some length in Part II of this book, are Thomas Hobbes (1588–1679), John Locke (1632–1704), George Berkeley (1685–1753), David Hume (1711–1776), and the economist Adam Smith (1723–1790). Among this group, David Hume stands out today as the giant of English-speaking philosophy, and perhaps as the greatest philosopher to write in that language. Hume's life, perhaps more than that of most other great thinkers of his time, was a very varied one. He traveled on the Continent, especially in France, knew most of the leading intellectuals of his day, served as a diplomat, carried on an extensive correspondence, and in later life achieved the literary fame he had been desirous of since his early youth. His greatest works are *Treatise on Human Nature* (1739–1740), which he later revised and published as *An Enquiry concerning Human Understanding* (1748), and *An Enquiry concerning the Principles of Morals* (1751). He was most famous in his day for his *History of England* (1754–62), but he was often criticized as an atheist and skeptic, and he decided to let his work on religion, the *Dialogues on Natural Religion,* be published only after his death.

Intellectual activity during the Enlightenment was especially intense in France during the eighteenth century. Mention has already been made of the great essayist Voltaire, and the encyclopedist Denis Diderot (1713–1784), and to them must be added Etienne Bonnot de Condillac (1715–1780), Jean d'Alembert (1717–1783), Charles-Louis de Sconday, Baron de Montesquieu (1689–1755), the Marquis de Condorcet (1743–1794), and the Baron d'Holbach (1723–1789). Of special interest is Diderot, who represents the spirit of the Enlightenment perfectly. He was optimistic and outgoing, dedicated to the cause of liberal social change, and critical of the church. His commitment to science and technology is evident in his efforts to produce an encyclopedia, that is, a reference work that would comprise the latest information about all areas of knowledge. Diderot was especially concerned to include scientific and technological knowledge, believing that the wide dissemination of science would produce inventions that would better human life.

In Germany, a great representative of the Enlightenment was Johann Gottfried Herder (1744–1803), whose *Ideas on the Philosophy of History of Humankind* (1784–1791) presents a remarkably liberal and appreciative view, for its time, of the achievements of non-European peoples and civilizations. Immanuel Kant (1724–1804) is considered the greatest philosopher of the modern age. His three great Critiques—the *Critique of Pure Reason,* the *Critique of Practical Reason,* and the *Critique of Judgment*—attempt to place philosophy and science, morals, and aesthetics on a secure if subjective foundation, that is, one that reflects the categories of the human mind instead of seeking what Kant thought was unavailable certainty concerning the ultimate nature of the world.

The Nineteenth Century

The nineteenth century is a period of romance and squalor, of great poetry, music, and art, but also of the enslavement of masses of people for the aims of industrial and technological progress; a period of war and foreign conquest, but also of a prolonged period of peace at home. Two characteristics of this century are of special interest to philosophers: the *growth of democracy* and the *industrial revolution*.

The Idea of Democracy

Democracy is a system of government with two central characteristics. First, the people with political power or desirous of obtaining power are required to submit themselves at regular intervals to the judgment of the people, who may elect them or remove them from office. Second, the people are guaranteed by law certain political rights, such as freedom of assembly, the right to bear arms, an unfettered press, and the right to think and to publish one's thoughts as one will. Democracy requires public education, for in order to vote or to exercise one's rights, a person must be able to read, write, and think for oneself. As people became more able to take part in the political and civic process by means of public education, a larger audience than ever before was provided for the creations of art, literature, and philosophy. People began to have a sense of themselves not as subjects of a monarch who ruled by the grace of God, but as citizens of a state who were responsible, in some measure, for the quality of the government they received. People also began to consider themselves members of a nation and a people with a unique fate in human history. Napoleon's armies spread about Europe the democratic ideals of the Revolution—Liberty, Equality, Fraternity—and the sense of national glory that led, in many cases, to pent-up hostility toward their neighbors by patriotic French, Germans, English, and Russians.

The Industrial Revolution

The Industrial Revolution had begun in England during the second half of the eighteenth century. The end of the Napoleonic Wars and the start of the new European order established at the Congress of Vienna in 1814–15 brought a peace that was to last, with a few minor wars in Europe, for a hundred years. The revolution in industry, banking, and technology that had transformed Britain a half-century earlier spread to the Continent. The changes in the lives of people that it produced was immense. Not all of those changes were negative ones; the Industrial Revolution extended people's span of life, gave them more secure dwellings, and provided wealth that was used to build universities and hospitals. Industry required, made possible, and made Europeans more aware of peoples and cultures existing beyond their own borders. Yet the Industrial Revolution also produced inner-city filth and disease, tied people to a workshop outside their own hearth and home, separated them for most of the day from their families, and put them at the mercy of the often rapacious men who owned the factories where they worked.

During the first part of this period, philosophy remained abstract, to a certain extent unworldly, and academic, in the sense that it became so technical that only persons who spent most of their lives as students and professors at universities could hope to master its intricacies or even its implications for human life. Of the greatest nineteenth-century thinkers, only those who were concerned primarily for social action, such as Karl Marx (1818–1883) or John Stuart Mill (1806–1873) were not university professors, or among those who aspired to join them.

German Idealism

The time was an especially fruitful one for philosophy in Germany, where the school known as German Idealism flourished. The ideas of democracy, nationalism, imperialism, and the Industrial Revolution had not yet struck deep roots in Germany, and yet the ideal of human liberty was a lightning-rod for German thought. It was the age of Schiller and Goethe in literature, and of Beethoven in music. German idealism attempted to reestablish the function of mind in nature by deducing all of reality from an absolute Idea, Self, or Spirit. Its chief representatives were Johann Gottlieb Fichte (1762–1814), Friedrich Wilhelm Joseph Schelling (1775 1854), and Georg Wilhelm Friedrich Hegel (1770–1831). Hegel's *Encyclopedia of the Philosophical Science in Outline* is one of the great speculative achievements of the human mind.

In the decades after the death of Hegel in 1831, the most vital activities of philosophy on the Continent were social and political in their purpose. A group of thinkers known as the Young Hegelians dominated debate about such questions as the foundation of religion, the future of the state, the social and political role of the newly emancipated Jews in European affairs, and the direction of human history. The greatest of the Young Hegelians of the left and, indeed, the greatest social philosopher of the nineteenth century, was Karl Marx. Marx attempted to leap beyond even the most radical of the Young Hegelians by turning Hegelianism on its head, or, as Marx put it positively, by "turning Hegel right side up." By this metaphor Marx signals that he intends to understand civil society—a nation's politics, law, culture, and morality—not as the expression of an absolute idea or even of the human unconsciousness, but as the products of human economic activity. Marx's epochal contribution to economics, *Das Kapital,* appeared in three volumes, the first in 1867, and the second and third after the philosopher's death, in 1885 and 1894 respectively. His more philosophical works, many not published until long after his death, reflect his critical sprit and moral idealism. They include *The Holy Family* (written in 1845), a critique of some of the Young Hegelians, and *German Ideology* (written 1845–1846).

Søren Kierkegaard

At midcentury there lived and wrote in Copenhagen a man to whom the earliest studies on themes that became vital to the twentieth-century school known as *Existentialism* are often traced. Søren Kierkegaard (1813–1855) saw his task in life as one of revitalizing Christianity by showing that it is not simply a belief that most of his contemporaries took for granted, but a way of life whose foundations are always uncertain and unfinished. We cannot be certain, Kierkegaard believed, either of God's existence or our own commitment to God; we must take a "leap of faith" and hold fast to our faith even in the face of objective uncertainty if we are to become Christians. Faith is an act of will, not an intellectual discovery, or an uncritical acceptance of some tradition. This attitude toward religious faith requires analysis of the human way of existence itself, an analysis that lays bare its temporal nature (a human life is always "unfinished business" until death), and each person's moral responsibility for both her actions and for the general shape of her life. An individual existence becomes a self (if it does so at all) by a kind of self-creation; its salvation, however, is not created by will, but by the leap that prepares one to receive the grace of God. Kierkegaard distinguished three such shapes of life, or what he called "stages on life's way," the aesthetic, the ethical, and the religious, and their categories of enjoyment, responsibility, and faith respectively. Kierkegaard wrote voluminously but was little known outside of Denmark until the beginning of the twentieth century. Then his works began to have an immense influence and were quickly translated into other European languages. His most significant contribution to philosophy is his critique of Hegel, which he called *The Concluding Unscientific Postscript* to the "system" of the universe created by the great German. No system can ever capture human life, Kierkegaard believed, for human life is essentially characterized by incompleteness.

John Stuart Mill

Great Britain's achievements in philosophy in the nineteenth century were less significant than its achievements in science and literature. Its greatest thinker was John Stuart Mill, whose works on moral theory and social liberalism continue to be discussed in the English-speaking world today. Mill accepted and extended the empiricism and utilitarianism of his great eighteenth-century predecessors, and he believed that all of our ideas are derived from sense experience, and all our motivations can be reduced to a desire for pleasure. His empiricism brought him into conflict with "intuitionist" philosophers such as William Whewell (1794–1866) and William Hamilton (1788–1856), who believed that there are necessary ideas in consciousness that are irreducible to sensations, and these constitute the foundations of our beliefs about the world.

Herbert Spencer

An important British thinker who attempted to develop the philosophical implications of evolutionary theory in the second half of the nineteenth century was Herbert Spencer (1826–1903). During most of his life he worked on a projected twenty-volume *System of Synthetic Philosophy.* Spencer generalized the notion of evolution and applied it to psychological and historical, as well as to biological processes. His thought contributed, perhaps against his own intentions, to the school of Social Darwinism, which teaches that the state should not interfere with the evolution of the economic system, even to relieve the distress of unfortunates who are unable to compete effectively within it. Such efforts (at welfare-statism, for example) are either useless or harmful, for evolution is a law of nature, and serves the health and viability of a species by weeding out the unfit.

Friedrich Nietzsche

The nineteenth-century thinker who has had the deepest and most persistent influence on subsequent philosophy is the German, Friedrich Nietzsche (1844–1900). Nietzsche is credited by some observers today as having initiated a thoroughgoing critique of the entire Western philosophical tradition, which finds expression today in what is called postmodernism. In the intensity with which he lived is life and pondered questions of human existence, he is also associated, as is Kierkegaard, with the later existentialist movement. In *Thus Spoke Zarathustra,* he announced the death of God and proposed to replace religious belief and its struggle for salvation with a hope in the coming of a morally and intellectually superior human being, the Superman. Human beings must be plunged in a constant struggle to realize their own capacity for power over themselves and the world. Two characteristics of the Superman are his readiness to demolish all Western metaphysics and epistemology, and his willingness to risk a complete reevaluation of all Western values and morals and dare to pass, as the title of one of his books tempts him to do, "beyond good and evil." This effort requires individuals to abandon any belief in objective and absolute knowledge, and to measure a belief against its ability to enhance their power over themselves and others.

THE CONTEMPORARY WORLD

General Characteristics

It would be a gross exaggeration to see in Nietzsche's work a prophecy of the philosophical obsessions of the century that followed his, as some observers have done. However, several theories that were argued by Nietzsche with special force have been assented to by most philosophers in the twentieth century. These notions are interrelated. The first is the *impossibility of metaphysics* as the science of ultimate reality. The effort to grasp the nature of that which is, as such, is a vain effort to step outside of humankind's perspectives and see reality as it is in itself. The second is a corollary to this position: *no absolute or certain knowledge exists;* what we call "knowledge" is derived from the peculiar standpoint of the creatures who lay claim to knowledge, namely human beings. Knowledge is always mediated by our senses and by the language that gives voice to our sense experience. It is not possible to stand apart from that perspective, or to achieve a perspective that is absolutely foundational—a "God's-eye" view of things (as, for example, Descartes believed to be possible)—or to find a kind of skyhook as a firm and certain foundation of being to which we could attach an edifice of knowledge that mirrors reality in an undistorted manner.

The third is the claim that *no system of moral knowledge is possible.* Philosophy cannot discover and justify principles that would validly dictate to the human will how persons should act and live. Socrates's belief that philosophy is the search for the Good Life is misconceived; there is no good life as such, beyond the simple satisfaction of humankind's material needs. There is no systematic answer to the question of what makes a person's life worth living.

Fourth, and finally, twentieth-century philosophy has *lost its connection to a concept of God* and abandoned the Jewish and Christian belief in an intelligent, holy, and supremely benevolent creator of the world. God may not be dead for all philosophers, but he does not undergird the picture of reality, knowledge, and morals as their final point of reference, as was the case since Plato first spoke of the Idea of the Good. Even the notion of an absolute mind or will, or an absolute anything, seems foreign to most thinkers today. Just as high art has not produced convincing representations of Christ since at least the middle of the last century, so has high philosophy not produced a convincing form of theism since at least the time of Hegel.

To make these claims about philosophy in the twentieth century is not to deny that there are dissenters from these four claims. But those who dissent have usually returned to earlier philosophies and religious doctrines for their spiritual nourishment, in the hope of infusing them with new vigor and using them to undermine and subvert what they believe to be the limitations and weaknesses of the prevailing views. Most creative philosophers have accepted the collapse, as it were, of Western metaphysics, epistemology, ethics, and the philosophy of religion, and located their efforts at human self-understanding in the wasteland that collapse has left behind.

The revolution they forged in philosophy was not the sole reorientation of human thinking and acting in the twentieth century. The beginning of the century—let us take the forty years from 1880 to 1920—saw one of the greatest outpourings of genius in western history, indeed in all of world history. Science was transformed by Max Planck (1858–1947), the originator of the quantum theory in physics, and Albert Einstein (1879–1955), the creator of the theory of relativity. Both theories were disquieting, in that they appeared to contradict common sense and had philosophical implications regarding the impossibility of objective and certain knowledge. There was a fundamental change in Western music during these years. Arnold Schönberg (1874–1951) developed a system for writing music in which the progression of musical ideas through keys, which was fundamental to Western music since the Renaissance, was abandoned in favor of atonality. In art, Pablo Picasso (1881–1973) and many other experimentalists broke decisively with the representation of objects in three-dimensional space, which again had been fundamental to painting since the Renaissance. Great breakthroughs in logic and mathematics were made, and an amazing attempt to unify the two was undertaken by Bertrand Russell (1872–1970) and A. N. Whitehead (1861–1947) in their *Principia Mathematica* (1917). During these years biology was also transformed by the young science of genetics and the discovery of chromosomes. We today are still living off the capital provided by these great discoverers and innovators of the early twentieth century.

World War I was not only immensely destructive of lives and property, it also had a profound influence upon the minds of Europeans and Americans. The confidence in progress that had been a legacy of the Enlightenment and supported by a century of astounding material and technological progress and peace was shattered by the experience of a war of attrition, in which men killed men from the trenches spread across France and Belgium. The sheer beastliness of the conflict, and its use of carefully contrived technology to kill and maim, led to demands for radical social and economic change, and yet also to defeatism, loss of confidence, and unquenched hatred among the combatants. Especially unsettling for intellectuals was the sight of men of different nations all praying to the same god for victory, and patriots arguing that justice itself was on their side.

Further, the economic structure of Europe was changed. In 1917, the Russian Revolution resulted in the first large-scale application of the socialist ideas nurtured in the nineteenth century, and the Western powers too began experimenting with socialist modifications of the capitalist system. People became dependent upon government for such things as health care, the construction of infrastructure, such as roads and airports, social security, and the regulation of the economy. The exploitive character of capitalism, in which the owners of the means of production paid armies of workers just enough to keep them working effectively, became less extreme with the rise of labor unions and of social legislation designed to protect the workers from unfair labor practices. The failure of these changes in capitalism to overcome the social misery of the economic depression of the 1930s, the linking of communism in Soviet Russia to the extreme despotism of Stalin, and the catastrophe of German and Japanese fascism plunged the world into the even more destructive Second World War. The shattering outcomes of this war—Europe was left in ruins, and the lives of an estimated fifty-five million persons were lost—cost Europe the intellectual, economic, and military superiority it had enjoyed since the sixteenth century. The colonial empire over which the European states had ruled collapsed, for the most part, within two decades of the war's end. It is perhaps not surprising that European philosophers came to believe not only in the Death of God, but in the death of philosophy also. Nothing remained to be said about its traditional themes of truth and goodness and beauty, of justice, knowledge, and even of the nature of the morally scarred and defeated human being.

One further change during the twentieth century of interest to the history of philosophy deserves to be noticed. The rise of mass armies since the time of Napoleon was accompanied by the growth of mass society. The complex class distinctions typical of earlier times was eroded, and individuals came to be distinguished only as the "haves" and "have nots." The usual separation of high-brow and lowbrow spiritual culture and popular culture was blurred because of new technological possibilities for the dissemination of information and entertainment. First newspapers, then radio, and later television, which could be read, heard, or seen by great numbers of people, created a kind of common culture among the masses. A process of leveling began that was first noted by the Spanish philosopher José Ortega y Gasset (1885–1955). The lowest standards of art, music, and philosophy eroded the prestige and authority of the higher culture. "Mass man," who has more time and money at his disposal than ever before, is unable or unwilling to learn to appreciate the higher culture, which sinks to his level to exploit his buying power. In such circumstances, nothing in tradition is viewed as holy or sublime. The vulgar, the tawdry, the violent, and the beastly begin to infect the common culture of all but a handful of people. The higher art, literature, and music began to turn inward; philosophers, for example, began to write only for other philosophers and lost their touch with the general reading public.

Pragmatism

In the early part of the century, this parochialism was not yet entirely characteristic of philosophy. In America, for example, the school known as *pragmatism* was intended for study by the average educated citizen, for it aspired to have a practical and beneficial influence upon the behavior and beliefs of persons and on the effectiveness of their civic institutions. Pragmatism as a distinctive way of doing philosophy is traced to Charles Sanders Peirce (1839–1914), who, in addition to technical works of great value on logic, published in 1877–1878 a famous essay in the popular press entitled "How to Make Our Ideas Clear." Here he argued that the methods of science should be brought to bear upon everyday beliefs. Beliefs should be measured according to their practical value; that is, we must always ask what the practical consequences are of maintaining some belief. In accord with the growing sense of the futility of any philosophy that attempts to grasp ultimate reality, Peirce noted that metaphysical beliefs such as Hegel's doctrine that the Absolute Idea realizes itself in history has no practical consequences whether it is true or false, so that entertaining it is useless.

Peirce's younger friend and associate William James (1842–1910) argued that some religious beliefs may, given certain conditions, have positive benefit to the life of the person who embraces them, and, where those conditions are fulfilled, a person may exercise his "will to believe" (1897) and live a religious life, even if the evidence for religious belief is not rationally compelling. Another philosopher associated with pragmatism is John Dewey (1859–1952), who also addressed himself frequently to a general audience. His works on the philosophy and practice of childhood education emerged in great measure from his experiences at the laboratory school he helped to found at the University of Chicago. During the middle decades of the twentieth century, most public school children in the United States were educated following ideas set forth by Dewey. For example, instead of having desks in parallel order all facing the teacher-authority, desks were arranged so that children could interact with each other. The teacher facilitated their learning while the children worked together on some activity, project, or experiment. As Dewey noted, you do not teach a child to swim by giving her a book on swimming!

Logic and Language in the English-Speaking World

Despite this continuing openness of philosophers to public issues, the orientation of most philosophy during the twentieth century was toward abstruse questions of logic or linguistic analysis. While examining the structure of human thinking in some area, be it mathematics or physics, religion or morals, philosophers followed up the implications of linguistic and logical structures, in order to make clear what otherwise might remain unnoticed by mathematicians, physicists, religious people, or moralists. Among the logical analysts were Gottlob Frege (1848–1925), Alfred Tarski (1902–1983), Rudolf Carnap (1891–1970), and Carl Hempel (1905–1997). More recent contributors to the structure and self-understanding of logical analysis are Willard van Orman Quine (1908–2000), and Hilary Putnam (1926–); the latter stands close to attempts to recover the philosophy of pragmatism for contemporary debates.

The majority of philosophers in the English-speaking world have turned their attention to an analysis of their natural language, as opposed to artificial, logical, or scientific languages, in an effort to solve traditional philosophical puzzles by demonstrating their origins in a misuse of language. Only a few English-speaking thinkers in the twentieth century would not fit under the rubric of linguistic analysis, notably Marxists and Catholic Thomists. To name them all would be to provide a list of most people who have contributed to academic philosophy in American, British, and Australian universities during the last hundred years. A list of a few outstanding analysts of the natural language might begin with Bertrand Russell (1872–1970), who deserves to be mentioned for his contributions to the practice of analysis itself as well as to the logical analysis of mathematical language. Ludwig Wittgenstein's (1889–1951) teaching, and his posthumous *Philosophical Investigations,* had enormous influence upon philosophers working first in England but then in the entire English-speaking world. Some philosophers working in the Witttgensteinian orbit are John Wisdom (1904–1993), whose article, "Gods" (1945), suggests that talk about God or gods may be meaningless insofar as such talk fails to identify possible experiences that would verify it. Gilbert Ryle (1900–1976) is celebrated for his *Concept of Mind* (1949), a deconstruction of Descartes's notion of the "thinking thing," mind, which he derided as a "ghost in a machine." Perhaps the most characteristic of the "ordinary language" philosophers was J. L. Austin (1911–1960), whose *Sense and Sensibilia* (1962) explored the understanding of knowledge and reality implicit in our everyday talk.

Nothing dies without a trace, of course, and the metaphysical spirit continued to live among some professors of philosophy. At Harvard, the British philosopher Alfred North Whitehead (1897–1947) initiated *process philosophy* in his 1929 work, *Process and Reality.* This philosophy attacks the notion of Aristotle that only individual substances are real and proposes to substitute processes and events as the fundamental realities. Paul Weiss of Yale University (1901–2001) founded the *Review of Metaphysics* in 1947. His colleague at Yale, Brand Blanshard (1892–1987) had ties to Hegelianism, and his critique of the prevailing empiricist and anti-metaphysical beliefs of his contemporaries appeared in *The Nature of Thought.* In England, the Oxford philosopher Peter Strawson (1919–) distinguished between "speculative" metaphysics, such as that of Hegel or Plato, which seeks knowledge of the structure of reality itself, and "descriptive" metaphysics, which seeks to reveal the foundational categories of language. Only the latter form of metaphysics is viable, in Strawson's view. In *Individuals* (1959), he argued that any view of reality will depend upon a language's possession of the category of individuals. A knowing subject must be able to distinguish basic particulars of various kinds if it is to have a world at all, especially one containing physical objects and persons.

Philosophy on the European Continent

On the European continent, a fundamental reorientation of philosophical method also took place. In *Logical Investigations* (1900–01) and *Ideas I* (1913), the German philosopher Edmund Husserl developed a method, known as *phenomenology,* of analyzing our direct and prelinguistic experience. The school he influenced had adherents and practitioners in most of the countries on the Continent. They included Max Scheler (1874–1928), whose *Formalism in Ethics* applied a method inspired if not adapted from Husserl to value theory; Martin Heidegger (1889–1876), whose *Being and Time* (1927) is a seminal work in the philosophy of the human being; and Jean Paul Sartre (1905–1980), whose *Being and Nothingness* (1943) drew upon both Husserl and Heidegger and is a comprehensive statement of the philosophy of Existentialism. Existentialism is founded in the phenomenological method. It is concerned with a description and evaluation of the human situation and the peculiar human way of existence. Historians have included many writers under the rubric of existentialism. Especially notable are, in Germany, Karl Jaspers (1883–1969) and the theologians and scholars Paul Tillich (1886–1965) and Martin Buber (1878–1965), who lived out the later years of their lives in the United States and Israel respectively. In Russia there was Nicolai A. Berdyayev (1874–1948), who emigrated to the West after the Russian Revolution. In France, Simone de Beauvoir (1905–1986), Sartre's longtime companion, was a major contributor to existentialist theory, and she influenced younger workers in feminist philosophy, perhaps especially in the United States. Albert Camus (1913–1960), a Nobelist in literature, was a writer of plays and novels as well as essays in philosophy, and Gabriel Marcel (1889–1973), a Catholic theologian, was noted for a treatise in the existentialist style entitled *The Mystery of Being* (1949–1950).

Also originating on the continent of Europe have been a variety of initiatives in philosophy classified under the general rubrics of post-structuralism and postmodernism. Although the term *postmodern* has received different interpretations depending upon the perspective a philosopher, an artist, or a literary critic takes toward the modern world, a common locus for the term is found in *The Postmodern Condition* (1979) by Jean François Lyotard (1924–). Other representatives of postmodernism include Jacques Derrida (1930–) and Michel Foucault (1926–1984). In America, Richard Rorty (1931–) has associated himself with Derrida, as well as with the pragmatists, especially John Dewey.

In postmodernism the anti-metaphysical and value-transformation themes in Nietzsche become most radical. Lyotard identifies the grand narratives or stories told by Christians, Marxists, capitalists, and other representatives of contemporary mainstream thought, who purport to give a single reading of history and to justify the social and moral arrangements they represent. These narratives must be examined for their genesis in power struggles, and deconstructed. Such narratives, and the concepts about which they are centered, contain in their margins elements that are excluded by them as unessential and yet necessary for their coherence. "Rationality," for example, as a part of the modernist narrative of progress, privileges linear thought and argument while marginalizing other legitimate and indispensable means of knowing and acting. Furthermore, each of the discourses that make use of the privileged concepts of the grand narratives is "incommensurable" by others, that is, they are mutually incomprehensible; no consensus, and no single truth could be advanced to unify these diverse speakers. The unity of Western civilization, which was in any case a myth, has now shattered completely, making visible to all the participants its centerless and pluralistic nature.

In the cause of human freedom, argue most of the postmodernists, this pluralism and diversity must be maintained. No one narrative must be allowed to usurp or marginalize all the others. A symptom of postmodernism on the economic and political level is the agitation against globalism and the rejection of the idea of a post-Soviet and post-colonial New World Order under a "pax Americana." No doubt philosophical thought will not be irrelevant to this debate.

PART II

The Problems of Philosophy

CHAPTER 4

Metaphysics

This chapter will address important aspects of the concept of metaphysics. It will provide discussion and analysis on the following topics:

- Aristotle and the Problem of Being
- The Early Greek Cosmologists
- Plato and the Origin of Metaphysics
- Aristotle
- Early Modern Metaphysics
- Metaphysics in Early Modern Great Britain
- Kant and the Critique of Metaphysics
- Hegel
- Metaphysics in the Twentieth Century

ARISTOTLE AND THE PROBLEM OF BEING

"First Philosophy," says **Aristotle**, "is concerned with what is both un-moved and separate from matter." This simple statement is Aristotle's first effort to define the subject matter of what has come to be called *metaphysics*. This name is purely accidental. An ancient editor of Aristotle's works gave the name of "after-the-Physics" (*meta-ta-physika*) to a collection of untitled treatises that he found after a book of Aristotle's called *Physics*. What it is that is both un-moved and separate from matter is not at first identified. Aristotle may be seeking to characterize reality as such, or that which *is* in itself and apart from the individual items that make up the world. Aristotle says in another passage that his theme is "Being as being," that is, of what it is to be in general, and not the being of specific things. After all, one might say that a dog exists, or this thing is a dog. If the characteristics of a dog that make it a dog are subtracted from it, and only its existence is considered, one is left with a sense of bare being. This bare being, if it makes sense to characterize it at all, would be that which is "unmoved and separate from matter."

ARISTOTLE: Aristotle was born in Stagira, Macedonia, in Northern Greece, in 384 B.C.E. His father was a physician to the court of the king of Macedonia. Tradition has it that he once served as tutor to the young Macedonian prince who was to become Alexander the Great. As a young man, Aristotle went to Athens to study with Plato and remained at the Academy for about twenty years, until Plato's death in 347. He lived for a time as the guest and as the husband of the adopted daughter of the ruler of Assos, an independent city-state in Asia Minor, and later on the island of Lesbos, where he conducted biological research. Upon the ascendancy of Alexander, Aristotle returned to Athens in 335, where he opened his own school, the Lyceum. Forced to leave Athens after the death of Alexander, he moved to Euboea, where he lived with, but never married, a servant-girl. It is said that she was buried next to him after his death in 324.

Can what Aristotle is looking for be put into words? His reasoning, which is typical of metaphysics, can be reconstructed as follows: If every attribute is subtracted from the dog but his mere existence, one is left, after all, with nothing. Does this apparent nothingness still characterize all things about which we correctly say that they are? If being is a character of all things, then it should be somehow knowable, just as we say that "having fur" is a knowable character of dogs, among other things. Yet if existence is a knowable descriptive character of things, isn't it then simply one characteristic among all others? It would be different only in that it characterizes all things that are, and not some specific class of them. However, if it is not a descriptive character of all things, then it cannot be an object of knowledge, and speaking of it is useless. To put the problem very simply, a person seems not to be *describing* a thing when he says of it that it is. Yet there also seems to be a difference between a dog that is and one that is merely imaginary. What is at stake in this problem? How would an answer to the question, "Is existence a character of things that are real?" make a difference trying to understand the world, which is the proper aim of science and philosophy?

THE EARLY GREEK COSMOLOGISTS

A clue to why Aristotle thought this question of being as being is the foundation of all philosophy can be found at the earliest beginnings of Western philosophy. Aristotle thought that philosophy began with a man named Thales, who had lived two hundred years before him. This ancient reflective man thought he could talk about the world in a new way. Many stories were attached to his name, but Aristotle attributes three pronouncements to him:

All things are made of water, and the Earth floats upon the water.

The magnet is alive, for it draws the iron to it.

All things are full of gods.

Aristotle does not tell us a great deal about the meaning of Thales's words. They suggest a concern with cosmology, or the structure, origin, order, and nature of the physical world. We know the ancient Greeks imagined the cosmos to be an orderly, harmonious, and, indeed, a beautiful thing. Thales's thought that the cosmos emerges from a single thing, water, was in keeping with this belief in the order and harmony of the world. His words also suggest some key issues that would occupy all of the later thinkers who lived in Greece before the time of Socrates. What is the nature of the physical world? How does one thing arise out of another? What is the nature or the source of the action and reaction that we perceive between things, and how does that nature or source make change possible? Magnets are, after all, not the only source of motion. What is the nature or essence of things (what are they "full of")? Aristotle found lurking in these questions the general problem of being itself.

There is something vast and new in Thales's claim that all things are made of water. The American philosopher **George Santayana** (1863–1952) once wrote that the idea that all visible, changing things are forms of an underlying substance such as Thales's water was perhaps the greatest idea that anyone has ever had. This is high praise, considering that Thales's notion is surely false: all things are not made of water. There must be a deeper reason for Santayana's remark than a desire to assess the truth of Thales's idea.

SANTAYANA'S ASSESSMENT OF THE ANCIENT GREEKS: "The [Greeks'] double experience of mutation and recurrence, an experience at once sentimental and scientific, soon brought with it a very great thought, perhaps the greatest thought that mankind has ever hit upon . . . It is that all we observe about us, and ourselves also, may be so many passing forms of a permanent substance. This substance, while remaining the same in quantity and in inward quality, is constantly redistributed; in its redistribution it forms those aggregates which we call things, and which we find constantly disappearing and reappearing. All things are dust, and to dust they return; a dust, however, eternally fertile, and destined to fall perpetually into new and doubtless beautiful forms."
—George Santayana, *Three Metaphysical Poets.*

The pre-Socratics represent what could be called the childhood, or at least the adolescence of Western thought. Would a child ask the question to which Thales's first statement is the answer: "What are all things made of, Mommy?" Most likely not, because the question does not seem to need an answer, or the answer is obvious: The world is made of all sorts of things, of the earth, of houses, trees, people, cars . . . one could call anything at all a partial answer to the question. Yet there is a logical error here, or at least a misunderstanding: the question that Thales asked himself was not, "What items are there in the world," but rather, "What are all these various items made of? What is their source, their origin, their nature?" Why would someone think that there must be some *one* kind of thing or substance that all other substances are made of?

Consider the following series:

acorn → oak → boards → desk → charcoal

This series has a temporal order, for an item to the right comes later in time than those to its left. It is not a causal series; oaks do not cause boards. Yet in some sense these items are interconnected. The acorn *grows* into a tree, the tree is *cut down* and made into boards, the boards are *nailed together* to make a desk, and the desk, when it has outlived its usefulness, is *burned in fire* to make the charcoal. As appearances, these items are totally different from one another, just as the earth, houses, trees, people, cars . . . are different in appearance from one another. What is it that ties these things together and makes them a series, and makes this series and others like it a *world,* and not just a pile of unrelated objects? Must there not be some connection between the items in the above series that makes them a series, and not just a collection of items that follow each other in sequence?

Because the Greeks thought of the cosmos as orderly and harmonious, Thales may have reflected that such order and harmony could not exist if the items that make it up are not related one to the other. An acorn does not simply stop being an acorn and an oak suddenly appears in its place; after all, nothing comes from nothing, so an oak tree cannot emerge from nothing. Yet an oak is *not* an acorn. On the level of appearance they are completely different. There must therefore be an invisible connection between them. Is there something of the acorn left inside the oak? Our eyes alone will not tell us. Could it be instead that the appearances are manifestations of the same underlying reality? This may be the thought that Thales had. He identified the underlying reality with water.

Aristotle wonders why Thales chose water as the root stuff of the cosmos. Perhaps a plausible answer can be found if one considers that in that same first sentence Thales tells us that the earth floats upon the water. Thales may have thought that the solid earth crystallized out of the original ocean, and all the other things of the world have grown out of the earth. If so, then all things would ultimately be water in some sense, although each thing would appear to our eyes as different. Thales might have thought of a series of visible changes, as that from the acorn to the charcoal, as being made possible only by changes in the underlying ultimate "stuff," water. The visible items are identical to each other in substance: they are all manifestations of the same underlying stuff. Of course Thales could not explain the nature of the transition from, say, an acorn to an oak. He could not say how the material that manifests itself as an acorn becomes the material that manifests itself as an oak.

Socrates. © *Thoemmes.*

It is difficult today to appreciate the puzzle that Thales discovered, just because most people think they know the answer to it. We have gone a long way down the road toward a rational understanding of change that Thales first wondered about. Our science tells us that changes are the result of lawful activity upon the microscopic, or atomic, level. In the acorn, DNA unfolds and directs cells to produce new kinds of cells out of themselves. These cells take on new functions in the living body. New chemical compounds form as the result of interactions among the atomic components of elements. The Greeks knew nothing of all this, of course. They performed no experiments and had none of the devices that enable us to extend our perceptions of the world, such as telescopes and microscopes. They were limited to formulating clever questions about the cosmos and speculating about possible answers to them. Yet the thought that substances and processes that the senses do not give us directly can explain the appearances of things is the root idea of all science.

PLATO AND THE ORIGIN OF METAPHYSICS

The revolution in Greek thought that is marked by the appearance of **Socrates** of Athens extended philosophy far beyond cosmology. Questions of how to create a just society and how to perfect one's own soul were central to Socrates's inquiries. His life was not spent in the investigation of the abstract questions of the nature of the physical world—indeed, he said that natural science, as the speculations of the pre-Socratics may be called, interested him hardly at all—but his was a philosophical life, a life guided in its actions by his discoveries in philosophy. He embodies not the scholarly life, but the life of intellectual and moral struggle.

SOCRATES: Socrates was born in Athens in 469 B.C.E. Not much is known of his early life, except his service in the war against Sparta and his apparent apprenticeship as a sculptor or stonemason. According to the account given in Plato's *Apology,* Socrates's life was strongly affected by the outcome of a visit to the Oracle at Delphi by a friend. The friend asked the oracle who was the wisest man in Greece, and the priestess told him "no man is wiser than Socrates of Athens." Socrates could not understand this response, because he thought that his wisdom had no substance and he had nothing to teach. Believing that the god who spoke through the priestess could not be wrong, Socrates began to test men with a reputation for wisdom to see if they were in fact wiser than he. He soon concluded that although these men thought they were wise, they were not, for they could not answer his questions about what they thought they knew. His wisdom, he thought, must consist in knowing that he was not wise. His persistent questioning of eminent men won him enemies, and he was tried for impiety and for corrupting the young before a tribunal of 501 Athenians. He was found guilty as charged, and sentenced to death. Refusing as base and immoral the opportunity offered by friends to escape the decree of a lawful tribunal, even from one that delivered an unjust sentence to him, he drank the poison hemlock ordered by the tribunal and died in 399 B.C.E. at the age of 70.

His great student, Plato, while continuing Socrates's quest for an understanding of what matters in human life, returned in his own way to the unresolved issues of pre-Socratic philosophy: What is the world made of? What exists really and ultimately? What is the nature and what are the mechanisms of change? In seeking to understand Plato's contribution to these metaphysical problems, some very general aspects of his thought must be first considered.

First, Plato is not studying what came to be called metaphysics; Aristotle in the generation after Plato's produced the first systematic works on First Philosophy. Consequently, Plato does not take up thematically the questions of being as being, or being as it exists independently of motion and of specific things. He is concerned with these questions, but he does not define them as an independent study within philosophy.

Second, Plato does not develop philosophical ideas in impersonal treatises, as Aristotle was later to do. His thought is presented via dialogues, that is, in imaginary conversations among contemporary people. Usually he depicts Socrates asking leading questions of persons presumed to know something about the subject in question. This procedure gives Plato's work the appearance of informality and, more important, permits Plato, the author, to place himself outside the discussions (he never appears in them himself) and take an ironic distance from them. He leaves us with the impression that one should never claim that an idea developed in the *Dialogues* was Plato's own. This procedure has a moral influence upon the reader: it shows him real people struggling to achieve understanding about some issue that matters greatly to them, and he is drawn into the struggle himself. The reader begins to ask himself: What would *I* have said at some point in the conversation, if I had been there? How would the others have responded?

Third, Plato accepts without question the apparent separation between the realm of appearance and the realm of reality that is implicit in the Milesian thinkers. The question of how the two are related—how some original stuff of the universe can be transformed into what it is not, the appearances—occupies his mature philosophy.

Fourth, and finally, Plato regards the cosmos in a spiritual or vaguely religious fashion. The pre-Socratic thinker, Parmenides, like Plato, distinguished between the Way of Truth and the Way of Error and Illusion, and both valued the former above the latter. Plato values the object of true knowledge, the ultimate reality that makes both being and knowledge possible, with a kind of reverence and veneration that, among the Greeks, had usually been reserved for divine things. Hence his attempts to appropriate the true, the good, the beautiful, and the real for his own life, and to realize them within his community, have a spiritual dimension that is unlike anything known in Greek philosophy before it. The word *Platonism* expresses an aspiration to the divine, and this aspiration has made philosophy religious and poetical, as well as analytical.

What is knowledge? A simple case of knowing can be considered. A person looks up from her work and perceives an object on a table, let us say a cup. She recognizes the thing perceived *as* a cup. She could formulate a proposition to state her knowledge: "That thing is a cup." Note in this everyday event the presence of three things: the person as knower, the object seen, and the idea or concept with which she identifies the object as something or other, in this case as a cup.

In general, for there to be knowledge there must be a *knower,* someone who has knowledge of something. The object of knowledge, the *known,* is in this case an object given to the senses with a shape and color, both of which may change a bit as the knower walks around the object. Despite the changing shape and color, she continues to recognize the object as one and the same thing. Yet in order for her to recognize the object as some specific thing, she has to apply a name to what she sees. Usually, these names take the form of words, although it is frequently not possible for a person to tell whether she is thinking in discrete words and propositions. Much of our thought goes on beneath the horizon of our direct awareness. In effect, she is comparing the color and shape she sees with one of the words or wordless ideas she carries about in her head. The result is grasping the thing that she sees as something to which she can apply the word *cup.* And this is a simple form of knowledge.

This notion that all our perceptual knowledge involves some knowledge of ideas or concepts or words (for Plato does not distinguish these terms carefully) raises difficult questions. How is it that people do not just see objects, but also recognize them as something or other? Where does one get one's understanding of the ideas we apply to objects? Are the ideas people in general have of things correct? Socrates had shown, by cross-examining people who thought they possessed true knowledge of courage, or justice, that their knowledge of these ideas, which they invoke when they describe individual objects or classes of objects ("Laches is a courageous man," "Athens has a just government.") is in fact unclear. Should we not distinguish between the ideas of courage or justice we have in our minds, and the real natures that our ideas imperfectly represent? Perhaps, Plato's Socrates suggests, true and ultimate models of courage or justice themselves exist in a realm of their own. Words point in the direction of those models, but they are not grasped in their truth. If this is so, then the world possesses a kind of two-tier structure. On one tier are things and events: courageous men and just cities, all of which have some physical embodiment and are changeable. On the other tier there exist the immutable and eternal Forms of things themselves, of which the individual things on the lower tier are the shadowy embodiments.

The suggestion that ideas exist apart from our minds seems strange to modern ears. Aren't ideas simply abstracted from our perceptual experience? Even a child who has not learned to speak must see similarities in the objects around her. Her parents eventually give her words as a kind of shorthand for referring to those similar items: a cup, milk, and so on. Plato is the author of a tradition that disagrees with this account of language-learning. His reasoning, versions of which are found in various points in his *Dialogues,* takes the simplified form in figure 4.1.

Observe this object.

Figure 4.1

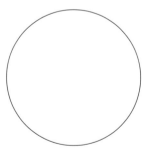

Most people would immediately identify it as a circle. However, a moment of reflection shows us that it is not. It is not a line, for it possesses width and not simply direction, and no printer could produce a circle that is *exactly* circular. In fact, no one has ever seen a perfect circle, only an approximation of one. But then how does one recognize in one's perception of the figure the representation of a circle? Only because people already possess a vague idea of what a circle ought to be and can see in the figure a shadowy example of that idea. People already have a vague notion of the Forms themselves, perhaps because they have seen them in a previous life, or before they were born, Plato speculates. The science of mathematics leads out of the "cave of ignorance" concerning circles, until one is able to contemplate the idea of circularity itself: a closed curved line, each point of which is equidistant from some central point. Similarly, one glimpses the Form of Courage itself in Laches's shadowy representation of it, yet without Socratic training in moral philosophy, which Plato calls *dialectic,* one is left in a cave of darkness where true courage cannot appear. Laches himself, who was an unquestionably courageous man, quickly became confused when he tried to account for the nature of courage in his conversation with Socrates. Yet courage and circles are real; people must therefore be looking with foggy mental spectacles at the structures presupposed by their identification of individual things as circles or as courageous. These structures are the Forms; they are immutable and abide forever in their own realm. They appear to possess, in Plato's view, a hierarchical structure, the highest member of which, the Form of Forms, he calls the Form of the Good.

In a passage in *The Republic,* Plato distinguishes four kinds of knowledge and correlates them with four kinds of being. He has Socrates tell the young men with whom he is discussing to draw a vertical line, divide it once, then divide each of the two segments, thus forming segments having the same ratio as the first two segments.

The left-hand side of the line represents the four kinds of knowledge. The higher of the two large sections is the place of true and certain knowledge. The highest segment of all refers to knowledge of the highest kind of being, the unchangeable Forms themselves and the Form of Forms, the Idea of the Good, which inhabits all Forms. The lower of the top division gives us knowledge of mathematical forms, which are formal structures of a simpler kind. The second and lower half of the diagram presents two kinds of "mere opinion," perception and illusion. Corresponding to them, on the right side of the diagram, are the kinds of being possessed by the world of appearance and becoming: perception gives us the changeable things of this world, and illusion gives us the objects of dream images and the representations of things in painting and sculpture.

With this theory in mind, Plato attempts to answer the questions posed by the pre-Socratic philosophers: What is the cosmos made of, and what is its source or origin? How is change possible? He argues that two kinds of things exist, things physical and things intelligible. The physical things, he says in his great dialogue on cosmology, the *Timaeus,* are made of the elements of earth, air, fire, and water. These elements are essentially **geometric** figures, specifically the four regular geometrical three-dimensional figures, not solids, although they appear to us as solids. The cosmos as a whole is also a geometric figure, the dodecahedron, made of twelve pentagons. For Plato the geometric figures, though stable, are mutable and can take the impression of form.

GEOMETRY: A high-school student who learns to prove theorems in geometry, or work out quadratic equations, may see intuitively that the reasoning she has run through is unquestionably correct and the theorems she has proven are true, but she may still wonder what it is about the world that makes them true. Is there a kind of mathematical structure to the world that the formulas of mathematics represent, or imitate in some sense? Plato thought there was. Could there be any world in which the base angles of isosceles triangles are not equal? Or do our beliefs in mathematics simply reflect a necessity of our thinking, rather than some necessity in the world itself? The mind of any schoolgirl or boy wanders off to another realm when she contemplates such questions, and so does ours. Socrates and Plato were citizens of that realm as surely as they were citizens of Athens.

The intelligible and rational structures of the world, the Forms, can be understood as the *blueprints* of all things. Just as there is a blueprint of a building and a circle, so too there exist blueprints of courage, of justice, of humankind, of all living things, indeed of all things for which there is a name, and perhaps of other things besides. In *Timaeus,* Plato's godlike Demiurge, a conscious, creative force, attempts to form the objects that make up the cosmos according to the ideal blueprints. Thus change comes about as the shifting geometric solids that create the visible realm are made to take on different formal patterns. The cosmos that results from his work is a shadowy imitation of the Forms, as an imitation is a copy of what it imitates. Impelled by the activity of the Demiurge, they are, in a sense, attempting to become more like their own blueprints, much as the efforts of human beings to be just in their actions and laws are an attempt to model their behavior after the eternal Form of Justice itself. No wonder, therefore, that Plato looked upon people who rely upon their senses for their understanding of the world as prisoners chained to a wall in a cave. They can see the shadows before them but are unable to understand the natures of which the shadows are a representation. The function of education is to turn our souls and minds toward the ideas dimly carried by things, to seek out the eternal Form in things, and to understand the structures and laws that make the world a cosmos. Plato's theory enshrines the highest capacities of the mind in a divine aura, and places it at the root of all being and knowledge.

Despite the fantastic complexity of Plato's thought, he left his followers with unresolved problems. He was well aware that his thought—which he appears unwilling to honor with the name *philosophy,* just because it is incomplete—could not account in detail for the tentative conclusions it reaches. Notice, for example, the use of the word *imitate* (*mimesis*) in the previous paragraph. The term is a simile: a mimic imitates the gestures of some celebrity as a desk imitates its blueprint (deskness itself), or as John and Mary's love for each other imitates the Form of Love. The comparison is amazing, jaw-dropping, inspiring. Yet how do physical things take on their formal properties? The simile does not help, because there is no obvious effort by boards to take the shape of a desk, nor are John and Mary imitating anything when they love.

ARISTOTLE

After long years of study and teaching at Plato's Academy, Aristotle was ready to tackle the questions of metaphysics that, in his estimation, Plato had not answered correctly. By his own definition of metaphysics, Aristotle must attempt to characterize the fundamental features of all existence, and, in consequence of his rejection of Plato's doctrine of the Forms, to deal anew with what is unmoved and separate from all matter. For the Forms are unmoved and separate from all matter, however much they may metaphorically participate in the material world, or however much the items in the material world imitate the Forms. If the Forms do not exist, as Aristotle maintains, then he must give his own accounting of unmoved and immaterial being. In one of humankind's great adventures of the mind, he sets out to do just that.

What exists? What is ultimately real? Does reality come in gradations, as Plato thought, one absolutely real and one a shadowy image of the other? Or are there even more gradations of reality, such that some things can be more real than others, in the way that one item can be heavier than another? Aristotle asserts that only substances exist—the individual things that make up the furniture of the visible universe: cups and saucers, mountains and rivers, Socrates, and Nemo the dog. This seems commonsensical enough: It is the child's answer to the question Thales asked himself: What are all things made of? Well, lots of things!

But what are these substances that are the very stuff of the world? Aristotle's answer must respond to three questions.

First, he must determine what their physical makeup may be. Each kind of substance may be unique, but many do not seem simple. A table, for example, is made of wood and nails and glue. Is a compound like a table a substance also?

Second, he must define the nature of mutability or change. A thing may change from, say, being the infant Socrates to being the old Socrates, and finally being Socrates in death. What underlies this process?

Third, he must tell us how the relative fixity of things may be accounted for, if there are no Forms. Substances also exhibit what appears to be a fixed nature. It may be true, as Heraclitus said, that you cannot step into the same river twice, but any given river possesses the character of a river during many eons, and a dog remains a dog throughout its life.

Aristotle's account of these three features of all existing things—their physical embodiment, their mutability, and their specific character—is as follows.

The Physical Make-up of a Substance

Aristotle accepts and adapts the famous theory of Empedocles, that substance is composed of Earth, Air, Fire, and Water. These material substances may exist on their own, or they may enter combinations with each other to form the material basis of complex substances. Aristotle is sensitive to the fact that these four substances vary in their qualities, the most important of which are the opposite pairs hot-cold and wet-dry. He places these qualities prior to the four elements. The qualities give rise to the elements; the elements do not give rise to the qualities. This point will be crucial for understanding Aristotle's account of change in the next section.

The four elements are simple and cannot be broken down further. (The ancients could not have known that water, for example, is a complex substance containing two discrete elements, oxygen and hydrogen.) However, Aristotle grants the possibility of an original unformed matter. This notion has questionable implications for the theory of substance, for Earth, Air, Fire, and Water are all visible substances with unique qualities, but matter as such—*prime matter,* as the ancient philosophers called it—has no qualities at all. It is therefore not intelligible, in Plato's sense: it cannot be grasped *as* something or other.

The Dynamics of Change

Aristotle does not claim to be able to account for the possibility of change, that is, to answer fully the question of how one can speak of becoming without involving oneself in the paradoxical claim that something comes out of nothing, whether the something be a mere appearance or a real object. Yet he believes the nature of change can be adequately accounted for, given the purposes of science. The first step is an analysis of the causal relation itself.

When it is said, "a causes b," where a and b are things or events, several things may be meant. One is that a was there before b, or a is temporally prior to b. Another is that a **conditions** b is some manner—that is, if there had not been a, there would not have been b, or, more broadly, a is responsible for b. Indeed, the Greek term for *cause* contains a suggestion of moral responsibility: of what or who was to blame for b. One also means to say, in certain cases, that a gives us reasons for b's happening. Thus one may say that the desire for John's money caused James to rob him. This causal claim refers to James's purposes in acting as he did. The cause, James's purposes, is temporally prior to the effect, James's act of robbery, but the cause also refers to an event that comes after the effect, James's enrichment by John's money. Again, causal claims may refer to the material out of which the effect is made. One says, for example, that the beautiful maplewood gives the table its luxurious appearance.

NECESSARY AND SUFFICIENT CONDITIONS: A thing or proposition a is a *necessary* condition of b if b could not occur or be true without a's having occurred before it or a's being true. Having fuel in the tank is a necessary condition of the motor running. A thing or proposition a is a *sufficient* condition of b if whenever a occurs or is true, b occurs or is true. Dropping a glass from a considerable height is a sufficient condition for breaking it, but it is not a necessary condition, for the glass can be broken with a hammer. In the hypothetical statement-form called material implication, "p ⊃ q", p is the sufficient condition of q, and q is the necessary condition of p. Causal claims are not mere logical conditions, however, since they require that a be prior in time to b, and a may not be a sufficient or necessary cause of b. Prinzip's shooting of the archduke, while neither a necessary or sufficient cause of World War I, contributed causally to it.

All of these different elements that may be found in the claim that "a caused b" are included in Aristotle's famous Theory of the Four Causes. Its elements can be listed as follows:

The *material* cause. This is what the substance is made from, as the desk is made of wood, nails, and glue.

The *formal* cause. This the nature of the thing. Thus a dog has the general shape and qualities peculiar to dogs.

The *efficient* cause. This refers to the forces that brought it about, as the volcano erupts because of the forces of pressure and heat upon stone.

The *final* or *teleological* cause. This is the purpose for which the thing is intended, as an ape's tail is intended to keep the ape balanced as it climbs.

These causes are most easily visible upon human products. Thus Michelangelo's *David* has marble as its material cause, the figure of the young David poised for action as its formal cause, the chisel of the artist as its efficient cause, and a variety of final causes: the glorification of David, the expression of the beauty of youth, the certification of the talent of the artist, or the money he might receive for the finished statue. These causal elements are also visible upon living things: Flesh and blood are the material causes, the species of which the individual is a member is the formal cause, the feeding that allowed it to grow the efficient cause, and the purpose of the species in the environmental niche it inhabits, or the uses people make of it, is the final or teleological cause.

Aristotle extends this thinking across all of the cosmos, and this extension results in his philosophy having an interesting similarity to that of Plato. Any object whatever is made of something, any object can be recognized as having some form or other, and any object can be traced back to the physical forces that produced it. Yet it is not at all clear that every object has a purpose, aim, or goal. To justify this doctrine that in fact all things have purposes, Aristotle notes that even physical motion has a natural end. Objects fall to the earth because they are seeking their natural or proper place in the scheme of things. The rock that lies upon the beach has a natural tendency to seek the lowest point that it can, a point as close to the center of the earth (which for Aristotle was the center of the universe) as possible, because that is the natural place of all objects in the terrestrial realm, that is, all things beneath the moon. Water flows downhill because it is straining to reach its natural place. Celestial motion, the motion of the planets and stars, is always circular, according to Aristotle, because objects in the celestial realm, being perfect, naturally move in circles, which, Aristotle believed, are perfect geometric figures. Thus everything in the universe is striving after the attainment of its natural ends, just as Michelangelo strove to realize his ends in the *David*. The study of the natural ends of things is called *teleology*.

The Fixity of Things

Aristotle was convinced that to account for any thing or event in nature it was necessary to establish all four of the causes of the thing. He is attempting to produce not simply a metaphysical picture of the cosmos as such, but a program for all thought that wishes to be truly scientific: to know the four causes of a thing is to understand it rightly and completely. However, it is still not clear how change is initiated. How is it that in Aristotle's view a thing with a fixed nature can change from what it is to something else, the acorn to the oak tree? To extend his notion of causality and to give further content to the notion of a teleological or final cause, Aristotle introduces the concepts of *potency* and *act.*

INTERPRETING ARISTOTLE: Scholars have a difficult time in dealing with apparent contradictions in Aristotle's thought. The difficulty is made worse by their inability to establish with any certainty the order in which his extant writings were written, and by the fact that some works seem to have been written as notes for lectures. Our strategy is to present Aristotle's thought as an attempt to give coherent answers to issues that troubled thinkers in his times.

Potency and Act

If we examine individual substances in the world around us, we notice that each of them possesses a set of characteristics and possibilities, some of which they share with things like themselves and even with some things unlike themselves, and others of which they share with no other things. A book, a log, and a wooden house all have the capacity for being burned in fire, while water, the air, and a stone do not. A seed or an acorn has the possibility of growing into a plant, while a nail or an egg does not. These possibilities are inherent in the things that possess them as such, and they may exist as potency even if they are not able to unfold: an animal may eat the acorn even before it has the opportunity to germinate. Act is the realized potency; the oak tree is the potency in the acorn now become act. In the human being, the situation is complex. A normal child, for example, has the potency to become a physician, and this potency she shares with all other children. Note, however, this potency is not the potential to practice medicine, but only to acquire the skill to practice it. The physician is a physician even when he is not practicing medicine (as when he is asleep), but he acts as a physician when he practices his skill upon patients.

This doctrine, Aristotle appears to have believed, enables him to respond to the Parmenidean problem of how, when a thing changes, something new comes into being. The notion need not be accepted that the only metaphysical categories are being and nonbeing. Potency is a legitimate category also. When an acorn changes to an oak tree, the oak tree did not emerge from nonbeing, which, of course, makes no sense at all. Rather, argues Aristotle, the oak emerges from a real potency in the acorn. The change is implicit as potency in the thing changed, that is, what it is was present in potency in that which it is not, the thing out of which it came. Science must begin, therefore, with the sensory exploration of the behavior of objects, and not, as Plato believed, with the intellectual exploration of the forms apart from their material embodiment.

Form and Matter

A further pair of notions central to Aristotle's metaphysics is that between *form* and *matter*. One can understand this distinction from Aristotle's description of the four causes. The formal cause is the nature or essence of what a substance is, as opposed to the material out of which it is made. According to Aristotle, form and matter do not exist independently of each other. Matter, as encountered by the senses, always possesses some form or other. A central question for Aristotle is the relationship of form to substance. Any given substance is an amalgam of matter and form, but what a thing is essentially or primarily is its form. Michelangelo's *David* is essentially a representation of David, and only secondarily a piece of the material, marble, of which it is made. Yet form cannot exist independently of individual things, except as an object of thought. It is this that distinguished Aristotle's notion of form from that of Plato, and gave his philosophy a primary concern for the empirical world. There are, no doubt, places in Aristotle where he seems to consider the forms as possessing a reality distinct from things, and it was this notion of what he called "substantial form" that influenced less empirical thinkers, especially during the medieval period.

Let us carry the form/matter distinction a bit further. People generally consider items in their experience as examples of something or other. A cup is not simply a physical object. It is a cup. As Plato might say, it participates in or imitates the universal nature or form of a cup. Universal natures, therefore, exist at least subjectively, that is, in our minds, if not objectively upon a higher or transcendental tier of the cosmos, as with Plato's Realm of the Forms. There is, for Aristotle, an objective basis in things for the subjective universals in our minds. These are the unique static features of all things of the same species. The mind can abstract these features from things and distinguish what is essential and what is accidental in them. A cup, for example, is *essentially* a piece of domestic crockery used for drinking hot liquids, such as coffee. It is *accidental* to its substance as a cup that it is white, for example, or made of porcelain, or holds eight ounces of fluid. In Aristotle's view, the *unchanging* features of an otherwise changing world of individual objects are the appropriate objects of science. Again, they must be studied as they appear in individual cases and not by means of abstract reasoning alone.

Evolution

Aristotle believed that each thing, insofar as it is what it is, has an unchanging essential nature. Big dogs have little dogs as offspring, and a dog has no potency to be anything else but a dog, that is, an animal with certain essential characteristics. This notion, which Aristotle shares with Plato, is one reason why a theory of evolution took a long time to dawn on Western biologists. For evolution asserts exactly what this ancient doctrine of essential natures denies; it claims that the world of living things is *not* static but is evolving. Evolution proceeds by a steplike accumulation of new adaptive characteristics of a population of living things, and there is no unique point at which a new species emerges from an older one.

The notion of the final, or teleological, cause is crucial for Aristotle's picture of the world. It connects the idea intimately with the notions of form and potency. The identity of an individual, its being essentially an acorn or a human being, is tied to the realization of its potency in a specific way. An acorn would not be an acorn unless it unfolded its potency for becoming an oak tree, nor would a human being be a human being unless it tended toward the exercise of specific physical, social, and intellectual functions. The physical object that is given form as a cup can be understood as a cup just as far as it functions by holding liquids for drinking them. No doubt the feature of a thing's form that governs its movement toward an end is most visible in living things. However, as the discussion of the four causes makes clear, Aristotle extends teleology across all things; everything in the universe is acting to achieve an end natural to it. The notion of teleology is therefore an essential feature of being as being. Again, therefore, to understand the world is to contemplate the static features of things, their form, and to be able to account for changes in individual things as natural or typical for the kinds of things they are.

Throughout history, metaphysics has attempted not only to explain the ultimate nature of the physical cosmos, but also to search for the ultimate source of the world in some ultimate reality or being. Aristotle's metaphysics is no exception. His idea of God is a strange one, and quite distinct from the Judeo-Christian-Islamic notion of God that is today familiar. It is not personal; one cannot pray to Aristotle's God. It is also not conscious of the world; it is conscious only of itself. It is connected to the cosmos not so much as its creator, but as its maintainer. God moves the heavenly spheres in the same way that a person moves his arms, by a kind of action that requires no effort, for it is a mental, not a physical action. All individuals in the universe find their ultimate end or *telos* in God; it is the ocean toward which all things naturally flow, each in its own way. Its awareness is only of itself: its existence is an eternal contemplation of its own nature.

EARLY MODERN METAPHYSICS

"To understand a thing," said *Francis Bacon* (1561–1626), "is to know how it works." This simple-sounding reformulation of what it is to know or understand was taken up by philosophers on the European continent and in Great Britain in different ways. The schools of thought they created, respectively, are called *rationalism* and *empiricism,* each of which implied a distinct metaphysical vision. Questions of being and knowledge are difficult to disentangle, because being is thought to be the ultimate object of knowledge, and knowledge aims at that which is. Since the concern here is with metaphysics, the conclusions of the rationalists regarding the ultimate nature of what is known will be discussed, and in the next chapter an account of their views on the process of knowledge and its limitations will be offered.

FRANCIS BACON (1561–1626): Bacon was a British philosopher, essayist, and statesman. He lived in the Elizabethan era and was a contemporary of Shakespeare. One of the first thinkers to be affected by the new science, Bacon believed that we must "put nature to the rack"—that is, perform controlled experiments—to make her reveal her secrets. Bacon was concerned almost exclusively with the practical value of science. Like most English philosophers he disdained speculation about the nature of things that had no connection to tangible reality and common sense. He was perhaps the first to speculate upon the proper method of doing science: We must amass a great deal of data about nature, and then construct inductive generalizations about them. This method has been criticized as insufficient for science, whose experiments are guided by preliminary hypotheses about the causes of some phenomenon.

Descartes

The break with the ancient and medieval metaphysical past is clear in **Descartes**. Chapter 1 told the story of his decision to doubt all he had learned at school, and all else that could be doubted, until he arrived at some bedrock truth that could not be doubted. This bedrock truth was the proposition, "I think, therefore I am." No doubt insofar as I think, I must exist, for thoughts cannot float freely; every thought must be thought by someone, and the only thoughts that I know directly and immediately are my own. I must, therefore, exist as the thinker whose thoughts these are. I surely cannot tell, with the same assurance of certainty, that the man next to me is thinking, even when he speaks to me about his thoughts. From the point of view of my immediate experience, he could be an automaton.

RENÉ DESCARTES: Descartes was born in France in 1596 and died in Sweden in 1650. He was educated at the Jesuit academy of La Flèche. He served as an officer in several armies during his youth, but he saw no action, dedicating his evenings to science and to philosophical speculation. His *Discourse on Method* (1637) describes the reflections of those evenings and how he arrived at his philosophical standpoint. This work, in French, was followed by his greatest philosophical treatise, the *Meditations on First Philosophy* (1641), in Latin, by which time he was famous throughout Europe. After 1628 he lived in Holland, but in 1649 Queen Christiana of Sweden requested that the great Descartes come to her realm as her teacher and as a leader of the circle of scientists and intellectuals

---

she was assembling at her court. The queen appears to have demanded her instruction at dawn. Descartes, used to staying in bed until midday and to a much warmer climate, fell ill and died within a year of his arrival in Sweden.

The idea that of all truths, the one most certain is the truth that asserts my own existence—not our own, for the only existence that I am directly or immediately aware of is my own—establishes subjectivity as the source of all knowledge. This turn to subjectivity characterizes both the rationalists and the empiricists in the seventeenth and eighteenth centuries. In the mildest sense, the turn to subjectivity resulted in the individual rational subject, rather than external physical evidence, becoming the ultimate criterion of truth and falsity. At its most rigorous, Descartes's turn suggests that the truth can be only in my mind; physical evidence, just because it is external to my mind, is mediated; I have no direct access to it. Access to the external world can only occur via the senses, which, as Descartes pointed out early in his writings, can *deceive* us: It is always possible to see things that are not there, and, when we dream, our dream world seems as real to us as the world does when we are awake—or think we are!

In metaphysics, the problem just sketched is called the *mind-body* problem. The problem arises not only from Descartes's belief that the most certain knowledge is of his own existence, but also from his further assertion that his thought is an attribute of his mind. "What am I?" asks Descartes, and he replies, "I am a thing that thinks." And what is thinking? It has many modalities: I reason, I love, I judge, I evaluate, I measure: all these are acts of a substance whose essence or chief attribute is thinking. Knowledge, as such, is a product of thinking. But what of the object of thought, the world the mind presumably inhabits and wants to know about?

Let us say that Descartes is thinking about the Egyptian pyramids. He calls up a memory-image of them, having seen them in person or in a picture once before. What is the relationship between the image of the pyramids in his mind and the physical pyramids in Gizeh? First, the two are clearly not identical. They may appear the same, that is, have the same shape and color, but there the comparison ends. The image-pyramid appears to have no mass, but the physical pyramid has mass. Similarly, the physical pyramid has a definite size and determinate position in its environment, but the image-pyramid has none of this. The two must therefore be made of different "stuffs"—the image-pyramid is a modification of thinking-substance, and the physical pyramid a modification of some stuff that Descartes characterizes as extended substance. Now even when he imagines himself to be looking directly at the physical pyramid, what he has of the pyramid, according to his account, is nothing more than a modification of his thinking via some input through the senses. This input is deeply problematic, for how can an extended thing make modifications in a thinking thing, that is, in something that is not extended?

Descartes's response to this problem is as ingenious as it is ultimately unsatisfying. He believed that he could prove the existence of absolute substance, or God, with greater certainty than he could prove the existence of extended substance, or the external world. He believed also that he could prove that God would not deceive his creatures if they did not deceive themselves by drawing conclusions too hastily, that is, before they saw the proposition they were reasoning about to be clearly and distinctly true or false. Therefore, the propositions about the external world that one asserts on the strength of clear and distinct evidence must be true: God's love of truth would not permit a person to be deceived fundamentally about what he sees and feels and touches, that is, what his senses represent to him about the world outside his mind. The place where extended substance and thinking substance meet, Descartes speculated, is in the pineal gland at the base of the brain.

Dualism, Materialism, and Idealism

This problem of mind and body has haunted Western philosophy since the time of Descartes, and philosophers have devised various strategies to solve it. The seriousness of the problem can be appreciated even today: mind and matter appear to be two fundamentally different kings of things. How can a physical substance interact with the senses so that a subjective image of itself appears in the conscious mind of a person? The problem seems to have three possible solutions, each of which has taken a variety of ingenious forms since Descartes, and the problem is still not resolved to everyone's liking. The three solutions are called *dualism, materialism,* and *idealism.* These are metaphysical theories as far as they characterize being as such.

Dualism

Dualism is the view that both minds and physical bodies exist and interact with each other. The means of this interaction is usually claimed to be the *causal.* An object outside of the mind causes modifications in the nervous system and ultimately in the brain. The modifications are caused by light, sound, tactile, olfactory, and taste signals from the senses. The modifications caused in the brain result in the sensible qualities apprehended by consciousness as colors, sounds, smells, tastes, and sensations. The mind is different from the brain, in this metaphysical account of the familiar phenomenon of perception. When a person turns on the stereo, she is not aware of her brain processing information about sound waves; she hears music. This interconnection seems mysterious, but then even the act by which her conscious decision to wiggle her fingers, or to cause her fingers to wiggle—almost by command, one might say, although she is conscious of no command—seems mysterious. Accepting the indubitable phenomenon that the mind and body interact, the dualist argues, is better than the two other options, which solve the problem neatly, but at the cost of our common sense.

Materialism

Materialism has its roots in the pre-Socratic thinkers and the later Stoics. Some later pre-Socratic philosophers called Atomists, notably Leucippus and Democritus, postulated that atoms, a class of microscopic, indivisible, and diverse material substances, and the empty space between them, are the ultimate constituents of everything that is real. Modern materialists apply this thinking to the mind. Holding that only material things (and, perhaps, forces and force-fields) exist, materialists deny independent status to the mind. Matter alone exists; the mind is simply what the brain does. There is no immortality: Since the mind is dependent upon the brain for its energy, when the brain dies, so does the person whose brain it was.

Idealism

Idealism responds to the mind-body question by denying the real existence of material objects. This odd position, first stated explicitly by the British empiricist **George Berkeley**, has its origin in Plato, who claimed that only the ideal Forms of things were genuinely real, not their material embodiment. Idealism in its modern form argues that what a person knows of the external world are ideas in the mind. A person has an idea of the cup sitting on the table next to him in his mind. Certainly he does not have the cup itself in his mind, nor does he have an idea of material substance as such, except by abstraction from perceptual qualities. The idea of the cup can be reduced to a varying set of visceral and tactile qualities, and all these qualities are said to be in the mind. Since qualities as mass and volume and shape can be perceived only via such mental qualities, then whatever measurements we make of its supposedly real qualities such as mass and velocity will depend upon these subjective qualities. Simply stated, if everything we look at lacked the subjective quality of color, we could not distinguish one thing from another by sight. So the idea that we have direct access to a realm of extended physical real objects beyond their subjective appearances is unacceptable. Berkeley went as far as to argue that he could make no sense of a thing having qualities other than the subjective qualities that appear to us. As those subjective qualities are in the mind, what is meant by a *thing* can be only a mental object. All that exists, therefore, are minds and their ideas.

GEORGE BERKELEY: Berkeley was born in Ireland in 1685 and educated in Dublin. He was ordained in the Anglican Church and was made Bishop of Cloyne in 1734. He was known during his lifetime more as a churchman and educator than as a philosopher, for his leading idea, that a material world outside of the mind does not exist, was thought absurd by many of his contemporaries. His *Three Dialogues Between Hylas and Philonous* (1713) was written in order to win converts to his doctrine, which he believed to be more acceptable to Christian faith than the common-sense materialism of

George Berkeley. © *Thoemmes.*

most people. He traveled to America with his plan for educating African and Native Americans on the island of Bermuda. He failed to win financial support for this idea from the English crown and his work was unsuccessful. He died in Oxford in 1753.

METAPHYSICS IN EARLY MODERN GREAT BRITAIN

The leading British philosophers in the eighteenth century reacted strongly against what they took to be the unjustifiable rationalism of the Continental philosophers. Descartes, they thought, was wrong to believe that thinking alone could prove fundamental truths about the physical world, apart from observation. For the British, all rational thought presupposes that objects and events are given to the senses. This empirical philosophy borrows an idea from the medieval Christian philosopher Thomas Aquinas: nothing can be in the mind that is not first in the senses. What is first given to the mind are the objects of the senses; we build up all mental contents, even abstractions such as circles or the idea of truth itself out of the data given to the senses. No ideas are innate, as Descartes and Plato had supposed; the mind at birth, John Locke famously argued, is a *tabula rasa,* a blank slate upon which are written the sense perceptions. Reality consists of the perceptual qualities that the mind, through repeated experience of them, associates with the physical objects that they represent. The great task of philosophy, for Locke, was to develop the mental laws by which we form a world out of our perceptions.

Locke

Two important observations about Locke's starting-point and his project can be ventured. First, one intellectual feature of the time in which the British empiricists lived was the overwhelming presence of the work of Isaac Newton (1642–1727). Newton's great work, *The Mathematical Principles of Natural Philosophy,* was the culmination of modern scientists' rejection of Aristotelian metaphysics. In place of the qualitative processes by which substances unfold an innate potential for development toward some fixed end, modern scientists saw events and processes in nature as resulting from the interaction of physical objects and forces according to quantitative mathematical laws. Real objects can be reduced to lawful microscopic interactions between corpuscles of some kind, the atoms, perhaps, which the ancient philosophers had speculated about, and which Aristotle rejected. For Newton, all events in the universe can be reduced to point-masses. His famous law of gravity describes mathematically a force that, when applied to aggregates of infinitesimal masses, produces an acceleration. It is hardly surprising, then, that philosophers who believe in the existence of minds would attempt to do for the mind what Newton did for matter: to reduce all complex ideas to the psychological atoms out of which they are made, and to derive the laws that regulate their interactions.

Second, the analogy between the composition of physical objects and mental ones—the notion that the ultimate building-blocks of all ideas in the mind are simple and indivisible perceptual data, just as objects are built from point masses or atoms—is difficult to maintain. It may seem that the cup upon the desk is given to us through specific atomic sensations: a color, a shape, a tactile quality of smoothness, and similar subjective qualities. From that fact it seems reasonable to infer that through repeated experience of these qualities there arises in us the general idea of a cup. Ideas are composed by association of the atomic sensations, yet can we specify how this process occurs? After all, what a person first sees on her desk is a cup, not colors and shapes. That she would not have the general idea of cup without having perceived the qualities of individual cups is no doubt correct. Yet it is not possible to observe the process by which a person goes from the qualities of an individual thing to the general idea of it. Locke thinks we can do so retrospectively. But to examine the mind is not the same as to examine the physical world. The method of analysis appropriate to physics may not be appropriate to psychology. Locke simply assumes that the mind is divisible into atomic ideas the way the Newtonian physical world is divisible into atoms, or atomic masses. Moreover, Locke's idea of mind leaves the question first raised by Descartes unanswered: How are our perceptions of a thing related to the thing of which they are the perceptions? Can a person ever grasp the nature of the substance that supports or causes the perceptions? For if the perceptions are the only data we have about things external

David Hume. © *Thoemmes.*

to the mind, then we cannot say what lies beyond those perceptions. Locke referred to the material substrate that supported the perceived qualities as a "something I know not what." Berkeley, writing a generation after Locke, scuttled the idea of a real material substance, while retaining the metaphysical notion of atomic ideas.

Hume

David Hume (1711–1776) encountered a further metaphysical difficulty emerging from the empiricist belief that what he called *impressions* and *ideas* are all we have of things. He notes that all causal claims (for example, that one moving billiard ball caused another ball to move) depend upon the synthesis of a series of independent perceptions. We see the billiard ball roll toward a stationary one. We see them touch, hear a click, and observe the stationary ball begin to move. However, we do not observe or have a perception of what seems necessary for any causal claim, the efficiency of the first ball upon the second. We think we can claim that the first ball made the second move, but we have no independent perception to justify that claim. The sequence of perceptions does not justify the claim that the motion of the first ball requires the motion of the second. If we had just sprung into existence with all our capacity for reason fully developed when the first ball began to move toward the second, we could not predict what will happen when the two balls meet. Our present conviction that the second ball will move results, Hume concludes, upon our having seen such events in the past: the two are constantly conjoined in our minds because of past experience. The causal claim is based upon habit, and not in reasoning about how the world is or must be. We cannot, says Hume, deduce rationally that bread will nourish us. Experience will assure us that it does, but since past experiences do not guarantee future experience, the universal causal claim, "Bread nourishes," is a practically but not rationally justified proposition.

Hume's analysis appears to invalidate all science, and for that reason it will concern us again in the next chapter, when the nature of knowledge will be studied. For science typically claims to be discovering truths about how the natural world operates, and these truths include causal claims. Science assumes causality to be a real feature of the world, but Hume relegated it to the mind and the mind's habits; it describes only psychological claims we make about the regularity of our experience and its practical effect upon our behavior. I am psychologically impelled, for example, to fear falling if I should jump from my window. I cannot prove rationally that I will fall, and, since the event is in the future, I have no sense-experience to support my belief.

The problem with causality that Hume stumbled upon in the second half of the eighteenth century had enormous implications for metaphysics. The question of necessity in nature had to be faced in the light of Hume's criticism. Whence the necessity of natural law? The term *necessity* is often used to refer to people's behavior: one must do this or that, either because it is morally obligatory, or because it seems to be a necessary means to a desired end ("If you want to do well in school, you must study hard.") But must this object fall when one lets it drop? Must things happen as they do? Rationalism had attempted to assimilate natural necessity to logical necessity, hoping that empirical laws of motion, such as Galileo's or Newton's, could eventually be shown to possess the same necessity as a theorem in logic or geometry ("an isosceles triangle *must* have equal base angles"), but it was unable to make good on that hope.

Could it be reasonably argued that physical laws themselves are not just generalizations about experience, but exist, and somehow constrain objects to behave in the way they specify? This, too, is a **metaphysical** or perhaps better **ontological** question, for it asks what kinds of things exist, and whether a given item of our experience, like natural laws or moral rules, exists independent of our experience. From the perspective of the early modern thinkers who questioned the status of natural laws, Plato's theory of the Forms seems less bizarre; it accounts for the regularity perceived in things. But Plato's theory does not solve the problem of the necessity of the laws of nature (taking those of Galileo or Newton as paradigms of the type) or of the blueprints of things that Plato called the Forms. Why these Forms, or these laws, and no other? Why must the world have the shape it does, and why do natural events take place as they do? Galileo, who asked himself these questions, had recourse to the Will of God. Berkeley had said that God accounts for the regularities in our perceptual experience. Yet such recourse to God was becoming strange and unsatisfying to the eighteenth-century thinkers. The problem troubled everyone who attempted to think of them. Without a foundation for natural necessity the world came to appear unintelligible, and every event groundless, a mere "brute fact." What holds the world in its inward depths together? Goethe's *Faust* wished to know. With Hume, philosophy returned, perhaps on a higher standpoint, to the notion of the pre-Socratic Parmenides that the changeable world given through the senses is a groundless illusion, a product, Hume adds, of human custom and habit.

METAPHYSICS AND ONTOLOGY: This presentation of metaphysics takes as its point of departure the definition of metaphysics by Aristotle. The references to "being as being" and to "that which is independent and separate from matter" are very vague. Some efforts have been made to specify the nature of metaphysics more narrowly. One such effort was the definition of a common metaphysical problem: What exists? How does it exist? This problem is called *ontological,* a term coined in the nineteenth century. Some familiar items pose no ontological problems: Cats exist, clouds exist, lightning exists . . . but what about ideas in minds? The empiricists thought their existence was unproblematic, but many philosophers today find ideas very problematic and attempt to reduce them to brain states or to dispositions or behavioral routines. What about values? Do they exist, and if so, in what ways? And what of natural laws, like Galileo's $= 1/2at^2$? Do they exist, and if so, how does their existence make a difference in the way nature appears to operate?

Metaphysics had reached an impasse. The Continental rationalists believed that rational speculation could provide a thorough account of what is, and of what is independent of motion and separate from matter. Their starting-point is the individual mind: the "I think" of Descartes. However, the Cartesian standard of indubitable, clear-and-distinct evidence as the highest criterion of truth failed to achieve an uncontroversial body of metaphysical knowledge. British empiricism seemed to result in a thoroughgoing skepticism regarding our knowledge of the external world, or in an idealism that flouted common sense.

KANT AND THE CRITIQUE OF METAPHYSICS

At this time, a thinker appeared to propose a new, startling, and very detailed solution to these metaphysical problems. His name was **Immanuel Kant,** a professor in the provincial city of Königsberg, then in eastern Germany. Kant proposed a Copernican revolution in philosophy. Copernicus had changed our perspective on the skies by placing the sun at the center of the universe and the earth on its periphery. Just so, said Kant, can we change our perspective upon knowledge. Instead of imagining, as philosophers had done consciously and purposely since Descartes, and unreflectively in the Middle Ages, that the mind is looking out upon a world external to itself and trying to describe the contents and understand the structures of that world, let us instead try to understand the

Immanuel Kant. © *Library of Congress.*

contents and the structures of our minds and how they determine the world as it appears to us.

IMMANUEL KANT: Kant was born in 1724 to a working-class family in Königsberg, East Prussia, in Germany, and died there in 1804. His life was remarkably uneventful, even for a scholar. At first forced to work as a tutor to the children of wealthy families, as a librarian, and as a private lecturer, he was finally made a professor at the University of Königsberg at the age of 46. Known for the great regularity of his habits—it is said that his neighbors would set their clocks when Kant appeared in the doorway for his afternoon walk—he read, prepared his lectures, dined with friends, wrote, and slept at the same time each day. He never married. He was an effective and beloved teacher, concerned with insuring that his students would always take away something useful from his lectures. His technical writing in philosophy is extremely difficult, and his *Critique of Pure Reason* is one of the most challenging books ever written, yet it won him an immense reputation in Germany during his lifetime.

This shift in perspective, Kant believed, will enable us to understand how we perceive the world the way we do. It proposes that the mind is not the passive observer of some fixed external reality that causes it to have perceptions of some kind, but rather that the mind is active in knowledge. The understanding gives structure to what would otherwise be a chaos of unordered sensible data. The concessions that Kant had to make in realizing this project, however, are considerable. He argued that although we can have certainty about the world as it appears to us (the "phenomenal world"), because that certainty lies in the sensible and rational structures of the mind that condition our experience (space, time, and the categories of the understanding). Yet, he conceded, we can never grasp the world as it is in itself, apart from our perception of it (the "noumenal world"). Kant abandons Aristotle's "primary philosophy," the study of being as being, as a misguided effort. Being as such—that which is ultimately real—cannot be known by us; only what can cross the threshold of the structures of human understanding can be known, along with those structures themselves. Kant's *Critique of Pure Reason* shows that unbridled reason will forever knock futilely at the **antinomies of pure reason** and necessarily engage itself in questions it cannot answer, just because the questions concern things as they are in themselves, and not things as they are given to us. However, the phenomenal world stands open to scientific exploration. As long as we limit ourselves to the kind of science done by Galileo and Newton, we will make progress in understanding. Any ultimate truth about the universe, if there is such, is knowable only to God, if such a being exists.

THE ANTINOMIES OF PURE REASON: Kant's argument that pure reason has fixed limits is illustrated by, though it is not limited to, what he calls the antinomy of pure reason. It is possible, he tries to show, to give equally good proofs of both sides of opposed theses that refer to things in themselves. These antinomies emerge inevitably from pure reason, when its ideas lead it to metaphysical questions. In attempting to answer these questions, it extends itself beyond the phenomenal, and has no information that allows it to resolve the antinomy. Kant identifies four such antinomies: (1) The world is limited in space and time/the world is not so limited. (2) There are ultimately simple substances/there are no ultimately simple substances. (3) Everything is determined by natural causes/Some things are not so determined [specifically, there is freedom of the human will]. (4)There exists an absolutely necessary being [God]/All beings are contingent. The futility of trying to prove either side of these antinomies encourages us to drop our efforts to prove propositions that require information beyond the phenomenal world.

Reason setting limits to itself—that is the legacy that Kant handed down to his successors. How reason sets these limits is a question of epistemology and will be discussed in the next chapter. His contributions to ethics are also considerable. But the dream of reason attaining to absolute knowledge had not been put to rest by Kant, even—or, perhaps especially—in his German homeland. Metaphysics in its largest sense—the search for absolute knowledge of absolute being—burst forth anew in the work of Johann Gottlieb Fichte, Friedrich Wilhelm Joseph von Schelling, and, most notably, in Georg Wilhelm Friedrich Hegel.

HEGEL

How does Hegel respond to Kant's challenge to all metaphysics? A key to this question may lie in the title of Hegel's first great work, *The Phenomenology of Spirit.* The term *phenomenology* suggests that he is going to take the world of appearance as his starting-point. But it is not enough to say, as Kant does, that an understanding of the appearance of things is the furthest that human understanding can penetrate. To posit something as a limit, as Kant does when he says the understanding is limited to the phenomenal world, is already to pass beyond the limit, said Hegel. Some sort of knowledge of things in themselves must be possible, even if it is merely known that they are beyond the reach of understanding.

Kant falsely assumed, according to Hegel, two things. He assumed that we can intelligibly regard reality as independent of the mind. It is not: Hegel proposes a system of absolute idealism. Reality is the self-thinking of absolute mind as its own thought, as thought externalized in Nature, and as thought becoming self-conscious in the fulfilled human Spirit. Second, Kant assumed that the categories of the understanding are fixed and innate. He did not realize, Hegel says, that the concepts of the human spirit are the products of a long history of humankind's wrestling spiritually with Nature. This process is called dialectic. In that struggle, the human mind constantly overcomes the limits it faces, until it understands its own structures as reflecting, ever more clearly, the structures of the absolute mind in Nature. Hegel's plan for a universal metaphysical system, to which the *Phenomenology of the Spirit* was intended to serve as a preface, would begin with a demonstration of how the basic categories of mind are generated. This demonstration he calls *Logic.* The body of the work was intended to be an encyclopedia that analyzes the logical interrelationships of all the categories of mind in nature and in the human spirit. Logic becomes metaphysics, for logic is the structure of a self-thinking absolute being as mind. All human activities (not just the logical categories that Kant thought condition human thought at all times and places) that aim at understanding and living in the world contribute to make Nature into a world that bears the impress of the absolute Spirit. Since reality *is* idea, the fact that laws and conceptual structures are the product of our own minds does not result in skepticism or relativism.

Hegel's early writings were in theology (he was born to a Lutheran family), but he seems to have thought that the theologian's concept of God was the same as the philosopher's concept of the Absolute, however differently it is formulated. Hegel's philosophical problem with the Absolute concerns its relation with the world, or, more generally, with the relationship between the finite and the infinite. In this respect, his philosophy is of a piece with the entire Western idea of metaphysics, for it attempts to discern how the changing contents of this world are related to unchanging, immaterial, and unconditioned being.

Hegel's starting-point is the conviction that reality is the objective order of an absolute mind, and that the absolute idea develops **dialectically** and teleologically in history, as in the famous example of **Master and Man,** toward its fulfillment in the developed human spirit. The world as a whole, Hegel believed, can be intelligibly reconstructed as the process in which Absolute Spirit, which

Georg Wilhem Hegel. © *Thoemmes.*

has attempted to externalize itself in nature, finally returns to itself as the philosophy and culture of humankind. For the Spirit comes to itself in the absolute idea that unifies subjectivity and objectivity: It understands the world that it thinks about, and the basic processes of its own thinking, as in Hegel's philosophy itself. His system thus incorporates, in a set of systematic logical interrelationships, all the conceptual structures that have been generated historically by humankind's efforts to understand itself and its world. It is a metaphysics aspiring to a vision of the entire universe as idea.

THE DIALECTIC OF MASTER AND MAN: An influential example of the dialectical process manifest in the becoming of the Absolute as Spirit is the dialectic of Master and Man. It is contained in a passage in Hegel's *Phenomenology of the Spirit,* where he considers the appearance of self-consciousness in human history. Self-consciousness requires the existence of another self-consciousness. If a person is going to become aware of himself as a self, it must place that self in relation to another self, which it negates. In the master-man relation, the master places himself in relation to a person he has conquered at the risk of his own death. The slave is a self that exists for the master, and the slave possesses his own selfhood through the will of the master, who creates him, as it were, as a being who sees himself in the self of the master. The master cannot destroy the slave, for then his own selfhood as master would be impaired. But the slave, in producing goods for his master's enjoyment, in effect comes to his

> objective selfhood, independent of the master, as the *maker.* In this way, the master becomes dependent upon the slave. Analogously, the master's way of life in the Old South was dependent upon slave labor and vanished when the slaves were freed. What was originally a matter of objective domination of one person by another eventually becomes a dialectical opposition of the two, and out of this opposition, Hegel argues, a higher form of consciousness emerges.

For Hegel, philosophy has moral implications; it is part of humankind's efforts to become free. Freedom requires, first, *self*-consciousness or awareness of oneself as an agent in the universal process through which the Absolute Idea becomes conscious of itself. Second, freedom requires less partiality, that is, less immersion in the peculiar and partial forms that the Absolute Idea has taken in one's own time and place, and it is more open to the entire dialectical process in which partial ideas confront their contradictions and are *sublated*—both overcome and preserved—in a higher synthesis. Such knowledge liberates us from our limited selves and partial cultures, and makes us willing participants in a necessary and universal spiritual process.

METAPHYSICS IN THE TWENTIETH CENTURY

Hegel's system generated critics and disciples in the hundred years after his death, leaving its mark on such diverse thinkers as the German Karl Marx, the Englishman F. H. Bradley (1846–1924), and the Italian Benedetto Croce (1866–1952), and even such existentialists as the Frenchman Jean-Paul Sartre. Yet it would be fair to say that one legacy left by Hegel and his immediate disciples was a deep distrust of metaphysics. Hegel's system came to be branded as a kind of vice: unbridled reason engaged in unverifiable speculations about the ultimate nature of things. This critique of Hegel, and its outcomes in the antimetaphysical stance that characterizes most of the important work in philosophy during the first half of the twentieth century, is one of the most fascinating episodes in the history of Western thought. The critique is based in the conflict between two convictions: that metaphysics is impossible, and that it is inevitable.

The European Continent

Friedrich Nietzsche

The first important figure in the critique of metaphysics is **Friedrich Nietzsche,** who argued that the Western metaphysical tradition was bankrupt and had reached its end in his own work. His attack upon the metaphysical tradition took four forms, each of which has had a lasting influence on the century that recently ended. It focuses on the Aristotelian idea of *essence,* the Hegelian idea of the *genesis of ideas,* the function of *reason* in philosophy, and the need to *transvalue all values.*

Friedrich Nietzsche. © *Library of Congress.*

FRIEDRICH NIETZSCHE: Nietzsche was born in Prussia, Germany in 1844. His father, a Lutheran pastor, died when Friedrich was a small boy, and he was raised by this mother, his sister, two aunts, and a grandmother. A brilliant student, he was offered a professorship at the University of Basel before he received his doctorate from Leipzig. Ill health forced him to step down from teaching in 1879, and he lived the rest of his working life as something of a recluse in the high Alps, and, occasionally, in Italy. His close friendship with the composer Richard Wagner ended after the publication of Wagner's last opera, *Parsifal.* In 1889, he collapsed on the streets of Turin, possibly the effect of tertiary syphilis, and lived the last eleven years of his life as a helpless and insane invalid, tended by his sister. He died in Weimar in 1900.

Essences

Aristotle's notion of the specific essence of a thing, its formal cause, was derived from Plato's notion of the Forms. Each substance has a fixed nature, according to Aristotle, which the mind can grasp by abstracting from specific instances of things. This notion has had a varied history. Aristotle's specific natures are related to the universals debated in the Middle Ages, the complex ideas of Locke, and the categories of Hegel. Are these essences real (a doctrine called realism)? Or are they a mere way of speaking, "breaths of air," as some medieval thinkers asserted (a doctrine called nominalism)? If nominalism is true, what holds things together, as it were, what makes a dog a dog, if not its participation in the objective nature of dogness? Are the words that refer to such essential natures as dogs or trees merely ways in which human beings deal with the chaos of experience, having no basis in reality? Nietzsche asserts the extreme nominalist position. He argues that there is no substrate, no formal cause that is the real nature of an object. There is no lightning that produces the flash; there exists only the perceived flash. Essences are creations of the human imagination, projections of the blind Will to Power, that for Nietzsche is the being of being.

In *Beyond Good and Evil,* for example, he accuses the philosophers of the error of assuming that permanent entities underlie phenomena.

> In the "in itself" [Kant's "noumenal realm"] there is nothing of "causal connection," nothing of "necessity" or "psychological unfreedom." The "effect" does *not* "follow the cause"; no "law" reigns there. We alone are the ones who have invented the causes, the sequences, the for-each-other, the relativity, the constraint, the number, the law, the freedom, the ground, the goal; and when we imaginatively read and mix this sign-world as a "thing-in-itself" into the things, so we are doing once again what we have always done, namely creating *myths.*

Things, for Nietzsche have no nature or form in themselves. He denies to nature an intellectual structure, and to all things an intrinsic potency for the achievement of form, as the phenomenal lightning-flash was thought to be the realization in matter of the form of lightning itself. Against this, Nietzsche asserts a fundamental distinction between a world-in-itself apart from mind, and the conceptual structures that we, to serve our biological need for survival, project upon the world-in-itself.

Since Nietzsche holds that we are prey to an all-encompassing and inescapable illusion, the world and our own self-image is for him nothing more than a myth. There are no essential facts; the world is a chaos of competing forces that seek only their own expression. Those essences that are central to a culture express its own self-identity, but they are not centers of any reality. The French philosopher Jacques Derrida stands in this Nietzschean anti-metaphysical tradition. He has attempted to deconstruct the various centers typical of Western culture such as *phallocentrism* (male domination) and *ethnocentrism* (cultural dominance of the European peoples) as examples of such myths built into the essential structures of our cultural self-identity. He wishes to find in the marginalia of the culture the underlying conditions of its myths, and to discover new essential metaphors that would allow a rebirth of philosophy in a culture with fewer myths, or one with a new notion of rationality. But there is no source of meaning beyond language, no absolute reality from which language and meaning are derived. "There is nothing beyond the text," is a familiar Derridaran phrase.

The Genesis of Ideas

Nietzsche reintroduced into philosophy Hegel's notion that philosophical standpoints arise out of an underlying conceptual process. But unlike Hegel, Nietzsche sees philosophies, not as the expression of Absolute Spirit becoming conscious of itself, but instead as the expression of the human struggle for power. This is the basis of his famous argument in *The Genealogy of Morals* that the Christian idea of humility and poverty as God-ordained virtues arose among the ancient Jews out of a resentment-laden desire to justify their impotent struggle against the proud and wealthy Romans. Their moral system allowed them to imagine the Romans burning in Hell while the faithful are called to eternal bliss in heaven. This thought is similar to Karl Marx, who identified philosophical theories as weapons in a class struggle, the twentieth-century French thinker Michel Foucault, whose writings explore the social and political forces that produced the ways we understand insanity, illness in general, or our own sexuality. What philosophers have conceived of as an impersonal search for universally acceptable and objectively valid truth turns out to be a veiled attempt to assert values inherent in human practices. For Foucault, all ideas have political force; cultures *valorize* some ideas at the expense of others, and systems of political dominance arise. Discussions about the true and the false, about what is good and what is evil, are simply camouflaged power struggles.

The Attack on Reason

Nietzsche's claim that all things, including metaphysics, arises out of a Will to Power, seems itself to be a metaphysical claim, with the Will to Power playing the role of absolute reality. But Nietzsche seems consistent: he recognizes his assertion of the Will to Power as the ultimate nature of reality to be itself an expression of Will; by asserting its truth, he wills it so. Truth, said Nietzsche, is a kind of lie that we tell ourselves to enhance our will to be; we believe those truths that are life-enhancing, unless we are weakened or corrupted by otherworldly hopes.

Transvaluation of All Values

Nietzsche taught that just as there are no essential centers to life or to reality, so too are there no real values; the values asserted by a culture or a person can be judged only by how they serve to enhance or detract from life. If this criterion is applied to the values of the modern world, if we "philosophize with a hammer," as Nietzsche put it, we will soon see that the values inherent both in Christianity and in the modern bourgeois state encourage a love of death, not of life. *Transvalued* values will have life and power at their center. It is not clear from his writings either how this transvaluation of values will take place, or what it will produce by way of new value-systems. But Nietzsche believed that in his time, "Nihilism was at the gate," and the human race was doomed to mass mediocrity and empty atheistic humanism unless some new prophet arrived on the scene. "Two thousand years!" he moaned, "and not one new God." When will our civilization produce a new locus of the divine and make possible the advent of the transvaluer of all values, the Superman?

Phenomenology

The most significant philosophical movement on the European Continent in the twentieth century reflected the antimetaphysical stance taken by Nietzsche. Edmund Husserl (1859–1938) is considered to be the originator of the phenomenological method and its greatest spokesperson. Phenomenology attempts to do no more than describe what is given to consciousness. Husserl argues in his *Logical Investigations* that philosophy must confine itself to a description to *what* is given to us, not to questions of how it can be given to us at all, as in Kant's philosophy, or of what the ultimate nature of what is given might be, as in Hegel's philosophy. Husserl's hope was to trace our conceptual structures back to a consciousness cleansed of all assertions of existence. Then the meaning-elements of cognitive structures can be seen for what they are. Phenomenology will then provide a clear and certain conceptual basis for all other knowledge, especially for empirical science. Yet he too could not escape metaphysics. He argued that all concepts in our minds, and thus all that human subjects consider to be real, are constituted in a transcendental ego.

This grandiose plan for a complete descriptive phenomenology of what is given in intellectual and perceptual experiences that found all scientific knowledge was taken into the areas of ethical and religious experience by the German thinker Max Scheler (1872–1928), and into the area of the philosophy of the human being by the work of another German, **Martin Heidegger**. Although both men were antimetaphysical in their initial philosophies, their own later work had clear metaphysical implications. Scheler developed a metaphysics of Spirit and Impulse, where the impotent Spirit eventually turns blind impulse to its own ends in the coming-to-be of the universe and of God. Heidegger's late work carries out the theme of ontological destruction mentioned in his early *Being and Time* (1927). Since the time of Plato, Heidegger argues, our experience of being has become skewed by the emphasis upon technology. Creating objects and transforming nature to our own practical ends has cost us the primordial sense of being possessed by the pre-Socratic Greeks. A new stance must be adopted, one that lets being be, that allows us to hear the call of being behind the objects that are manipulated and transformed for the sake of human practical designs. Heidegger noted the affinity of the spirit of his philosophy with that of Zen Buddhism.

MARTIN HEIDEGGER: Heidegger was born in Baden, Germany, in 1889. In 1927 he startled Europe with his *Being and Time*, one of the seminal works of philosophy in the twentieth century. A professor at the University of Freiburg after 1928, Heidegger was named Rector by the new National Socialist regime in 1933. At first an enthusiastic follower of Hitler's regime, his support for Nazism waned in later years. The American occupying forces refused to allow him to teach at Freiburg after the war, but they permitted him to lecture privately and to write. His later works represent a turning from the problems posed by *Being and Time.* Instead, he attempted to carry out a destruction of ontology, which was an important influence upon the postmodernist and deconstructivist movements after 1970. He died in 1976.

Metaphysics in Great Britain and the United States

The English-speaking tradition in metaphysics is strongly empirical, in that it believes all knowledge to come from the senses. It tends to confine philosophy to the realm of practical objects and to be critical of any claims to surpass that realm intellectually. Experiments with events in nature are clear examples of the empirical approach to knowledge. We cannot make advances in knowledge in an armchair, or by means of discussion of abstract matters among groups of scientifically unprepared people, as in Plato's *Dialogues.* Observations of and generalizations from what we can clearly see and feel during experimental or controlled observation is the only secure road to knowledge. This tradition assumes also that scientific knowledge is paradigmatic for all other knowledge. Philosophy is not the queen of the sciences, but merely science's handmaiden. Its only remaining problems are those of the analysis of language. It must do this with the same rigor and disinterest as science itself. Because of this demotion, philosophy has become quite technical, and often irrelevant to the affairs of everyday life.

Furthermore, as the success of science has been due in part to its indifference to, or elevation over, human values, English-speaking philosophers were encouraged to make a rigorous metaphysical distinction between facts and values. We cannot show scientifically the truth of moral claims ("Never tell lies!"). Consequently, science never asks about the value of what science achieves, but only about the evidence for its claims, and philosophy should do likewise. Metaphysics, too, as far as it carried on the Aristotelian task of an inquiry into ultimate reality, seemed to many to be the height of human vanity: A human race that could not hold itself back from the abyss of slaughter and ruination, from genocide and hate, aspired to understand the whole of reality! Some—the existentialists, for example—argued that it would be better for humankind to accept the groundlessness of our own existence and recognize that we have to create the meaning of our lives by throwing ourselves into projects that our own deepest impulses make meaningful to us, rather than imagining that there is a transcendental structure and purpose to things, or that purposes and values exist independently of our choices and desires.

History and Metaphysics in the Twentieth Century

The twentieth century also saw the massive encounter of cultures that were formerly geographically and spiritually cut off from each other. The culmination of European imperialism by the end of the nineteenth century had opened the possibility of the interaction of intellectual cultures. Europeans began to learn in detail, for the first time, the large Asian philosophies called Hinduism, Buddhism, and Confucianism. These great religious, cultural, and intellectual systems began to make themselves felt among European intellectuals, and not simply among historians, linguists, and scholars. Buddhism, especially, seemed to many in the West to be a significant alternative to its own religion and philosophy. The dawning of the idea that the Western culture of philosophy was not the only candidate for adherence by rational men and women seeking answers to the perennial questions of people caused a thoughtful reassessment among Europeans of the aspirations of their own culture. The belief, central to Western metaphysics, that there had to be only one truth about the world and only one means of obtaining it, namely by rational science and philosophy, came to appear narrow and parochial.

We are, as yet, a long way from a world metaphysical outlook. The commitment of many of the world's great cultures to their fundamental dogmas and their dogmatic insistence upon a single set of spiritual truths and a single set of valid styles of life, politics, and community, may make such a world outlook seem a distant dream. Still, the current situation for metaphysics is far from discouraging. Human beings have been brought into direct contact with each other's cultures as at no other time in history, and even if that contact is not loving and intimate, it at least requires all parties to think through the intellectual commitments of their fellow human beings and their total vision of the world contained in their various beliefs and practices. There is no reason to believe that this encounter will result in a mutual destruction of all intellectual and spiritual beliefs aspiring to universality. The metaphysical impulse, the need to explore what the world rests upon ultimately, will not be lost in the future, even in the face of its near abandonment by Western thinkers presently. Metaphysics arises out of real human need, and takes shape in the physical, cultural, and intellectual experience of persons. The brave new world of humankind's cultures, now forced to sit on each other's doorsteps, may yet produce a rebirth of metaphysics in the century that has just begun.

CHAPTER 5

Epistemology

This chapter will discuss epistemology, or the theory of knowledge. The following topics will be considered:

- The Problem of Knowledge in the Ancient World
- The Challenge of Skepticism
- The Problem of Universals in the Middle Ages
- The Modern Formulation of the Problem of Knowledge
- Twentieth-Century Epistemology on the European Continent
- Contemporary Epistemology in the English-Speaking World
- Metaphysics and Epistemology

THE PROBLEM OF KNOWLEDGE IN THE ANCIENT WORLD

The most technically difficult part of philosophy, although perhaps not initially the most engaging, is *epistemology*, or the theory of knowledge. One cannot explore the higher reaches of the field without having done extensive preparatory work. In this past century, epistemology has come under intense scrutiny by some of our best professional philosophers. For that reason, this chapter will attempt to make intelligible the source of the perennial perplexity and conflict that epistemology has caused. At times, this conflict appears to outsiders to degenerate into absurdity—into claims that the world may be a dream, or that there is no genuine knowledge at all. Gorgias, who lived in the time of Socrates, is reported to have said: "There is no such thing as reality, and even if there were, we could not know it, and even if we could know it, we could not communicate our knowledge of it." Why would anyone seriously propose such a notion, which makes hopeless all our aspirations to know, and not simply to be? Yet Gorgias's dictum emerges naturally from our efforts to understand what we mean when we say we know something. How do skeptical challenges to the very possibility of knowledge arise, and what form have some responses to these challenges taken?

Modern philosophical analysis was illustrated earlier by the example, "Johnny knows that p," where "p" is some factual claim or proposition, such as "Fire is hot." The analysis led to a familiar account of knowledge as justified true belief. This account says that the interrelated claims that Johnny believes that p, Johnny has good reason to believe that p, and p is true are all asserted when one claims that Johnny knows that p. This account may be criticized. For example, it does not cover cases of knowledge that are not expressed in language, or non-propositional knowledge. The proposition, "Johnny knows how to play baseball," may be true without Johnny knowing many factual claims (for example, "The distance between home plate and first base is ninety feet"), although he must know at least the purpose of the game, and some of its rules (for example, "Three strikes and the batter is out"). Knowing how to do something may also require some physical skill, whereas propositional knowledge does not. Attributing knowledge to higher animals is possible, but only this nonpropositional kind. The dog knows how to hunt rabbits, a complex task, without being able to formulate how he does it in a set of propositions. This chapter confines itself to problems surrounding claims to know that a proposition is true or false.

The chief problem for epistemology arises out of the second part of the above definition of propositional knowledge: What is justified belief? Can we specify the conditions when, if ever, a person is justified in claiming to know something? What reasons are good reasons for believing something? Surely a child is justified in claiming to know that fire is hot, once he puts a hand into it, or that the base angles of an isosceles triangle are equal, once he has gone through the proof. Yet both these examples assume something: that sense experience or logical argument are sources of knowledge. What guarantees those assumptions? It is difficult to say. Then again, a person may have very good reasons for believing some proposition, and yet the proposition is false (for example, when she does not notice an error in some otherwise carefully conducted calculation). Similar examples can demonstrate that there is a problem in asserting that a belief is justified in the strong sense that any justified belief must be true.

Consider the metaphysical theory proposed by some pre-Socratics as Parmenides, who argued that all change is impossible, for a thing must either exist or not exist; becoming, he seems to have thought, is an incoherent notion poised between being and nonbeing. Nonexistence is unthinkable, for it implies that "what is not" can be an object of thought and figure in our judgments. Further, the argument that all things about us come out of some original stuff (Thales's water, for example) does not answer Parmenides's charge. For whether the original stuff is water, or prime matter, or whatever, it cannot intelligibly become what it is not, namely the many things of the world. If it exists, it simply is what it is, not what it is not. And Thales does not show us how change is possible, or what happens when water becomes something that appears not to be water. The universe, Parmenides concluded, simply is: unchanging, undifferentiated, unmoving Being itself. All things are one; no cogent distinction between reality and appearance is possible, as Thales assumed.

This remarkable doctrine is unstable, however, for it generates objections that threaten to undermine it. Consider the proposition, "All is one." This cannot be a true proposition, for there must be at least two things, the One Thing, Being itself, and the assertion that there is one thing. If Parmenides were to counter that observation by claiming that assertions themselves are a part of being, then he admits that being has real parts, which it was not supposed to have. If, instead, he argued that assertions themselves are illusory, or a part of the Way of Error, then he is unable to assert the truth of anything, even his own doctrine, for doctrines are propositional assertions. We are left, therefore, with the necessity of asserting the reality of at least two things, assertions, and that about which they make assertions—or, more generally, of knowledge and reality.

The gap that this line of reasoning opens between knowing and being has plagued Western philosophy almost since its beginnings. The gap has taken many forms: It is said to exist between knowledge and reality, between language and the world, between assertions and what assertions are about, or between the mind as an instrument of knowledge and the physical world of which it presumably has knowledge. How can two fundamentally different things interact?

Metaphysical idealism, studied in the last chapter, asserts that there is no gap between knowledge and reality, for reality is itself idea. Yet if we argue, for example, that the world is mental, or in minds, as idealists do, we do violence to our common-sense notion that the mind and its objects cannot be the same thing. An idea of an object may be in the mind, but we have a strong sense that the object it represents is not mental. Besides, there might still be a gap between a mind and its ideas. Are the ideas in a mind, taken collectively, the mind itself, or does the mind or the person whose mind it is have its ideas as objects of its consciousness? If the latter, there would again be a gap between subject and object, in which errors in knowing could arise.

Metaphysical materialism also tries to eliminate the gap between knowing and being by arguing that the mind is nothing more than a manifestation of the physical brain. Yet this doctrine again does violence to our common-sense notion that our ideas, beliefs, and feelings, and our sense of ourselves, are different in kind from brain-states, no matter how complex these brain-states might be. The dualist theory that minds and their objects, and objects in the world that give rise to ideas in the mind are different in kind, yet causally interact, does violence to the common-sense notion that a nonphysical idea cannot cause something that is physical, or vice versa. How could my thought of writing a letter cause my body to move in various ways? How could a physical object cause me to have a certain perception and then entertain certain ideas about it? Thinking is different in kind from what is thought about. In sum, how could Parmenides's Being be the only reality—and yet Parmenides know that?

THE CHALLENGE OF SKEPTICISM

Those philosophers who challenge common sense by identifying specific barriers to knowledge are called skeptics. The challenges raised by the earliest skeptics, men such as Protagoras and Gorgias, did not have a determining effect upon the greatest of ancient thinkers, Plato and Aristotle. Both men seem to have considered skepticism self-defeating. Plato, for example, argues in Theaetetus that the skeptic's claim, "No knowledge is possible for human beings" refers also to itself, as to all claims to knowledge. Yet then, paradoxically, if the claim is true, it must then be false, because it asserts at least one proposition as knowledge—the proposition of skepticism itself! Yet Plato's clever counter-argument does not settle the questions raised by the skeptical challenge. It establishes only that skepticism fails as a theory of knowledge, as indeed it would have to. A theory cannot account for what it says does not exist. At its best, skepticism just points to logical difficulties inherent in the idea of justified knowledge. What follows is an account of some of those difficulties.

SEXTUS EMPIRICUS: The skeptics, a school of ancient philosophy derived from the teaching of a certain Pyrrho, about whom little is known, but who is thought to have accompanied Alexander the Great (356–323 B.C.E.) on his expedition to Persia and India. The best known figure of this school is Sextus Empiricus (early third century C.E.) because two of his works have come down to us. Skeptical arguments, or *tropes,* were intended by him to show that there is equally good evidence for both sides of a proposition in philosophy. The presentation here of the ancient skeptical challenge to knowledge follows the stronger of these tropes.

A common-sense approach to justified belief might challenge the skeptic in this way: "It is one thing to say that knowledge as justified belief is impossible, another to show why one should accept such a view. No doubt there is a difference between the knower and the known—otherwise how could there be knowledge?—but what of the obvious facts just referred to: 'Fire is hot.' 'The cup on the table in front of me is white.'? Aren't these propositions adequately justified by our senses? Why, in heaven's name, not?" The skeptic answers with two kinds of commonsense answer of his own. One response attacks the notion of justified belief and tries to show that no belief can be sufficiently justified to warrant the claim of knowledge. The other challenge analyzes the nature of the gap or the barrier between the knower and the known. It uses that analysis to explain why all attempts to bridge that gap and justify belief must fail. One example makes both these challenges clear.

The Tree in the Forest

A standard conundrum posed to introductory students in philosophy is, "If a tree falls in the forest and no one is around to hear it, does it make a sound?" Two problems are inherent in this question. The first concerns justification: If no sentient creature with ears is in the neighborhood, then we have no way to put the matter to the test. Naturally, if someone had been there, that person would have heard the tree fall. However, that response begs the question of what happens when no one is there. Putting a recording device in the forest would not help even if we hear the sound upon playback. For the recording device did not hear the sound, it simply recorded the sound waves as electromagnetic impulses. The skeptic concludes that we do not have sufficient grounds for the belief that the tree makes a sound when it falls.

The gap between the knower and the known is seen in the standard scientific account of the situation of hearing a tree fall. On that account, the falling tree causes transverse waves to form in the air. These waves, when they enter an ear, cause these vibrations to be transformed into electrochemical impulses that, when transmitted by the auditory nerve, result in the perception of a crashing sound by the hearer. Apart from that perception, there is no sound, although there are sound waves.

Given this account of hearing and sound, the skeptic raises his second challenge. "There are times when we 'hear' sounds that are not 'really' there, as with a hearing impairment. It is therefore possible that when we judge a tree to be falling because of what we hear, the cause of the sound is something internal to our ears, and no tree at all is falling." The mere possibility that an internal event triggers the sound cannot be eliminated. For the same reason we may wonder whether a falling tree makes sound at all, for when we see a tree fall, we may just happen to be hearing sounds internal to our ears, and falsely projecting them beyond our hearing apparatus and onto the falling tree. To show causation, we must always examine both the cause and the effect. Here, however, we can examine only the effect, the sound that we hear. We cannot examine the sound apart from the hearing of it; to do that we would have to go outside our capacity of hearing sound, to the sounds as they are apart from our hearing them. And that we cannot do, says the skeptic.

Illusions

Even if we grant that the senses give us access to a real world of physical objects, the reliability of the access may be questioned. The access itself may distort what is accessed, much as the glasses we wear may distort the image of what we see. And what if we cannot remove our glasses? We are all familiar with the phenomenon that a pencil extending out of a clear glass of water appears cut at the point of its exit from the water. Now perception is usually taken as a warrant for knowledge. Our seeing a bent pencil is taken to be a warrant for the truth of the proposition, "The pencil is bent." Yet here the refraction of the light has deceived our senses. How can we be certain that similar obscure tricks of nature do not always result in our seeing things other than they really are? Our senses may trick us unawares. When we have shown a source of knowledge even once to be unreliable, the skeptic asserts, we must always doubt whether it is reliable in any given instance. Even worse, if perception is the only possible source of knowledge—it may be that all other thinking is based upon it—then knowledge in general is not possible. Perhaps, as Hinduism teaches, the world is a "magic show" produced by our own animal natures, conjured up, as it were, by our desires and fears.

A Chinese philosopher is supposed to have said, "Last night I dreamed that I was a butterfly. And when I awoke, I was uncertain whether I was a philosopher dreaming I was a butterfly or a butterfly dreaming that I was a philosopher." When a person dreams, he never questions the reality of what he is dreaming. He is immersed in the content of his dream as deeply as he is in his ordinary waking world. Of course, in retrospect, when he is awake, those dream-images seem shadowy, and, in their relation to each other, they are usually less coherent than the objects in our waking world. Yet the differences in clarity and coherence are relative ones. Perhaps, the skeptic may argue, some godlike beings perceive reality with far greater clarity, coherence, and certainty than we can in our waking life. So we can never be certain that what we perceive is more real than a dream image.

THE PROBLEM OF UNIVERSALS IN THE MIDDLE AGES

In the European Middle Ages, the skeptical challenge was not taken with great seriousness, any more than it had been by Plato and Aristotle, but for different reasons. Most of the medieval thinkers believed themselves to be in possession of indubitable knowledge, namely holy Scripture. The belief that God exists and has revealed his ways to humankind was taken by most people as an absolute certainty. Besides, all of Scripture assumes the mind's direct involvement with reality. How could there be salvation for anyone if the possibility of knowing anything, especially God and righteousness, were denied? The question must therefore be not whether knowledge is possible, or how the term *knowledge* can be defined, but what is the nature of knowledge?

Here the medieval thinkers found room for a powerful debate. In their debates, the gap between knowing and being again appeared. Their idea of what knowledge is was derived, of course, from the ancient thinkers, as Scripture contains no analysis of the definition, the nature, or the possibility of knowledge. Plato had taught that knowledge is possible only by means of the general notions that are carried in our minds. These notions are shadowy imitations of the Forms, which are both the highest reality and the structural features of individual things. We derive knowledge of the Forms from a pre-birth experience of them, but that knowledge becomes shadowy after we are born; therefore our need for science and philosophy to clarify what we once knew well but have now in part forgotten. Aristotle believed that the active intellect abstracts general notions of individual substances from experience. Both men assumed that our general ideas—for Plato the Forms; for Aristotle the abstracted universal natures of things—were what is intelligible about reality. We cannot know individuals as such in their uniqueness. Science or systematic philosophy therefore begins with a study of these Forms, or general natures.

Thomas Aquinas. © *Thoemmes.*

Now the universal is neither the particular, nor the particular the universal. We know the object on the table is a cup by applying the universal idea, cupness, referred to by the word *cup,* to what we see. Yet what is the existential status of these forms? Both John and Mary are human beings. Is there a third thing, *humanity,* that they have in common, and that they do not share with dogs or trees? If so, how is this third thing related to the two individual things that have it in common? That is, how does Mary participate in or imitate the universal idea of humanity? In the Middle Ages, at least three theories were advanced to solve this problem of the apparent gap between the universal nature and the particular thing.

St. Augustine, the first great Christian philosopher, believed that Plato's Forms were ideas in the Mind of God. All individual things are related to the ideas in God's mind as an individual building is related to the blueprint of an architect. Just as we can build any number of buildings according to a single blueprint, so are the myriad things constructed from the formal or structural patterns in God's mind. Of course, Augustine, no more than Plato, could recount in any detail how the Divine Architect realizes his blueprints. We are left with a metaphor. We call Augustine's theory of universal Forms a realist theory, for he says universals really exist, as Plato did.

Aristotle claimed that the universal is subjective, that is, it exists in the mind only, not additionally in some transcendental ground. The subjective essence of Aristotle nonetheless has a basis in reality in the individual existing objects. The active intellect, a part of the mind, can abstract these real features by studying carefully the features of individual substances. St. Thomas Aquinas developed this idea in the High Middle Ages. Aquinas wished to provide a transcendental ground for universals, but he denied that universals have the status of Platonic Forms in the mind of God. His theory of universals is called moderate realism. The senses are the source of all knowledge, but the senses cannot perceive universals; as in Aristotle, only the active intellect can discern the common features in things given through the senses. Only individuals exist as such, and they are given to us through the senses in the form of what Aquinas calls phantasmagoria. Universals therefore exist only in the mind. Nevertheless, they have a basis in the common form shared by like objects, as creations of divine reason and will. The active intellect distinguishes us from animals, and makes language possible for humankind. Animals are only the passive recipients of data given to the senses. Since they lack an active intellect (as far as our closest examination of their behavior can tell), they are unable to discern the common features of things and thus become capable of propositional knowledge. Aquinas does not tell us in detail how the mind assembles its universals out of the sense-data, and so the gap between intelligible natures and the unintelligible phantasmagoria received from the individuals is not closed.

Later medieval thinkers, notably William of Ockham, denied both an objective and transcendental foundation to universals. The theory Ockham developed defies simple formulation and classification. It was derived in part from a lesser eleventh-century thinker named Roscelinus (1050–1125), who said that universals were only words, puffs of air. This theory of universals, called *nominalism,* represents a softening of the quest for knowledge of absolute reality. It denies the reality of the very means those ancient thinkers declared to make intelligible the objects given to us through the senses. If only Jacks and Marys, and not their common humanity, exist, then all talk about humanity is subjective, and without ground in the nature of Jacks and Marys themselves. According to nominalism, speakers use the word *humanity* to organize their experience in ways intelligible to them. Such words are the product of convention. Yet if this is true, then all claims to knowledge are themselves mere human conventions, because all such claims employ universals.

THE MODERN FORMULATION OF THE PROBLEM OF KNOWLEDGE

Descartes: Rational Knowledge

Rationalism and empiricism were two epistemological theories that emerged from the new metaphysical philosophy that had arisen after the scientific revolution of the sixteenth and seventeenth centuries. Descartes, the first rationalist philosopher, believed that absolute and certain knowledge is possible, if only we acquire a reliable method for seeking truth. The British empiricists tended towards skepticism in at least some areas of inquiry. However, Descartes and the British empiricists, with one notable exception, Bishop George Berkeley, accepted the dualist metaphysics of mind and body. Both agreed that external objects cause ideas to form in the mind. Rationalists and empiricists are, however, opposed in the roles they assign to mind and body in knowledge. Rationalists stress the role of reason, or other mental capacities such as intuition, in justifying belief. Descartes, a rationalist philosopher, held that clarity and distinctness are criteria of the truth of a proposition (not, it should be noted, of the existence of a physical object). He believed also, as do most rationalists, in an idea borrowed from Plato: that the mind contains **innate ideas**, that is, ideas that are inborn and native to the mind. By means of these ideas, we have a source of certainty that we can never obtain from sense experience alone. No doubt, Descartes believed, the truthfulness of God prevents the ideas of material objects outside the mind from being merely fictitious or illusory, at least in cases where we carefully attend to our experience. Yet the ideas of individual external objects, as far as they are not innate to the mind, are subject to error or at least confusion. Innate ideas, where they are part of the mind's activity to scrutinize its experience, serve to guarantee the truth of the propositions that a person may assert after that scrutiny.

INNATE IDEAS: A simple example may clarify this notion, which first appeared in Plato's dialogue *Meno*. When children learn a simple proposition in arithmetic, such as "2+2 = 4," they are usually given examples of the relationship to help them visualize it. The teacher will show them two apples and again two apples, put each pair together, and ask the children to count them: of course, the result is four. Suppose that one of the children took an eyedropper and put two drops of water through a funnel with another two drops of water. Only one drop would be found where the drops collected, so 2+2 = 1! Our experience, therefore, cannot assure us of the truth of "2+2 = 4." Descartes (and Plato's) point is that the mind can recognize the truth of "2+2 = 4" because it possesses innate structures that are activated upon seeing an example of the relation, but the mind does not have to resort to experiments with apples or drops of water to know that the proposition is true. Empiricists deny the existence of innate ideas and generally claim that all the mind's ideas, even mathematical ones, are derived from sense-experience.

Primary and Secondary Qualities

This guarantee is possible because of another idea initially shared by both rationalists and empiricists, excepting, again, George Berkeley: that of primary and secondary qualities of objects. Some qualities of things appear to be essentially subjective, in that they exist only to a perceiving mind. Colors, for example, exist only when there is light and would not exist as such without perception. We see colors, and not the waves of light that presumably produce them in our minds. The situation is similar for the other senses; we do not hear sound waves, we hear sound, although we would not hear the sounds without the waves. However, such qualities as length and mass and velocities exist apart from our perception of them; they are objective qualities of things. The distinction is marked by calling such qualities as colors and sounds secondary, and such qualities as velocity and mass primary qualities of extended substance.

The distinction supports a specific concept of reality, namely one that conceives of physical objects as really possessing only such qualities as volume, mass, and velocity. Now if the real qualities of things are such measurable ones as volume, mass, and velocity, then we can justify the view that physical science, which, at least since the time of Galileo, was insistent upon the use of mathematics as the language of science, has pride of place among all other forms of knowledge. If the qualities of things we can measure are their real qualities, and if the mathematical knowledge we apply to these measurements is certain because it is not derived from the senses, then we can insulate genuine knowledge from subjective sources of error. By extending the reach of our mathematical ideas to the real qualities of sense-objects, we will penetrate more deeply into the nature of things, so far as they are knowable by us at all. For the rationalist, knowledge may be had by thinking alone; experiments merely illustrate aspects of the physical qualities of things that the mind can know without their assistance. And yet Descartes, a rationalist, appears to have overlooked a question that the empiricists would drive home: Don't we know the primary qualities of things by means of their secondary qualities? If so, the primary qualities are not insulated from uncertainty.

Locke: Empirical Knowledge

The empiricists, beginning with John Locke, subjected Cartesianism to serious criticism. Locke's first critique centered precisely upon Descartes's doctrine of innate ideas. No ideas in the mind, he argued, were not first given through the senses. Locke's great work, *An Essay concerning Human Understanding*, is in four parts. After arguing against innate ideas in the first part of this work, Locke tells us what knowledge is and how we obtain it. The senses apprehend simple ideas, such as colors or shapes. The mind, born without ideas innate to it, a *tabula rasa,* reflects upon its own operations and associates these simple ideas, noting which ideas normally appear together, and which not. For example, by associating such simple qualities as "solid," "yellow," and "easy to shape," we get our complex idea of "gold." Our complex ideas are of various kinds. We have complex ideas of substances, of relations between them, and of such abstract ideas as those in mathematics, ethics, and religion. All these complex ideas are derived from the simple ideas given through the senses, although they do not apply to physical reality.

According to Locke, knowledge is, in a sense, formed by us. We use the material of sensation given through the senses to build up our picture of the external world. What causes the sensations? External objects, no doubt. What is the nature of these external objects? Locke's answer is skeptical. The idea of gold represents an external object to us, but we cannot obtain knowledge of the real nature of gold itself. It must be, argued Locke, that subtle and perhaps microscopic elements and powers of physical objects cause primary and secondary qualities that we mentally associate as the complex idea that represents gold in the mind. But since it exceeds the power of our senses to experience these qualities directly, they cannot be known with any certainty. We know only our ideas of them, not the objects themselves. Hence the gap, opened by Descartes, between the nature of a physical object and its subjective appearance, cannot be closed.

"We know directly only our ideas"—not the things of which they are the ideas, or representations. This key notion was unavoidable for Locke, since the Newtonian science of his day subscribed to a corpuscular theory of reality: all physical things are made up or defined by point-masses, and particles of light. It was no longer possible for Locke to imagine, as did Aristotle and Aquinas, that a comparison of individual substances will give us a common essence. For the Forms of Plato and the essences of Aristotle were defined not in terms of quantifiable if subtle particlelike forces and processes in things, but qualitatively, in terms of forms and purposes. No doubt Locke's idea was suggestive to scientific minds. In fact, today we can give a good, though incomplete, account of the forces and processes on the microscopic level that cause in us sensations of color, sound, and smell. Yet in Locke's day, these forces and processes were still unknown and apparently unknowable. Locke was left, therefore, with a new and seemingly unbridgeable gap between knowledge and the world. If we know only our own ideas, we cannot be certain that the causes of our simple ideas resemble their effects, just because the ideas originate in sensation internal to our minds.

Hume and the Problem of Induction

More than Locke, David Hume embraced what he called a limited skepticism. He thought such unlimited skepticism as that of Sextus Empiricus was impractical and even unhealthy. We can rely upon habit or custom to carry us through life. Our ideas of the world have at least enough consistency to enable us to live, but we have no way of knowing whether what Hume called "impressions" and "ideas"—the mental events through which objects are presented to the mind—represent the world to us the way it really is.

A centerpiece of Hume's theory of knowledge is a familiar distinction that he used in a new way: that between propositions asserting matters of fact and propositions asserting relations of ideas. He found here a means of criticizing the whole of past philosophy and limiting all future philosophy to the few things that he thought the mind is genuinely able to understand. Propositions asserting matters of fact refer to items of experience, either individual items ("The object next to me is a cup") or general ones ("All swans are white"). As an empiricist, Hume naturally insists that we derive all the materials of experiences from sense experience, from "simple ideas copied from a precedent feeling, sensation, or sentiment." Propositions asserting relations of ideas simply analyze the implications of their subject matter. Thus when it is asserted, "All bachelors are unmarried men," one is simply analyzing the meaning of the term *bachelor,* not stating any facts concerning bachelors. Note that the denial of a proposition asserting a relation of ideas is a contradiction. This fact, for Hume, is characteristic of all propositions asserting relations of ideas and serves as a warrant of their truth as certain and necessary: "John is a bachelor and has a wife" contradicts itself and cannot be sensibly asserted. In contrast, no contradiction is generated if one denies the truth of the matter-of-fact assertion, "Bread nourishes."

All reasoning about matters of fact must be traceable to some sensation, whether outward (of things) or inward (of states of mind or body). If we cannot trace an idea to some sensation, then it is illegitimate: it represents a leap beyond what is given to the senses. Here Hume has discovered the basis for a method of doing philosophy, and for a critique of philosophical doctrines that are quite different from Descartes's. In the *Inquiry concerning Human Understanding,* he offers the following idea for a method:

> When we entertain, therefore, any suspicion that a philosophical term is employed without any meaning or idea (as is but frequent), we need but inquire, from what impression is that supposed idea derived? And if it be impossible to assign any, this will serve to confirm our suspicion. By bringing ideas in so clear a light, we may reasonably hope to remove all disputes which may arise concerning their nature and reality.

Now most reasoning about the world is based upon the cause-effect relations between things. To take again Hume's own example, a person normally believes that when she sees a billiard ball roll toward a second ball, the two will meet, and the second one will necessarily move off at the angle it was hit. This conclusion is based upon past experience of similar situations. Yet is the reasoning legitimate? Hume believed that it presupposes that future experiences will necessarily resemble past ones. Yet that proposition is not based on any outer or inner impression. We have no impressions of future sensations, nor do we have an impression of necessity in nature. Such reasoning about matters of fact is therefore always uncertain; we believe such assertions as "Bread nourishes" only by force of habit. Skepticism about the order and structure of the physical world is therefore vindicated. Hume subscribes to the view that a belief is a kind of feeling-state, or, as he puts it, "belief is something felt by the mind." It arises not through the operation of reason, except in mathematics. It arises when impressions of the senses take hold of our minds. Resemblance, nearness, and frequent repetition of the same associated impressions and ideas give a greater liveliness and importance to some ideas more than others, and this generates the feeling of belief, argues Hume. The notion that belief is a psychological state derived from custom, rather than from a chain of necessary reasons or compelling evidence, cements the view that knowledge is justified belief. For a belief can be warranted only by psychological necessity, and not by compelling rational evidence.

Hume's deepest epistemological problem, one which he could not imagine being solved, is proving the rational validity of most of our beliefs concerning matters of fact. And, indeed, it cannot be solved on its own terms—terms that require every valid belief about matters of fact to be traceable to individual sense-impressions. For we surely have no sense-impression of the necessity that bread will nourish us, or that our moving billiard ball must transmit its notion to a stationary one. These are simply matters of brute fact. No doubt Hume would agree that as a practical matter we will go on buying bread in the expectation that it will nourish us when we eat it. But Hume's skeptical problem arises from the fact that a factual claim such as, "Bread nourishes" contains elements of necessity and universality that go far beyond the supporting evidence. We have no experience of a necessary relation between bread and nourishment, and yet the proposition "Bread nourishes," just because it pretends to be true, lays claim to necessity and certainty. Also, we have no experience of future cases of our bread eating, and yet the proposition, "Bread nourishes," asserts a relation among all cases of bread and nourishment, past, present, and future.

This skeptical issue is called the problem of induction. Induction is the process whereby we go from an observation of the properties of some class of things to a conclusion about all members of the class. As an argument, it has the following form:

A is a case of x and has property p.

B is a case of x and has property p.

C is a case of x and has property p.

. . .

N is a case of x and has property p.

Therefore all cases of x have property p.

Imagine that A, B, C are Fluffy, Pickles, and Tom; X is the class of cats, and p is the property of catching mice. Our conclusion attributes the property of catching mice to all members of the class of cats. It does not refer to any specific individuals, it refers to all things that are properly characterized as cats. Now clearly the conclusion passes far beyond the evidence given, and that would be so even if we examined thousands of individual As, Bs, and Cs down to N. Here is a new gap, then, one between the evidentiary warrant and the propositions asserted based on that warrant. If all beliefs about matters of fact are based on limited evidence of this kind, then they are not guaranteed by reason; we are convinced only out of habit.

Hume was persuaded that his reasoning had given him a clear measure of epistemological sense and nonsense. He concludes the inquiry with the following words:

When we run over libraries, persuaded of these principles, what havoc must we make? If we take in our hand any volume—of divinity or school metaphysics, for instance—let us ask, Does it contain any abstract reasoning concerning quantity or number? No. Does it contain any experimental reasoning concerning matter of fact and existence? No. Commit it then to the flames, for it can contain nothing but sophistry and illusion.

This method of tracing philosophical claims back to the experiences that gave rise to them has become central to the practice of philosophy in the twentieth century in English-speaking countries. These philosophers have, like Hume, consigned works of metaphysics, theology, and even ethics to the dustbin, for many of their foundational claims cannot be traced back to simpler givens of experience. The objection that Hume's *inquiry*, by its own criterion, would be committed to the flames is psychologically effective, but hardly sound. The skeptic's denial of knowledge may result in a paradox, but the objections he raises to justified belief remain in place.

Kant and Transcendental Idealism

The great watershed figure in modern philosophy, in epistemology as in metaphysics, is Immanuel Kant. Kant's epistemology may be regarded as a synthesis of empiricism and rationalism. It borrows from rationalism at least two things: a belief in objective rational knowledge, confined to the world of appearance, and the notion of innate ideas, understood not as propositions, but as the categorical structures of the human mind. From British empiricism Kant borrows the idea of representation of objects by means of data given to the senses. We require both data and categories for knowledge: a famous aphorism of Kant says, "Thoughts without content are empty, and intuitions [that is, perceptions, not simply internal sensations, such as twinges, but of objects having spatial and temporal form] without concepts are blind." The mind cannot weave any truths about the world out of itself, as Descartes thought to be possible. It must be given some content from incoming sense data, as it were. But the sensible data themselves cannot carry or produce all the conceptual structures we apply to them, as Locke believed to be possible.

Kant assumes that natural science, such as Newton's, gives us objective knowledge of the world as it is presented to the human mind. By "objective" he means not certain or absolutely true, but "intersubjectively valid": It is knowledge that all people who examine the evidence can and will agree upon. Kant's great work, *The Critique of Pure Reason*, asks how such objectively valid science is possible. How does the activity of the mind synthesize such valid knowledge from the data given to the senses? What structures must our minds possess, such that our awareness of the world is not chaotic, a random and unorganized aggregate of sense and thought? His answer to this question is called *transcendental idealism* because it proposes to study the mental structures that transcend our everyday awareness of the world but that are the ideal conditions of our having a world at all.

Figure 5.1

KINDS OF PROPOSITION	KINDS OF KNOWLEDGE	
	A priori	**A posteriori**
Analytic	Analytic a priori	Analytic a posteriori
Synthetic	Synthetic a priori	Synthetic a posteriori

For example, Kant held that we cannot derive intuitions of space and time from sensation. The intuition of space and time, from which we derive the sciences of geometry and arithmetic, cannot be abstracted from the sensations of primary qualities, but must be inherent in some form of apprehension belonging to the mind. We necessarily apprehend objects as in space and as in time, that is, as manifolds of sensible qualities arrayed in space and time, and unified under some empirical concept. We recognize this cup as a thing having size, shape, and duration in time. Our knowledge of space and time must be prior to our knowledge of objects in space and time. But what of our knowledge of things as something or other, as a cup, for instance? Kant would agree that the idea of a cup can be worked up by the imagination based on repeated experiences of a cup. But the idea of a cup and its spatial and temporal arrangement is not all that is involved in knowing this thing to be a cup.

To help us understand what else is involved, Kant reintroduces some crucial distinctions. Hume had distinguished between propositions expressing relations of ideas and those expressing matters of fact. Let us call the first kind of proposition, such as "All bachelors are unmarried men," analytic; they give us information not about bachelors, but about what the word *bachelor* means. The second kind of proposition, such as, "Most bachelors are under twenty-five," we will call synthetic. These propositions give us information not about the term "bachelor," but about bachelors. Gottfreid Wilhelm Leibniz had distinguished between two kinds of knowledge: A priori knowledge is rational or intuitive knowledge, derived by the mind alone and not by means of the senses, and a posteriori knowledge is empirical knowledge, derived from sense experience. One sees the relation between these two kinds of knowledge and two kinds of statement in figure 5.1.

All a posteriori knowledge is synthetic. Analytic propositions are always knowable a priori since they are about relations of ideas, which we can analyze rationally or grasp intuitively. There can therefore be no analytic propositions that are known a posteriori. The chief question, for Kant, concerns synthetic a priori knowledge. Is there knowledge that arises entirely from the mind but applies to facts about the world? His task is to show that synthetic a priori knowledge is a condition of valid objective knowledge of phenomena, but not of what he calls noumena, the things-in-themselves, which are the metaphysical objects of pure reason.

Kant must now do four things: He must first demonstrate the foundational synthetic a priori ideas, native to the human being, which he calls the categories of the understanding. This occurs in a passage in the *Critique of Pure Reason* called the "metaphysical deduction" of the categories. He shows there that the mind's a priori categories are the fundamental categories of the science of logic. In the passage entitled "transcendental deduction," Kant shows how these logical categories function as specific ways of ordering and structuring the judgments we make of the phenomenal world. They are the necessary conditions of such judgments. Then, in the passages concerned with the "schematism" of the acts of the understanding, he shows how we can apply the categories to individual objects in the phenomenal world. Finally, he shows how a human subject may assert judgments. For this task, he develops the notion of the "transcendental unity of apperception." This is the notion that a subject must be able to assert her own continuity in time. However orderly phenomena may be, they would not be coherently experienced by a person attempting to assert propositions about them unless she was able to synthesize her continuous selfhood. For every cognition of an object and every assertion about that object, the "I think" of Descartes must be potentially in the person's mind, otherwise the assertion would have no coherent assertor. Kant responds to Hume's observation that we have no impression of a continuous self by claiming that the phenomenal self is a transcendental condition of all phenomenal knowledge and is not an object of perception. A noumenal self—traditionally called the soul—is unknowable, according to Kant.

A simple example may clarify this complex undertaking. If we can identify the object we see before us as a cup, we must not only perceive it as a thing in space and time, we must also perceive it as a unity within a plurality. If not, we could not distinguish the cup as the specific thing that it is from the table beneath it and the telephone next to it. Now the notions of unity and plurality are central to logic and to arithmetic. In logic we say a thing is what it is, or a proposition materially implies itself, "$p \supset p$," or "A is A," and we add unities, "$1 + 1 = 2$." These are extremely abstract notions, but they clearly structure not only the a priori knowledge of logic and arithmetic, but of the phenomenal world as well. And these are surely not derived from the sense-data—Hume's ideas and impressions—alone. The sense-data would not be coherent without them; they must therefore be prior to (a priori) our synthesis of objects.

Similarly, in logic we have the relation of ground and consequent, "$p \subset q$." This abstract relationship, called material implication, and defined in Chapter 2, structures some relationships of the kind, "if A, then B," especially causal relationships. "If I do such-and-such to this thing, then this thing will be changed in such-and-such way." The schematism of these structural categories show how the mind can apply abstractions such as these to phenomena via intermediate schemata and make such valid judgments about phenomena as, "If I drop this cup upon this stone, then the cup will break." Note that the specific reference I make to myself in this proposition is unnecessary for the assertion to be true, but any such assertion must refer to someone making the judgment. If people did not have a sense of themselves as continuous subjects of the "I think," they could not unify phenomena as a coherent world of events.

In this way, Kant attempted to respond to the skeptics' argument by conceding the impossibility of absolute knowledge to them: We cannot know things in themselves, the nature of things apart from their being-an-object to us. The gap between the phenomenal realm and the noumenal realm, if, in fact, such a realm of things-in-themselves exists, cannot be bridged. Yet we can be assured that valid and objective knowledge is possible, for the stability of objects in the phenomenal world that is necessary for knowledge arises from the abstract categories that structure our apprehension of phenomena.

Hegel and Absolute Idealism

Kant was the last great Enlightenment philosopher. The cultural period in Europe after Kant in Europe is usually called the Romantic Age. Romantics are always storming castles without a worried regard for the formidable barriers in their way. Fichte, Hegel, and Schelling, quintessential romantic thinkers, believed that the human mind is at the center of reality, and that center, to them, was spiritual in its deepest nature. Hegel believed that in human thinking the Absolute Idea comes to know itself. For Hegel, no unbridgeable gap exists between the human mind and the world. The categories of the Absolute work themselves out first in nature, and then, in a higher synthesis, in the art, culture, and religion of human beings. All the concepts of reason, whose limits Kant tried to establish, are traceable to and are founded in the Absolute Idea. Thus, Hegel believed, the idea of something absolute and in-itself, which Kant had rejected, is restored to philosophy. In coming to understand in philosophy the categories in which we think, we come to know the Absolute.

TWENTIETH-CENTURY EPISTEMOLOGY ON THE EUROPEAN CONTINENT

The growth of the human sciences—psychology, anthropology, and sociology—in the waning decades of the nineteenth century and the start of the twentieth aroused interest among epistemologists. If it is possible to give a coherent and lawlike account of human behavior, it might also be possible to view the philosophical quest for knowledge and understanding in a scientific, external, and dispassionate way. Now there is no doubt that the beliefs of people concerning the general features of the world and humankind's place and role in it have varied considerably from culture to culture. The study of the understanding of ideas in history and how ideas evolve in the changing circumstances of life is known as *historicism* when it attempts to understand how beliefs become embedded in a culture and how they happen to change within that culture. It is known as *hermeneutics* when it interprets the texts left by earlier or distant communities. When it attempts to show relationships between the social forms of a culture and the world-views of that culture, it is known as the *sociology of knowledge*. In all these cases we see philosophy losing its autonomy as the queen of the sciences and becoming an object of historical inquiry, that is, simply another human activity to be accounted for by social science.

Hermeneutics and Historicism

The German philosopher Wilhelm Dilthey (1833–1911) is known for the distinction he drew between natural science (for example, biology, physics, or chemistry) and the human sciences (for example, psychology, economics, or anthropology), of which the latter were first being developed at the end of the nineteenth century. Dilthey generalized the Marxist notion that the beliefs of a culture play a role in the class struggle that is fought out within that culture. All knowledge, he believed, emerges from what he calls a "form of life" and is necessarily situated in or is relative to a historical and cultural context. This may be a form of skepticism, because it suggests an unbridgeable gap between the beliefs, knowledge, or more generally, the consciousness typical of our own culture and that of others. We cannot know foreign cultures directly; universal human knowledge is not possible. Many philosophers influenced by Dilthey did, in fact, draw such skeptical conclusions.

Dilthey himself, however, stressed the difficulty, not the impossibility, of understanding other cultures. The radical distinction between scientific attempts to understand the physical world and historical attempts to understand human culture and history simply point to the necessity of developing methods of properly interpreting other cultures. Dilthey extended the application of the term *hermeneutics,* which was formerly used to designate the technique of interpreting historical documents, especially sacred Scripture, to the effort to render intelligible any text whatever, along with the meanings of the techniques, taboos, rites, or moral codes of peoples other than the interpreter's own. The epistemology peculiar to Dilthey's hermeneutics supposes that it is possible for an interpreter to enter empathetically the whole of a prior culture and relive the elements of knowing and meaning that were peculiar to that culture. Dilthey's goal is to achieve sympathetic understanding of that culture on its own terms.

Max Scheler (1872–1928) approved of Dilthey's project, although he believed that we must carry it out based on his phenomenological procedure. For Scheler, it is possible to grasp in reflective intuition the essences and essential relationships that function within the conscious culture of a people. Many of these essences are disclosed to us not by reason or by the understanding, but by feeling. Through feeling we come to know aspects of the world—especially in the realm of the cultural values that typify a culture—that remain hidden from a purely logical or scientific standpoint. Scheler, for his part, believed that humankind's feelings are in a certain sense universal. It is one task of the sociology of knowledge to explore by reperforming in reflective intuition the feelings and cognitions from which the intellectual and moral structures of a culture's world-view arose. We can in this way, and in principle, understand a foreign culture the way the members of that culture understood it.

Despite the optimism of Dilthey and Scheler regarding efforts to achieve a perfect understanding of other cultures, the notion that each culture is situated in or is relative to a historical and cultural context suggests that we cannot speak of truth or falsity outside the system of culture in which beliefs appear. Cultures may differ, after all, even regarding what they take to be adequate evidence warranting its systems of knowledge and value. Let us assume, against Dilthey and Scheler, as many contemporary epistemologists do, that we can have no direct sympathetic understanding of foreign systems of belief and value. Any attempt to understand these systems requires an imaginative leap of the mind. But then it is always possible that our leap has taken us in the wrong direction. Furthermore, it may be that our own system of knowledge and culture is incommensurate with that of the foreign culture in the sense that we lack a common language by which the belief systems of the foreign culture might be translated into the notions familiar in our own culture. Then we would not be able to understand them as they understood themselves.

These skeptical consequences were drawn later in the twentieth century by such men as Thomas Kuhn (1922–) and Paul Feyerabend (1924–1994), who applied historicist and hermeneutic principles to a study of communities of modern scientists. Kuhn argued that the paradigms or ruling models of scientific knowledge today are defended, attacked, and overthrown, but not by the discovery of new facts. Power struggles among the scientists generate these clashes among scientists themselves. A paradigm (say, Newtonian physics) is abandoned and replaced by a new one (say, general relativity) simply because the new theory reflects the prevailing social, political, and historical conditions of the scientific establishment under which the substitution arose. The new paradigm does not represent a more profound truth that scientists have discovered but simply represents a different way of doing business among scientists. The new way is incommensurate with the old; the scientists working out of different paradigms are unable to conduct research with each other, for the very assumptions that undergird their researches have no common center.

These notions suggest that knowledge is formed by or within the political and moral struggles of a culture and are not uniquely determined by the world. We can describe the world in any number of ways that correspond to the known facts. A later hermeneutical thinker, Hans-Georg Gadamer (1900–2001), adopted the view that the documents and artifacts of foreign cultures cannot be understood on their own terms. Rather, our very efforts to interpret the values and knowledge of other peoples that are communicated to us through the veil of history are a part of our own ongoing efforts to create knowledge. Our dealings with the past are a kind of dialogue; we ask of distant or dead authors questions that are important to us from our own historical perspective. This dialogue generates a history of interpretation; different interpreters at different times will see different things in a historical document. There is no privileged position from which to ask questions about the meanings of texts, it is impossible for us to get rid of the cultural beliefs that define our own age, and there is no timeless meaning to find in a historical document. Historians were mistaken in the belief that they were trying to get it right when they described the nature of a culture. Instead, they were trying to describe those cultures in ways that made sense to them.

This outcome, however, may be less skeptical in its implications than it appears to be, for if our knowledge were not shaped by the past—if we came to inquiry entirely bereft of culturally shaped beliefs—we could not begin the process of interpretation. Gadamer argued that all propositional knowledge is laden with the expectations and desires that our culture has shaped. These expectations are prejudices, no doubt, but they are correctable by future experience. These future experiences may lead us to correct our earlier theories, but they themselves may be based on further presuppositions that have not yet been subject to criticism. Yet without these prejudices, the work of inquiry could not begin. We have to stand somewhere or other when we begin to dig into the earth; the spade must be turned in some direction. This is true even for this book. The ideas, endless in number, that make up the history of philosophy must be sorted in some manner. The author must choose facts to narrate, pick and choose organizing themes, judge what is significant and what is not. All these efforts are conditioned by the author's education and philosophical beliefs, and by what he takes to be the interests and expectations of his intended audience.

In the wake of the collapse of Hegelianism and the tremendous impact of natural science both on the Continent and among English-speaking philosophers, new theories of knowledge emerged. On the Continent, late nineteenth-century thinkers attempted again to place the origin of knowledge in the activity of the human mind. Schools of neo-Kantianism and psychologism appeared. The latter group had an affinity to Hume rather than to Kant. Its members tried to show how beliefs, even purely logical or analytical ones, arose out of innate psychological structures in the human mind, structures that evolved from the efforts of human beings to deal with the environment. However, the great mathematical logician Gottlob Frege (1848–1925) questioned the possibility of justifying truths of logic in a Kantian, or even in a psychological manner. Such obvious logical rules as "$p \supset p$," he argued, are believed to be true because they are true, not because they reflect structures in the mind or help people to adapt to their environment.

Phenomenology

One twentieth-century school of philosophy believed that the certainty of our knowledge could be attained by a new philosophical method. Such an attempt was made in the phenomenological philosophy of Edmund Husserl (1859–1938) and applied to diverse spheres of human understanding by such thinkers as Max Scheler in Germany and Maurice Merleau-Ponty (1908–1961) in France. Their epistemology is founded upon three considerations. First, consciousness is always intentional, that is, consciousness is always directed at an

Bertrand Russell. © *AP / Wide World Photos.*

object. We can distinguish between the conscious act in which we apprehend such truths as "p ⊃ p" and the object of the act, the essence or essential relationship designated by "p ⊃ p."

Second, the correct method of apprehending essential objects is intuition: I reflect intuitively upon my mental acts and their objects until both are given with complete clarity. The similarity to Descartes's notion of clear and distinct knowledge is apparent, although Husserl's intuitions are not of the truth of propositions, as in Descartes, but rather of essential states of affairs that can be given with indubitable clarity or self-given in intuition. In "p ⊃ p," not the truth of the proposition but its content is self-given. "Truth," Scheler quotes Spinoza, "is the criterion of itself and of the false." Thirdly, the object of phenomenology is to get at the essences or essential states of affairs that underlie our languages, whether specialized scientific languages or the natural languages of everyday life. Such knowledge will provide the basis for empirical studies of science, of human behavior, or of the human situation in general.

CONTEMPORARY EPISTEMOLOGY IN THE ENGLISH-SPEAKING WORLD

Russell

In the early twentieth century the leading thinkers in the English-speaking world who contributed to new efforts in epistemology were G. E. Moore,

Bertrand Russell, and Ludwig Wittgenstein. In the last decade of the nineteenth century, Moore and Russell had slowly retreated from the influence of Hegelianism and moved toward forms of realism. For the early Russell and for Moore, the term *realism* designates the view that language refers to objects in the world, and those objects really exist apart from our designation of them. There are facts about cups, and true sentences containing that word really capture those facts. For example, "The cup is on the table," picks out a feature of a really existing cup and does not simply utter an idea or a mental construct. Moore took himself to be defending common sense when he asserted that we have direct knowledge of items in the external world, and that we have direct intuitions of such properties as "red" or even "good" when, for example, we eat a fresh strawberry. The proposition, "This strawberry is red," is true because the strawberry is red, that is, since the proposition corresponds to its object, the red strawberry. Nonetheless, the possibility that I may be in error limited Moore's ability to affirm that what I perceive directly in perceiving a thing as a red strawberry is the red strawberry itself. The red strawberry-looking thing I am holding in my hand may turn out to be a plastic strawberry. Therefore, Moore appears to have concluded, we have direct apprehension only of qualities of things, rather than the things themselves. Yet perhaps we can learn to control and distinguish rigorously what our propositions claim about such things as cups, the structure of propositions about them, and the perception of their qualities.

In the face of this problem, Russell proposed to examine the language we use when laying claim to knowledge about the external world. Russell's concern was for the particular facts themselves and how they can be organized into a logical language that affords rigorous control over what propositions in that language assert. Such a language must (1) specify such terms as *meaning* and *reference*, and (2) provide an account of how true propositions can refer to nonexisting items, such as unicorns or square circles.

This latter problem is especially acute. Russell's famous example of a proposition referring to the qualities of something that does not exist was the sentence, "The current king of France is bald." This sentence picks out a singular item in the world—the current king of France—and says something about it. A realist takes this "picking out" to be a fundamental function of propositions. Yet this proposition, which is immediately understandable to speakers of English, picks no item out, for there is no current king of France. Russell responds to this curious situation with his theory of definite descriptions. It is intended to express precisely what assertions of the existence of things come down to.

The analysis takes complex and vague statements and reduces them to truth-functional complexes of simple statements. It replaces terms that name items ("the current king of France," for example), with variables ("for all x"; "there is an x such that") that range over incomplete descriptions ("is bald"), that is, over formulas that have no reference. The above sentence translates, for Russell, into "There is at least one current king of France, there is at most one current king of France, and whatever thing is the king of France is bald." This statement picks out nothing as its logical subject, as the original statement does. It does not name a nonexistent thing. The descriptions, "the current king of France" and "bald" are incomplete symbols, not propositions, and therefore do not pick out objects. The analysis provides a structure for an abstract logical language, and it relates all claims that a thing asserted to exist has qualities designated by incomplete symbols, to what we can know by direct acquaintance: not with kings of France as such, but the notions of "king" and of "France." The logical language thus allows us to trace what our propositions assert back to the atomic sense-data or impressions that are the bedrock of all empiricism.

The Influence of the Vienna Circle

In the period between the two world wars, a group of philosophers working in Vienna developed the epistemological implications of Wittgenstein's ideas. Under the general leadership of Moritz Schlick (1882–1936), they established logical positivism. This school developed the celebrated verifiability criterion of meaningfulness: a proposition is meaningful if and only if we can verify it. The expression permits a variety of interpretations that depend upon the interpretation of the key term *verifiable*. Usually, philosophers interpreted verification empirically, that is, by scientific observation and test. In the early writings of the English philosopher A. J. Ayer (1910–1989), whom the Vienna School deeply influenced, the term was used to debunk not only claims in religion and metaphysics, but in moral philosophy also. For example, the moral claim, "It is wrong to tell lies," cannot be empirically verified—there appears to be no sensible experience that corresponds to "wrong"—and it is therefore said to be meaningless.

The verification principle ran into the same difficulties as the skeptical principle that no knowledge is possible. This principle, if it refers to itself, cannot be known to be true or false. Similarly, if the positivist criterion of meaningfulness refers to itself, it would need to be verified, and there may be no way of doing that without circularity.

Wittgenstein

In the *Tractatus Logico-Philosophicus* (1922), **Ludwig Wittgenstein,** strongly influenced by Russell, argued for a kind of metaphysical atomism, the contents of which—atomic particulars and their relations to each other—would be charted in their relationships by a powerful logical language. This procedure appears to limit what language can say to atomic facts, that is, to simple cases of what Russell calls knowledge by acquaintance. The only genuine propositions in this analysis would be the factual claims empirical science makes.

LUDWIG WITTGENSTEIN: Wittgenstein was born in Vienna in 1889 to a wealthy and cultured family and was trained as an engineer in Austria, Germany, and Great Britain. His studies for his first great work, *Tractatus Logico-philosophicus* (1921), much impressed his teacher at Cambridge, Bertrand Russell. He returned to Austria to serve in the First World War and afterwards worked as a school-teacher. Returning to Great Britain in 1929, he lectured at Cambridge for most of his life thereafter, until ill health and depression caused him to retire in 1947. He had immense influence upon the development of linguistic analysis, which dominated Anglo-American philosophy for most of the second half of the twentieth century. His major work of those years is the *Philosophical Investigations,* which was published in 1953, two years after his death from cancer.

Wittgenstein nevertheless began an exploration of ordinary language in his *Philosophical Investigations* (published posthumously in 1953). In everyday contexts, language is not used only to describe purported facts, it is used to pray and to tell a joke, to play guessing-games, and to praise and blame people. The key notion here is that we must understand language in the context in which it is used. Scientists and religious people, for example, may use the same words drawn from their common language, but the context in which they use them is different. These differences may be incommensurate, but in a sense different from the use of the term by the writers on hermeneutics. Wittgenstein suggests it is impossible to translate a phrase of language easily grasped in some context into a different kind of context. Each context—morals, science, theology, metaphysical speculation—makes up a unique language-game. In each language-game, the rules of successful communication vary. If so, then the original project of the *Tractatus,* to develop a logical language that could be used to express simple atomic facts would, if successful, give us only a part of human experience. The fullness of life expressed in the various language-games each culture plays would not be touched. What we can hope to achieve as philosophers (and not simply as logicians) is nothing more than the resolution of philosophical puzzles that arise out of the language-games that people play. There is no single privileged language-game to which all truths about the world could be translated.

Pragmatism

Having wrestled themselves free from the influence of Absolute Idealism, as Moore and Russell first did in England, American thinkers at the turn of the past century began to philosophize in a new key. Much like their English counterparts, American thinkers became convinced that philosophy could not answer the skeptical challenge on the terms in which the Enlightenment thinkers had posed it. Those earlier thinkers were looking for the wrong thing—certainty concerning matters of fact and morals—in the wrong place—in philosophical speculation—and they were finally forced to the conclusion that knowledge was impossible. Yet perhaps they had thought that certainty in philosophy was not

William James. © *Bettmann/Corbis.*

achievable only because they had viewed philosophy metaphysically, as the analysis of being and the quest for certainty, rather than simply as another practical activity. These Americans turned to action, activity, and the practical satisfaction of practical problems, where all solutions are experimental and provisional, as the new key to philosophy. These efforts collectively became known as Pragmatism. Its leading representatives were Charles Sanders Peirce, **William James,** and John Dewey. It continued its influence in America in the work of such very different thinkers as Willard van Ormand Quine (1908–2000), Richard Rorty (1931–), and Hilary Putnam (1926–).

WILLIAM JAMES: James was born in New York City in 1842. His father, Henry James Sr., was a scholar and theologian, and his brother, Henry Jr., became a major American novelist. James took an M.D. degree at Harvard but rarely practiced medicine, remaining instead a professor at Harvard for most of his life. Turning to the study of psychology, he produced *The Principles of Psychology* (1890), which was for many years considered the greatest American contribution to his field, and *The Varieties of Religious Experience*, a book that has few peers as a study of spiritual experience. James was a very popular public lecturer, and the book for which he is best known, *Pragmatism: A New Name for Old Ways of Thinking* (1907), emerged from a collection of his lectures. He died in New Hampshire in 1910.

The spirit of Pragmatism is the spirit of American life. It rejects an absolute distinction between theory and practice and insists that no theoretical inquiry is completely divorced from the interests of life, or, more broadly, from human happiness. All useful human projects are, like life itself, open-ended and uncertain. The universe is pluralistic, not monistic, and it is not possible to organize all human experience under a single set of categories, theories, or laws. Yet to the active mind, practical problems suggest fruitful directions for theoretical inquiries. All genuine inquiry, Dewey insisted, arises out of a practical dissatisfaction with one's present state of understanding and points beyond itself. However, when we argue about metaphysical issues—about, for example, the reality or unreality of universals, or the mental or material character of reality—we think, mistakenly, that we are looking for a single correct answer to a straightforward question. Yet words like *reality* and *matter* have no clear meaning unless they possess a clear relationship to human practice. "Every difference must make a difference," said James. But what practical difference would there be if universals were real or not? Or if reality itself were ultimately mental or material in character? The phrase, "Reality is material in nature," lacks importance, thought the Pragmatists, for it does not relate to any practical consequences for human activity or inquiry. One should not ask: Does God exist? for that is an unanswerable question, but rather ask: Should I believe in God? for this is a question that has immense practical implications for how I will live my life.

James illustrates this anti-metaphysical attitude of pragmatism by a story he tells in his collection of essays entitled *Pragmatism* (1907). The story concerns a hunter and a squirrel. The hunter spots the squirrel in a clearing, and the squirrel quickly dashes behind a tree to evade the hunter. The hunter continues to circle the tree in hope of spotting the squirrel, always keeping the distance between himself and the tree constant (a very poor strategy for the hunter, we might note). The squirrel hugs the tree meanwhile, and always keeps the tree between himself and the hunter. At last the hunter returns to the spot from which he began. Now consider the question: Does the hunter go around the squirrel?

This story and its question inspired a fierce metaphysical struggle between some friends of James's on a picnic. All participants in the struggle demanded a single true answer to the question, but they were not able to arrive at one; the dispute continued for hours without a resolution, until James returned from a walk. His solution to the problem requires us to look at this matter practically. The answer depends upon a practical choice of what sense of "to go around" we use in describing the situation. "To go around" may mean to go from the north to the east to the south to the west and back to the north of a thing, or it may mean to be in front, to go to the right, to go behind, then to the left, and return to the front of the thing. In the first usage, the hunter goes around the squirrel, and in the second he does not.

In the late twentieth century, some philosophers have modified pragmatism, notably Richard Rorty. In a celebrated book entitled *Philosophy and the Mirror of Nature,* Rorty denies that language represents items in nature. His study of linguistic structures reveals metaphors that enable our practical dealing with reality. Like James, he believes that philosophy does not mirror nature—we cannot draw a single correct portrait of it. Like all pragmatists, Rorty holds that foundational metaphysics is impossible; there is no God's-eye view of the world. Our efforts to understand the world and to live, politically and morally, in the human community, should be experimental, open-ended, and ready to embrace directions of thought that promise to be practically satisfying. Pragmatism aspires to be an antimetaphysical metaphysics; it holds that no comprehensive views of reality are possible. Yet as our experience of the world extends itself over new areas of thought, the beliefs that satisfy our needs in dealing with these new matters will be more inclusive as well. We may not eventually discover the ultimate truth about things, but James encourages us to retain our courage and good humor in the face of a universe that refuses to sit still so that we can take the measure of it.

METAPHYSICS AND EPISTEMOLOGY

It has frequently been remarked how intimately metaphysics and epistemology are intertwined. To verify this relation, one has only to look at the debates among contemporary theoretical physicists. Albert Einstein spent much time in the second half of his life searching for a unified field theory that would reduce the theorems of general relativity and quantum mechanics to a single set of formulae. This theory-of-everything continues to elude physicists. It is not mere historical speculation to see in these efforts a modern-day version of Plato's quest: the unification of the Realm of Forms, which everything in the universe imitates, according to its own measure, in the Form of Forms, the Idea of the Good. Today's seekers after the Unified Field Theory are pointing upward, like Raphael's Plato, to the single object of all speculation, the Idea of Ideas that will unify all other knowledge. They seek to deduce specific phenomena from general postulates encompassing relativity and quantum mechanics. Their method is frequently intuitive, like Einstein's famous **thought-experiments**.

THOUGHT EXPERIMENTS: Imagine two persons, one at the very midpoint of a fast-moving train on a straight and level track, and the other on the ground next to the track. Just as the two men pass each other, the man on the ground notes two flashes of lightning, one striking the rear of the train and the other the front end. He says that the two flashes occurred simultaneously. Would the man on the train agree? No, because he is moving toward the flash at the front end of the train and away from the flash at the rear. It will seem to him that the flash at the front occurred earlier than the flash at the rear, because the flash from the rear had to catch up with him, while he was moving toward the flash at the front. Who is right? The problem would be easy to solve if we measured the speed of light and found that the speed of light from both flashes was the same for the man on the ground, but different for the man on the train. For him, the speed of light from the front and the rear should be different proportional to the speed of his train. But experiments show that measurements of the speed of light in a vacuum are not affected by the relative motion of the measurer. Therefore, Einstein's Special Theory of Relativity asserts, there is no way of telling which of the two men is moving, and judgments of simultaneity of separated events are relative to the person making the measurements.

But there are theoretical physicists today who doubt the outcome of this quest. These thinkers, physicists, and mathematicians are engaged in chaos theory, which assumes that the edges of things are fuzzy and defy any reduction to a single set of formulas. Rather, the shapes of things in the world emerge unpredictably from events in prior stages. The original state of the world, if there was such a thing, was random. Just as the populations of similar organisms, according to Darwin's theory of evolution, take advantage of chance events in the physical environment to bring forth something wholly new, so too do forces in the physical world take advantage of complex but random events to produce a world. Our efforts to understand events must therefore be piecemeal; our procedure must be inductive (generalizing from individual substances) rather than deductive, and empirical rather than intuitive. These scientists, like Raphael's Aristotle, point downward at the individual and frequently chaotic events on the earth.

The way one seeks knowledge, therefore, reflects what one takes to be real. As yet, we are still unable to decide what is the deepest reality in the universe: simple equations governing everything? Or chaotic randomness that unfolds stable structures in an unpredictable manner? If we don't know what is ultimately real, how, then, shall we decide what questions to ask, and what sort of spectacles to put on when we try to answer them? And which language-game shall we play?

CHAPTER 6

Ethics

Sigmund Freud noted that all human communities have a taboo on incest. If so, that is a striking fact. Is the rule forbidding incest hard-wired in the human brain, as a kind of instinct, or is it an adaptation of social evolution? There is a big difference between instincts and taboos. Instincts are unvarying behavior routines that every member of a species must follow. Never does a bird decide not to fly south in the winter, if that is what its instinct requires, but many human beings have committed incest, however much they may be condemned by others, however much they may feel guilty later, and however much they may have to accept the consequences of such behavior, especially the likelihood of producing defective children. Some features of morality may be universal to humankind, but our adherence to it is never automatic.

An even more striking fact, of which Freud did not make mention, is that never has there been a human community that did not have moral rules of some kind. There may not be a single set of moral rules to which every human community has professed allegiance. Yet every community has some set of moral rules and moral values that it passes down to the next generation through lesson and example. Did this morality arise from our social if not our biological evolution? We do not know. But we experience our lives in moral terms; we all praise and condemn the behavior of ourselves and others. The philosophical exploration of moral experience will be the subject of this chapter. It will study and discuss the following topics:

- Moral Experience
- The Subject Matter of Ethics
- Normative Ethics
- Contemporary Issues in Ethics

MORAL EXPERIENCE

We are oriented to moral values by our emotions especially, and most generally, by the emotions of love and hate. Love is a joyous response to the actual and possible positive values we sense upon a thing; hate is a painful response to actual and possible negative values we sense upon a thing. We feel concern for the well-being of our friends and desire their well-being (sympathy), and we turn away from our enemies and wish them ill (antipathy). We respond to those emotions and the values given with them by praising and blaming, condemning and admiring the people and things we think possess those values. Such experience is inescapable for human beings. It gives rise to moral judgments: "This government is unjust"; "John is a liar"; "Tom is a good cook"; "Mary is a saint." Ethics considers how such judgments arise out of shared values, and it considers how they may be justified.

The terms *ethics* and *morals* are sometimes used interchangeably in everyday talk. Morals or morality is the collection of value-judgments, usually stated as rules, that a community makes concerning the behavior of its members, and which that community views as binding upon its members. So, for example, in most American communities, we are taught such general moral judgments as these: "Turnabout is fair play"; "Do unto others as you would have others do unto you"; "Do not tell lies." We are not taught these rules as a matter of fact. We are taught them as standards for our behavior, and we are taught that the community will reward or punish us in a variety of ways for our adherence to or failure to behave in ways specified by these judgments, or as children we are simply subjected to them. Children are cheerfully encouraged to embrace them, and they usually come to understand why these rules are, on the whole, reasonable ones.

Ethics is the philosophical reflection upon morals and human moral experience. It brings the techniques of philosophical analysis to bear upon moral experience and the rules such experience leads to in human communities. Normative ethics tries to provide a theoretical basis for the justification of moral judgments, or to demonstrate the rationality or reasonableness of them. Theories of right and wrong action may emphasize the concept of virtue and identify such moral predicates as courage, honesty, greed, or trustworthiness as central to the moral value of persons. They may also locate moral values in the motives of the person acting (the desire to do good or evil), or in moral rules for action (either of these are called deontological ethics), or in the consequences of actions (these are called teleological ethics). Normative ethics sometimes concerns itself with deciding individual ethical conflicts—whether, for example, some person did wrong in telling a lie to save his friend's feelings. This effort is called **casuistry**, and it usually takes place within some set of moral assumptions shared by the debaters.

CASUISTRY: In the early modern period, the Jesuits, an order of priests in the Catholic Church, were accused by their critics of creating specious or false moral arguments to justify morally questionable actions of the church or of one of its powerful patrons. There is a wonderful scene in Verdi's great opera, *Don Carlo,* where the Grand Inquisitor tells King Philip that he should have the Crown Prince, Carlo, killed as a traitor and heretic. "May I, as a Christian," asks the King, "have my own son killed? Will you absolve me?" And the Grand Inquisitor responds, "God sacrificed His son, Jesus, you will do the same as He." Philip prepares to commit infanticide by signing a death warrant for Carlo.

Casuistry relies frequently on analogies between a morally questionable situation (Philip's sacrificing his son, Carlo) and some other morally clear situation (God's sacrifice of his son, Jesus). Does the Grand Inquisitor's argument provide an adequate warrant for Philip's act?

THE SUBJECT MATTER OF ETHICS

Choice

Human beings are not self-sustaining like such imaginary beings as angels. Angels need nothing, and they want nothing they do not have. People, like all animals, must act if they are to live, and how they must act is not always clear: people must make choices. In themselves, choices may have no moral implications. Whether a person chooses to write words with a pen or a word-processor is morally indifferent, and the choice will be made on the basis of what is available to her, what is more convenient, and other like considerations. Animals also make choices. The cat is sleeping on the cable box because it is warmer there. When the house warms up a bit, she may move to the sofa, because it is softer and more comfortable. None of her choices have any moral implications either. But now we come upon an interesting consideration. Although a person's choice of a word-processor over a pen to write with has no more moral significance than the cat's choice of the cable box as a bed, some things a person may choose to do have moral significance. A writer may choose to plagiarize someone else's work, for example. What about the cat's actions? Is it possible for them to have moral significance? Here there is much controversy, but the opinion of many observers is that the behavior of animals cannot be sensibly praised or blamed morally. No doubt people can admire animals for their beauty, or strength, or simple animal well-being, but those are nonmoral values. Even a nonliving thing, like an automobile, can be admired for its beauty or its power or its fuel efficiency. Why should this be so? Why does it appear to make no sense to say that it was right or proper, or wrong and wicked for a cat or an automobile to have acted the way it did?

Freedom

We assume, for most human beings at most times of their lives that they are free to act in one way or another. *Freedom* in this context does not mean simply physical freedom. A person may be physically free just now to leave the room to take a walk, but she would not be if she were tied to her chair, or had her legs in a cast. Rather we are thinking of freedom of choice, where a person can choose to act in one way or another, where she can give reasons for her choice, and where those reasons alone determine the choice. Whether this freedom is ever possible for a human being is a large issue and will be discussed in the final chapter. But we must note at least this: If human actions are always determined by psychological, genetic, or indeed by any kinds of events over which the individual has no control, then we could not attribute **moral responsibility** to individuals. One could not blame a bank robber for robbing banks any more than one could blame a volcano for erupting when it did. If we normally refuse to attribute moral responsibility to animals (and to such unfortunate human beings as the retarded, infants, or those who are insane), it is because we think that they are determined by causal laws to behave the way they do, just as the volcano is. We tend to think normal adult human beings are free to act in the way they do because they make choices by exercising their reason, or their free will. They can consider various courses of action that are available to them in a given situation, figure out such things as what will probably happen if they act in one way rather than another, how they and other people will be affected by that action, and how the people affected will respond to the action. These considerations and others like them serve as reasons for acting one way rather than another. If a person chooses to act based upon those reasons, then he is morally responsible for his action; he could have done otherwise. Animals cannot reason about their choices in this way, and therefore we think them not morally responsible for their action.

MORAL RESPONSIBILITY: Note that moral responsibility is different from responsibility in general. We may say, for example, that the eruption of the volcano was responsible for the destruction of the city. However, we do not mean to blame the volcano for the destruction. Praise and blame specifically refer to moral responsibility, and our analysis attempts to make persuasive the idea that only human beings, if even they, are proper objects of praise and blame. If, of course, the determinist is correct in her belief that all human actions are determined by factors beyond the individual's control, then human beings would appear not to be the proper objects of praise and blame either—though one doctrine, soft determinism, denies that.

The subject matter of ethics, then, is free human actions. But not all such actions are of interest to ethics. When a person decides to scratch her head or take a nap, she acts freely, no doubt, but there is no moral relevance in these acts, at least at first sight, for they are not done for any specific purpose. Of course we scratch our head because we have an itch, or take a nap because we are sleepy, but there is no deliberation about the choice; we normally do not have to give reasons for it. Only some of those free acts done for a purpose, where some deliberation concerning means and ends is required, have moral relevance. People may at times act randomly, carelessly, without thinking. The child who breaks a valuable vase while playing roughhouse thinks he can defend himself by saying, "It was an accident! I didn't mean to!" But that may not be much of an excuse if there is reason to think that the child should have known not to be so careless, should have been deliberating about what he was about to do, and should have been aware of the possible consequences of his roughhouse play. Probably on some level of his mind he was aware of those possibilities. True, he didn't mean to break the vase, that was not part of his intentions; but he did mean to play roughly when he must have known that such play can damage valuable items. So his mother blames him for the destruction of the vase over his protests of moral innocence.

But again, not all actions that a human being freely performs after due deliberation and for some purpose have moral relevance. Suppose a person is bored and looks about for something to do. He considers calling a friend, reading a book he just purchased, taking a walk, or cleaning his apartment. After some thought, he decides for the book. Let us assume that no one but himself is affected by his action. Then surely there is no reason to praise or blame his action; it is morally indifferent. But if we change the context a bit, moral relevance may enter. Suppose, when choosing the book, he had carelessly forgotten about a promise to prepare a presentation for a meeting the next day. Then his action takes on moral significance. What gives such deliberate and free human actions their moral relevance? That is a question that ethics tries to answer: What are the norms upon which our judgments of rightness and wrongness are based? Why ought these norms matter to us? Can we give a coherent account of these norms that is consistent with our moral experience?

Moral Relativism

But wait, a skeptic might object. Are not moral norms relative to each individual society and culture? Moral relativism asserts that they are. It claims that it is impossible to establish universal rational moral rules, for the values upon which moral predicates, such as *is good* or *is unjust,* do not exist. Moral rules and values are the products of the customs and habits of a community. They are not based upon reason or perception, but upon sentiment or feeling. Moreover, the customs and habits that give rise to values and moral judgments are chaotic and nonrational and vary from time to time and place to place. There is no such thing as moral knowledge, in this view. Moral judgments have sway only within a given community and are therefore relative to that community. Consequently, there can be no rational basis for the criticism of one community's moral standards by another's. The principle of "diff'rent strokes for diff'rent folks" is invoked. In the early books of the Bible we read of miscreants being stoned to death on order of the town elders, and the stoning is said to be approved or even demanded by God. In our culture, we would condemn the act of executing a person by stoning him to death as cruel. Neither party to this dispute is right, the moral relativist claims; how could it be right or wrong to feel a certain way about an action? Yet perhaps both parties are right in the sense that it is understandable that a person will judge himself and others on the basis of the moral feelings that are typical of his community.

Moral relativism claims that what is called right and wrong, or values in general, are metaphysically unreal or subjective in the way imaginary objects are. If the moral relativist claims that we have no knowledge of the values upon which moral judgments are based, he is taking an epistemological position similar to that of logical positivism. A contemporary statement of the metaphysical and epistemological foundation of moral relativism is the following, by the philosopher J.L. Mackie in his book, *Ethics: Inventing Right and Wrong.*

> When we look in detail at the demands which moral discourse places on the distinctive qualities with which it putatively deals, we find that these demands are unsatisfiable. . . . Semantically, it [moral discourse] is representational thought, true or not true according to whether certain real properties apply or fail to apply in the world. But the truth is that there are no such properties; reality is simply empty of all states of affairs whose representation would require thought of distinctively moral content.

We think we are representing items in the world when we say, for example, "Hitler was an evil man"—that is, we think we are describing Hitler as we do when we say, "Hitler had a little moustache." But, as Mackie argues, there is no property such as "evil" in reality, as there is the property "having a moustache." No doubt, Mackie is assuming he knows about the nature of reality, about what exists and what does not exist, and about what we can and cannot know or assert. Perhaps Mackie's assumptions can be challenged; perhaps the world does contain "moral facts" that we can grasp in some way, just as we grasp "having a moustache" through our senses. If Mackie's position or any other form of moral relativism is accepted, then ethics is impossible. We cannot theorize effectively about norms and values if it turns out that they do not exist; we can only do **descriptive ethics**, or what is called in high schools *values clarification*. We can discuss what moral beliefs we or others appear to have, but we cannot justify or give adequate warrant for those beliefs.

DESCRIPTIVE ETHICS: As its name implies, descriptive ethics attempts to describe the moral beliefs of historical communities, including our own. A descriptive ethicist might undertake, for example, to write a history of western morality, or to describe the moral vision of Hinduism, or of classical Greece. These studies are not the same as sociology or anthropology, which try to explain the moral beliefs of a community on the basis of an understanding of the broader social conditions in which they lived. No doubt a hunting and fishing community will have a need for a different kind of moral rules than those, say, of early Middle Eastern kingdoms, where the conditions of life were different. Descriptive ethics is not explanatory; like the efforts of hermeneutics, which was discussed in Chapter 5 it tries to create sympathetic understanding of the moral values of communities quite different from our own.

Ethics requires us to assume that purposeful human actions are in many cases freely done, that the persons who do them are responsible, in some measure, for their actions, and that there are universal rational standards available for judging degree and kind of moral responsibility the agent has for his action. Some of the theories that try to organize, explain, and justify those universal rational standards of responsible moral action will now be discussed.

NORMATIVE ETHICS

Moral theories cannot be reduced to a single kind. The western tradition in ethics is very complex, for it has been formed by two very distinct cultures, that of the ancient Greeks and that of the ancient Hebrews. What we today call Judeo-Christian morality is, in a very general way, based upon rules and is traceable to the **Ten Commandments**. Again, very generally, the Classical tradition established in Greece what is called a virtue-based tradition. It aims to evaluate behavior on the basis of values that embody standards of excellence of character thought appropriate to human beings in their social lives. The oldest theories of this kind are those of Plato and Aristotle. A study of normative ethics should begin with them.

THE TEN COMMANDMENTS: These are just ten of over five hundred laws that God gave to Moses on Mount Sinai. Some of them give us models of moral rules. They are: (1) I am the Lord your God; you shall have no other gods before me. (2) You shall not make idols to worship. (3) Keep holy the Sabbath. (4) Do not take the name of the Lord in vain. (5) Honor your mother and father. (6) You shall not steal. (7) You shall not commit murder. (8) You shall not commit adultery. (9) You shall not lie (bear false witness). (10) You shall not covet your neighbor's possessions.

We would not call all of these commandments moral rules today. It does not seem to be a question of right and wrong, for example, to keep a Sabbath day holy, or not to curse in the name of God. These commandments, and hundreds of others, are found in the first five books of the Jewish Bible, which together are called the *Torah*.

Theories of Virtue

Plato

In the discussion of metaphysics it was seen that Plato assumed the existence of Forms, ideal structures that constitute the essence of specific things. A line, for example, is a circle just insofar as it participates in, or imitates, the Form of Circularity. In this way, Plato gives to every individual thing an ideal end, the achievement of a perfect standard by which it can be compared and criticized, and a nature that enables us to understand that thing as the kind of thing it is. When we encounter persons, or laws, or forms of government that we call just or wise, we do so with implicit reference to the Forms of justice or wisdom. For to be truly just or wise is to imitate in an exemplary way the structure of these Forms.

Of course, persons or governments or laws can imitate better or worse the forms of justice or wisdom. And the features of life that can hold back a person or a form of government from participating more fully in the Forms of justice or wisdom are considerable. The human soul, Plato argues in *The Republic*, like most civil societies, is neither simple nor unified. A kind of internal war goes on between the different desires of our souls, and similarly between the different purposes of the classes and political groups within the state. Such warfare makes the achievement of virtue, in persons and in states, as difficult as it is rare. The human soul desires understanding, it desires to be accepted by our fellows, and it desires the satisfaction of our physical needs for food and sex and shelter. If we are not sufficiently wise, we will try to satisfy all these desires at once, or one desire in ways that conflict with the satisfaction of others, and we will fail. Two simple examples will clarify what Plato has in mind. On one level, a person may desire to be healthy, but on another level, she desires cigarettes. On one level, she desires to be admired by her companions, but on another level, she desires to do shameful things. How can she get all her desires in step with each other, so that all three of these kinds of desire—for health, for honor, and for satisfaction—can be satisfied in the fullest way possible? This is the way Plato states the question of what the good life is all about. And his answer is simple, but very hard to carry out. The good life is a life of happiness, in which all my desires are under the control of the highest part of my soul, the reason, which instructs each part of the soul, including itself, in the best way of satisfying its desires in complete harmony with each other. Such a human being would be virtuous, or excellent, a superior human being, thought Plato. She would be truly free, because she would be in charge of herself. She would be wise and courageous and just and temperate and pious, beyond all temptation to do what is shameful or cowardly or foolish or dishonest, for, as a wise person, she draws the norms for her behavior from an understanding of the Forms of virtue themselves.

A virtue-based ethics does not ignore the relevance of action to moral theory. However, the Greeks did not think that virtue or excellence (the Greek word is *aretē*) consisted in the conformity of one's actions to a divine moral law, as the ancient Jews did. The Greeks saw virtue as embodied in a person and in a state or governments possessing the formal qualities of justice, courage, piety, wisdom, and temperance. For Plato, virtue is not simply a possession but an active capacity for conducting one's affairs well, both as a citizen and as an individual. Justice is that kind of order of the soul that allows each of these functions to achieve its optimum success in attaining the objects it craves: respectively, knowledge, honor, and the satisfaction of the appetites. Justice is inseparable from the other virtues, but especially from that of wisdom, which enables the individual to plot his course in life and to achieve a maximum of happiness that the changing events of life cannot destroy. Just as wickedness and wretchedness are byproducts of ignorance, as Socrates maintained, so too is the tendency to virtuous action the natural byproduct of a life of wisdom that enables harmony within oneself and with one's fellows in society. The achievement of such harmony, and the happiness it makes possible, make the requirement to adhere to universal moral rules, given by society or by the gods, independent of the achievement of virtue, unnecessary. The virtuous man does what is right through knowledge of the Good.

Aristotle

What Aristotle calls the good or virtuous life is also the rational life. The kind of life we all want to live he calls *eudaimonia,* a Greek term that is usually translated as *happiness,* but it means something more specific. It can be called the state of well-being, or the sense of being healthy, strong, able to affirm the value of one's activities, and confident in one's powers to carry them out. Perhaps the term coined by the twentieth-century psychologist Abraham Maslow may be used to describe what Aristotle has in mind: the "fully functioning person." The following passage by the English philosopher Herbert Spencer (1820–1903) expresses nicely the kind of person most of us would want to be, and contrasts that person with another whose vital well-being is considerably lower.

> Bounding out of bed after an unbroken sleep, singing or whistling as he dresses, coming down with beaming face ready to laugh on the smallest provocation, the healthy man of high powers, conscious of past successes and by his energy, quickness, resource, made confident of the future, enters on the day's business not with repugnance, but with gladness; and from hour to hour experiencing satisfactions from work effectually done, comes home with an abundant surplus of energy remaining for hours of relaxation. Far otherwise is it with one who is enfeebled by great neglect of self. Already deficient, his energies are made more deficient by constant endeavors to execute tasks that prove beyond his strength, and by the resulting discouragement. Besides the depressing consciousness of the immediate future, there is the depressing consciousness of the remoter future, with its probability of accumulated difficulties and diminished ability to meet them. Hours of leisure which, rightly passed, bring pleasures that raise the tide of life and renew the powers of work, cannot be utilized: there is not vigor enough for enjoyments involving action, and lack of spirits prevents passive enjoyments from being entered upon with zest. In brief, life becomes a burden.

Excellence, or *aretē*, however, is an achievement that appears only in the active political and intellectual life. Virtue is the means by which the natural potency of a person is actualized, as would be expected from the discussion of Aristotle's metaphysics. Anyone, for example, may be capable of being a physician, but he actualizes that potency through the study of medicine. Human-as-we-are is contrasted with human-as-we-could-be if we achieved the full potential native to the human being, our *telos*. Life is initially a challenge that engages all of our latent potentials, but as we struggle through life and habitually practice the various virtues, we choose to develop one or more of those potentials, and in that way we become something specific and play wisely, honestly, courageously, and temperately a specific role in our community.

Eudaimonia, or vital well-being, is a byproduct of this movement from potency to act, from potential achievement to actual achievement. The good life is a life of rational activity according to virtue in a context that gives scope to one's talents. A person's virtue is recognized by one's fellows in the *polis* as an achievement in self-mastery, and in the capacity for making useful contributions to the important common causes of life. The concept of virtue is given content by the nature and purpose of those activities. Specific virtues, such as justice or courage, cannot be defined apart from them, and they take different forms in the changing activities of life, as people face new challenges. For example, courage is a virtue that may appear on the battlefield and in a courtroom. Aristotle reminds us early in the *Nicomachean Ethics* that the subject matter of ethics is not capable of the kind of rigor, clarity, and universality that are available in other disciplines. Ethics cannot prescribe precisely what one should do or how one should live, as the Bible does. Rather, in his practical activities, the person of virtue will seek a **golden mean** between the extremes to which passion may drive him. We recognize the courageous person as giving in neither to foolhardiness nor to cowardice despite a strong desire to do so, and as seeking the mean, courage, to which reason directs him. He reflects upon the good of his own soul and the good of the *polis* and knows, from practical experience, when to restrain himself and when to impel himself toward his objectives. We may think that Spencer's happy, energetic man could be an axe murderer or some less spectacular kind of criminal. But Aristotle would reject that possibility out of hand. Crime arises out weakness; a man with the wisdom and strength of character he equates with virtue would not be tempted to criminal action. Sin, crime, and vice—*akrates*—are simply beneath the virtuous person, who knows that they are incompatible with the realization of his *telos* and the enjoyment of *eudaimonia.*

THE GOLDEN MEAN: Aristotle thought that one of the functions of reason was to discover appropriate behavior in situations in which our passions are strongly engaged. All of us feel passionate about money; we never have enough, and we spend much of what we have on pleasures. We are driven to opposite extremes by this passion for money; not just that we will do anything to get it, but when we have it, we are liable to hold on to it greedily (the miser) or to spend it unwisely (the drunken sailor). The extremes to which we are driven are miserliness and waste; the golden mean, says Aristotle, is generosity: knowing how to spend one's money wisely and for good causes.

For Aristotle, man-as-he-is is found always in a state, or *polis*. Virtue is possible only in a political context, where people struggle together to produce things of value. Aristotle famously remarked that a man who could live outside of society would have to be either a beast or a god. There would have been little admiration for hermits or monks, as there was little admiration for social dropouts—men who called themselves **cynics**—in ancient Greece. Such men, when they appeared, were often the objects of amusement and derision when they were not admired for their indifference to luxury.

THE CYNICS: During the period following the decline of Athens, there appeared a school of philosophers who called themselves Cynics, a word that is probably derived from the Greek for "dog." These men professed contempt for the values of most Greeks, many of which we today share—a love of luxury, respect for men of wealth and power, and a willingness to honor one's native land or *polis*. Diogenes, the most famous of them, is said to have chosen to sleep in a tub and lived a life of great poverty, simplicity, and independence. Cynics believed that the good life was the natural or simple life, and they often treated with insolence and disgust social institutions that they believed to be artificial, contrived, and unworthy of a free and wise man. Among artificial and contrived social practices was philosophy itself, and the school consequently never developed a broad theory of social justice or of the good life to justify their social attitudes as Plato and Aristotle attempted to do.

Life within the *polis* is conceived by Aristotle as a kind of *agon,* or competition, in which the rules of play are clearly set forth, and where victory is assured, apart from tricks of fate, to the superior player. The ultimate object of virtuous action in a competition is not, however, mere victory, but rather the personal satisfaction and the admiration of one's fellows obtainable from playing well. The capacity to achieve the values implicit in the nature of the competition constitutes the difference between good and bad players. The degree of virtue of the players is hence completely determinate, though of course relative in their existence to the political and social nature of the game being played in that *polis*.

Unlike Plato, then, Aristotle's theory of virtue makes the forms that courage, justice, temperance, wisdom, and piety take in some community relative to the game being played, and the game in turn is relative to the constitution of the *polis*. It is one thing, after all, to be an excellent statesman, another to be an excellent physician, and still another to be an excellent baseball player. No doubt Aristotle considered the important features of human excellence to be more or less the same in all cultures. The necessary inherent condition of playing well he considered to be the possession of reason and character, which is universally though not equally distributed among members of the human species. Aristotle's theory of virtue, therefore, does not involve Plato's universal Forms of the virtues, but, like Plato's theory, it offers us a picture of moral virtue founded in the victory of reason over appetite or impulse in the achievement of qualities of soul that manifest themselves in a disposition to do right and in the capacity for effective action, the byproduct of which is optimal happiness or vital well-being. Plato and Aristotle offer magnificent visions of a society of happy and free rational people of action. They appeal to our sense of what we are, what we can become, and what we want to be.

Virtue and Education: Socrates

All virtue-based moral theory requires an education for children that will inspire them to strive for excellence of character and capacity for achievement, and for the wisdom to grasp what is significant in the life of their community and what not. An example of moral education is given in Plato's dialogue *Euthydemus*. Socrates is observing two professional teachers instructing a schoolboy named Clinias in knowledge and virtue. It is not possible to learn knowledge, they tell him, for if one possesses no knowledge or is in a state of ignorance, one cannot learn, because to learn is to possess knowledge. But then, if one possesses knowledge of a thing, then one has nothing to learn about it. This kind of reasoning seems to derive from the metaphysical problem of how something can come out of nothing. If something is what it is, then it cannot become something else. How can ignorance become wisdom, if ignorance has no wisdom in it? The poor boy is left intellectually perplexed, despite all his efforts to think about such serious matters. The lesson has resulted in nothing but absurdities. He is, perhaps, in a state like most people when they begin their studies in philosophy. His efforts to learn about wisdom and knowledge have not affected him personally, as they must, if he is to become wise and good. But then Socrates begins to speak with the boy, and he quickly achieves what the Sophists promised but failed to do.

Socrates begins by asking Clinias questions with obvious answers: Does not each of us desire to do well in life? Of course. And to do well, one must have plenty of good things. But what are those good things? Wealth and health, of course, and Clinias agrees; but we also want such moral qualities as courage and honesty and self-control, and perhaps also, he says, a measure of good fortune. Socrates encourages Clinias to modify that last notion. He asks whether wisdom is not an important possession for doing well in life, more important than good luck. "If you were ill, with whom would you prefer to run risks—a wise physician or an ignorant one?" A wise one, of course. Now think of the many other good things we thought we needed to do well—wealth and health and the like. Is just possessing them enough to give us benefit? Don't they have to be used, as the physician has to use his knowledge of medicine if it is to do anyone any good? Otherwise there is no benefit in having these things. Now wealth in the hands of a man who does not know how to use his wealth wisely might be harmful. But what do we call that which produces the right use of one's possessions? Knowledge and wisdom, of course, as we noted in connection with the wise physician, whom we trust more than the ignorant or foolish one. We get no benefit from his knowledge unless he knows also how to use it wisely, and that is all the good fortune he needs. Plato himself can finish the conversation. The translation is by W.H.D. Rouse.

Socrates:	Does any benefit come from the other possessions without intelligence and wisdom? Could a man get benefit, possessing plenty and doing much if he had no sense—would he not benefit more by doing little with sense? If he did less he would make fewer mistakes, if he made fewer mistakes he would do less badly, if he did less badly he would be less miserable? . . . Then to sum up, my dear Clinias . . . the truth is that in all those things which we said at first were good, the question is not how they are in themselves naturally good, but this is the point, it seems. If ignorance leads them, they are greater evils than their opposites, inasmuch as they are more able to serve the leader, which is evil, but if intelligence leads, and wisdom, they are greater goods, while in themselves neither kind is worth anything at all.
Clinias:	It seems to be so, as you say. . . .
Socrates:	Then let us consider what remains. Since we all desire to be happy, and we have been shown to be happy by using things and using them [rightly], and rightness and good fortune were provided by knowledge, what seems to be necessary, you see, is that every man in every way shall try to become as wise as possible. . . . For wisdom's sake, Clinias, there is no disgrace, no reproach . . . for a man willing to give honorable service in the passion to become wise. Don't you think so?
Clinias:	I think you are quite right.
Socrates:	Yes, Clinias, if only wisdom can be taught, if only it is not something that comes to men of itself—for that is a point we have not considered. . . .
Clinias:	Well, Socrates, I think that wisdom can be taught.
Socrates:	Well said, admirable boy! . . . Now, then, since you think it can, and that wisdom alone in the wide world makes a man happy and fortunate, don't you say it is necessary to love wisdom, and don't you mean to do it yourself?
Clinias:	That I do, Socrates, as hard as ever I can!

"Oh, yes, Socrates, as hard as ever I can!" Most people feel the same glow in the heart left by the boy's desire to be wise, so that he can be righteous, just, courageous, and in all things good. This Greek notion of virtue is the capacity to do good—the sense we may have of our own capacity or strength of character to do what we know to be right. There is a remarkable parallel to this thought in Confucius, who, in describing the course of the moral struggle of his own life, says he found that at age seventy he could follow his heart's desire without fear of transgression against what is right. Let us hope that it does not take Clinias so long to become sufficiently wise so that virtue in him is as spontaneous as in the old Confucius! How few are the teachers, like Socrates and Confucius, who can inspire in their students this moral aspiration for excellence in all things, but especially in wisdom and goodness.

Rule-Based Ethics

The Judeo-Christian moral law was secularized as it became part of the tradition of modern Western moral thinking. Several kinds of rule-based moral theories have been developed by philosophers, and some technical terms will have to be introduced to make them clear.

When a person tries to judge the rightness or wrongness of some action of some human being, either one that has been performed or one that is being proposed ("Should I have told my girlfriend that her boyfriend is cheating on her?" "Is it OK to take an umbrella from the pile of them at the restaurant if it is raining and I've forgotten my own?"). There are three ways of judging the action: its motives, its kind, and its consequences.

Motivationalism

The term *motives* refers to the conscious reasons that a person performed the action. *Kind* refers to the maxim of the action, that is, to some moral rule, moral right, or **obligation**. By *consequences*, we refer to the benefit and harm given to the persons who were affected by the action. Any moral theory that holds the value of one's motives, or the rules one obeys, or both to be the source of right and wrong is called deontological. Any moral theory that holds consequences alone determine right and wrong is called teleological.

OBLIGATIONS: Traditionally, obligations are divided into perfect and imperfect. A perfect obligation is one we have at all times, such as the obligation to tell the truth, or to help someone in distress. An imperfect obligation leaves open how it to satisfy it. We have the general imperfect obligation to be charitable, but we are not obligated to give charity to this person at this time. Obligations are frequently linked to rights: if John has an obligation to Mary, then she has the right to demand you fulfill it. Obligations may be self-inflicted, as it were. If John freely promises Mary something, he puts himself in a state of obligation to her.

The first standpoint from which an action can be morally evaluated is that of its motives. Why was the action performed, or why would a person be inclined to perform it? Some answers come quickly to mind: The person is inclined to do this action because there is profit for her in it; she is afraid that she will be harmed if she does or doesn't do it; people expect it of her; she thinks it is the right thing to do. There are words for praising and blaming motivations to act and the persons who act on those motives. Some people may be called cowardly, others brave; still others are praised as compassionate, or condemned as selfish.

But how are rules involved in such judgments? Recall that not all actions done for a purpose have moral relevance. If it begins to rain, and we put up our umbrellas because we don't want to get wet, we act for the purpose of not being harmed, but our action would not for that reason be called cowardly, nor would we be condemned for weakness of character. No moral rule was involved. But if we see a child drowning in a pond, and we don't jump in to save it just because we are afraid of drowning, or are simply afraid of getting wet, then we would likely be called cowards, or worse. Motives are morally important when some moral rule is at stake in what a person is motivated to do or to refrain from doing.

Why not just consider the rule, then, and not the motivation? Many ethicists focus on motives because they seem morally important in certain respects. In the case in which the child is drowning in the pond, the passerby may think: "The poor child, I must help him." She feels an obligation to help people in distress, and she jumps in the water and saves the child's life. Doesn't her motivation count toward her being a heroine? If people found out that she saved the child not because she felt sorry for it, or because she felt an obligation to help out, but only because she hoped to get a reward, would they then be as willing to praise her?

A typical form of motivationalism is that of Jesus, who presents a kind of moral theory in his **Sermon on the Mount** (Matthew 4, 5). Jesus says, rather famously, that he comes not to destroy the Law, but to fulfill [it]. He adds to the Jewish law one new one, the commandment to love one another, and love is a motive: our behavior toward our neighbors and all other people must be motivated by a charitable concern for their well-being in this world and the next. Jesus makes this point clear via the formula, "You have been taught [the law] . . . but I tell you this [the spirit of charity with which you are to carry it out] . . . " which he repeats many times. One of the most famous can be used as an example: "You have been taught, 'You shall not commit adultery.' But I tell you this: a person who looks after a woman with lust in his heart has already committed adultery with her."

THE SERMON ON THE MOUNT: This Sermon is a description of the Christian life given by Jesus to his disciples. It begins with the eight Beatitudes, which declare the blessedness of the meek, the poor, and the humble, and tell of their rewards: they will inherit the earth, or be called the children of God. The body of the Sermon describes the Christian motivation: charity (*agape*) toward all, perhaps especially toward one's enemies. God, Jesus says, is not concerned as much with behavior that adheres to the letter of the law, but of the spirit that inhabits the souls of his followers.

Jesus is obviously concerned with motivation here. It is not enough just to refrain from adultery, one must not even contemplate doing such things. There is a deep truth in this. A married man who spends his days dreaming lustfully about other women may not be hurting anyone, but he is showing a crudeness of soul and a disposition to treat other human beings as mere objects of his lust that Jesus, and many others, find discreditable. No doubt it seems odd to condemn this man on the basis of his motivations alone, as Jesus seems to do. Even worse, Christ does not make a clear distinction between the immorality of a man who dreams about committing adultery, and one who actually does commit it, or even one who plans an adulterous liaison but fails to carry it out. At another point in the Sermon, Jesus says that not only the man who murders his brother, but also one who calls his brother a fool, will pay for it in the fires of hell. No doubt the discreditable motive in both cases is similar: hatred of my brother, or love of his possessions. The problem, however, is not merely that Jesus is overly harsh in his condemnation of humans, but that he does not help us distinguish clearly between what appears to be an important moral distinction, that between murdering a man and insulting him.

Legalism

Some moral theorists see in moral rules alone the essential difference between right and wrong actions. Such deontological theories are called legalistic. The Ten Commandments give an example of a legalistic morality. We are not told to act on these commandments because of our feelings toward them, nor are we told that if we act according to them we will experience good consequences, except, perhaps, a reward from God for our obedience. Characteristic both of legalism and of the God who speaks in the early books of the Jewish Bible, we are not told why we should adhere to these commandments, or why it is morally good to do so; we are just told to obey and be holy. This should hardly be surprising, for our own statutory law does not contain long descriptions of why we should obey it, or justifications of its rightness; even the Constitution does not do that. And no doubt frustrated parents have responded to their frustrated teenagers who ask why they can't smoke marijuana by shouting, "Because it's against the law!"

Not all legalism is based upon a belief that God has given us commandments that we are to obey. But if not, how do we know what the moral rules are, and why should we obey them? Some legalistic moral philosophers have argued for a form of intuitionism, that is, the idea that human beings possess a moral sense that enables them to grasp the truth of moral rules by the mind alone. Thus they would argue that, "Keep your promises," or "Do unto others as you would have others do unto you," are moral axioms that we know to be true in the same way that we know "The shortest distance between two points is a straight line" to be true. Still others have argued that rational moral rules are established by deducing them from a general principle of obligation that is innate. This notion was developed in a very refined form by Immanuel Kant.

Natural Law

Other legalists have argued that we can deduce, as it were, moral rules from the nature of things. Such theories are called naturalistic. A form of naturalistic ethics that developed in Europe in the early modern period is called natural law theory. It had many adherents, and it remains an important school in the philosophy of law. The English philosopher, John Locke, developed an influential version of natural law theory, so influential, in fact, that it became a fundamental part of the American Declaration of Independence.

That document contains the line: "We hold these truths to be self-evident, that all men are endowed by their creator with certain inalienable rights, among which are life, liberty, and the pursuit of happiness." To say that such rights are self-evident means that a rational person who looked at life and the ways of men and women would affirm that each human being has a right to be free. However, many ancient peoples, the Greeks and the Chinese, to take two examples, surely had rational minds among them who did not think freedom a self-evident natural right of all persons. The early Americans themselves, who claimed that it was, failed to apply what they called a self-evident right to slaves and women—a fact that may make us wonder how self-evident, natural, and binding they really thought them to be. But the claim that such moral rules and political rights are guaranteed by nature and are self-evident to any rational person collapses under the objection that human beings are unable to agree on the scope and the content of natural law. Is homosexuality unnatural, for example? Nature seems to have created persons of two sexes for the purpose of reproduction and designed the sexual organs accordingly. Many people around the world have thought the natural order of things to condemn homosexuality, but most of us today find the idea repugnant. It is surely not self-evident that nature commands us to express our sexuality in a certain way, and that to do otherwise upsets the natural order and deserves condemnation. The fact that people do not easily agree about such matters shows that we are not dealing with self-evident truths.

Teleological Theories

A powerful form of naturalism called utilitarianism arose in the late eighteenth and early nineteenth centuries. This theory eventually obtained the allegiance of the majority of writers on ethics in the English-speaking world until, perhaps, a few decades ago. Utilitarianism is a teleological theory of right and wrong action, that is, it measures the morality of actions or of rules to action by their consequences. The natural characteristic that all right actions, or all positive moral rules, have in common is the goodness of their consequences. Utilitarians vary somewhat in their identification of good consequences, but as the name of the school indicates, good consequences are utile ones, that is, of use to the person or persons affected by an action, and bad ones are useless or harmful. Two early utilitarians, **Jeremy Bentham** and John Stuart Mill, argued that thinking about right and wrong in this way has tremendous advantages. It makes morals concrete, in the sense that one can test any claim that an action is right or wrong by inquiring what its consequences are. What makes the moral rule "Do not tell lies" a good one, for example, is that lie-telling in general is harmful—it produces disutility in most cases—and for that reason, and no other, lying is wrong.

JEREMY BENTHAM: Bentham was born in England in 1748. Intending to follow in his father's profession of law, he studied at Oxford and at Lincoln's Inn and was called to the bar, but he never took up the practice. Concerned by what he took as the failings of British jurisprudence, he set about the development of a revised system of law, one philosophically grounded upon the moral theory now called Utilitarianism. His work, however well-intentioned and humane, remained rather fragmentary, for he seemed temperamentally ill-suited to the demands of his grand ambition. Many of his works were left unfinished or were edited by others. His greatest theoretical work was the *Introduction to the Principles of Morals and Legislation* (1789). Yet his unusual personality attracted many followers, and the Benthamites, as they were called, exerted considerable influence upon the theory and the reform of British legal practices for many decades. Bentham died in 1832. His embalmed body and a wax model of his head are kept in University College, London, which his disciples helped to found.

Bentham: Utilitarianism

The simplest form of utilitarianism, and one of the oldest, is that developed by Jeremy Bentham. His theory, like most forms of utilitarianism, is **hedonistic**. It defines the utile as the pleasurable, and holds that pleasure is the only thing that is intrinsically good, that is, desirable for its own sake, and pain the only thing that is intrinsically bad. All other things are only instrumentally good and bad. Money is desirable, not for its own sake but for the sake of the things we can buy with it, things we want to buy because they cause us pleasure. Even monks and hermits who live in misery and isolation do so because they believe that they are earning the kingdom of heaven, a life of unceasing happiness. Since the good is happiness or pleasure, it is only natural that a morally good action should be the one that produces the greatest amount of pleasure and the least amount of pain for the greatest number of people.

HEDONISM: The idea that the good life for a human being (and perhaps also for animals) is pleasure has a long history. Disputes among hedonists frequently concern the kind of pleasure we ought to pursue. The earliest of the hedonists were the Cyrenaics. They believed that strong physical pleasures were best, such as food, sex, and wine. The Epicureans disputed this idea, holding that physical pleasure inevitably brought pain in its wake (as drunkenness is followed by a hangover). They pursued instead mild pleasures, such as simple food, music, conversation, and the contemplation of the happiness of the gods, for many of such pleasures could be enjoyed in a single day. Such activities make a life more pleasant and give us more pleasure in the long run.

We stand under two great taskmasters, wrote Bentham: pleasure and pain. They determine not only what we will do, but also what we ought to do. Furthermore, his utilitarianism is a moral theory, for he holds that we are obligated always to so act as to produce the greatest tangible balance of pleasure over pain for the greatest number of people, always counting our own desire for pleasure to be no greater or less in value than the desire for pleasure of all other people. This is called the greatest happiness principle. If, for example, through your

Jeremy Bentham. © *Library of Congress.*

action you can cause a great pleasure for yourself while doing only a small harm to someone else, then you ought to perform that action. For then you will have produced the greatest balance of good; through your action, the world will be enriched with pleasure more than it will have been made poorer. The idea of balance is important, because we cannot always avoid inflicting pain when we try to produce pleasure. A dentist, for example, produces pain by drilling into a patient's tooth. But we do not think the dentist does wrong, for her action prevents much greater and long-lasting pain. If she did not, we would find another dentist. People naturally prefer pleasure to pain, and it is reasonable to sacrifice some pleasures and accept some pain if the total pleasure or absence of pain that results from the behavior is greater.

Bentham believed that it was possible to calculate the amount of pleasure and pain that was likely to be produced by some action. He called this procedure the hedonic calculus. Imagine that a person is thinking about voting for a piece of legislation, or trying to decide whether to cancel a promised visit to a sick aunt and go to the theater instead. Courses of action such as these are going to affect the pleasures and pains, burdens and privileges, happiness and unhappiness of at least some human beings, and these must be considered in deciding how to act. Pleasures and pains can have seven dimensions.

Pleasures and pains can be more or less intense, of greater or less duration, can be more or less pure (pleasure unmixed with pain, pain unmixed with pleasure), more or less certain (more or less likely to have the expected or intended effects), more or less fecund (able to produce new pleasures or pains), nearer or farther from us (how far we have to go to get pleasure or avoid pain), and greater or less in extent (the number of people who are affected).

In each of these seven dimensions we must estimate the value, as quantitatively as possible, for each of the alternative actions. The morally right thing to do is to act on that alternative that our calculation leads us to believe will result in the greatest happiness for the greatest number of people affected. Again, a person is to count his own happiness as having no greater or less value than that of any other person.

The strength of this notion, as Bentham points out, is that we all think in these terms already. What other outcome than pleasure could we rationally desire? Yet since we may become confused and think of right and wrong in terms other than profit or the general happiness, we fail to apply this technique of reckoning consistently and systematically. Perhaps we are afraid to admit to the hedonism we naturally assume and hide behind hypocritical saintliness. Yet if we are honest, when we think about visiting our sick aunt or going to the theater, we will consider such matters as how intense the pain to my aunt will be if she breaks her promise; how entertaining the theater is likely to be that night; whether the aunt will be affected for the long term in her feeling for us if we fail to show up that night; whether our absence will cause further suffering for her (she may need us to run an important errand); whether she will get over it quickly; whether we will long remember with pleasure this night at the theater, and entertain other people by telling them about it. This is not a complete calculation, no doubt, but Bentham might ask, isn't this what rationality in moral decision-making comes down to? And, if we are moral persons, and the calculation comes out on the side of giving up the theater and visiting our aunt as the course of action that will produce the greatest happiness for the greatest number, then we will go to the aunt's even if we are pained by the boring evening and the loss of the night at the theater.

Bentham was subject to ferocious criticism even during his lifetime. Utilitarianism was called a philosophy suitable only for pigs. One reason for this claim was that Bentham believed that all forms of pleasure are equal in value. As far as pleasure is concerned, "pushphin (a silly game) is as good as poesy," he wrote. Both poetry and games cause pleasure in the people who enjoy them; why should anyone think that one kind of pleasure is better" than another? No doubt the pleasure of a pig cavorting in his muddy sty with his sow is greater, at least by the measure of intensity, than the pleasure a fine mind feels while reading Shakespeare. But if utilitarianism recommends the life of a pig as equal in value to, say, the life of a human mind steeped in culture, then, the critics said, utilitarianism is hardly a good guide to human efforts to live morally. The notion of hedonism that underlies all utilitarianism was therefore thought unworthy of human beings: a person's soul can never be satisfied by a life of pleasure alone.

A related assumption of Bentham's may be untrue: that human happiness is built with *hedons* of pleasure as a house is built with a number of bricks. The more bricks, the bigger (but, noted the critics, not necessarily the better) a house. The life of some person that contains more pleasure than the life of another person is not for that reason alone a better life. Happiness is a long-term state of well-being, as was seen in Aristotle. A person who considers herself happy does not do so because of the number of pleasures she has enjoyed. No doubt, a life without any pleasures at all would be a mad and lamentable affair. Yet happiness involves at the very least a sense of having lived well, of having achieved something worthwhile. The more pleasurable life may be better in the sense of being more desirable as a life (but not necessarily so), but it is surely not for that reason more worthy or morally better. The pleasures enjoyed by one person may have been purchased with the blood of other people. Of course Bentham would agree that a man is unworthy whose pleasures are obtained by the suffering of others; after all, the morally good or worthy act is the one in which a person considers his own desire for pleasure to be of no more value than anyone else's. But his hedonic calculus suggests he does not realize that a society that achieves the greatest pleasure for the greatest number of it members will not always be a morally superior, or even a happier society.

John Stuart Mill

Utilitarianism had its most talented defender in John Stuart Mill. Mill wished especially to respond to two intertwined criticisms of utilitarianism: (1) it was a hedonist philosophy suited only for pigs, and (2) it requires us to approve of obviously immoral actions that happen to provide more pleasure than pain to those affected by them. In response to the first issue, he argues that there are higher and lower pleasures, and we should measure the moral value of an action upon its tendency to produce more of the higher kinds of pleasures. In response to the second issue, he argues for what he calls *rule utilitarianism*, that is, we should apply the hedonic calculus not to single actions, but rather to a rule that governs many actions of its type.

Most people would disagree with Bentham's claim that the pleasure we get from playing a childish game with gusto is no different from the pleasure we get from reading Shakespeare or Plato. They are both pleasures, but there the comparison stops. And yet it is difficult to describe what the difference in these pleasures consists in. Playing the game causes more visceral pleasures: we laugh or shriek as the game takes an unusual turn; we may feel a certain satisfaction when we win a game that was all but lost; we are observant and focused, wickedly or gaily, upon the game; some of our talents for quickness, agility, fraud, or strategic cleverness are brought into play. In contrast, the pleasure we get from reading Shakespeare seems almost entirely mental: We enjoy the unique turns of phrase, the elegance of the language, the conflicts in the plot, the unfolding of character, and the deep insights into human nature and the human condition. We enjoy the puzzlement we may feel when we try to understand the motivation of the characters' actions, or the relation of the characters to each other. Such enjoyments do not come as naturally to us as do the visceral pleasures of the game. It requires more effort to remain focused on Shakespeare's text, and a subtle mind is needed to perceive clearly all that is going on in his works. In sum, the pleasures we obtain from Shakespeare are the pleasures of

John Stuart Mill. © *Thoemmes.*

the human spirit, whereas the pleasures we obtain from the game are based in our animal and social natures.

Bentham wished to measure quantitatively the pleasures and pains that were likely to result from some action. Is there some way of measuring the quality of pleasure obtained from some action? Mill is a bit cagey about this question. He sees that the advantage of utilitarianism is its placing of right and wrong in the natural physical events of pleasure and pain. Bentham, of course, included such mild pleasures as those of a walk in the spring or a poetry reading in his calculus, but he believed such pleasures are thoroughly measurable in intensity, duration, and the other parameters as are the visceral pleasures of sex and play and eating. They are different in degree, but not in kind. Mill thinks the "higher pleasures" are a different type entirely; they are mental and not visceral in nature. Then how are they to be measured? He says that we must rely upon the judgment of those persons who have enjoyed both kinds of pleasure. Those who know nothing but the pleasures of sex and gambling and drunkenness are unable to judge the pleasures offered by the works of Mozart or Shakespeare or Rembrandt. Further, Mill believes that people who have enjoyed both kinds of pleasure are consistent in their judgment that the spiritual pleasures are higher, and hence more valuable, than the lower.

Granting Mill that there is a difference between higher and lower pleasures, what is the significance of the distinction for moral theory, in Mill's view? Mill was a social philosopher, like Bentham before him, and he wanted to influence politicians in their policymaking and social legislation. In *On Liberty,* perhaps the most important document in the history of modern liberalism, Mill argues for mandatory elementary education for all Englishmen, commonplace today, but far from being a reality when Mill wrote. Mill wished to make most citizens at least minimally literate, so they could participate intelligently in the democratic process. But part of his concern in demanding universal literacy was to make what he called "higher pleasures" available to more people—to raise, as it were, the standards of enjoyment of the common people. If people are attracted to such depraved pleasures as the spectacles of the Roman Colosseum, perhaps this is because they are unaware of the more refined pleasures that are available to educated and literate persons, and it is a legitimate aim of government to raise the level of pleasure in the land. If we cannot eliminate pain or maximize pleasure, we can at least enhance the quality of the pleasures we enjoy.

Another problem left to Mill by the legacy of Bentham concerned the possibility that an action producing more pleasure or utility than pain or disutility may be patently immoral. For example, throwing one Christian to the lions for the amusement of thousands of **Romans** assembled in the Colosseum would produce more pleasure than pain for the greatest number. To show how such an act is immoral, one might argue that the Christian did not deserve to be so treated, for he was innocent; the Roman mob showed no compassion for the victim, and that is wrong; we are told, "Thou shall not commit murder," and this surely is murder; persons have the right to equal treatment under the law; and so on.

MORAL CONCEPTS OF THE ANCIENT ROMANS: The Romans might have found some of these criticisms unjustified. They had no clear concept of equal rights for all citizens, and they would have viewed the Christians they sacrificed as dangerous influences, if not as lawbreakers. We might respond by criticizing them for their failure to grant people a right to their religious beliefs and to treat religious nonconformists with compassion and justice. The Romans might still disagree with the way we conceptualize the situation, but a reasonable Roman would hardly insist that the act of tossing Christians to the lions was a morally good one. Yet this is what Bentham's theory appears to state.

The problem for the utilitarian is that all these objections are deontological in kind, for they refer to maxims of action, rights, obligations, and motives, and these are not relevant to a utilitarian analysis of right and wrong, which refers only to pleasures and pains. Terms such as *right, innocence,* or even *justice* do not seem to be easily expressible, if at all, by descriptions of pleasures and pains alone. The only obligation we have, according to utilitarianism, is to maximize pleasure and minimize pain for all persons who may be affected by our actions, and that obligation, both Bentham and Mill believe, follows from the natural fact that all humankind prefers pleasure to pain. As Mill puts the matter, the only argument we have for the preferability of a thing is that people prefer it. So, presumably, we ought to prefer, and favor, the quantitatively higher pleasure of the Roman mob over the intense pain of the sacrificed victim. But this presumption, Mill will argue, is wrong.

The error made by Bentham, according to Mill, is that he performs the hedonic calculus on a single action. *Act utilitarianism* is the moral theory that proceeds in that manner. It results in such aberrations as favoring the Romans over the Christian. Since Mill believes that pleasures and pains can be distinguished according to their quality, he is skeptical of Bentham's calculus. But if we are to make a calculation, we should make it with reference to the rule of which the action is an example. This theory is called *rule utilitarianism*. The rule, or maxim, of the action proposed by the situation in which one man is tortured for the amusement of many seems simple to formulate: "It is morally acceptable to send some individual, whom we do not like or think dangerous for some reason, to be tortured (perhaps devoured by lions)." And the outcome of the calculus applied to this rule seems clear also: The long-term effects of a society with such practices is liable to be negative, that is, more productive of pain than pleasure. The rules set forth in the Ten Commandments, or our normal sentiment of justice, provide good maxims for action, and they ought to be fostered in our educational system. But they are justified only by their tendency to produce greater pleasure or happiness measured both qualitatively and quantitatively. What justifies the rule against murder, for example, is not that it is God's will or is intuitively evident, or a natural law, but that adherence to it results, in the main, in the greater balance of pleasure over pain.

Some thinkers will still be repelled by rule utilitarianism because of its hedonism, even with Mill's effort to factor in the higher pleasures in the hedonic calculus. Others, especially those committed to the Christian tradition, will reject utilitarianism for its failure to appreciate the value of suffering—Christianity's main symbol is a man suffering the agony of crucifixion—and its apparent reduction of the human being to its physical nature, as though the only thing that mattered to us humans is our physical and psychological well-being. Even rule utilitarians seem unable to account for the fact that a moral obligation matters to most people, even if the only way a person could meet the obligation were by bringing pain to himself and to everyone affected. The German philosopher Nietzsche sneered at utilitarianism, noting that man does not pursue pleasure—only an Englishman could think that. But there are also at least two logical problems infesting Mill's version of the theory that must be noted.

Take again the torture-for-amusement situation. Rule utilitarianism formulates the maxim of this action and then attempts to measure the probable outcomes of adherence to it. What guides it in formulating the maxim? At first the matter seems unproblematic: the maxim is, "It is morally acceptable to send individuals, whom we do not like or think dangerous for some reason, to be devoured by lions for the amusement of the citizens." The consequences of following this maxim seem clearly bad: No one could feel safe in such a community; arbitrary murder by mobs for the sake of their amusement would be common; the people would become brutalized by such spectacles.

Yet many cases are not as clear as this one. Suppose several people could be saved by telling a lie to someone, let's say to a deranged killer who is holding people hostage. What is the maxim of this rule? It is justifiable to tell lies, perhaps. But if the hedonic calculus is performed upon that rule, the outcome will be negative; more people would be harmed than benefitted. So the rule utilitarian would conclude that we should not lie to the hostage-taker. This is not good; lives are at stake. Perhaps then this maxim: It is justifiable to tell lies to save the lives of people. But what if telling a lie in some circumstances would save the lives of some people while sacrificing the lives of others? Will the rule have to be modified again? Or what if, in other circumstances, the lie would destroy the willingness of other people to trust us (as, for example, if the liars were police officers, and public trust of the police is necessary for its effective work in the community)? Can we so formulate the maxim of the action so that all cases of obvious wrong would be eliminated? The maxim would have to become very long, indeed! Rules may have exceptions, but if we were told to act only on those rules for which all the relevant exceptions were stated, we might wonder whether we could ever formulate those rules adequately. Besides, if the rule has exceptions, then we must ask by what rules we are to judge what the exceptions are. If the reply is simply that in this case (of the hostage-taker), the harm is greater than the good, and therefore we should lie to the killer, then haven't we returned to act utilitarianism?

Deontology

The three theories of right and wrong considered here—motivationalism, legalism, and teleological utilitarianism—each take a different perspective upon an action that is being evaluated for its rightness or wrongness. Motivationalism and legalism are both deontological theories. A theory is called teleological if it finds the source of right and wrong in the consequences of the action. Jesus was named as an example of a motivationalist position, Moses as an example of a legalist position, and Bentham as an example of a teleological position. Do these three positions always come to the same conclusions regarding the rightness or wrongness of an action? In many cases they do not. Imagine the following situation: A person is walking down the street with a friend when she is accosted by a beggar who asks her for $5 for a cup of coffee. She gives him the $5. Her friend praises her morally for this action; he says it was the right thing to do. Since she is a philosopher, she asks her friend why he thinks so. If her friend were a motivationalist, like Jesus, he would probably say that he could see in her heart that she was concerned for a suffering fellow human being, and that loving concern motivated her action of giving the beggar the $5. Her heart was in the right place, and it is that heartfelt charity that alone gives our action moral worth. If her companion were a legalist, like Moses, he would probably say that the divine (or natural, or moral) law obligates all persons who can do so to help the needy, and because she followed that law in giving the beggar $5, her action has moral worth. Finally, if her companion were a utilitarian like Jeremy Bentham, he would probably say that the $5 made the beggar happy—more happy, indeed than she was made unhappy by being $5 poorer (on the assumption that she could afford the loss).

At least her three friends all agree that the action had moral worth, although they agree for different reasons. Imagine that the situation was a little different: She is walking down the street and is asked for $5 by the beggar. This time she takes $5 from her purse, throws it at the beggar, and says, "Here, take it, you drunken bum." Jesus, no doubt, would condemn this action, for it is done without charity, concern, or a good heart. That the beggar would be benefitted would make no difference to Jesus, for benefit is not to the point in morals; for him, the only thing that matters is the quality of our souls. Moses would have to say, at least, that she had obeyed the moral requirement to help those in need. The traffic officer, after all, does not care why a driver is driving within the speed limit. It may be because he is afraid of getting a ticket, or because he is concerned with public safety. The officer judges people only by the rules that they are required to follow. Bentham would have to ask whether she had injured the beggar by insulting him, and whether the act of insulting him made her feel better or worse, but, if after considering those matters, he concluded that her action produced more pleasure than pain for those affected (herself, the beggar, the friend, perhaps the owner of the place where the beggar spends the $5), he would have to conclude that her action was a good one. In this version of the situation, at least Bentham and Jesus would be at odds, with Moses most likely on Bentham's side, regarding the moral value of our action. It is hard to see how the sides could be reconciled. This conflict between deontologists and teleologists in ethics occupies the efforts of many writers on the theory of right and wrong today. Perhaps if these two theories were given in a more detailed account, they could overcome some of the objections that have been made of them.

Kant

People who are convinced that utilitarianism has insurmountable flaws may turn to one of the deontological theories for a different account of right and wrong. The most powerful of modern deontological theories was developed by Immanuel Kant in the century before Mill.

The Good Will

Kant wishes to demonstrate that what is valuable about a human life is its moral worthiness, not its happiness. To be morally worthy is to do what is right, even if doing so produces no tangible benefits, that is, benefits that can be measured in terms of pleasure, or happiness, or usefulness. A life of pleasure can never be worthy or sufficient in itself, even if the pleasures are obtained justly or rightly. A worthy person acts rightly for the sake of right alone. Kant's subtle and difficult moral theory can be approached by unpacking a famous passage from his *Fundamental Principles of the Metaphysic of Morals*, written in 1794.

Nothing can possibly be conceived in the world, or even out of it, which can be called good without qualification, except a good will. Intelligence, will, judgment, and the other talents of the mind, however they may be named, or courage, resolution, perseverance, as qualities of temperament, are undoubtedly good and desirable in many respects; but these gifts of nature may also become extremely bad and mischievous if the will which is to make use of them, and which, therefore, constitutes what is called character, is not good. It is the same with the gifts of fortune. Power, riches, honor, even health, and the general well-being and contentment with one's condition which is called happiness, inspire pride, and often presumption, if there is not a good will to correct the influence of these on the mind, and with this also to rectify the whole principle of acting and adapt it to its end. The sight of a being who is not adorned with a single feature of a pure and good will, enjoying unbroken prosperity, can never give pleasure to an impartial rational spectator. Thus a good will appears to constitute the indispensable condition even of being worthy of happiness.

The purpose of this complex passage is to establish that one thing alone is good without qualification, namely the good will. This claim comes somewhat as a surprise. Most people, if asked what is good without qualification or exception would reply with a laundry-list of exactly the same kind as Kant's own: Happiness, gifts of fortune, such as wealth or health, talents of the mind, such as intelligence or wit; these are the things that we all want to have in as great an abundance as possible. They seem to be the conditions of living a life that is worth living. Yet, Kant argues, they are not unqualified goods; each of them comes with a "but" attached. Wealth is good, but not if we use our wealth to obtain unfair advantage over others; intelligence is good, but not if we use our intelligence to fool others less intelligent than ourselves; wit is good, but not if we use it to make fun of or demean other people. All those things are good only if they are turned to uses determined by the good will, that is, only if the person possessing them has a will to use them in the right way. The good will itself is always, unqualifiedly good: It is always good to try to do what is right, regardless of the consequences for our wealth, health, intelligence, wit, or even our own happiness.

To support this remarkable idea, Kant calls upon what he calls a "disinterested rational spectator." Imagine that we are observing the happiness of a man who has no good will at all, who enjoys the suffering he inflicts upon other people, or who is simply unconcerned with the injustice he does while he enjoys all the pleasures life has offered him. Imagine also that we are completely disconnected from him: we have nothing to fear and nothing to gain from him. Would we feel pleasure at the sight of his happiness? Kant is certain that we would not, although common sympathy would cause pleasure in us if we were to observe the happiness of a morally good man, just as the sight of the suffering of such a man would cause pain in us. The goal of life for Kant, therefore, is not pleasure but righteousness; is not success but adherence to the demands of duty; not happiness, but being worthy of happiness, even if in fact no gifts of fortune, no talents of the mind, no happiness, are ours to enjoy. Alas, experience teaches us that a worthy person is not always a happy one.

But what is good will? Or, more specifically, what does the good will will to do? The short answer is that it wills to do its duty: the morally good person chooses to do what it knows to be right or obligatory for him. But what is his duty? We all know, Kant believes, what our duty is. We already possess moral knowledge, and there is no need for a revelation from on high of the moral law. For there is a moral law inscribed upon our hearts; we may not know where that law comes from, but every human being senses the weight of moral obligation upon him or her, and knows, in general, what those obligations are. "Two things fill me with awe," wrote Kant, "the starry heavens above and the moral law within."

Duty and Inclination

Kant is a deontologist, but he makes use of both forms of deontological theories: motivationalism and legalism. Kant believes that we must obey the moral law, and we must obey that law for the right reason, that is, out of respect for the law. This respect for the law is, for Kant, the good will: The good will wills to do its duty because it is its duty, and not because the person acting thinks that it is in her interest to obey. Of course, the problem for every human being is that she may be inclined to break the moral law for the sake of her interests—for the sake of the interest she has in being happy, for example. She knows what the moral law requires of her, but she may not have the strength of will—the good will—to carry it out, because she cannot do her duty and get what she wants at the same time.

Kant offers us some examples of the conflict he has in mind, and how the good will may shine forth in such situations. A child is sent by its mother to the baker's to buy some bread. The baker, on receiving the money from the child, thinks to himself: "This child is so young, it cannot count as yet. I could give the child the incorrect change, and make a greater profit." Despite this thought, the baker gives the child the correct change. Has he done the right thing? We can't tell as yet, according to Kant. It is clear that he has acted according to the moral law, but perhaps not for the sake of the moral law. Maybe his thinking continued, "I'd better not cheat the child. Its mother may find out, and I will get a bad reputation and lose some of my business." In this case, the baker was inclined to do his duty; he acted for the sake of his business, but not for the sake of the moral law and the action it requires. He deserves no moral praise. What if he thought as follows: "Why should I bother cheating the child? I don't need the extra money." Again, he will have acted according to the moral law, and yet not for the sake of the moral law. He is simply not tempted, and he deserves no moral praise for that. Does a person deserve praise for never having committed murder, if he was never tempted or had an opportunity to do such a thing? This question will receive further consideration in a moment. Now what if the baker thought in the following way: "I could cheat the child, and the mother will never find out. And I do need the extra money very badly. But I will not cheat, because it is wrong to cheat." In this case, and only in this case, Kant says, the good will shines through. The baker knew his duty, was inclined to do otherwise, but acted according to the law for the sake of the law alone.

The analysis of these scenarios may seem persuasive, but some lingering doubts about the coherence of Kant's theory remain. Why, for example, can a man or woman not claim some moral worth for never having committed murder or some other immoral or illegal act just because he or she was never tempted to do such things? After all, motivations are supposed to matter morally for Kant, and if a person is not motivated to break the moral law in many instances, shouldn't that count to that person's credit? She may be one of the fortunate persons to whom thoughts of murder and mayhem do not occur. Would we be better persons if such thoughts of murder and their working-out as plans of action came to us frequently, and we always had to struggle against them by reminding ourselves that they are evil? Is the worse person the one who is, as it were, born with angelic qualities and would never dream of hurting a fly? Most of us would prefer the company of the angelic person, no doubt—we'd be safer with him or her—although, we have to admit, there is great nobility in a person who is able to struggle with great temptations and in the end does what he knows to be right.

A passage from the Christian Gospels is illuminating in this regard. Christ has been speaking to tax-gatherers and other unsavory characters, and the Pharisees criticize him for the company he keeps. Jesus responds to them with the story of the Good Shepherd (Luke 15: 4–8). When the Good Shepherd finds one of his sheep missing, he leaves the other sheep in the open pasture and runs after the one that is lost. When he finds it, he rejoices. So, says Jesus, "there will be greater joy in heaven over one sinner who repents than over ninety-nine righteous people who do not need to repent." Perhaps Kant had this story in mind when he argued that the good will shines forth only from the darkness of the human inclination to crime and wickedness. We are not angels, and moral struggle is necessary and perhaps good for us. When we succeed, the moral grandeur of the human being becomes visible.

The Categorical Imperative

A key to understanding the conflict between a Kantian moral theory and a teleological theory is Kant's famous distinction between categorical and hypothetical imperatives. An imperative sentence is one that directs or commands action. "Please shut the door," is an example of a sentence in the imperative mood; it asks someone to shut the door. "The door is open," is not an imperative sentence; it asserts a fact about the door. A categorical sentence asserts something thought to be a fact: "The door is open"; "All Frenchmen are Europeans." A hypothetical statement is more complex. It asserts a relationship between two sentences, one of which, called the consequent, is conditional upon the other, called the antecedent. Our sentence about Frenchmen can be asserted as a hypothetical statement: "If a person is a Frenchman, then that person is a European." This sentence has the same logical shape as the material implication "$p \supset q$," and it asserts that being a Frenchman is a sufficient condition for being a European. "A person is a Frenchman" is the antecedent, and "That person is a European" is the consequent.

What are hypothetical imperatives? They are statements in which the imperative is a consequence of an antecedent categorical statement. Thus, "If you want to lose weight, go on a diet." "You want to lose weight" is the categorical statement that serves as the antecedent of the hypothetical statement, and "Go on a diet" is the imperative. Now the imperative, "Go on a diet," applies only to persons who want to lose weight, not to all people. Going on a diet is a requirement only for those people who want to lose weight. Compare this to the categorical imperative, "Do not tell lies." This imperative is universal; it applies to all rational men and women, and its application is not contingent upon some hypothetical antecedent, such as, "You want people to believe you (or trust you, or like you)." Your desires are not to the point here; you must not tell lies no matter what your inclinations, desires, or wishes are. That is one characteristic of all moral law, according to Kant. It does not apply only to some people, to those, for example, who wish to achieve some end other than the moral life itself. It applies to all indifferently, whatever a person's situation or desires: You must not tell lies.

But surely not all statements in the imperative formulate moral rules. "Shut the door" is an imperative and is asserted categorically, but it is not morally incumbent upon anyone to do as it orders. How do we distinguish moral rules from other kinds of imperatives? To answer this question, Kant develops his notion of a Categorical Imperative—emphasized this time, for we are not speaking of any specific imperative that is asserted categorically, such as "Do not tell lies," but with the idea of moral law itself, of which "Do not tell lies" is an example.

The Categorical Imperative is the abstract form of all moral duties. It functions as the ground of the possibility of a system of moral duties in general. All specific duties make implicit reference to it. It contains no reference to specific duties but it provides a kind of criterion for deciding whether some imperative is in fact a moral rule that ought to bind the will of all persons. Kant formulated the Categorical Imperative several times. Perhaps the final formulation is easiest to understand: "Treat all human beings as ends in themselves, and never merely as a means." For example, say we are going to tell a lie to a person in order to obtain some advantage for ourselves. We would then be treating the person to whom we lie as a mere instrument to our own ends; we are not respecting him as a person who has ends of his own, or purposes that matter to him. No doubt, if a man pays a taxi driver to take him somewhere, he is using him as a means to his end, getting where he wants to go. But he is not treating him the taxi driver merely as a means; he may respect his autonomy as a person and as a working man when he pays him. But when he lies to the taxi driver, he denies his autonomy; he takes advantage of him and does not respect his interest in hearing the truth. The extreme case of denying a person's autonomy is the institution of slavery, where a human being is treated as a mere instrument of the slaveowner and is denied all rights and autonomy. He is stripped of his dignity as an end in himself and made to function only as a means for the owner. The fundamental principle of all morality for Kant, therefore, is the respect for the

Ethics

autonomy of persons, each of whom lives for his own ends, and not merely for those of others. When we are in a moral quandary regarding our treatment of others, we must always ask ourselves what his dignity and autonomy—perhaps we may say his intrinsically valuable selfhood—requires of us in our treatment of him.

Kant's other formulations of the Categorical Imperative are a bit more complex. He states one as follows: "Act always so that the maxim of your action could be made by your will a universal law that all persons would follow." Let us say that a person is considering breaking into a home and stealing the owner's property. Clearly, the thief is treating his victim as a mere means to his end, the possession of the owner's property; he is not concerned at all with the ends to which the owner wishes to put his property. But now he asks himself: "What is the maxim of my action?" Presumably it is the rule that it is morally acceptable to steal. Could he will that this rule become a universal law that all people would follow? He could not; for if all persons stole, no one could maintain private property, and there would be nothing to steal. The maxim of his action is therefore logically incoherent. He wants to make an exception to the rule, "Thou shalt not steal," for his own advantage, but he knows that if everyone were to steal as he does, then no one, including himself, could steal.

Take the case of telling a lie. The maxim of the action is that it is morally acceptable to lie. Yet again, the maxim shows itself to be rationally incoherent. One feature of telling a lie is that the liar expects his hearers to believe him. But if everyone lied always, no one would believe anyone, and it would become impossible to tell lies.

Kant's theory has several advantages over teleological theories. Since the consequences of actions are not considered to be relevant by him, it is not necessary to change our judgment about the rightness and wrongness of an action as its consequences unfold. It is wrong to lie, everywhere and always, regardless of the consequences the lie may have. The difference between right and wrong is unvarying and clear. Kant is also able to make the point that although the moral laws are engraved upon the hearts of every rational man and woman, we do not have to postulate some special moral sense such as intuition that enables us to know the moral law. The moral law is knowable by reason, as Kant insists: Maxims of action that are morally wrong are rationally incoherent and cannot be willed by a rational person. Finally, the moral law does not stand outside our own persons as a foreign imposition, say, as an imposition by God or by Nature. We legislate the moral law to ourselves as autonomous rational beings. We are essentially rational beings, and our own reason dictates to us how we must act in order to be moral. No doubt, we also possess beastly inclinations toward what our reason tells us is immoral; but the rational will, the good will, has the power to turn those inclinations toward its own ends. The good will can "rectify the whole principle of acting, and adapt it toward its ends," to return to the passage from Kant quoted above.

There have been many objections to Kant's theory, not the least of which are those developed by John Stuart Mill himself. The utilitarian objection to Kant reaches into the very premisses of his thought. Kant refuses to consider consequences as having moral worth, because he believed that actions prompted by thoughts of good consequences are the products of our inclinations. But, the utilitarian responds, our inclinations ought to be considered when we are formulating moral rules. Suppose we are asked about the whereabouts of his wife by a maniac who is looking to kill her. Are we supposed to act on the maxim, "Tell the truth!" and in that way help the maniac to kill his wife? Kant would say that you must so act. The death of the wife is in any case not your moral responsibility, but that of the killer; you simply did your duty in telling the truth. Kant might agree that you could respond to the maniac's query by saying, truthfully, that you do know where his wife is, but you will not tell. Then you risk having the maniac kill you. But no matter: you have done your duty. Florestan, a hero of Beethoven's opera, *Fidelio,* starving to death in a dungeon where he has been placed by a powerful man he tried to oppose in the name of justice, sings to himself: "Sweet consolation in my heart, I have done my duty."

Presumably Florestan's efforts to do his duty had some beneficial results. Yet what if doing his duty had in fact no positive consequences for anybody at all, made no person happy, or saved other persons from grief? Would Florestan find such sweet consolation then, or would he decide that he was dying for nothing? A utilitarian surely would so decide; Florestan's action would have no cash value, as it were; it did not create a positive balance of happiness over unhappiness or pleasure over pain. Why would anyone be willing to make such sacrifices in the name of the moral law if the consequences of the sacrifice were painful to all those affected?

Alas, this perplexing question, which both Kantians and utilitarians try to answer, each in their own way, has no easy answer. We all want to be happy, but most of us also want to be worthy persons. Remember the promise to visit our sick aunt one evening, when, during the same day a friend gives us tickets to a play we're especially interested in. The evening at the theater will give us more pleasure than the pleasure we will give our aunt by going to see her, but our minds are still divided: after all, we promised! And a promise has to make some kind of difference. Kant, of course, says it makes all the difference in the world. By keeping our promise, we assert our autonomy as rational beings and will do what we know to be right: Keep your promises! Our good will shines forth through our disappointment at missing the theater. And yet we ponder in our own conscience: Weren't we fools? Would it have made that much difference to our aunt if we had called her and asked to reschedule our evening together? Even if we'd told her a little lie, what harm would it have done? Wouldn't there be a greater sum of happiness in the world if we had attended the theater and gone to visit the aunt another night? That may all be very true, but she will still be very unhappy. So we ponder and agonize over our righteousness, question our virtue, and add and subtract the points on the side of happiness, until we manage to satisfy our conscience in one way or another.

CONTEMPORARY ISSUES IN ETHICS

During the years extending from the Second World War to the Vietnam era, moral philosophy in England and America was in deep disrepute for its apparent failure to produce verifiable statements of moral obligation. Value predicates—*good* and *bad*, of course, but also such "thicker" terms that refer to qualities of character or of action, such as *noble, just*, or *brave*—were said to be a class of terms distinct from physical predicates like *hard,* or *hot*, or *green*. As there is no experimental way of verifying the judgments in which they appear, value judgments were thought to express only the likes and dislikes of the speaker and a request to the hearer to feel the same way. According to this doctrine, called ethical emotivism, all normative ethics is based upon the logical error of confusing facts and values. Statements of fact are either true or false; value judgments, as expressions of prejudice or taste, are neither.

Moral Skepticism

By the 1970s, new initiatives in ethics were appearing. First, a new historical understanding of the sources of the apparent failure of normative ethics was emerging, and with that new understanding, limited alternatives for ethics became available. One important step was taken with the appearance of Alasdair MacIntyre's celebrated book, *After Virtue*, in 1981. MacIntyre (1929–) argues that the "Enlightenment project" of Kant, Bentham, and others, which attempted to provide a secular and rational foundation and binding force for the moral injunctions passed down by the Judeo-Christian tradition, was doomed from the start to failure. It thought it could rest value judgments upon pure practical reason, or upon some form of naturalism, or again upon tangible outcomes, which all rational persons could take as valid measures of the goodness or badness of actions. Sadly, each effort created more controversy than agreement. The collapse of the Enlightenment project, and the slow evaporation of the Judeo-Christian framework to which it referred, has resulted in the current disarray of our moral language and in skepticism regarding the possibility of moral knowledge.

MacIntyre makes two crucial claims at the start of his analysis of the historical situation of ethics. First, our moral culture is derived from incompatible and different sources—as we noted earlier, it is derived from the Greeks, the Jews, and also from modern technology-driven capitalism—and each source is deeply involved in the historical conditions of the intellectual culture from which it emerged. This moral pluralism is not "an ordered dialogue of intercepting viewpoints, [but] . . . an unharmonious mélange of ill-assorted fragments." Since the moral beliefs and preferences of Western thinkers have no common source, the "fragments" of contemporary moral philosophy cannot be traced back to a universal realm of values. The morals of the Jews, Greeks, and moderns are "incommensurate," to use the term from hermeneutics. There is no common currency, no moral gold standard, that would allow us to express cross-cultural moral disputes in ways that are equally intelligible to each of the disputants. In the face of an inability to offer universal theoretical guidance for the resolution of pervasive transcultural social and individual moral conflicts, philosophers must assert moral relativism, the claim that, "There is no single consistent set of principles that people have reason to regard as having [moral] authority in all contexts," to use a phrase of the Harvard moral philosopher Thomas Scanlon. Moral judgments have no foundation in anything but the varying needs and social situations in which they function, and from which, presumably, they emerge.

A second crucial claim of MacIntyre's analysis is that the source of the current value-skepticism is the high standards of rational justification of ethical claims demanded by the moral theories of Kant, Bentham, and Mill. These standards are derived from logic and science, and they do not and cannot apply to moral judgments. Secular philosophers expected too much certainty of ethics, and turned their backs upon it when it failed, dismissing it as prejudice. Moreover, the growth of a democratic spirit in Europe undermined the sacred authority of morality as the commandments of kings, priests, and Scripture. Yet all universal moral commandments, even the secular categorical imperative, refer at least hypothetically to the authority of some commander, be it God, or reason itself, as in Kant, or the natural taskmasters of pleasure and pain, as in Bentham. The rise of the equalitarian spirit led to value-subjectivism; each person is the sole source of her own moral authority.

Another step toward a new understanding of ethics was taken by Bernard Williams (1929–2003). He is skeptical about the value of ethics in the guidance of life that has been attributed to it since Socrates. Morality is only one of many things that are important to living well. He argues in his *Ethics and the Limits of Philosophy* (1985) that ethics has lost its significance in human affairs and can survive only by turning inward upon itself, and by becoming academic and self-serving. But then, he thinks, ethics will sever its legitimate ties with other things people consider important. The problem is not just that the values to which value predicates refer do not exist, but that ethics has no hold upon the world beyond its own talk about rules, obligations, and ideals. A good life is not only a moral life, and moral philosophy is not an adequate guide to living well or even being a worthy person. In fact, Williams writes, "we have deep and persistent reasons to be grateful that we do not live in a world where morality is universally respected and all men are of a disposition to affirm it." No doubt a constant and unflagging concern for strict righteousness by everyone would result in a madhouse. But the corollary to Williams's notion would seem to be that we should be thankful for human wickedness, a frightening thought. Williams is far from Socrates's confident notion, which he communicated so well to Clinias: knowledge of virtue, wisdom, and goodness are the necessary and sufficient conditions for living the good life.

New Efforts in Moral Theory

Some of the new work in ethics has not produced only relativism and moral skepticism. Thinkers like MacIntyre and Williams may have cleared the soil for new plants: ethicists, it seems, had been digging in the wrong way for the wrong things. However, what has arisen of a positive nature for moral philosophy out of the ashes of the Enlightenment project is rather modest in its claims. While accepting wholeheartedly the historical relativism implicit in MacIntyre's criticism of the past, ethicists in the English-speaking world attempt today to develop normative ethics by exploring the supposed common moral understanding implicit in the language of their own culture, and by recovering the moral insights of other times and places through historical and genealogical studies. MacIntyre himself attempted to develop a virtue-based theory of morality, while insisting, in his *Whose Justice? Which Rationality?* (1988), that all moral theories, and even their most general concepts, such as justice and rationality, are inseparable from the cultural communities that articulate them. Moral theory has been reinvigorated by the attempt to found morality not in Reason, or Nature, or Happiness, as the Enlightenment naturalist thinkers attempted to do, but rather in the common moral assumptions of the shared culture of the modern post-industrial world. These efforts at a moral philosophy for a new age can be expressed in six key questions.

Adjudicating Moral Disputes

What are the sources of moral disputes, and how can they be resolved? Thomas Scanlon argues in *What We Owe to Each Other* (1999) that when persons disagree about the moral responsibility of an agent for an act, three issues are at stake. The first is concerned with the force of reasons we give for the attribution of moral responsibility of an agent about what is to count as a good reason. The second concerns the range of cases in which we have reasons to be constrained by the requirement of justification to others. The third concerns the question of whether any of the principles that figure in the attribution of moral responsibility could reasonably be rejected. Moral conflicts about responsibility arise from the core values and the priorities assigned to them by different parties to the conflict. They are unresolvable, unless some of the parties alter their core values.

Moreover, a moral situation may also be unresolvably ambiguous if we cannot decide which moral rules, ideals, outcomes, or values apply to it. Moral judgment refers, no doubt, to publicly available facts and principles that are elements in the unwritten social contract, but, as in law, people may disagree systematically about the scope of the social contract, the relative force of its provisions, and the applicability of those provisions to specific cases. Scanlon attempts to secure a foundation for moral judgment and a procedure for justifying it. Justification must provide an account of the reason to do or not to do some action that is not founded in some nonmoral value, such as being well-looked upon by one's fellows. It must be founded in a moral concept of what it is to be wrong. For Scanlon, the reason-giving force of a judgment of right and wrong is the moral importance of standing in some positive relationships to others, such as those relationships characterized by trust, respect, and mutual autonomy. The function of moral reasoning is hence to establish those relationships firmly in the moral community.

Another simple strategy for the exploration and possible resolution of moral problems that has become familiar today is the analysis of simple, if abstract, moral situations about which there is likely to be a consensus, and then the extrapolation from the moral insights that formed the consensus to more complex and concrete cases of moral conflict. Those moral thought-experiments, as they may be called, enable us to isolate the moral content of political and personal conflicts, as the material with which philosophical reflection must struggle as it attempts to fight its way through to a normative position regarding the conflicts. The celebrated **"trolley experiment"** has attracted the attention and tested the intellectual acumen of many moral philosophers.

TROLLEY EXPERIMENT: Compare the following two structurally similar scenarios with respect to their moral content. Try to determine whether they are dissimilar in morally relevant ways so that one of them might be the right thing to do, and the other the wrong thing.

1. You are the motorman on a cable car (such as the ones in San Francisco). As you bring the car down a steep hill, the brakes fail. Five people are standing on the track in front of you, and you see that you will inevitably kill all of them unless something stops the car. At the last moment, you are able to shunt the car via a switch onto another track upon which you see only one person is standing. The car kills him, and the other five people live.

2. You are a surgeon in a hospital. Five of your patients will die shortly unless they receive organ transplants. One needs a kidney, another a lung, the third a heart, the fourth a liver, and the fifth a stomach. A person wanders into the hospital looking for directions to some other part of the city. You anesthetize him, remove his vital organs, and transplant them into your five patients. They live, and the man from whom you took the organs dies.

Other ethicists believe that when we agree about right and wrong, we appeal to moral imperatives that are sufficiently broad to be universally shared, but which may give rise to different moral injunctions, such that reasonable persons could take either of two conflicting sides in a moral dispute. An attack on the supposed insurmountable relativity of moral belief is found in Bernard Gert's *Morality Its Nature and Justification* (1999). His aim is to show the inherent reasonableness of the public system of behavior and accountability, which he calls the "common morality," whose best metaphor is what is called the natural law. He proposes a kind of moral minimalism that founds its broad maxims in human needs so fundamental that they are universally shared. No one could rationally disagree, for example, with the maxim that any person in any culture has an interest in the preservation of his or her own life. If we can state all such broad maxims, we will at least have established the range of rational disagreement about the moral content of a situation without falling into the pit of incommensurability that makes further debate useless. It is absurd to argue with a person whose language we do not and cannot understand. But Gert's point is that any person can understand any other person because we share the broad maxims he articulates. When we disagree, we can understand just why we disagree. On this view, Kant's disinterested rational spectator could not provide a unique adjudication of a moral conflict, but she could at least give us a range of possibilities to which any morally acceptable resolution of it must conform. Such a theory is conducive to a democratic system, because it helps us understand why other people reason about moral matters the way they do, and, in such moral disputes as those about capital punishment or the right of a person to an abortion, it precludes the demonization of opponents, or the condemnation of one side by the other as irrational.

A similar proposal for the democratic adjudication of moral disputes is what Charles Taylor has called an *ad hominem* ethics, notably in his article "Explanation and Practical Reason" in *Philosophical Arguments* (1995). It is useless to apply abstract moral rules to specific situations without reference to the "moral universe" of one's interlocutors. We must appeal to their own moral perspectives at the points where we can agree. Often, this strategy comes down to nothing more than pointing out the inconsistency of their position (because we all agree that an inconsistent position is worthless), or the special pleading it represents (because we all agree that bias is unfair). Before moral criticism can take hold on a deeper level and have motivational value for the persons affected, Taylor says, an appeal must be made to the shared values that pervade our world and that of our opponents. To make such an appeal is, no doubt, to argue in an ad hominem fashion, for the appeal is not simply to the moral facts of the case, but to the nonmoral fact that one's hearers and oneself have some stake in these moral facts; both sides have given at least some prior approval of them, however tacit. To argue without such an appeal, and to pretend that logic or fact alone has a claim upon one's will, apart from the values to which one has always made implicit reference in arriving at moral judgments, is to make ethics an alien imposition upon persons rather than a statement of their own foundational moral beliefs. In sum, our first question to an ethics for a new age asks: Do all persons share some foundational moral values, and can we formulate them adequately and apply them to moral conflicts successfully?

Feminist Ethics

A feature of twentieth-century life that has cast new light upon this question of foundational values is women's liberation: the increase in the number of women working outside of the home, independently of their husbands or other family members, and in many cases, in positions of great responsibility in government, the professions, and business. Naturally, this development has resulted in a reevaluation of the responsibilities of civil society in insuring that justice be done to women entering the job marketplace, and in providing assistance to women who both work and raise children. Philosophers have played a role in articulating these new social responsibilities and have frequently written on top-ics relating to such social issues as affirmative action for women, the ethics of marriage and its shared responsibilities, and other broad issues relating to the nature of human sexuality and **gender**.

GENDER ISSUES: It has become commonplace today to refer to is-sues concerning the conflicting interests of men and women as gen-der issues, to distinguish them from more narrowly sexual issues, which concern matters of sexual activity and reproduction. The no-tion of gender, however, is derived from grammar and was not in-tended to designate interests specific to the two human sexes, but rather the distinction between masculine and feminine (and, in some languages, neutral) words or forms of words. In contemporary philosophy, however, a sexual issue refers to problems concerning, say, the role of sex in marriage or the morality or immorality of adultery, while a gender issue is one that is of special concern to men or to women, as, for example, the existence of a *glass ceiling* blocking women from top posts in a hierarchy.

Feminists have argued that the theories of virtue and of right and wrong action characteristic of Western civilization are inadequate for understanding the full range of human moral experience. These theories have failed to consider the nature of women's moral experience because of the covert sexism of our civili-zation, or simply because women have not been encouraged, have failed to take the initiative, or have not had either the leisure time or the professional standing to develop that experience in the form of a considered philosophical theory. Why, according to modern feminism, are the traditional theories of virtue and of right and wrong action inadequate? What do they lack?

The theory of virtue developed especially by Aristotle, but also other an-cient schools of philosophy, applies to autonomous individuals placed in com-petition with each other. The virtuous man is the one who is successful in performing valuable tasks in the political contexts of his time. The individual competitor finds activities within that context that give scope to his talents, con-forms his emotions rationally to a golden mean, and wins recognition among his peers as virtuous or excellent by his superior performance. This struggle for achievement and self-justification is a dim historical reflection of the Homeric heroes' struggle for distinction in war or the Olympian athlete seeking glory for himself and his city-state. Feminists do not deny that women can and have been entirely successful in such competitions. But the rules of the competitive game have up to now generally been set by men to conform to their own dispositions and their sense of their own talents. Important elements of human excellence are either entirely absent from or marginalized by a theory of virtue that concen-trates exclusively upon competition for whatever prizes a society may set for success.

Similarly, the various forms of the deontological and teleological theo-ries of right and wrong action all suffer from the limitation of an excessive and one-sided concern. Deontology is primarily concerned with the justification of rules of action that can be applied to kinds of individual cases, and teleology is primarily concerned with the calculation of benefit and harm, and it attempts to direct human action toward the maximization of profit—happiness, pleasure, or another kind of benefit. These theories of right and wrong were adapted to the context of the modern bourgeois, who struggles within the law to advance himself economically. Both require rational assessment of situations and a calculation of the actions required within those situations if they are to be morally right ones. Feminists do not argue that these procedures are wrong because they are loaded with masculine bias, or follow naturally from a male-dominated model of action. They will argue, however, that a fair assessment of right and wrong must consider forms of moral experience and moral evaluation that emerge from a perspective that is as natural to women as the rule-based moral theories are to men.

The models of action most often proposed by feminist ethicists focus upon the notion of care. Feminist strategies for evaluating moral quandaries are based in empirical studies of men and women as they attempt to formulate their responses to those quandaries. But the purpose of feminist ethics is to determine the validity of a particular strategy from a moral point of view. Is the strategy proposed by the care paradigm that is said to be typical of women superior to the male strategy proposed by the paradigms of the virtue- and rule-based moral theories? The social psychologist, Carol Gilligan, claimed in a 1977 essay entitled "In a Different Voice" that earlier studies of moral growth in children fail to recognize that boys and girls think of moral situations in different ways. The studies measured moral growth against a yardstick provided by boys, and this procedure led them to conclude that girls (and, by extension, women) were inferior in their capacity for moral reasoning. But what if girls' thinking about moral choices employs a different yardstick, one that places unstated emphasis upon the concern for, and the responsibility to, other persons?. Following this initiative from a psychologist, feminist moral philosophers have developed an ethics of care and interdependence that contrasts with the autonomy of the individual that characterizes most Western moral theories. Feminist morality is a search for ways of living comfortably together, with each individual appropriately cared for by his or her immediate community. Care, concern, and a sense of mutual responsibility for each other's well-being give us a moral paradigm that takes us out of the context of autonomous individuals striving for distinctions or rewards and places us in a more humane and peaceable moral milieu, feminists argue.

For example, in the case of the conflict between a promised visit to our aunt and our desire to use a friend's gift of theater tickets that same night, an ethics of care would seek out possibilities of resolving the matter in the best interest of both of us. We could confide in the aunt the problem we are having, but we should not ask her for forgiveness if we were to fail to come that evening, or to beg her to "let us off the hook" just for today. Either of those requests would put the aunt on the spot. She would probably agree to either of them, but she would be harmed in any case. Caring for her implies looking at the matter from her point of view. We should ask her whether she needed something special from us that evening that we were not yet aware of, whether we could come by before the theater to provide her with a meal or a purchase of something she needs. We could suggest doing something special for or with her on another evening that week, something that would go beyond what she could have expected from us that evening, something the anticipation of which would soften the burden of our absence that evening. We would make clear to her our sense of responsibility and concern for her and make clear to ourselves that we must be ready to drop the evening at the theater if we become convinced that this evening with us means more to her than our evening at the theater means to us. Such a caring solution requires a great deal of open communication with those to whom we are responsible and certainly requires just as much moral commitment to the right course of action as do the virtue- and rule-based theories. It makes us active participants in the lives of others, far more than the autonomy and disinterest affirmed by rule-based theories. Care requires favor toward those to whom we are tied by family, work, and interdependence. It supplements, by the emotion of sympathy, the rational calculation of consequences and the application of coherent moral rules.

No doubt there are problems with claiming that morals are gendered, and that an ethics of care emerges from a specifically female moral experience. The care model of moral responsibility seems, for one, to be derived from female perspectives that feminists claim to be stereotypical of women at best, and oppressive to women at worst. If women are subject to conditions of psychological, economic, and physical oppression, then it is possible that the feminine moral perspectives that arise from this oppression express those very conditions and will contribute to their continuation. An ethics of care might require the agent's docile submission to the needs of those perceived as needing care (husbands, children, elderly parents), more than the virtue- or rule-based theories do. Would women who fight against sexism and wish to excel at professions formerly limited to men do better to abandon an ethics of care and adapt, say, a male rule- or virtue-based theory that has evolved within the battleground they are entering? Or might it be possible, our second question to twenty-first century ethics asks, to assimilate feminist ethics to the moral theories that are being developed by nonfeminist thinkers today and generate a paradigm of moral reasoning appropriate to both men and women?

Freedom and Equality

Respect for the freedom and moral equality of other persons is a necessary condition of all moral discourse. We must assume that our opponent in a moral dispute is our equal in some sense and is at least as free and self-governing as we are, if our dispute is to respond to rational analysis and not simply to the imposition of power by the stronger party upon an opponent thought to be irrational and unworthy. In this connection, Scanlon notes that for Kant, the justification of a moral action always requires a respectful appeal to free and equal persons to accept the grounds of some action as rational or as justificatory. We treat a person as an end in himself just insofar as we recognize the need to justify, in his eyes, the action we are taking regarding him. When we deal with another person from a position of weakness, we are frequently more inclined to be remiss in the obligation to justify our behavior than when we are dealing with an equal. We may, for example, resort to deceit in order to level the playing field between us. Scanlon models his moral theory in *What We Owe to Each Other* upon a kind of contractarianism, where the moral contract fosters, as must all acceptable contracts, a reasonably successful way of life, the standing in a valued relationship with others that includes mutuality, impartiality, and trust, and where the individual is required to justify morally his or her actions by presenting grounds for them that other agents could not reasonably reject. Any moral theory must supply the conditions for such a contract that can be used as a standard and a corrective measure in evaluating moral conflicts where the parties are not equal. This third question for an ethics of the future asks: Can we state the terms of a reasonable moral contract between autonomous and equal persons that can be the foundation of their lives together?

Moral Action

Where an agent's intentions in his performance of an action are thought to have moral implications, problems arise about how to describe such intentions. Are the wellsprings of human action reasons, or motives, or passions, or something else? The classic expression of this problem is David Hume's famous declaration, "Reason is and ought to be the slave of the passions." Reason, he believed, may enable the passions to envision their maximum gratification, and to find means to achieve it, but it cannot motivate action on its own. The notion is usually contrasted with that of Plato, who argued that enlightened reason can and must rule over the passions, for the sake of one's ideal self-interest. Bernard Gert has argued, in opposition to Plato, that acting rationally and acting out of self-interest are quite different. It is always rational for a person to desire that other people adhere impartially to the broad maxims of morality that condemn depriving persons, without cause of life, the ability to act, freedom, pleasure, or the inflicting of pain upon them. However, according to Gert, a true alienated individualist, it is not irrational to wish these moral prohibitions not to be applied to one's own actions, if it is in one's self-interest to act immorally. Moral action is, after all, frequently burdensome to us, and wickedness is often profitable. To resist the demands of morality may be discreditable, but it is not irrational.

The separation of reason and passion divides the human agent in two: we are hybrid creatures, rational animals whose two parts, reason and passion, do not get along with one another. Perhaps human motivation is far more complex. A variety of morally legitimate motives beyond both reason and passion may prompt an agent to meet her moral obligations. Such motives as sympathy, fellow-feeling, or the desire for glory or recognition may figure in our decision to tell the truth, or to save a drowning child. Perhaps such inner conflicts that are the sources of human beings' hybrid nature are to be sought elsewhere than in the simple reason-inclination distinction of Kant and Hume. We need a new theory of the human being as moral agent, a philosophical anthropology that enables us to see more clearly what motives are involved in human moral action, and to grasp more effectively what kinds of social arrangements contribute to the flourishing of the rational human animal. Our fourth question for ethics in the twenty-first century is: Can we establish a coherent theory of human motivation that enables us to recognize in moral theory the means to achieve our own highest good?

The Limits of Moral Responsibility

Even given a theory of motivation, the question of moral responsibility has not been settled. Most people today would assent to the thesis that the social context of the motives of autonomous persons may determine, to some extent, those motives and the actions they prompt. This social context may mitigate the responsibility of a person for her actions. Scanlon argues, for example, that an agent may be responsible for the harmful effects of her intentional actions, yet she need not always be subject to punishment, but rather offered social help. The community can and must take on some responsibility for the autonomous actions of its members. Persons may, for example, freely and with full knowledge of the implications of their actions, cause harm to themselves and to others by engaging in unprotected sex, or by the use of dangerous drugs or alcohol. They may become the voluntary victims of some social scourge, such as AIDS or drug addiction or drunken driving. It is impossible to fix the extent of their responsibility, for they may, at least in part, be subject to cultural factors over which they have no control. This possibility was rarely confronted by ethicists earlier than the last century. Another question for the new century asks: Can we interpret the notions of autonomy and responsibility to allow for a reasoned decision as to the nature and limits of social involvement in fostering the moral obligations of its citizens?

Why Should I Be Moral?

A final question concerns the binding force of moral rules. Why should a person do what she ought to do—if she does not want to? Bernard Williams seems to applaud the inability of ethics to answer questions of this sort when he says that moral theory, if it existed and could provide a binding force to its rules, would claim the right to legislate to the moral sentiments, that is, to tell a person how he ought to feel, and in that way deprive his feelings of rightness and autonomy. Presumably he means that the autonomy of individuals—their freedom from moral commandments—is to be preferred to the rightness of their sentiments, which agrees with his observation that we should be grateful that all people are not of a disposition to act morally. But perhaps this is due to the content of the common commandments, and not to ethics as it is properly conceived—

as the study of the means of attainment of our own highest good as rational social animals.

How can universal moral obligations impose themselves upon an individual acting agent? And, if they cannot, are we not forced to admit a kind of moral anarchy? What good, then, are the strategies of moral philosophers that we employ to show others—and perhaps ourselves—the moral error of their ways? What can moral philosophy say to a man preparing to plunder the investments of his employees to enrich himself? That it is wrong to do wrong? Indeed, asks Williams, what is there to say about promise-keeping beyond the thought that a promise is a promise? If there is no justification of moral propositions beyond the assertion of the tautology that promises matter because they are promises, then morality in general is of little value in our search for a life that is worth living.

Plato believed that a morally excellent person—a balanced, harmonious, well-ordered soul—could not be overwhelmed by disaster. As Socrates says at the end of his trial, "Nothing can harm a good man in this life, or in any life to come." If true, that is sufficient reason to be good! But it is not enough to say that virtue is its own reward. We cannot assume that happiness and worthiness are compatible, or that although our personal happiness may at times be at odds with our moral obligations, virtue in the end pays off in happiness, and our sacrifice of temporary happiness or benefit will contribute to the long-term flourishing of a society and of my own life. Goodness may require the sacrifice of other interests—to be rich, for example. Is the sacrifice worth it? The final question for the new ethics is: Can we recover in some form the Platonic idea that a certain kind of strength and happiness, perhaps quite different from what we think those things to be, is only possible in a life dedicated to moral goodness?

CHAPTER 7
Social and Political Philosophy

The branches of philosophy often focus upon some broad notion. Philosophers have analyzed the meanings and implications of these notions and specified clearly what phenomena they refer to. These exchanges among philosophers have a history, and it is impossible to enter today's discussions of them without a sense of the discoveries and, perhaps, the mistakes made during that history. In metaphysics, the notion that focuses the discussion is *reality*. Epistemology is concerned with the nature and limits of *knowledge;* ethics with *right* and *wrong*. Aesthetics analyzes as primary notions *art* and *beauty;* in the philosophy of religion, the notions are *God* and *faith in God*. In social and political philosophy, the central concept is *justice*. This chapter will consider the following themes:

- Theory of Justice: Characteristics
- Plato: Justice As Harmony
- Aristotle: The State and the Individual
- Social and Political Philosophy in the Middle Ages
- Idealism and Realism: The Early Modern World
- The Nineteenth Century: Radicalism and Liberalism
- Social and Political Philosophy in the Twentieth Century

THEORY OF JUSTICE: CHARACTERISTICS

The term *justice* has currency in ethics, for it concerns a kind of moral relationship among persons. It is unjust, for example, to treat others prejudicially, that is, favoring or disfavoring them for irrational or irrelevant reasons. We treat the person about whom we have prejudices merely as a means to our ends, the satisfaction of our prejudice. The person injured or benefited by our prejudice did not deserve to be harmed or favored; she had done and could do nothing to earn such treatment, she received it because of the prejudice. Her right to be treated fairly and equally had been injured. All these reasons emerge from the general notion of injustice that functions in the background when people condemn prejudice.

In **social and political philosophy**, justice takes on a much larger role, although one that is parallel to its role in ethics. A just society or a just political and legal order is one that is regulated by principles and laws that all those living in that society or that political order can or should, if they are rational, recognize as a reasonable and fair basis for their life together. Such principles and laws may be written down. The Constitution of the United States is an effort to embed the principles of justice in a set of regulations to be adhered to by the government in the making, execution, administration, and enforcing of the laws. Or they may be unwritten customs and precedents that citizens tacitly but consciously adhere to. The theory of justice attempts to analyze and criticize such principles with reference to an abstract notion of justice. It asks, "What is justice, and is our system of laws, principles, and institutions a just one?"

SOCIAL AND POLITICAL PHILOSOPHY: The terms *social* and *political philosophy* are interrelated. Every society up to now has had a political structure, and the political structure has always attempted to regulate the affairs of the members of the society as citizens of the state. By *political* we refer to the administration of the state. The state includes such organizations as congresses, government administrative bodies, the judiciary, and the police and military. By *social* we refer to the institutions and affairs of the people, their churches (where they are not a part of the state, as, for example, in ancient Egypt), corporations, private land holdings, clubs, labor unions, and the like. Social and political institutions, though highly interactive, are usually quite different in their functions and purposes. A theory of justice is intended to offer means to evaluate the nature and quality of the justice provided by the institutions of the society and the state to their members and citizens.

How can what philosophers are looking for in a theory of justice be characterized? Two broad questions that guide inquiry into the nature and function of justice come immediately to mind.

First, what is a theoretically sound conception of justice based upon? Here philosophers have considered a range of possibilities. A theorist may derive a concept of justice *empirically,* that is, from an observation of how justice is administered in her own or foreign lands. Justice would be, in that view, simply what it is called in those states. A philosopher may also try to derive a concept of justice in an a priori manner, that is, by working out her deepest moral intuitions of what justice is and ought to be. Another may rely on a concept of the Will of God, or, as with Natural Law theorists in ethics, on an assessment of the foundational natural needs and desires of human beings, or the requirements of nature itself.

Second, what is the *purpose* of a theory of justice? Most theories have been prescriptive; they are intended to establish standards of justice against which states and societies can be evaluated. In some cases, philosophers have demanded a complete overhaul of state and society in order to achieve their concept of justice. They are the revolutionaries. In other cases, philosophers have used a theory of justice either to support the existing institutions of societies and states, or to demand a return to an earlier social structure. They are conservatives and reactionaries, respectively. Still other theories of justice are intended to offer ideals to societies for altering their institutions in the direction of greater or more evenly distributed justice. They are liberal. Still other theories may be called utopian, in that they make demands for justice upon human beings and their social and political arrangements that seem not to come naturally to them. The utopian aspirations of Marxist-Leninists to produce a classless society and a workers' paradise in the Soviet Union or in Communist China appear to have failed without hope of eventual resurrection.

PLATO: JUSTICE AS HARMONY

In *The Republic,* Plato describes Socrates in conversation with several young men at the home of an old friend. They begin an analysis of justice by clearing away two notions of justice that are as familiar today as in fifth-century Athens. The poet Simonides (circa 556–468 B.C.E.) is quoted has having defended the idea that justice is giving others what is owed to them. And what do we owe others? Young Polemarchus replies: "Good to one's friends and harm to one's enemies." In this view, if someone has been harmed maliciously, it is only just that the victim harm his attacker in return. Similarly, if someone performs a spontaneous act of kindness to another, justice requires that person to repay his benefactor with some other kindness. In both cases, justice requires a balancing out of a kind of moral debt between two persons or groups of persons. No doubt the notion of revenge lurks in the background of this kind of justice. However, Socrates does not criticize Polemarchus's definition of justice simply because of the support it gives to blood feuds. He thinks that the concept does not capture the immense social and political importance of justice. Besides, he says, we may not always know just who our own friends and our enemies are (especially if we are uncertain or mistaken about what is in our own best interest). Further, he argues, it is unjust to harm an enemy in the name of justice, if the harm makes him worse as a human being. How can a good thing like justice produce essential harm? Many people wonder today whether our system of criminal justice is justice at all, if people come out of jail worse men and women than when they went in.

The second notion of justice that Plato wishes to clear away emerges from an unfriendly encounter Socrates has with a Sophist among the group, named Thrasymachus. This man had argued that justice, not as it is generally understood, but as it really functions in the affairs of people, is nothing more than the advantage of the stronger. The strong man, or tyrant, makes the law to suit his own advantage. He calls these social arrangements justice, and the common people either obey his commands or are killed. Thrasymachus's notion is close to the modern saying, "might makes right." Those who control the institutions of the state choose whatever measures will guarantee the continuation of their own privileges. The citizens are so deluded that they regard as just those very arrangements that privilege the rich and powerful and confine the poor to a life of misery. "The weak minister to the interests of the powerful," says Thrasymachus, "which is very far from being their own."

Socrates points out that Thrasymachus's strong man, or tyrant, is in reality not the happy man that Thrasymachus takes him to be. Happiness, strength, and success in all aspects of life, Socrates thinks, is not possible without virtue or excellence of soul, and **justice** is the greatest of the virtues. The tyrant damages his own soul as he damages those of others. Thrasymachus is finally defeated in this war of words by Socrates, and he leaves the discussion, at least for awhile, in a huff. But two other young men present, Adamanteus and Glaucon, are not satisfied that the issue is settled. Is the unjust tyrant, who is revered as a leader even as he corrupts and enslaves his fellow men, really worse off, from the point of view of his own best interests, than a poor and disliked but genuinely just man? After all, the tyrant has all of society serving him at his pleasure; how could he not, apart from some tricks of fate, be the happiest of men? And what is justice, such that its possession, by a person or by a state, is the most valuable possession of all, as Socrates believes? To answer these questions, Socrates leads his two young friends on a discussion that ranges over almost all significant features of human life. They first try to show what justice is and how it functions in an ideal state and then attempt to define the just individual. In the end, they discover why the life of such a person is much to be preferred to that of an unjust person.

JUSTICE: The claim that justice in the state is the same kind of thing as justice in the individual is a remarkable assumption. It is related to Plato's conception of the Forms. Justice, he believes, must be one Idea that manifests itself in the things that we properly call just. A just person, a just government, a just law, a just action, must all participate in the single structure that is ideal justice. From this it follows that *justice* in the state is isomorphic with justice in the soul of an individual person, and if we understand the former, we will understand the latter. Another assumption is related to but does not follow from this one: If justice is the highest good, and if justice is everywhere the same, then the good of the state and the good of the individual will necessarily be in harmony in the just state. Conflicts between the individual and his government are only possible in unjust societies. Certainly Plato must have thought that the deadly conflict between the historical Socrates and his *polis,* Athens, was due to the injustice of Athens. A key question for Plato is how people can create a just *polis* in which a just man like Socrates would naturally function as one of its leading men instead of being put to death.

Socrates, Adimantus, and Glaucon begin their search for the just society by examining how a simple society arises out of families and villages, reaches an optimum phase of development, and then begins to go wrong—it begins to develop the features of injustice that are typical of the states these men were familiar with. The simple society becomes corrupt when it becomes large and produces more goods than its people need. It creates luxuries and the citizens develop the taste for them. This wealth gives rise to the need for an army to protect the people's property. Yet this development, which threatens to dissolve the society by external warfare and internal envy, can, they speculate, be checked by the proper education of a new kind of army, one trained in virtue and in war. Its members are called the Guardians. Out of their ranks will come a new leadership elite, called the Philosopher-Kings. The Guardians will place limits on wealth, and luxuries will be rare and generally not desired by anyone, for everyone will have enough to meet their needs and simple tastes. Thus what appeared to be a danger—the need for an army to protect the possessions of the citizens—turns out to be the strength of the society. The Guardians will insure that the greatest threat to internal stability, the class war that arises from great differences in the distribution of wealth, will not occur. All depends upon the proper education of the Guardians, and a large segment of *The Republic* is dedicated to the theory of education. Higher education of the proper kind is possible only as a state undertaking, not a private one, as it had been in Athens, where it was conducted by the Sophists. Through discussion, the three men write up a kind of constitution for their ideal state, in which the outlines of justice itself appear.

Two key concepts are central to Plato's theory. First, the ideal society will be divided into three classes, and each class will have a different function, which is defined by the ends they pursue. Membership in a class is determined by an individual's aptitude for the training needed to carry out the functions of that class. The producers have the function of producing the material necessities for all members of society. The Guardians' function is to guard the *polis* against internal and external threats, and the function of the Philosopher-Kings is to rule. The authority of the Philosopher-Kings is total and absolute, for they alone have knowledge of the nature of the Forms of all things. Plato's idea is similar to the modern notion of a meritocracy, in which positions of authority are given only to those who possess the character and knowledge needed to rule rationally and well. If a person is to work as a surgeon, she must have acquired knowledge and competence in that skill, and her knowledge and competence will be tested by licensed surgeons before she is permitted to practice. Since we know what the function of each class is, we can determine what training is needed for each function and judge how well each class is performing its assigned task.

Second, Plato assumes that there is no happiness without virtue, or human excellence. Since the function of government is the fostering of human happiness, Socrates and his friends turn to the question of what constitutes virtue or excellence in government. They attempt to determine what virtues, or excellences, each class must possess in order to function well. In the case of the Philosopher-Kings, that virtue is *wisdom:* this class embodies the knowledge that makes possible the functioning of the state and its creation of the conditions of human happiness. In the case of the Guardians, that virtue is *courage:* that class embodies the high spirits and freedom from irrational fear that makes for effective warriors. The producers possess no specific virtue, although they possess the practical knowledge needed to do their jobs. What gives them virtue is their willingness to accept direction by the Philosopher-Kings. A state embodies the virtue of *temperance,* when each of its classes accepts the order of things that the rulers, in their wisdom, decree. Plato notes that temperance, unlike the other two virtues, must be a quality that inheres in the entire city, and not only in one of its classes. It is, he says, like self-mastery, where the worse part is ruled by the better part, and both parts consent to this rule. In the ideal city both the ruler and the ruled are of one mind as to who ought to rule. This is similar to the situation in which a plaintiff in a lawsuit takes direction from his lawyer, believing that the lawyer knows better than he how his interests in the suit should be pursued.

But what of justice? Plato's answer amazes: It does not call for a fair distribution of goods and burdens, for the establishment of a constitution upon which all citizens of the society, acting as each others' equals, could agree upon, or for the defense of legitimate entitlements, as our major contemporary theories of justice maintain. Justice, for Plato, occurs when each of the three classes of society strives to achieve its proper ends. Justice in the state is therefore the doing of its own business well by each social class, and injustice will be the disunion caused by the attempt of persons to perform the tasks assigned to a class other than their own.

What does this mean in terms of the practices of this state? One interesting practice was criticized by Aristotle. This great student of Plato thought that his teacher had sacrificed too much for the sake of the unity of his society. This criticism is confirmed if one looks only at the concept of temperance. Plato desires a society in which all persons are of a single mind regarding social and political policy, for in such a society there will be none of the strife that characterizes almost all human societies, and that tends to weaken them. And Plato does have Socrates say, in *The Republic,* that the greater the unity of the state the better. This premise is used by Socrates to argue for a specific practice, that of state communism, at least among the guardian class. The Guardians are to have all property in common and to eat in a common mess, as did the Spartans. Moreover, they are not allowed to form families, for the family causes a conflict of interest in the Guardians. Plato feared they might become more faithful to their wives and children than to the state, thus causing disunity. For this reason, men are not to know who their children are; they are to have sexual intercourse at night and in groups, when lovers cannot see who their consorts are. The children that result from this adventure will be raised in a common nursery. Aristotle's criticism is that this society will deny its citizens the sense of ownership that gives them a personal stake in society. One result of the lack of personal property even in children will be that the children, instead of being tended by all, will be tended by no one. For Aristotle, what was intended by Plato to produce unity will result instead in indifference and chaos.

Plato's ideal state gives a monopoly of power to the Philosopher-Kings. This idea assumes that the Philosopher-Kings will possess such acute and total knowledge of human affairs that their rule over ignorant men can be justified. People today are unwilling to grant that such knowledge is or can be possessed by their leaders. Moreover, another of Aristotle's trenchant criticisms of Plato rings true to us. The citizens of a society are each other's equals, Aristotle said, and a man must rule and be ruled in turn. Plato's Philosopher-Kings are a permanent ruling committee that takes new members only upon the assent of current members. Democracies like ours today may not allow for all the citizens to take public office at some point in their lives, but it does require that public officials be responsive to the wants and beliefs of the citizenry. Every so often the people's representatives must put themselves up for election. Plato would denounce such a process as nothing more than a popularity contest in which the ignorant choose the candidate that makes the most flattering promises. Would we choose a lawyer or surgeon in that manner? And, he asked, what function is more important for human happiness than good leadership? But Aristotle is right: the citizens of a state must have some empowerment; justice requires some measure of free consent to the laws on the part of the governed. Plato's citizens are more like ignorant patients or clients than like free men. Perhaps he believes that most men lack reason and must be treated like children for the sake of their own happiness.

No doubt unity and conformism for the sake of stability are not the primary aims of Plato's ideal society; its purpose and end are preeminently the happiness of its members. Plato nowhere thinks that the producers are to serve the Guardians; rather the reverse is true. Happiness, and not just stability, is only possible, he believed, if justice as harmony of functions has been achieved and each citizen is excellent in his specific function as a member of a class and as an individual. Then we will have rulers who will not **abuse their power.** Human individuals are rational creatures, they are social creatures, and they are animals, and each of these different natures must be allowed to flourish in its own way if there is to be happiness. The problem is not that there is strife among these functions—as when a man desires to be healthy and at the same time desires to smoke cigarettes—but that the individual, like the state, lacks the wisdom to see that his interest lies not in suppressing the desires either for health or for cigarettes, but in directing these desires so that they all can be satisfied to the greatest degree possible. That can only happen when the lower functions accept the direction of the highest function, the reason, which, if enlightened, allows the desire for knowledge, for honor among one's fellows, and for food and sex and shelter all to be satisfied according to some proper measure. This is not unity for its own sake, it is for the sake of the highest happiness, possible only through the life of reason.

ABUSES OF POWER: One of the chief problems of any political system is the corruptibility of persons by power. "Power corrupts!" is not just a populist slogan. History is filled with examples of benevolent men and women who, when accepting a public office, take advantage of all the easy and usually safe ways to use their power for their own advantages. Plato's *Republic* may be read as an attempt to answer this question: How does a *polis* protect itself from "strong men" who undermine the system of laws and take absolute power over the state? The problem is especially acute for Plato, for he despised democracy, which he identified with a kind of mob rule, but he feared tyranny as well. His answer is to rely on the Guardians' knowledge of virtue. A good man, he thought, would not be tempted to abuse his authority, for he knows that tyrannical rule is not in his highest interest.

ARISTOTLE: THE STATE AND THE INDIVIDUAL

Aristotle's crucial criticism of Plato's ideal state was its sacrifice of individual freedom in the name of social order. But can men and women conduct their political affairs democratically, either by direct participation in the institutions of government, or by representation, or must they be directed by the state from above, where the state is placed in the hands of a small number of wise men (such as Franklin D. Roosevelt's "Brain Trust"), or of monarchs or dictators masking as wise men? Plato no doubt favors the power of the state over that of the individual, for most people cannot rule themselves, that is, achieve happiness, on their own. The situation in Aristotle's *Politics* is far more complex. Aristotle, like Plato, is concerned with training young men in virtue. For Aristotle, however, virtue is a life of rational activity that includes both prudential (or practical) and theoretical reason. The life of virtue requires a developed reason, practiced in self-control and concerned for the good, that is engaged in both the political and scientific enterprises that attract the attention of the superior men in a *polis*. Citizens must be given adequate scope for their rational activities. Since practical reason can be exercised only in the political arena, the free man must be given the opportunity to rule and to be ruled in turn, according to Aristotle. Happiness, or *eudaimona,* requires the self-realization of the free citizen in a life of reason according to virtue. To exclude most people from politics, and to place all political activity into the hands of a handful of aged men (for Plato insists that the education of a Philosopher-King requires an education that continues into a man's sixth decade), is to deny to most citizens one of the greatest satisfactions that people can have: the opportunity to exert authority in the political arena.

Aristotle's analysis of the ideal state draws on his *Nicomachean Ethics* for its picture of virtue in the state and in the individual. In that treatise, he teaches what are the human virtues, the role of reason in achieving them, and the education and training needed to turn boys into free men with the desire for excellence in all worthy things both political and intellectual. The *Nicomachean*

Ethics can be read not simply as a philosophical treatise on ethics, but as a teaching instrument, for the goal of education is to foster the good life, and to allow men to become happy. Aristotle's theory of justice is not, like Plato's, concerned with making men and states conform to an external standard of righteousness, but of giving boys the education and training needed to develop, each in his own way, his intellectual and political virtues in an atmosphere of freedom and friendship. Justice is "complete virtue in its fullest sense because it is the actual exercise of complete virtue" (*Nicomachean Ethics* V. 1, 1124b). It is the virtue through which the other virtues manifest themselves in our dealings with other persons. For example, it takes courage or magnanimity to do justice to others in difficult situations. In fact, why would there be a need for courage, if people owed nothing to anyone, that is, if there were no obligation to be just?

For both Plato and Aristotle, the good ruler is the good man. But Aristotle does not place all power in the wisdom of the good man. Justice in the state appears as the justice of its citizens in their dealing with each other. It may function as universal justice, or *lawfulness,* or, in particular cases, as the treatment of individuals fairly and equally. In the second case, it involves *distribution* and *compensation.* Justice in *exchange* involves reciprocity, giving back equal value. *Political* justice refers to fairness in one's dealings with one's associates, friends, wives, children, and slaves. Finally, Aristotle refers to a *natural* justice that produces men with the capacities for intelligence and virtue.

Just as Aristotle emphasized the development of the freedom and self-sufficiency of individuals, so in politics he was concerned with securing the practical success of the institutions and laws of a *polis* in creating the conditions of human happiness. Aristotle denied Plato's metaphysical theory of the Forms and insisted that the only things that exist are substances. To understand the natures of individual substances, we must study those substances directly; we cannot begin, as Plato seems to have begun, with the nature of things apart from their physical embodiment. Aristotle's work is more empirical and requires the use of our senses to understand the nature of things. Hence we see him, in his *Politics,* examining the nature of existing systems of law in the cities and among the peoples of which he knew. He is, of course, interested in discovering what kind of constitution is best for humankind, given our desire to be happy. But the complexity of the world around him made it impossible to discover a single set of laws and institutions that would achieve this end. He did not believe, as did Plato, that one system is best for all. Nations survive under varying conditions, and some possess many great men to be their leaders and others few. A constitution must therefore be suited to the conditions of its state. Where a nation is especially warlike, or where it possesses very few good men, monarchy may be the best system of government, Aristotle believes, while a nation favored with many able leaders would prosper under a democratic system. *Timocracy,* or rule by the rich or by the generals (a *junta,* as we would say today), and tyranny are everywhere the worse kinds of government. Aristotle's political philosophy is experimental, open-ended, and evolutionary in nature, as is an individual human life. Just as the rules of the game in any given state may determine the forms of excellence displayed by the men who strive to achieve the good life for themselves and their fellows, so too will natural conditions, and not an eternal model of justice, determine the kind of constitution best suited to a given people.

SOCIAL AND POLITICAL PHILOSOPHY IN THE MIDDLE AGES

Saint Augustine

Augustine disagrees with Aristotle that the state, or government, is natural to humankind. It is natural only to our present fallen state for in that state our natural desires are perverted by sin. Men and women require political control if they are to be humbled by the higher power of the state and be prepared by the state at least in that way for their eventual redemption. But individuals are not all perverted to an equal degree. The extent of a person's corruption is measured by what he loves. Most people love themselves more than they love God. Some people seek their nourishment and delight in God; others find the things that delight them in the world. Some of us live for eternity, but most of us live for today and tomorrow. No doubt many of us reach out in both directions: Since humankind learned of good and evil in Eve and Adam's sin, we have been of unsteady mind. We know and are attracted to the goodness of God and abhor the wickedness of sin, but we are attracted also by the goodness of earthly pleasures and repelled by the badness of physical pain. In a famous metaphor, Augustine says we at once are citizens of two cities, and we must eventually choose our final allegiance and take up residence with the things we live for and love. Some of us reside in the City of God, and some of us live only in the Earthly City. The City of God is God-ordained Jerusalem, now represented in the world by the Roman church that was established by Christ. The Earthly City was once sinful Babylon; now it is represented by the state, which for Augustine was the Christianized but decaying Roman Empire. Are those who live primarily in the City of God and those who live primarily in the Earthly City the saved and the damned, respectively? Yes, in that the loves and hates of a person indicate his eventual membership either in the Heavenly City or in hell. No, in that the church is not made up only of saints; it may have evil members—false priests, as it were. The state, also, may have functionaries who are just and love the Lord, and by that love will be among the elect in heaven.

SAINT AUGUSTINE (354–430): Augustine left his *Confessions,* a book that gives us a deep insight into his inner emotional and intellectual life. He narrates his life story, beginning with his childhood, from the perspective of his newly achieved state of grace in Christ. He recalls the childish delight he took in stealing, with some other lads, a few pears from a neighbor's orchard, an action that he now knows was sinful. He and his friends did not *need* the pears, they were not hungry; they stole only because they wished to steal, to do evil for its own sake. As a young man, Augustine further confesses, he had a great sexual appetite. He had a child by one of his mistresses, whom he eventually sent away. In a touching passage he recalls having asked God to cure him of the sin of lust—only not yet! But the greatest of his early struggles was to find spiritual nourishment. He enjoyed the secular Roman authors, became a teacher of rhetoric, and experimented with astrology and with one of the many cults that had spread about the declining Roman Empire. One day it seemed to him that he heard a voice calling, "take up the book and read." As an open Bible was lying on a table, he reached for it and began to read the passage that first struck his eyes, and there, in Paul's Epistle to the Romans 13, he found the words that were to mean salvation for him. He was ordained a priest and was eventually called, against his will, to be Bishop of Hippo, a city in northern Africa.

The tangible difference between the two cities here on earth is shown by their respective functions. The City of God has the task of leading people to their salvation, while the Earthly City provides persons with their material needs, so that they can seek their salvation. The state is not abandoned by Augustine for being inherently wicked, or as a stumbling-block to Christians on the way to heaven. Christians need not become hermits or monks and choose to live outside of the Earthly City. But the Earthly City is devoid of saving grace unless it plays its debt of Christian justice to God, for it must allow itself to be suffused with the light of God on earth. Just as, for Augustine, knowledge is possible only because the light of God is always present in the mind, so must civil society turn toward the light of God's justice, if it is to achieve whatever justice is possible in humankind's fallen state.

As a matter of practical politics, Augustine's downgrading of the function of the state in the procurement of human happiness and virtue may have led to a loss of interest in political matters. At worst, the state came to be identified with the works of sin and depravity and, believers held, had been consigned by God to the ash-heap of history as unnecessary to the work of redemption. A wise man, therefore, will turn his back upon the state and seek refuge in the church. Because of this attitude, the church came to obtain a political power it was ill-prepared to wield. Indeed for Augustine, the church was the only safe haven for a person who loves God in a world grown mad with wickedness, and whose secular government has been abandoned to the barbarians. This is not to suggest, as Edward Gibbon (1737–1794) does in his great history, *The Decline and Fall of the Roman Empire,* that Christianity itself was a major cause of the crisis of government that led to the downfall of Rome. Yet a key to Rome's fall may be due to a crisis in self-confidence that derives from Christianity's reliance upon divine grace for the achievement of human ends instead of relying upon the work of autonomous, secularly educated citizens working through rational and just institutions.

Saint Thomas Aquinas

At the far end of the long period of European history known as the Middle Ages is the colossal figure of the Christian theologian and philosopher **St.**

Thomas Aquinas. Aquinas was the beneficiary of newly available writings by Aristotle that entered Europe in the century before he lived, at first via Latin translations of Arabic versions of Greek texts. Aquinas was thoroughly Aristotelian in his philosophical, if not his theological, convictions. He abandoned Augustine's notion of a divine illumination as a necessary condition of knowledge and emphasized the role of sense-experience in knowledge. This shift was accompanied by a similar departure from Augustine in political philosophy. For Aquinas, it is possible for the state and its citizens to achieve, apart from the grace of God, a just arrangement of institutions that serve human happiness and virtue, for the state is ordained of God, and its role is not merely the negative one of restraining wickedness or the practical one of providing for our material needs. Humankind would require by nature to live in civil society even if it were not in a fallen state. The church, no doubt, has the nobler function of leading people to salvation, but the state functions morally in the spiritual uplift or virtue of its citizens. The achievement of virtue is humankind's natural end. The key to the state's contribution to this end, according to Aquinas, is the concept of law. In this he shows himself again to be a good student of Aristotle, though one whose fundamental worldview is clearly Christian.

SAINT THOMAS AQUINAS: Aquinas was born in Italy to noble parents in 1225. Determined to become a Dominican monk over the opposition of his parents, he joined that order in 1243. His mother, seeking a more brilliant church career for the young man, had him imprisoned for almost a year, but he refused to leave the Dominicans, who allowed him to continue his education at the University of Naples. He later studied with Albertus Magnus in Paris and in Cologne. He became a priest in 1250, earned his doctorate, and eventually became a professor at the University of Paris, where he taught theology until 1259. He traveled to Rome to teach at Dominican monasteries but returned to the University of Paris in 1268. His last two years were spent again in Naples, where he helped to found a Dominican school. He fell ill and died in 1274 while on a journey to Lyons.

Aquinas accounts for three levels of the law, and he uses his account for a theory of the limits of the power of the state. The first and highest law is the eternal divine law, which is an expression of God's reason and is the foundation of the creation and governance of the world. Then there is the natural law, the idea of which emerged in Roman jurisprudence, and which Aquinas thought to be derived from the natural ends that God ordained for all things at the creation of the world. So, for example, a natural human right to liberty is derived from humankind's divinely ordained possession of free will, a necessary means to our final end, salvation. Then there is the human positive law, which, as in Aristotle, will vary depending upon the natural conditions under which people live. Aquinas seems to prefer monarchy as the best foundation for the human positive law, but he concedes that people may live rightly under other forms of government, and the positive laws in each will vary, if the government is a just one, within the range permitted by the natural law. The positive law is thus subject to criticism by reference to the natural law. The monarch is responsible to God and to his citizens for his actions and for the laws he makes. People become to some extent active in and responsible for the quality of the government under which they live. Aquinas expressly states that a monarch can be deposed by his people, as a last resort, if the laws made by the monarch are unjust. The state's control over the individual is therefore not only limited by the church, a function of which is to support the social and governmental conditions under which humans can best achieve salvation, but also by the natural moral law. The monarch, although the maker of positive law, is not the source of that law. All law comes from God, and human laws must conform to the higher law. The monarch must listen to both the church and to his citizens to retain his legitimacy.

IDEALISM AND REALISM: THE EARLY MODERN WORLD

Thomas Hobbes

The first great contribution to modern social philosophy came from the English thinker, **Thomas Hobbes**. Just as the Christian world-view and its notions of fallen humankind, our supernatural vocation, and our redemptive history had, in the hands of Augustine and Aquinas, their effects in social philosophy, so too the spirit fostered by capitalism and by mechanistic technology had a tangible effect on philosophy. Of course, philosophy is never simply a response to, or an expression of, the new ideas and institutions that form the intellectual atmosphere in which people live and write. Consideration of the scientific and economic trends in the early modern world can make intelligible some of the more unfamiliar and, to us perhaps, bizarre features of Hobbes's philosophy. But there were dangerous political struggles in his day to which this thought was a direct response.

THOMAS HOBBES: Hobbes was born in England in 1588. The son of a clergyman, he studied at Oxford and supported himself initially as tutor to the son of Lord Cavendish, who took Hobbes on journeys to Europe. He associated with the intellectuals of Europe, even traveling to Florence to meet Galileo. He was invited to submit criticisms of Descartes's *Meditations,* which led to some acrimonious debates with the French philosopher. Indeed, Hobbes often involved himself in such polemical exchanges during most of his long life of 91 years. A supporter of King Charles I in the civil war that engulfed England after 1642, Hobbes went into exile in France. His greatest work, *Leviathan,* was written in France and published in England in 1651. A year later, Hobbes returned to England under the Commonwealth, which sought to make use of his political philosophy for its own ends. Yet when King Charles II was placed on the English throne after the fall of the Commonwealth and the Restoration, Hobbes was honored by the new king, whom he had served as tutor during his exile in France. Hobbes died in 1679.

Thomas Hobbes. © *Archivo Iconografico, S.A./ Corbis.*

Hobbes wrote his greatest book, *Leviathan,* during a period of civil war in England (1642–1648), when the legitimate king, Charles I, was beheaded by Puritan leaders. Civil war, to Hobbes, threatened the lives and safety of Englishmen. Government may not be natural to human nature, as Aristotle believed, but it is obviously necessary as a practical means to peace and security. How do we deal with the centripetal forces among humans that threaten to break down civil society and return humankind to the law of the jungle, to a war of all against all?

Consider first the notion of human nature. If the state is not natural to human beings, then what is natural for us? Hobbes asks us to imagine human life in the raw: our existence in a state of nature, outside institutions of government. Here human beings appear unadorned with civilization or morals. They are egotistical individuals, concerned only for their own welfare and fearing and mistrusting others. They naturally seek to obtain as much as they can from nature and from each other, and to hold it unless or until someone takes it from them. People are not invariably selfish, Hobbes believes, but each of us assumes as a natural right that one must survive as best one can. It is psychologically impossible to sacrifice one's life and limb for the benefit of another. Human psychology is a simple thing to Hobbes. Each person wants two things: success in competition with others, and glory, if possible; and each person mistrusts all others, knowing each to have the same passions and desires as himself. Civil society and government are built up out of such lawless individuals, much as a clock is built up out of its crude parts. But given this egoism and moral distrust, how is it that the state of nature did not endure forever, but humankind allowed for the rise of civil society? How were the parts of the social mechanism combined to create something more than and different from the sum of its parts?

For Hobbes, two things allowed for the transition to civil society, that is, to organized government. First, we are aware that no individual is able, on his or her own, to master all others. All persons, however strong they may be, must not only mistrust but fear other individuals. Gangs of weak men may conspire against and kill a strong man, if they are lucky. No one is safe; all must fear all others. In a famous passage in *Leviathan,* Hobbes describes the conditions in the state of nature that make humankind long for a measure of security:

> In such condition there is no place for industry; because the fruit thereof is uncertain: and consequently no culture of the earth; no navigation, nor use of the commodities that may be imported by sea; no commodious building; no instruments of moving and removing such things as require much force; no knowledge of the face of the earth; no account of time; no arts, no letters, no society; and, which is worst of all, continual fear and danger of violent death; and the life of man, solitary, poor, nasty, brutish, and short.

People love not only themselves, they also have a natural passion for the works of civilization. It is interesting that Hobbes includes in the list of things that would be absent in a state of nature not only practical things such as commodities and comfortable housing, but also knowledge, art, and literature. It follows from this psychology that despite men's otherwise rapacious and undisciplined nature, they will seek a means to end their "war of all against all."

Second, we have not only a passion for civilized existence, we possess reason, which points to a way of achieving peace. Reason gives us a sense of what the natural conditions of such peace would be. These conditions Hobbes calls by the name of "natural law"; but these natural laws differ markedly from what we have come to consider under that heading. People usually think of natural moral laws as prescriptions that require people to obey them, even if so doing threatens their own security. They constrain people's behavior toward each other and form the basis of the moral authority that requires governments to grant such rights as life, liberty, and the pursuit of happiness, and to pass laws protecting them. For Hobbes, natural laws are simply the natural conditions of secure existence that are discoverable by reason, and from which the general structure of government can be deduced. They are the necessary conditions of peace among us. For example, one of the nineteen laws he lists in *Leviathan,* indeed the second and perhaps the most important, reads as follows: "that a man be willing, when others are so too, as far-forth, as for peace and defense of himself he shall think is necessary, to lay down this [natural] right to all things; and be contented with so much liberty against other men, as he would allow other men against himself." This is not a moral law so much as a condition of any system of justice and **common law**. In a state of nature, no rational person would obey it; but it is reasonable for one to obey it in a state in which others are willing—indeed, have made themselves forced by law—to obey it also.

> **COMMON LAW:** The Roman idea of law as civil statutes that judges were obliged to refer to in deciding individual cases was influential on the early modern social theorists. However, in Hobbes's time, many jurists assumed that the decisions of a judge would be based not upon statutes, but upon the legal precedents established in England since the medieval period. This unwritten law was called the *common* law, for it was assumed to have grown up naturally from the people's and judges' sense of custom and right, and the administration of law was assumed to be the flexible application of the precedents to cases at hand. Hobbes attacked the notion, and assigned to the sovereign the obligation to make statutes in all matters affecting the citizens.

The thought that the laws of nature do not have authority over our actions in a state of nature seemed shocking to many of Hobbes's contemporaries, and it still has the power to shock today. It denies the existence of moral law and justice outside of the laws established by the sovereign power in an established state. Yet the motive of his thought was not to destroy common morality. In a state of complete anarchy, as Hobbes envisaged the state of nature, persons have no time or thought to obey moral laws. How can a person be inclined to keep promises, or to tell the truth, or to restrain his own desires for the sake of helping others, if everywhere he is threatened by other persons who have no inclination to tell the truth or to be generous? A person may know what is right in theory (what Hobbes calls *in foro interno,* or in conscience) but not be able to be righteous in practice (*in foro externo*) for fear of his own destruction at the hands of others. The only solution to the war of all against all is the creation of the Leviathan itself, the State, which will be the conscience of individuals and establish itself as the authority over them.

Thus men enter into covenants with each other, in which they establish one person as the king, or a parliament of men, as the final political and moral authority. Each individual gives up his natural freedom to do what he wants and transmits that freedom to a king or parliament who will enforce the peace between them. The covenant is hence the product of the prudence and reason of egocentric individuals, each seeking his own benefit. Hobbes seems generally indifferent to whether the state authority takes the form of a monarchy, an oligarchy, or a democracy. The important point is that all enter into a covenant with each other, turning their natural freedoms over to the sovereign who, himself, is not party to the covenant. The sovereign power thus has the authority to make law, form an army, and, backed by force if necessary, require each party to the covenant—now the subjects of the sovereign—to obey the law. In this way, the foundations of civilization and of commodious living conditions are established.

What liberties will individuals retain after the creation of the Leviathan? Can individuals withdraw from the covenant if they are unsatisfied with the sovereign? Can a sovereign act in such a way that renders himself illegitimate, as the American colonists claimed in justification of their rebellion against their sovereign, George III? Hobbes is not entirely clear, but his answer to these questions seems to be as follows: The sovereign's authority is absolute. He alone makes the laws and, as we would expect from Hobbes's account of natural law, is the source of all authority in the state and hence of all administration of justice. Sovereignty cannot be divided, for if it were, the sovereign's power would not be absolute, and again anarchy and civil war would arise. Only if unable to assure public safety will the sovereign lose authority over the citizens, for that was the main purpose of the covenant that created the state. Hobbes would not have considered the American colonists' demands justified, whatever George's abuse of power, as long as he possessed sovereign power in England and maintained order in the colonies.

Clearly there can be no moral challenge to the state's authority, for no moral law exists in itself, apart from the decrees of the state. However, Hobbes imagined that the state would rarely seek to interfere in most citizens' private affairs, such as the choice of employment, the enjoyment of private property, or the choice of how to pass one's leisure or to spend or invest one's money. Yet if the state chooses to involve itself in such matters, the individual cannot demand freedom from interference or justice for himself, for right and justice come from the state. Then, too, Hobbes thought, the laws will give people stable expectations concerning what the state will or will not do. That is the obvious advantage of the rule of law. However, the state is under no external constraint to keep the laws constant, or even to adhere to them itself. Since the sovereign is not party to the citizens' covenant, its actions cannot be challenged.

It is striking how modern Hobbes's political philosophy appears when it is contrasted with the medieval word that was being supplanted by new ways of thinking and acting. His theory denies that the state is founded in God's will. The state does not have a purpose or teleology beyond the security it offers its citizens, that is, the satisfaction of their passion for peace. It is subject to no higher law than the natural laws of human behavior. He insisted that the civil authorities must decide matters of belief in a way that minimizes religious strife. Also modern is the notion that the law is the decree of the sovereign, which is a doctrine fundamental to legal positivism, or the concept that law is founded not upon a natural moral law, but upon the sovereign's command backed by force. And Hobbes's theory seems to be an application of the methods of the sciences that so impressed him when he visited Galileo in Italy. Hobbes's "laws of nature" can be viewed as axioms in a deduction of the state from the passions of its people. Human passion and need are the forces that create government; they are its efficient cause, in Aristotle's sense, and it has no other cause or justification. This is a naturalistic picture of human society, one based in visible, physical conditions of life. It looks forward to theories that attempt to discover the foundations of economics, and, indeed, of human history itself, in humankind's animal egoism, and not in a divine providence that directs all things toward a supernatural end.

John Locke

Hobbes's writings drew intense criticism even during his lifetime, and he is still the object of caricature because of his belief that human nature is corrupted fundamentally by egoism, and that the state is beyond effective moral criticism. Some of these objections were unfair to Hobbes's arguments, and to the considerable insight, nuance, and reasonableness of his writing. John Locke's critique of Hobbes's social philosophy is noteworthy. His moral, social, and political philosophy was developed in two of his greatest works, the two *Treatises of Civil Government* and the *Essay Concerning Human Understanding.* Both these works appeared in 1690, shortly after the Glorious Revolution placed William of Orange on the throne of Great Britain, gave Englishmen peace from religious strife, and limited the arbitrary power of the monarch. Locke does not attack Hobbes directly in most cases, but his thoughts on civil government clearly have their roots and their targets in the works of the older man. Like Hobbes, Locke was concerned with establishing the state on a naturalistic rather than a religious footing, and he approved of Hobbes's attempt to discover the foundations of civil society in a covenant made by men in a state of nature. However, the state of nature (which he apparently believed to be a matter of historical fact) had a very different character in Locke's thinking.

For Locke, the state of nature is characterized by liberty, but not anarchy. Men and women constrain their actions by a natural moral law that prescribes benevolence toward others and the practice of human brotherhood. In general, people are also required by the natural law to preserve the peace and not harm others arbitrarily or for their own advantage. The problem with the state of nature is its instability. Some individuals will not freely bind themselves to the unwritten natural law and will try, by fraud or force, to take the lives and property of others. Civil government comes into existence for Locke as for Hobbes through a covenant, or social contract, in which people invest a king or a parliament with legislative, judicial, and executive power for the sake of the advantages of peace. As in Hobbes, therefore, the state arises not upon the natural condition of humankind—our social nature, as in Aristotle—or the decree of God, but as the result of a modern economic invention applied to politics, the contract.

PROPERTY RIGHTS: Both Hobbes and Locke agree that one of the functions of government is to defend the rights of property of its citizens. The notion of property rights naturally requires some analysis and defense. What if a person did not acquire his property legitimately? What if a person uses his property to harm other persons, for example, by using his ownership of a factory to employ workers at very low salary? What, theoretically, *entitles* a person to the use of his property? However, Locke's theory of how property is acquired is interesting: He says that when a person uses his own labor to make something out of what was originally communal property, he lays claim to it. For example, if a person settles on unclaimed land, builds a house and barn, and begins to cultivate as much of the surrounding land as he can, then he is entitled to that land in perpetuity, that is, he can bequeath it to his children.

John Locke. © *Thoemmes.*

A central purpose of social and political philosophy in Locke is an analysis of justice, and, by extension, of the legitimacy of a government's claims to enforce justice against the will of those individuals it indicts as criminals. The notion of a social contract offers an account of justice: justice is manifest in the will of the persons who made themselves citizens of a commonwealth by the social contract. As a child reaches maturity, he or she implicitly adds his or her name to the contract by remaining in the commonwealth and is obligated to observe its terms, and assent to whatever the sovereign power decrees, as long as it holds power in fact. Yet Locke thought that assent need not be absolute. There is a standard of justice external to the state that can be used to measure the justice of its laws.

Locke believed, against Hobbes, that we have objective knowledge of natural moral laws that are external to the state and the covenant. He also denied Hobbes's dictum that sovereignty must not be divided. In Locke's view, the state has three organs, each with its own function: the legislative, which has the task in specific circumstances of enacting laws that reflect the natural moral law; the executive; and a third organ that is concerned with making war. Further, he appears to have believed that people make not one but two covenants. The first is the covenant in which individuals agree to sacrifice some of their natural liberties and enter a commonwealth under natural moral law. The second is where the members of the commonwealth agree to form a government to rule over them. This separation allows Locke to maintain that when the members of the commonwealth agree to overthrow the government that exists by their consent, they can do so without overthrowing civil society itself. If the governing body or sovereign having authority does not enforce laws according to natural law, a majority of the people may then legitimately dissolve the government. Locke would have taken quite seriously the American colonists' claim to a right to rebel against George III, and his doctrine inspired the reference in the Declaration of Independence to "inalienable" rights; that is, rights that cannot be taken from individuals by the command of the sovereign without his forfeiting his legal and moral authority. He does not take rebellion lightly, however. He no doubt also inspired this passage in Paragraph Two of the Declaration: "Prudence, indeed, will dictate that governments long established should not be changed for light and transient causes; and accordingly all experience hath shown, that mankind are more disposed to suffer, while evils are sufferable, than to right themselves by abolishing the forms [of government] to which they are accustomed."

No doubt, for Locke, the legislature is the highest power in the commonwealth. It makes or promulgates the laws. Yet Locke was perhaps the first to see the validity of an idea that was developed at length by the French political philosopher Montesquieu (1689–1755), and which is assumed in most democracies today, that of the separation and balance of governmental powers. In America, the Congress (legislature), President (executive), and the Supreme Court (judiciary) are each assigned "sovereignlike" powers in their own domains. The hope is to prevent any one power (the king or the president, especially) from taking all power in its hands and ruling from a position above the law. All three of these points—the subjection of the sovereign to the natural law, the two-covenants theory, and the division of powers—are intended to establish limited, not absolute, government among humankind.

Locke's view of human nature was far more positive and optimistic than that of his great predecessor in social contract theory. People are not innately inclined to war, or motivated by egocentric passion limited only by prudence. People possess a genuine love of their fellows. Perhaps such a view could easily be entertained during the period in which Locke published (under a pseudonym) the *Two Treatises on Civil Government*. The long years of civil war in England seemed to have passed, religious ardor had cooled somewhat, and Englishmen could look forward to the cultivation of the arts of peace. Even more, the influence of modern science had undermined the religious certainty that so often inspires fanaticism. People were coming to realize that a claim to truth must be supported by evidence of reason and experience that is unavailable for religious doctrines. Although a Christian, Locke was nevertheless one of the first to attempt to formulate a kind of stripped-down view of Christianity, which has come to be know as **Deism**. He asserted the existence of God as creator of the world, who is the proper object of worship by communities of believers who should be free to worship God according to their conscience. Such worship is the condition of salvation, and also a condition of a firm moral attitude. Locke claimed that atheism should be illegal, as atheists lack an important motive for doing good and obeying the law, namely the fear of hell.

DEISM: Although in Locke's day, and for long afterwards, the methods and the success of science were making a belief in the historical correctness of Biblical teachings difficult for most educated people, few wished to abandon Christianity entirely. Many men and women who lived during the Enlightenment became deists, in many cases through the influence of Locke's essay, *On the Reasonableness of Christianity.* Some deists believed God to be like a cosmic clockmaker, who created the great mechanism of the world and then set it running by itself. Such a God is not concerned with the everyday affairs of people; the mechanism God created runs by itself without constant divine interference. This view provided people with what seems to be an explanation for the world's existence. "If God did not exist, we would have to invent him," wrote Voltaire, for otherwise we could not explain where the world came from, how life came to be, and what the purpose of existence is. At the same time, Deism achieves this explanatory power without speculating upon God's motives, worrying about the details of Scripture, or what he may desire people to do. It is a reasonable religious belief, one that encourages tolerance of persons of other faiths. A noted deist in America was its third president, Thomas Jefferson.

But there is a further cause of Locke's confidence in the success of limited sovereignty than his optimistic belief in human benevolence and goodness. People are *reasonable,* in his view, and can be trusted to judge the quality of government they are receiving. In the affairs of humankind, the interpretation of the natural moral law and its application to specific conflicts is quite difficult and uncertain. Yet Locke places the ability and the right not only to create the commonwealth, but to judge the morality of laws and policies in the *people,* and not simply in the persons of philosophers and lawmakers and judges. This measure of confidence in the intelligence of the people and the value of individual autonomy had enormous consequences for the centuries ahead. It led, among other things, to the beliefs in the rights of individuals enshrined in the American Bill of Rights, and similar documents in other countries. These beliefs in the people and in the benefits of freedom were developed by another philosopher of the early modern period, Jean-Jacques Rousseau (1712–1778). He too placed the origin of law and government not in the will of God or the will of the sovereign, but in the will of the people.

Jean-Jacques Rousseau

Rousseau heralded the beginning of the Romantic Age in Europe. Like most romantics, he valued feeling, spirit, and the adventure of freedom more than reason, scientific naturalism, and a stifling conformity. His deepest concern was to find a way of justifying the existence of civil society, which necessarily limited the very freedom that he looked upon as the greatest human good. He tells us in his *Confessions* that he came upon his core political and social ideas while on a walk to visit a friend near Paris. These convictions took shape in the *Discourse on the Sciences and the Arts* (1755), the *Discourse upon the Origin and the Foundation of Inequality among Men* (1758), and the *Social Contract* (1762). These three works are, however, quite different in the picture they give us of the individual and the citizen. The two earlier works offer a trenchant criticism of the society of his day. The later work attempts to devise the principles of an ideal and uncorrupted civil society. In effect, the earlier books diagnose the problem of contemporary civilization, and the later book attempts to find the means to cure it.

JEAN-JACQUES ROUSSEAU: Rousseau was born in Geneva, Switzerland, in 1712. His *Confessions* give us, he says, an unembellished portrait of a poor young man's early travels and loves, and his later conflicts with the intellectuals of his day. He describes his life as thriving under the patronage of Madame Louise de Warens, his break with her, his earliest success in French letters and music, and his receipt of a prestigious award from the Academy of Dijon in 1750. He was a friend of some of the other noted thinkers of the day, such as Denis Diderot, who gave him work writing articles for his *Encyclopedia,* yet many of these friendships ended with bitter quarrels, such as those with Voltaire and David Hume. Deciding to leave France, he moved first to Prussia and then to England, finally returning to France in 1768 under an assumed name. Rousseau died in France in 1778.

The State of Nature

Rousseau's picture in the *Discourses* of the moral character of human beings, as it exists in society and even as it may have been in a state of nature, is somewhat negative, although not as negative as that of Hobbes. People are brutish and instinctive, but they possess compassion for others and are not rapacious. Natural man lives outside of morality and the law, but he is not immoral or criminal by our civilized standards. People are initially good but are corrupted by civilization, which creates artificial barriers to our natural liberty, and by civilized religion, which stigmatizes as sinful the truant, but still benevolent, natural desires of human beings. The state of nature is not described by Rousseau in any detail. However, in his novel in the form of letters, *Julie, ou La Nouvelle Héloïse,* Rousseau paints a charming picture of people who are no longer isolated individuals living a in a natural but barbarous state, but living in a kind of intermediary position between primitivism and a corrupt civilization. These people, who inhabit an Alpine region not far from Rousseau's native Geneva, live with a simplicity and peaceful tranquility that express themselves even in their treatment of outsiders. The translation is by Philip Seward and Jean Vaché.

When I would arrive in the evening in a hamlet, everyone would come so eagerly to invite me to his house that it was very hard to choose, and whoever received the

Jean-Jacques Rousseau. © *National Library of Medicine.*

preference seemed so pleased by it that the first time I mistook such eagerness for cupidity. But I was quite astonished when . . . The next day [my host] refused my money. . . . Their disinterest was so complete that in the whole journey I never managed to [spend money]. Indeed how can money be spent in a country where masters are not paid for their expenses, or domestics for their work, and where no beggar is to be found. Yet money is quite rare in the upper Valais, and it is for that reason that the inhabitants are well off: for foodstuffs are plentiful without the slightest trade to the outside, without luxury consumption within. . . . If ever they have more money, they will infallibly be the poorer. They have the wisdom to sense this . . .

These qualities of kindness, naturalness, freedom, and spontaneity give great scope to these people's innate individualism, while at the same time they allow for the achievement of the moral and spiritual benefits of membership in a community with others. How can we be bound in a contract with others, and yet be free, even more free, than when we bound ourselves? That is Rousseau's fundamental question.

The General Will

By the assent of each person to a social contract, Rousseau believes, people went from a life of isolation as separate individuals to a life as a member in a kind of corporation. A corporation, even a business corporation, brings something new into the world, something with a life of its own beyond the individuals who make it up. This thing created by the social contract is not a government, but civil society. It does not even create a sovereign body, as in Hobbes and Locke; rather the people in assembly alone are sovereign. The socialized person, for Rousseau, is a new kind of person, different from the instinctive person of nature. In civil society, a person's identity as a citizen of a society cannot be imagined apart from solidarity with one's fellows. One's will and one's conscience are inseparable parts of the whole.

Crucial to Rousseau's picture of this sovereign assembly of the people is the concept for which he is celebrated, that of the *volonté générale,* the general will. The social contract creates a superindividual moral will, the general will of the persons who bind themselves by the contract. This superindividual wills the good of the entire society, that is, it wills the highest degree of personal liberty consistent with the social good. This is not to argue that the de facto laws of a society, or the decisions of a tribunal, cannot be criticized by the citizens. They can, but only on the basis of an argument that the laws or decisions are *not* the expression of the general will. The general will is not to be identified with the will of the majority, because the majority, in most societies, is tainted with partial ends and unenlightened passions. Individuals, too, may be slaves to their passions, and partial to their own goods, and not see the higher good that is expressed in the general will. The general will, when it is the product of enlightened individuals in a society where all persons have impartial allegiance to the society they have created, is infallible as a guide to the public good and to the making of social and political policy. Justice is embodied in the laws that correspond not to any external natural or divine law, but to the general will. Government becomes necessary when a civil society is so large that its problems cannot be addressed by a meeting of all the subjects, or by a referendum. Individuals are then deputized by the people to make and execute the laws in their name as the sovereign general will. Some deputies, more than others, will be able to give expression to the general will and make the citizens aware of what they sense to be in their common and individual interest without themselves being able to formulate it.

Even in this brief sketch of Rousseau's philosophy of society, large tensions and ambiguities can be noted. He insists as much as any thinker ever has upon the rights and the freedom of the individual, and yet he has created a political context in which the individual is in danger of being submerged in the general will—or, perhaps, of emerging unexpectedly as something vastly different from the picture of the individual as the atomic, instinctual, natural individual that we encounter in Rousseau's description of the state of nature. As a result of this uncertainty, great disagreement has arisen among scholars as to what his position implies regarding several urgent issues. We can identify those issues under the following headings. First, what is the relationship between a human being in the state of nature and that same person in a society established under the social contract? Second, how do we distinguish, in the established society, between the will of the majority of its members and the general will itself? Third, how do we justify constraining the freedom of individuals (which Rousseau admits will be necessary) in the established society? Fourth, what limitation, if any, is placed upon the power of the people's deputies to conduct the affairs of government?

The Individual and Society

Rousseau is often credited with having been the first to develop what came to be called the "organic theory of the state." The metaphor *organic* suggests that the state, like the body of a living organism, is more than the sum of the parts that make it up. The human arm, for example, would be useless without the rest of its body; it could neither function nor live as an arm without the other parts, and the other parts would be lacking without the arm. The organization of the parts brings something into existence beyond the collection of parts, namely the living organism. Similarly, when people come together to form a society by entering into a social contract, a new moral spirit and will among the participants come into existence. The individual becomes part of something greater than himself, the general will. He senses that it expresses his own conscience, and even his deepest sense of what is fitting and right. The general will is an objective reality that makes it possible for the individual to become a social being.

In this way, Rousseau dissolves the separation of the individual from the state and embraces the individual in something that he himself has created for the sake of the benefits of civilization, fellowship, and liberty under law. Civil society alone can develop the natural sympathy among persons that Rousseau believed to be native to humankind. His use of the notion of *solidarity* among nations and groups, so important to many intellectuals in the twentieth century, reminds us of the threat to our social natures by reducing society to its legal and contractual components, and thinking of them as external and foreign to the citizen. Yet Rousseau's ideas also contain the seeds of totalitarianism. The nineteenth and twentieth centuries give us many examples of human beings swept up enthusiastically in the general will, and led to disaster by charismatic figures that pretend to give voice to the general will. These mass movements were very romantic in their inspiration, however dangerous they also were, and Rousseau must be considered part of their philosophical pedigree. He was a Romantic himself and was perhaps too distrustful of reason and too trusting of human feeling and sensibility, and he failed to sense how the individual person may become not only uplifted by, but also submerged in, the general will.

An extreme example of a partial general will—one belonging to a distinct group within the society, rather than the society as a whole—is a lynch mob. Perhaps inflamed by the speech of one of their fellows, the members of the mob lose their individual conscience as they join enthusiastically with the mob in acts of violence and injustice. Later, of course, they may come to regret what they have done, and even wonder how they could have done it. Now Rousseau is very sensitive to the dangers of mob rule. His response to it, however, seems impractical: he will prohibit the formation of private organizations. They, like the mob, may win more allegiance from their members than the society as a whole is able to do. Sovereignty belongs to the people as a whole and ought not to be divided. When a society is divided into competing organized groups, even the laws promulgated by the people as sovereign may be the product of compromise and not represent the general will. A citizen observing the behavior of a lynch mob may therefore justly criticize the actions of the mob because of its motives, if they are partial and not representative of the general will of the entire society. But then is it not at least possible that the general will of a people may function as a lynch mob and try to impose its destiny upon its neighbors? Rousseau's position does not seem to allow for criticism of acts in which an entire society becomes a lynch mob, by reference to some moral law that is higher than the general will. For moral law is brought into existence only by the social contract.

"Forced to Be Free"

In signing the social contract, individuals agree to be bound by the law, that is, to renounce their natural freedom to do just what they want to do. Yet in Rousseau's theory the scope of individual **freedom** is unclear. He is perhaps right in asserting that the mere freedom to follow one's impulses is a form of slavery. He is also perhaps right in declaring that it is difficult in a corrupt society for a person to know what he really wants beyond the objects of his impulses. Yet there seems to be little room in his theory for moral autonomy, for the right to exert one's capacities for framing judgments about right and wrong, about the just and the unjust, and to act according to them even in disagreement with one's fellows. Freedom, it may be asserted against Rousseau, must allow not simply for an individual to come into the possession of his true self by immersion in the will of the whole, but also for him to stand on his own feet intellectually, and to resist the general will on the basis of conscience and reason. In Rousseau's philosophy, the individual self appears so intertwined with the individual created by the general will that it becomes impossible to identify oneself as distinct from one's social self. It may be true that one cannot form a clear picture of oneself apart from one's social existence. But that need not mean that a person cannot be correct in her expression of judgment and will over against the general will. Rousseau says, for a person to obey herself is simply for her to obey the general will. Yet Rousseau's slogan, "forced to be free," serves to describe far too many political policies since the time of Rousseau where men and women were told that their highest happiness consists in conforming to some supposed historical necessity, such as the "manifest destiny" idea in the United States a century ago, or in contributing to the victory of the proletariat, or to the plans of some "glorious leader."

POSITIVE AND NEGATIVE FREEDOM: This is a distinction first observed by Kant. In a celebrated essay, the English social and literary critic Isaiah Berlin (1909–1997) distinguished between them as follows: *Positive* freedom is the freedom to be released from one's "lesser [private] self" and its impulses, and, with the aid of the laws and the state, to grow into the ideal selfhood that is only possible through membership in the society, or the general will. *Negative* freedom is the freedom from compulsion by governmental interference. Negative freedom is freedom *from* (say, coercion), while positive freedom is freedom *to* (become what one really is and desires). Rousseau supports positive freedom as the freedom to realize one's true interests in the general will.

The Political Process

How is the power of the persons whom the sovereign people deputize to run the affairs of government exercised and limited when the entire people are not in session? Rousseau appears to believe that the general will may appear clearly in the words of a gifted individual. This is a new idea in the modern world, and one that was to have a great and infamous history. The right of kings had not been conceived as expressions of the general will. A man anointed king was thought to be the legitimate ruler by the will of God, or by virtue of his conquest of the land, or of his being the successor of the previous legitimate king. Dictators and tyrants in the ancient world might occasionally have been glorified as great leaders by the people because of their seeming superhuman qualities as leaders, especially in war—Julius Caesar was such a person—but they were surely not perceived as the embodiment of the general will. Now if, as Rousseau says, the general will is infallible, and if those who express that will are the deputies of the people, then, without an external standard to limit the power of the people's deputies, a charismatic leader might justify the measures he takes as the infallible expressions of the general will, and make his embodiment of that will the object of a civil religion. When a politician wraps himself in the flag, he pretends to embody the will of the people as symbolized by the flag of the nation. Men such as Hitler and Stalin claimed to embody the general will, although they called it by other names: the "destiny" of the German people in Hitler's case, the "wave of the future that is communism," in Stalin's case. They created a state religion in which the individual came to his or her "true self" by discovering themselves in the symbols of the state.

No doubt this is a very negative reading of Rousseau, for his intentions were never to submerge individual freedom in any form of state totalitarianism. But then no social theoretician would want Nazism or Soviet Communism as an outcome of their thought. Philosophy must question what the theory allows, not what its author wants or hopes for. Rousseau simply could not imagine a natural law that exists apart from the social contract, and he could not imagine a citizen who exists as an individual apart from the society that he creates as a citizen when he signs the social contract. The idea is encountered in Hegel that concepts do not exist in isolation from each other, and the concept of an isolated human being surely implies as its antithesis the collectivity of humankind of which he is a part. When the isolated human being reappears as a citizen of the state, he is, like the state itself, something new, something that did not exist before the social contract was signed, and he can no longer be thought of in isolation. Hegel read Rousseau very carefully, and his own social philosophy bears Rousseau's imprint, although applied to the Prussian state of which Hegel was a citizen. Hegel was a great influence upon Karl Marx, whose social philosophy became, in the twentieth century, an ideology that came to power as the Soviet and Communist Chinese states.

THE NINETEENTH CENTURY: RADICALISM AND LIBERALISM

Karl Marx

Born in 1818, **Karl Marx** was seventeen when Hegel died in 1831 at the height of his influence. And Marx, growing up intellectually in the ferment of ideas that Hegel left to posterity, slowly fought himself free of Hegel's influence. He established a new and radical way of conceiving of the individual and the state, and a new concept of justice as a means of criticizing established societies.

KARL MARX: Marx was born in Trier, Germany, in 1918, of Jewish ancestry. Educated at the University of Bonn in the Rhineland, he was known for his volatile temperament and for the force with which he would debate issues with others. His friendship with Friedrich Engels (1820–1895), the son of a wealthy industrialist whom he met in Paris in 1844, was expressed in the many books published under both their names. Their *Manifesto of the Communist Party* appeared in 1848, a year of revolutionary uprisings across Europe. Marx survived as a journalist and took personal part in the developments of the revolutionary Communist League and later in the First International Working Men's Association. Forced into exile by the German authorities as the editor of the radical *Rheinische Zeitung,* Marx settled first in Paris, then in Brussels, and finally in London. At the British Museum, Marx did the research that was to result in his greatest contribution to economics, *Das Kapital.* He died in London in 1883.

The first challenge by Marx of Hegel and Rousseau was directed at the organic theory of the state. Unlike Rousseau, Hegel had included corporations and other private organizations in his picture of civil society. The individual exists both within the natural relationships of the family, and also within the family's antithesis, the objective external contractual relationships typical of civil society. Both are taken up in the state as the objective expression of the rational will of the individuals that produce it. In the state, the individual remains a particular person while existing in and through its institutions and its spirit. The individual understands herself as a part of the state, and is elevated above herself by it, even while she reflects upon her particular fate as a part of both natural and contractual communities.

Karl Marx. © *Perry-Castañeda Library.*

Marx's response to this organic picture of the individual and the state is to cut right through it. The individual person does not "come to himself" in solidarity with others in the state, he is *alienated from it*. This term has a long history. It suggests that a person or group may feel separated from some aspect of the world instead of feeling at home. Thus a man may be alienated from God, or a teenager can feel alienated from her parents. Something is separating them from a proper relationship, the first person by sin, perhaps, or a sense that God has abandoned him; the second by the need to establish a selfhood separate from her parents. For Marx, the state is the external bureaucratic mechanism, equipped with power and the threat of force, which exploits and alienates the individual worker and his natural needs and desires. Far from there being a social contract to which all members of the state are parties and to which they give their free consent, the laws and the state are the products of a small group of people interested in controlling and reducing to the level of commodities the lives and fortunes of the many.

This claim that the individual is alienated from the state, as it existed in Marx's time, first requires a theoretical treatment and justification. Second, Marx must identify the nature of the conflict, or class struggle, in civil society between those who utilize the state for their own ends, and those who are its alienated victims. Third, he must provide a new view of history that incorporates the dynamism of this conflict between the state and its victims, for history, Marx believed, is driven by this conflict, and it aims at a new form of justice in a new form of civil society.

Alienation

In a collection of essays published only long after Marx's death, the *Economic and Political Manuscripts of 1844,* young Karl Marx justified his opposition to the political realities of his day by arguing that the workers under capitalism are alienated in several ways from the world around them. Marx's analysis makes clear why he believed that happiness or a feeling of being at home in civil society was impossible for the working class.

First, the workers are alienated from their *work.* In a capitalist factory system, a worker is given his work, he does not select the work he is to do. Consequently, the worker cannot express his personality in his work, for he is simply doing what others tell him to do, and not what he would choose to do if given the opportunity. Contrast the workers' lot with that of the artist; the artist selects his medium, develops his own style, expresses the necessities of his own nature, and is completely absorbed by the process of creation.

Second, the worker is alienated from the *product* of his labor. This is not only because, in many cases, the worker cannot afford to buy what he has produced; an artist, too, may be unable or unwilling to pay the market value for one of his own works. Rather, the worker has to look upon the product of his labor as his enemy, even though he produced it by his own hands, for the product is owned by the capitalist. The capitalist has provided the worker with the raw materials, the workplace, and its tools, and given him a salary. The factory owner sells these products to the highest bidder. Some of the money he recovers goes into the upkeep and overhead of the factory, the purchase of the raw materials, the salaries of the laborers, and his own maintenance. But some of the money is reinvested. If he is successful, the capitalist becomes richer relative to the worker and, through his riches, becomes more powerful socially and politically. Meanwhile, the worker remains at a subsistence level. So when the worker looks at what he has produced—a pair of shoes, perhaps—he sees an item that is being used against him, used to assure his continued impoverishment, while his employer becomes, by means of these items, better able to exploit him.

Third, the worker is alienated from his *fellow workers.* In a capitalist economy, there must always be a pool of unemployed workers from which the capitalist can draw his workforce. The worker is thus faced with insecurity: he can be replaced. His fellow workers are therefore his competitors for work, salary, and survival. If one worker thought aloud of rebellion, his unemployed fellows could betray him for the sake of taking over his job. No one is safe in such a system, and no one can be trusted. Marx apparently believed that the workers would never be able to rebel against their bosses on their own; they would have to depend upon disaffected capitalists who were ruined in the struggle for profit. They would bring their resentment, their knowledge, and their intellectual skills to the revolution.

What a sad picture! Precisely at those points at which a person should feel unalienated and fulfilled in his life—his work, his products, his fellows—the worker is forced to feel separated, an outcast, as it were, from the way things ought to be. Marx's simple but powerful analysis of the underlying structures of his state and society makes a mockery of Rousseau's romantic notion that the people are sovereign and are brought to their own true self by participation in the social contract and the general will it creates. Moreover, Marx wishes to show that alienation is not simply a perversion of the capitalist market economy, or a transitory phase that can be overcome by political action. Alienation exists necessarily at the core of capitalism itself, in the very consciousness of the workers who are exploited by a system concerned only for profit, and not at all for humankind. This analysis, for Marx and his followers, justifies the attempt to overthrow the state.

The Class Struggle

In the *Communist Manifesto,* which Marx produced in 1848 with his friend, Friedrich Engels, the history of the world is presented as a history of class struggle. This struggle is illustrated by the conflict, up to then suppressed by the ruling class, between the owners of capital and the propertyless masses of people, called the proletariat. Class struggle took place also between patricians and plebeians in ancient Rome, between the feudal barons and the serfs in the Middle Ages, and between the bourgeoisie—the city-dwelling merchants and property-owners—and the king and his aristocrats that culminated in the French Revolution and the victory of the bourgeoisie. One form of life gives way to another as the means of production are altered by economic and technological factors. In a book with the interesting title, *The Poverty of Philosophy,* Marx wrote: "The hand-mill gives you society with the feudal lord; the steam-mill, society with the industrial capitalist." Hegel had shown that the dialectical progression of ideas in history, the coming-to-be of the absolute idea in nature and in humankind, is no accident, but a necessary unfolding of the Absolute Idea. Marx "stood Hegel on his head," and substituted for the Absolute Idea what he considered to be the material conditions of human history, the productivity of the essentials of life in an economic system. It is not reason that expresses itself in human history, it is humankind's struggle for food and power; the world is not determined by ideas, but by economics.

Marx argued accordingly that civil society is erected upon an economic base. As changes in the economic base occur, corresponding changes in the superstructure take place. Civil society consists first of a political structure, the government, and second of the legal system. Actions of the government do not affect economic policies, rather the acts of the government and its courts certify economic realities. The dominant economic class expresses its interests in government and law; these exist only in order to carry out policies on its behalf. The educational structure, even the art, culture, and religion of an age, reflect the interests of the economic leaders. At his most extreme, Marx insists that the very consciousness of an age expresses the economic balance of power, and if revolutionary ideas should arise in the minds of any of the people, these ideas would necessarily reflect the growing interests of an economically deprived class that is seeking inroads to power. Philosophy, in Marx's view, is a tool in the class struggle; philosophical theories justify the power, or the grasping for power, of the parties to the class struggle. Philosophy is not autonomous; it cannot conjure new ideas out of the ground; new ideas are the effects, not the causes, of the class struggle.

Business Cycles and Their Outcomes

The greatest contribution of Marx to economics is his theory of business cycles, published in *Das Kapital.* Tied by Engels to Marx's theory of history as the history of economic struggle, it was a crucial element in what would later be called *dialectical materialism,* the state philosophy in the Soviet Union under Stalin. Dialectical materialism predicts the fall of the capitalist class, and its replacement by a workers' state in which there would be no class distinctions at all. This prediction is based upon the inherent instability of capitalism. A market economy, Marx argued, is always subject to cycles of boom and recession. A perceived increase in the effective demand for commodities results in increased use of labor, increased factory output, and a general rise in the economy's total wealth. However, the boom cannot continue. Overproduction occurs, commodities find no takers, and the capitalist producers are unable to pay their bills. Some go bankrupt, there is widespread unemployment, and production slows down. Of course, some capitalists survive the downturn, and those that do are able buy up the businesses of their failed colleagues, who fall into the working classes. Eventually, effective demand rises, and the process begins all over—but this time capital is concentrated in the hands of fewer people, among those owners who survived the downturn. Since nothing can be done to alter this process, Marx believed, eventually all the capital in a given economy will be concentrated in the hands of a small group of the super-rich. They will find themselves confronted by a great mass of impoverished workers. Under such circumstances, the power of the state would fall out of the hands of the capitalists; the workers would rebel, sweep away this system, and establish a dictatorship of the proletariat. No class distinctions and no class struggle will exist in such a society, since only one class, the proletariat, will rule. In the final classless society, the state apparatus itself will "wither away," because governmental authority is needed only to secure the privileges of the economically dominant class.

Marx was always impatient with what he considered to be the abstract questions of philosophy, as can be seen in one of his *Theses on **Feuerbach***: "The philosophers have only interpreted the world . . . the point, however, is to change it." In this might be seen an unwillingness to struggle intellectually with the concept of justice, and, in a certain sense, he does not. His concern was with the origins of what he considered to be the obvious injustice around him, the legal, political, and economic exploitation of the workers. He provides us with a method of uncovering this exploitation, which he utilized in the analysis of alienation. Marx does not proceed by developing an ideal concept of justice and the state, as, say, Plato and Rousseau both do each in their own ways, or by examining the conditions of justified rebellion against the state, as Locke does. The workers need liberation, not legal justice, which is impossible in a state dominated by the capitalists; they need economic revolution, not political rebellion, for the source of their misery is the unjust distribution of capital, not political power itself, which merely reflects the interests of the ruling class.

LUDWIG FEUERBACH (1804–1872): Feuerbach was a student of Hegel. His break with Hegel's idealism was a momentous event in German philosophy. Against most German thinkers of his time, he insisted upon the material basis of human wants and needs. In his *Essence of Christianity* he argued that the image of God in Christianity is an ideal image of man himself, and that by worshiping God we were worshiping our own deeper nature. In a famous aphorism, *"Man ist was man ißt"* (One is what one eats; the "ist" and "ißt" are pronounced the same), he suggested that human consciousness is influenced by the way our material needs are satisfied. Such beliefs mark a turn from the ideals of the Romantic Age, and toward the political and social philosophies of the age of revolutions, national movements, and social experiments that were to follow.

The Workers' Paradise

Marxist social criticism proceeds by analyzing the material structures internal to an economic system. It shows how the economic structure shapes the values, the practices, and the consciousness of the people who live within it. It explores how those with economic power wield their power; how they are yoked to, while struggling against, other capitalists; and how they are able to manipulate the masses to achieve their own ends. When these raw features of capitalism become apparent, the working classes can easily be brought to see that their only hope is revolution. "Working men of all nations unite," say Marx and Engels at the end of the *Manifesto,* "you have nothing to lose but your chains."

The *Manifesto* asserts a vague ideal of just social organization as the guiding principle of the workers' struggles: "We will write on our banners, 'To each according to his needs; from each according to his abilities.'" After the revolution, everyone will receive the same share of the benefits and burdens of life—that is, everyone will be economically equal—except where some members of the society require additional things in order to do the work they have been assigned. The ditch digger will be given his pick, while the engineer will be given her workshop and the means of transportation she needs in order to get to the places where she is supervising the workers. Marx also wished, at least in the early *Manuscript,* to cut back as much as possible the "sphere of work from necessity," that is, the number of hours a worker must contribute to the common social needs in the course of a day. The less people have to work in order to live, the freer they are, and, for Marx and Engels, freedom from work is a great value. Perhaps they remembered a wonderful saying of the Roman orator Cicero: "The very fact a man has to work for a wage is a measure of his slavery."

Marx never developed a clear picture of the future workers' state. He writes tantalizingly on this topic in *The German Ideology* that life there will be like work in the artists' colony mentioned earlier: a person will work in the fields in the morning, go hunting in the afternoon, and write critical articles for the newspapers in the evening. He does not address the obvious problem of limiting the power of the workers' deputies in such a state, thus risking dictatorship. Many of the bourgeoisie in Marx's day were haunted by the specter of communism, not simply out of fear of losing their privileges to the workers, but also because of a commitment to democratic rule. A politics that attempts to improve the plight of the working class should require that social justice be done without "forcing men to be free," in a system that permits the real freedom of the citizens to pursue their own ends without paternalistic interference by the government. Such a political theory is at the foundation of what today is called liberalism. Its great nineteenth-century theorist and approximate contemporary of Marx was the Englishman, John Stuart Mill.

John Stuart Mill

John Stuart Mill was a utilitarian moral philosopher who wrote extensively on contemporary social, political, and economic matters, and he was active in liberal causes such as women's suffrage, birth control, and social programs for the working classes. He was elected to Parliament, and served as a member from 1865 until 1868. His great work on social theory, *On Liberty,* appeared in 1859.

The Concept of Liberty

For Mill, social justice requires the greatest extent of personal freedom that is compatible with the greatest good of the greatest number of people. He formulated a principle that has been the guiding notion of liberal democracy ever since: Each person should be permitted, by law and by social forbearance, to do whatever he pleases as long as his exercise of freedom does not interfere with other persons doing whatever it pleases them to do. The concern for social forbearance, or tolerance, shows Mill's love of individual freedom and his opposition to what he called the "tyranny of the majority." His mentor, Jeremy Bentham, had pointed out that personal freedom is not limited only by the laws. Laws sanction many forms of behavior; we cannot steal or commit fraud without the threat of arrest. But the opinion of others may also sanction activities which, while legal and harmless, are outside of the social norm. The sanctions of public opinion are directed at private vices, like adultery, fornication, or immoderate drink. People who do those things have to fear not only public condemnation, but public ridicule. No doubt, such sanctions may be justified if the behavior in question is really loathsome. However, condemnation and ridicule may also be directed at the lonely genius, great visionary, or noble dreamer whose eventual contributions may benefit the entire society. Mill therefore argues for greater *negative freedom.*

Society should decriminalize what we call today "crimes without victims," such as pornography or sexual license; it should teach the toleration of nonconformists, foster the participation of women in civil society, and limit the power of government over the private affairs of its citizens. The importance of education in the development of a truly liberal society is emphasized in *On Liberty*. Indeed, one of the few places where Mill was willing to limit the freedom of men as the heads of families was his requirement that all persons be forced to educate their children. His efforts to develop public education in England for members of the working classes and his leadership in the creation of the founders of the University of London were in keeping with his liberal vision.

Mill's notion of justice is not founded upon a divine or natural moral law. It arises instead from public utility, or expediency. Laws are justified only insofar as they serve the public good. But there is more to moral judgment than the mere calculation of expediency, as with Bentham's hedonic calculus. Mill had a very positive view of human nature, and he believed that the sentiment of justice—and the repugnance most people feel at the sight of social or personal injustice—is widespread. People are inclined to act for the greatest good for the greatest number, and desire to live in a society under law that permits the greatest possible freedom for individuals that is compatible with the greatest material good for the citizenry. There is thus a concrete and objective human need for justice that derives from the permanent interests of humankind. And it is upon this practical basis that our laws and any political agitation for changing them must be justified.

The expedient satisfaction of permanent needs may at first sight seem as vague a concept as that of justice itself. Mill recognizes that what may be expedient at one time and place may not be at another. His point is rather to show that arguments about justice and injustice are, in the end, arguments about utility and disutility and not about divine ordinances or intuitive principles or purported social contracts. Mill means to foster laws and policies that can be shown to be in the collective interest of persons affected by some policy or law. Presumably, there will be a consensus about the content of those interests among the persons affected by public policy. The establishment of such a consensus about the larger interests of the community is the purpose of the political process and should result in laws and policies that further those interests. The universal interest of humankind is, of course, to be happy, but unlike Bentham, Mill does not identify pleasure as the sole constituent of happiness. He once wrote in his diary:

> The only true or definite rule of conduct or standard of morality is the greatest happiness, but there is needed first a philosophical estimate of happiness. Quality as well as quantity of happiness is to be considered; less of a higher kind is preferable to more of a lower. The test of quality is the preference given by those who are acquainted with both. Socrates would rather choose to be Socrates dissatisfied than to be a pig satisfied. The pig probably would not, but then the pig knows only one side of the question; Socrates knows both.

Just laws do not further all pleasures equally but rather favor those pleasures constitutive of a happiness appropriate to a human being. Enlightened discussion among equal parties will again permit a consensus concerning the Good Life and the fostering of conditions that make a better life possible for everyone.

Justice and Distribution

Mill is offering a theory of *distributive* justice. He believed that justice consists in an expedient distribution of the **benefits and burdens** of civilized existence among the citizenry. Mill attempts to specify what such a just distribution might consist in. He argues that the following elements form the basis of legitimate demands that the individual may make of his society.

BENEFITS AND BURDENS: Utilitarians do not speak of wealth and poverty alone as the benefits and burdens that citizens must enjoy or bear. To borrow a phrase from debates today, they mean to include in the benefits to be distributed among the citizenry primary social goods that are under the control of the state, such as basic liberties, and the means for the pursuit of the good life for oneself, whatever the specific goods one is striving after. Those means include equality of opportunity, health care, meaningful work, and of course, food and shelter. The utilitarian thinker is trying to measure, or to bring under the possibility of measurement, some standard of a full and rewarding life, or well-being.

First, *distribution of needed goods ought to be based upon the value of the contributions made by individuals to society.* Those whose contribution to the well-being of the community is greater than others should receive greater privileges. That utility is the basis of this principle is easy to see. If we distribute all goods equally, there would be a loss of incentive to work harder. If people do not work hard, there will be less social progress. And social progress, it may be assumed, improves the lot of all members of society. However, Mill recognizes a further requirement of justice that would limit this principle.

Second, *the principle of equality conditions distribution.* Each of us is capable of fellow-feeling; we experience it especially toward friends and family. We should direct that feeling at each person, without regard for his wealth, social status, or achievements. True fellow-feeling teaches us that each person has an equal claim to life, liberty, and the pursuit of happiness. Hence, if one is not able to claim special treatment by virtue of one's contributions (Principle 1), distribution must be equal. "Each person," Mill wrote, "maintains that equality is the dictate of justice, except where he thinks expediency requires inequality." Modern utilitarians argue at times that this principle of equality applies without exception to some goods, though not to others. Medical care, for instance, should be distributed equally to all. However, if one person has more money than another (presumably because of a greater social contribution), the former should be free to buy a Rolex rather than a Timex.

Third, *distribution ought to be based on demonstrated need.* The minimal benefits of society that each of us need are, of course, food, clothing, and shelter. When an individual perhaps through no fault of his or her own is unable to provide for those needs, then society or the government ought to provide them. The basis for this principle is not any abstract moral law, but the concrete social utility that follows from not having people at the outer limits of starvation or other dire need. People do not live by bread alone but need the spiritual goods of freedom, dignity, and equality of opportunity to be happy. Hence justice requires that these goods, too, be distributed to all members of society as extensively as possible.

Fourth, *distribution ought to be based upon merit.* This is sometimes expressed as the principle of *desert.* It says that a person may lay claim to more goods than others because he or she deserves more. This principle is familiar to all of us today. We usually do not dispute the granting of a scholarship to a fellow student if we think that he did better on the scholarship examination than we did. On the contrary, we feel that it would be unjust because it is inexpedient to distribute a limited number of available benefits to persons who had not demonstrated the ability to make good use of them. We tend also to believe that a person who has done harm deserves the penalty that he receives. This sentiment is again justified by the social utility that will most likely result from the deterrence of other criminals that incarceration will produce. The sentiment of approval that we feel for someone who gets his just deserts tends itself to be highly useful.

SOCIAL AND POLITICAL PHILOSOPHY IN THE TWENTIETH CENTURY

Critical Theory

In the period after the First World War, some radical philosophers on the European continent who were not committed to the orthodox Marxism preached by the Soviet Union developed a social philosophy that came to be known as Critical Theory. The term was devised by Max Horkheimer (1895–1973) of the Institute for Social Research in Frankfurt; its members came to be known as the Frankfurt School. A remarkable group of philosophers and social critics assembled there during the Weimar Republic. They included such men as Ernst Bloch (1885–1977), Walter Benjamin (1892–1940), and Theodor Adorno (1903–1969). Forced after 1933 by the Nazis into exile or death (Benjamin committed suicide when he was about to be detained by the Gestapo), some of the Critical Theorists regrouped in Frankfurt after the Second World War, and were later joined by the young philosopher and sociologist Jürgen Habermas (1929–). One man who was briefly a member of the school, Herbert Marcuse (1898–1979), eventually settled in California, where he became a lightning-rod, gathering the energies of rebellious students during the tumultuous 1960s.

Critical Theory has a deep legacy in the philosophy of Karl Marx. Critical Theorists emphasize Marx's early moral stance—his documentation of the injustice done to the working class, and his exposure of how the alienation and exploitation of the workers are inevitable in a capitalist market economy.

They continue his technique of unearthing the tensions and contradictions in the capitalist system, such as Marx's discoveries of the labor theory of value and of business cycles such as the recurrent crises of capitalism. Critical Theorists are less messianic than orthodox Marxists, less confident of their riding the "wave of the future," and more empirical, scientific, and piecemeal in their assessments of the economic and political situation of the day. They tend to reject Marxist dialectical and historical materialism, for they think it led to inflexible dogmatism. They thereby jettison the Hegelian dialectic, and the notions that capitalism was fated to collapse and the workers' state destined to put a final end to class war. They also resist Marx's claims that philosophers simply reflect the interests of the class to which they belong and cannot initiate social and economic change. Whether Marx himself believed that the only justification of a revolutionary idea is that it is fated by economic laws to succeed, that is, to be on the victorious side in the class struggle, is uncertain. Social theory, he thought, is not intended in any case to provide a blueprint for the future revolution: At the end of *Das Kapital,* Marx wrote that he was not writing recipes for the cookbooks of the future.

Critical Theory, in contrast, attempts to reestablish the link between theory and practice. At the time of its inception by Horkheimer, the efforts of the Institute of Social Research were dedicated to the creation of an empirical sociology of capitalist practices that can give substance to the workers' demands for change. It studied the conditions for the self-understanding of revolutionary movements within capitalist states that can enable Critical Theory to escape from the charge that its claim to objective knowledge is undermined by its inherent class-based relativism. It applied social criticism to normative ends by instructing the exploited and alienated victims of capitalism about the forms that exploitation and alienation take within the prevailing social and economic system. In sum, Critical Theory aspired to be *scientific* and base its claims concerning social and economic structures in rigorous empirical evidence; to be *explanatory,* to show how the forms of exploitation and alienation arise; and to be *emancipatory,* in that its normative evaluations and explanations of the means of oppression serve the ends of radical social change.

The adoption of social science for normative ends was a crucial strategy of Critical Theory. It is an attempt to turn science against the ends posited by modern industrial society, which had appropriated all human reason and science as its own creation and its own method of dominating the world. Knowledge, for Critical Theory, is not power, but the means to liberation from power. But why should anyone take more seriously the Critical Theorist's exercise of rationality in the service of justice and emancipation than that of social criticism from other standpoints, given the relativity of human consciousness to one's class? Critical Theory's response to this question takes several forms. Adorno's response is perhaps especially revealing of the tenor of the early Frankfurt School, and the ideas he represented were to surface in the thought of later radicals.

Theodor Adorno

Adorno distinguishes between critical reason and instrumental or *identitarian* reason. The latter is typical of the uses of reason in the technology-dominated world of late industrial capitalism. It attempts to absorb disparate and individual objects under convenient rubrics for the sake of efficiency, clarity, and practicality. It makes no effort to understand itself but organizes means for the sake of ends that are thought to be self-evident, such as the increase of material wealth and military power. In identifying apparently different things just because they can be made to serve the same ends, identitarian reason misses both the sphere of freedom and the uniqueness of the individual. For freedom arises out of a person's self-awareness of herself and her social and economic condition. By concerning itself only with organizational efficiency, identitarian reason does not expose itself to the contingency and specificity of human existence. Marxism itself was threatened by this kind of identitarianism, for it attempted a global diagnosis of history, economics, and politics, much as Hegel demanded a totalizing theory of the world. Such totalizing forces the theorist to round off ends that do not quite fit into his theoretical picture. It is a rational system in a world whose diversity and particularity eludes summation as a system.

Critical reason places itself in the flow of events. Its analyses of specific forms of capitalist practices make visible the individuality that is hidden under general categories, and it diagnoses the conditions that distort, impoverish, and emmiserate the concrete life that takes place under those categories. This "new form of cognition," as it was called by Horkheimer, refuses to agree to the separation of the individual from his civil society in the name of technical efficiency. Adorno's general name for his procedure, which he developed through his entire life, was *negative dialectics*. Unlike the dialectical idealism of Hegel or the dialectical materialism of the communists, Adorno refuses to absorb contradictions in a higher synthesis, for that would precisely close the door to the individual and the specific that appears at both poles of the contradiction. We must instead keep open the contradictions in things and be willing to swing back and forth between them. Similar to the American philosophy of pragmatism, critical theory opens itself to the world in an experimental way, insisting always on the practical value of philosophy as critical reason in the effort to liberate humankind from oppression.

Naturally, the Second World War and the cold war between the United States and the Soviet Union that followed it challenged the implicit hopefulness of Critical Theory. The world appeared to have lapsed either into barbarism, or into the managed control of citizens enjoying a comfortable unfreedom from which there was no escape. Adorno, who had always believed in the redemptive power of aesthetic experience, wrote many fine, if difficult and often obscure, essays on music and literature, in whose creations may be found an irreducible individualism and an effort to transcend the very historical conditions that make them possible. Emancipation is still possible, for nothing is fixed or absolute, and even economic realities are not determined by immutable laws, as Marx believed. Critical Theory must still assess the available means for producing a

structural change in the institutions of civil society in the direction of emancipation from oppression and unnecessary toil.

Jürgen Habermas

Habermas's massive contributions to Critical Theory address these last
issues. Crucial to his undertaking, and decisive for his break with the older Critical Theorists, is his attempt to reinstate, in a modified form, Enlightenment rationalism. During the Enlightenment, reason was seen as an instrument of truth
rather than as a form of consciousness subject to class bias, or as conditioned by
different socialization processes in different human cultures. It was put in the
service of what were taken to be the universal interests of humankind. Of course,
Habermas agrees, there is an element of interpretation in all efforts to "tell the
story" of how universal human needs and interests have realized themselves in
history, and no doubt the understanding of terms such as *justice* or *legitimacy* or
freedom may be distorted by the political, economic, and historical situation of
the storyteller. But Habermas resists both the movement toward the mere analysis of tensions within capitalism—the "interpretative" or storytelling analysis of
capitalist practices—and the efforts of scientists to subject civil society to an external analysis by the accepted methods of psychology, sociology, economics, or
political science. Rather Habermas wishes to locate Critical Theory within the
capitalist democracies themselves, as did Mill, rather than remaining outside of
them as their critic and naysayer. To achieve this shift in perspective, Habermas
developed two distinct notions, that of *communicative action* and *discourse
ethics*.

Critical Theory, in Habermas's view, has tended to see the individual
person in isolation, rather than as engaged in political discourse with others
about the interests they share and the policies that will further those interests.
The kind of rationality contained in discourse, where it is conducted among
equals under no practical constraints, is different from the kind of rationality that
had been co-opted by industrial capitalism. The capitalist technocrat views reason as involving only means-ends relationships. Any questions that arise within
late industrial capitalism can involve only the application of technical means that
will leave the ends of capitalism—the amassing of wealth and power—intact.
But the kinds of debates that go on in a democratically structured environment
are different, Habermas argues in *The Theory of Communicative Action* (1981).
Here the application of reason is not to means-ends relations, but to a resolution
of problems by appeal to the shared interests and the common modes of rational
evidence. Parliamentary debates are of this kind. We must only remove the conditions of unequal power and ingrained prejudice that Marxists claimed infested
all discourse between members of different economic classes. The relationship
of Critical Theory to democratic practices consists in its fostering of the free
communicative interaction of the parties to the debate and the citizens they represent. The meaning of claims to validity in practical matters consists in the
shape they take in discourse among free and unbiased parties. The institutions of

government must be shaped to the conditions of unbiased communicative approach to political consensus. The theory of education must explore the socialization of individuals so as to make them capable of an undistorted formulation of their needs, and of understanding the needs of others. People must be enlightened so that they possess insight and can accept of reject the policies discussed without coercion. For only when the parties to a parliamentary debate can assume that their fellows are sincere, open-minded, willing to listen, and not biased in their speech by private self-interest can the debaters hope to come to a rational consensus about the truth of their beliefs and the justice of their actions.

A democratic debate must arrive at a consensus about just action. Habermas developed a theory of justice founded upon what he called *discourse ethics.* The notion of justice requires a social context. Some questions of right and wrong, or all questions about what the good life is, may be decided by individuals. But social justice involves discourse among the parties to a debate about the best way to resolve conflicts over their diverse interests. It is always interpersonal, and always conducted in a specific historical context. Habermas's discourse ethics borrows from both American pragmatism and from the moral philosophy of Kant. The references to pragmatism show that Habermas does not believe that the aim of communicative rational discourse aims at an absolute truth. The truth it requires is simply one that rational parties to a dispute can agree to as the best basis for action that conduces to the common good of the group in some situation. The appeal to Kant refers to Habermas's notion that the principles of justice adopted by a state, or by any group of individuals, must be genuinely universal. Those principles must reflect and protect the interests of all parties to the discussion. They must be principles that they can accept as a moral basis for their common action, or, more generally, for their living together. The question of justice must be answered by the parties to a continuing political debate under conditions of undistorted linguistic competence. Critical Theory nevertheless must not abdicate its responsibility for criticizing the institutional arrangements in the existing society that hinder undistorted communication, and for fostering procedures for decision making through which competent and equal citizens can formulate policy and initiate common action.

Recent Social and Political Philosophy in the United States

Philosophers do not normally attempt to provide justifications for partisan politics in their home country. They speculate on the nature of the principles of justice, equality, fair distribution of goods, or the foundations of government itself. However, the theoretical principles they develop may be useful to partisan politicians who are looking for a general justification for the policies their parties support. During most of the twentieth century, Americans have conducted many of their political disputes under the headings of **liberalism** and **conservatism.** These social and political debates have been so intense and so prolonged that we would expect that they would occur also on a philosophical level. American contributions to political and social philosophy were very limited until after the middle twentieth century, but a large amount of work has followed in the wake of two books published in the 1970s: John Rawls's *A Theory of Justice* (1972), and Robert Nozick's *Anarchy, State and Utopia* (1974). Rawls's work gives substance and support to liberal politics, and Nozick's to conservative politics.

LIBERALS AND CONSERVATIVES: *Liberals* tend to give an activist role to government in the achievement of a fair distribution of social benefits and burdens, usually by means of such policies as the graduated income tax, social welfare, and affirmative action. They adopt experimental social programs to solve such problems as poverty, urban blight, crime, or drug addiction. *Conservatives* tend to limit the role of government to the provision of internal and external security, the establishment of civil courts for adjudicating disputes among citizens, and the maintenance of infrastructure. Their aim is to extend the freedom of citizens from government interference or oversight as far as possible, and to foster the freedom of individuals to own and to dispose of property according to law. Conservatives are less concerned with distributive justice than are liberals, for the redistribution of benefits interferes with the freedom to dispose of property, as far as redistribution requires by law that those who have many benefits give to those who have few. For similar reasons, conservatives have less concern with economic equality than liberals; conservatives want only to ensure that those with many economic holdings have acquired those benefits legitimately and can dispose of them freely, while liberals fight against large disparities of income as unjust.

John Rawls

Much American thinking about liberal government was derived from John Stuart Mill, who believed that questions of justice are related to questions of public utility. His initiative drew may Americans away from the earlier contract theory of Hobbes and Locke, for it is *equalitarian,* asserting that the claims of all persons to social benefits are at least at first sight equal in value, and it is *progressive,* measuring the justice of a society by its efforts to respond flexibly to the claims of citizens. Differences in distribution must be justified by reference to claims of equality, merit, need, or desert. No generation need be tied to contracts signed by earlier generations. However, John Rawls (1921–2002) reverts to the notion of the social contract in his theory of justice. He argues that the notion of a fair contract between free and equal citizens, rather than utility, lies at the root of any adequate account of justice. Like the Critical Theory of Habermas, Rawls's theory borrows from Kant rather than utilitarianism, for, like Habermas, he is seeking a set of principles that rational agents would dictate to themselves as a basis for their living together.

Rawls's theory of justice begins with a thought-experiment that has become famous. Imagine an "original position," in which a group of persons meet to create a new society. This position, as described by Rawls, has two central characteristics. First, the participants are placed behind a "veil of ignorance" regarding themselves. They do not know what their own abilities and interests are, or what role they will eventually play in the society whose rules they are creating. Second, the participants in Rawls's experiment are each other's equals. They are able equally to arrive at, and make felt, their own concept of a just social order. Rawls refers to this condition as the *symmetry* of their relations to each other. If both these conditions are met, Rawls argues, then the social structure the parties eventually agree upon will be a fair one.

What principles of justice would rational people in the original position adhere to in their efforts to draw up the terms of their contract with each other? A contract is a document that stipulates an agreement between individuals concerning the benefits and liabilities they will enjoy and bear in some common undertaking. A social contract involves an exchange of benefits and liabilities between participants in society and the governmental and institutional structures that this participation creates. Imagine a person is contracting with a construction company to build an office building. If she is to bear the burden of paying the company, she will, if she is rational, first assure herself that she will get what she is paying for. If she is going to bear any special burdens, such as buying or producing the raw materials, she will demand that those burdens be to her eventual benefit. She will require that the cost of the building be less, or the eventual product be a better one, than if she did not bear those burdens. The construction company, similarly, will consider its interests in negotiating the contract. The final contract will specify what the contractor and the owner both consider to be a fair exchange. In determining its fairness, it is relevant to consider whether the owner, or anyone in her position, would sign the agreement even if she did not know whether she was in fact the owner of the building or the contractor.

Now the burdens and benefits that arise from participation in society involve a kind of exchange also. Some persons benefit more and some less; some bear heavier burdens and some lighter ones. What makes such exchanges fair ones?

Rawls sketches two principles regarding the fair exchange of benefits and burdens that rational persons in the original position of symmetry and ignorance would choose as fundamental to justice and write into their social contract.

First: Each person is to have an equal right to the most extensive total system of equal liberties compatible with a similar system of liberty for all.

Second: Social and economic inequalities are to be arranged so that they are both (a) to the greatest benefit of the least advantaged, and (b) attached to offices and positions open to all under conditions of fair equality of opportunity.

Note how the concept of contract relates to these principles. If a person is to engage in a fair contract with other persons, all must be in some sense upon an equal footing of power and competence. The contract must not be imposed upon one participant by others stronger or smarter than him.

The second principle addresses the question of desert, which was raised by Mill in the context of his utilitarianism. It assures the cooperation in the common purposes of society of those less advantaged by assuring them that any in-equities in the society are in their interest, that is, conducive to the greater good. If a person is to be subject to burdens while others live in prosperity, she must be convinced that the advantages of others eventually work to her own betterment. Why should she, as a rational person, agree to others being richer than her, or possessing greater social benefits, unless their riches benefit poorer persons like herself? One might object that those richer than she have earned their riches and hence deserve them. But Rawls insists that desert is a contingent feature of the cooperative scheme that cannot justify any inequalities of burdens and benefits prior to the adoption of the contract. There must be grounds for rational assent to that scheme independent of, and prior to, desert. Once a person has studied the contract—the rules of the game, so to speak—and sees that its provisions can be reasonably expected to be to everyone's advantage, then if he wins benefits by adhering to the rules, he deserves to enjoy them. The question of the fairness of the contract had already been answered affirmatively before its provisions went into effect, and individuals were able to exercise their talents under the contract.

Politics is the attempt to achieve rational consensus on practical solu-tions to social problems. Rawls's book is a study in social theory and appears to stand outside of the political fray. Yet the political situation may influence what people consider to be rational. Can a rational contract be drawn up outside a con-crete historical situation? Of course, Rawls considers the original position to be a merely hypothetical starting point for reflections on the nature of social jus-tice. It is not a situation, he insists, that real persons in a real historical situation could replicate. Yet how can we then be certain just how such imaginary persons in an imaginary situation would act? Whenever any group performs Rawls's ex-periment, its members are always already situated in specific historical and so-cial circumstances that the contract is supposed to respond to in some tangible way. Is this abstract rational neutrality necessary for choosing primary princi-ples that are just or possible at all? No doubt, we have to begin our ruminations on justice somewhere, and exploring Rawls's thought-experiment could strengthen our capacity for a reasoned apprehension of the structures of a just social contract.

Robert Nozick

A related criticism of Rawls's initiative in *A Theory of Justice* is not so easily responded to with sanguine hopes for a future of just distribution of ben-efits and burdens. Recall that the contract theories of Hobbes, Locke, and Rousseau all assumed that the social contract was signed by persons who had no history of civil society behind them. They had possessions, but they had no legally protected property. They owned only what they were able to take by force, or by their own labor. But in fact, all efforts to write constitutions or so-cial contracts are done by persons in a state of civilization in which they already possess or lack certain rights to property. Can justice demand that a party to the agreement be forced to give up that to which he is already entitled? The notion that it cannot is vigorously argued by Robert Nozick (1938–2002).

Naturally, Nozick will first have to account for the notion of property rights, or what he calls one's *entitlement* to some good or some benefit. The French **anarchist** Pierre Joseph Proudhon (1809–1865) had famously declared that "all property is theft," a notion which, if put into a political program, would require the liquidation of all private property without compensation from those who possess it (for they are thieves). Most people would find that seizure to be unjust. Many people become wealthy, not by theft, but by hard work and by such personal attributes as intelligence or cleverness. Nevertheless, a critic might observe, surely wealthy persons owe a debt to the society in which they enriched themselves. Nozick responds that this uncertainty about the justice of allowing individuals to amass large fortunes without incurring serious social or legal obligations, or even to use their native capacities and talents for purposes that are purely selfish, is uncalled for. He admits at the beginning of his book that he once shared such compunctions about the limits of entitlement until he was convinced otherwise by the force of the arguments he was able to muster.

ANARCHISM: Proudhon is considered to be the father of anarchism as an alternative to the systems of government that have prevailed throughout history. Anarchists, who include such men as the Russians M. A. Bakunin (1814–1876) and Prince P. A. Kropotkin (1842–1921), believe that governments enforce unjust limitations upon human freedom and protect the power and property of the few at the expense of the weak. Very few concrete proposals for anarchist social arrangements exist, and the philosophy is associated in the public mind with violent attacks upon the established order: The assassin of President McKinley, for example, identified himself as an anarchist. The association is unfair, for most anarchists are pacifistic in their philosophy. In general, they hope to organize human society in local associations for the common good, rather than in nation-states. Today's opponents of a global economy often identify themselves as anarchists.

Second, Nozick will have to account for the just acquisition of property. Nozick's idea of entitlement borrows from Locke's idea that a person becomes entitled to a piece of property by adding his labor to it. He raises curious questions about this notion, wondering whether, for example, by adding a cup of tomato juice a person happens to own to the ocean, he thereby comes into possession of those parts of the ocean touched by the juice. By building a fence around some unclaimed land, do we become owners of the land enclosed, or only of the portion of the land directly beneath the fence? Despite such lack of clarity in Locke's original notion, Nozick believes the notion of entitlement has great force, and claims to entitlement in specific cases can be settled by reference to principles of the right acquisition and transfer of property. Certainly, he believes, a proper definition of entitlement will give us all we need by way of a theory of social justice. True, the fact that the current possessors of property may have obtained their property by unjust means presents a difficulty. Ownership has a history. Though Nozick grants that the matter of justice in original acquisition and transfer of holdings is a "complicated truth," its thorough exploration will allow many past injustices to be rectified.

Justice in acquisition is subject to the important Lockean proviso that there be "enough and as good left in common for others," or, more broadly, that the appropriation of some previously unowned good will not worsen (without adequate compensation) the position of others, except insofar as they will not be able to use the good appropriated. This is a stronger restriction on appropriation than might at first appear. For example, Nozick says that a man may not, under the conditions of this proviso, appropriate the only oasis in the desert and charge people what he wants for its use. Entitlement, if it is to be just, may not have as its consequence the deprivation of the conditions of life to other persons. Nozick holds that "the operation of a market system will not actually run afoul of the Lockean proviso."

Third, Nozick has to respond to the demand for a fair distribution of benefits and burdens. He argues that a "wholly just" world would not meet what liberals call one requirement of distributive justice, namely that the entitled income of individuals be redistributed, by means of taxation and in the form of welfare, to those who are less well off. Nozick argues his position upon the basis of liberty, that is, that such redistribution interferes with the freedom of individuals to acquire and make use of property as they see fit. He calls "patterning" all efforts to specify a principle of redistribution according to some criterion. Say we choose to redistribute holdings according to a person's "moral merit, or needs, or marginal product or how hard he tries . . . " Any of these patterns, if enforced, will prevent some people from using the talents or the wealth to which they are justly entitled. Even in a society in which all people's basic needs are satisfied, some individuals will still desire further benefits, which they seek to obtain by labor that goes beyond that required to satisfy their needs. To take those extra benefits of their labor and put them in a common pot for redistribution according to the preferred pattern would be unjust, Nozick asserts. Moreover, if individuals are entitled to use the benefits that have been redistributed to them under this pattern, the preferred pattern could be subverted, for those people may choose to distribute their possessions to persons not entitled to them under the pattern.

It follows from this thinking that the taxation of earnings is a form of forced labor. The redistribution of the earnings of productive individuals to those in need is, Nozick argues, an attempt to extend to the entire society those voluntary relationships of love and assistance that are appropriate to the family. Redistribution schemes focus upon the recipient of the distribution rather than upon the provider of it and, in that way, generate people's rights to the distribution rather than upon the more questionable source of the obligation of the provider to contribute to the social pot. Self-interest will, perhaps, dictate to persons with wealth that they contribute voluntarily to the needs of the less fortunate. But there is no "social need" as such that private parties must contribute to; needs are always those of individuals, and individuals are never served well, Nozick argues, by threatening their entitlements and distributing their holdings to an anonymous social being.

Nozick's distinction between the providers of distributions (those with many holdings) and the recipients of them (the needy or less well-off), and his focus on the former, suggests one line of criticism of this theory. It may be far too one-sided a concept of justice that defends only the right to legitimate entitlements while neglecting the rights to assistance of those in need. Even if it is true that the patterned redistribution of benefits is self-defeating, destructive of initiative, and a threat to liberties, the notion that others have no more claim upon the holdings of other people than the request for voluntary charity (or upon nonvoluntary and mandatory Good Samaritanism in limited cases, where, for example, a person owning a rope is required to give it over to save a drowning man) conflicts with a deep communitarian notion, evident in most societies, that justice requires at least some redistribution of primary goods.

The flood of writings on social and political philosophy in the United States since the appearance of *A Theory of Justice* in 1973 has engaged philosophy in the democratic process, in political struggles, and in the fostering of a political vision of justice, the Great Society, and the Good Life. The new vigor of political philosophy has helped save philosophy from the irrelevance into which it was falling at midcentury. It fosters both the will and the ability to formulate clearly the aims and aspirations of the democracies in an increasingly hostile and dangerous world. And it has returned philosophy from immersion in the technical detail of argument to the political questions and perplexities that gave rise to political philosophy in the ancient world. What are the true interests of human beings? What kinds of social arrangements will best enable us to be happy, or fully functioning organisms, or at least at peace with ourselves and with one another. What do we owe to each other?

CHAPTER 8

Philosophy of Religion

GOD AND PHILOSOPHY

The philosophy of religion is concerned with the critical examination of two groups of concepts that refer to items found in every civilization. The first group centers about the concepts of the sacred or holy. In Western civilization, these terms especially, although not exclusively, refer to what is called God, the sacred divine being who is thought to be active in human history, and who calls on each of us to worship him. The second group refers to practices that have the sacred and divine as their objects. They are grouped under the heading of religion. Philosophers may ask about the first group of ideas: What is the nature of the being that Jews, Christians, and Moslems call God? Does this being exist? How can we know that? And they may ask about the second group: What is the nature of religious belief? How is it different from other beliefs people may have? How does religious belief function in an individual's life, or in that of society?

Students entering the philosophy of religion may wonder whether the effort to master its complexities is worth any possible outcome. After all, they may think, isn't a belief in God a matter of personal faith? Faith is something you have (or do not have), and religion is something you do, and not merely think about. To try to justify rationally a belief in the existence of God is useless, for if there were such rational justification, we would all know that God exists, and there would be no room for faith. Having faith in God implies at least having a belief in God's existence without proof. It is a belief in which a person may be sustained not by reason, but by Scripture, or by personal experience with God. Even more, if such a proof of God's existence were available, how could philosophy demonstrate that one form of religion was better than another, that, for example, Jewish practices were in some important sense better than Islamic practices? The whole effort of philosophy of religion seems therefore misconceived and doomed to failure.

This objection would have considerable weight if the purposes of the philosophy of religion were only to demonstrate God's existence (or nonexistence) and to evaluate ways of worshiping God with respect to their adequacy. But these are not its aims. The philosophy of religion is intended first to bring coherence to our talk about God, so that when believers or nonbelievers reflect on the content of their beliefs, they will be able to do so effectively; they will know what they do and do not believe in, and what are their reasons for their beliefs. The second purpose is to make clear how religious beliefs relate to, or stand beyond, our moral, political, or scientific beliefs.

Yet even more than these two practical ends of coherence and clarity, the philosophy of religion offers to our reflection some of the most engaging and profound questions of human life. It is not by chance that most people are brought into philosophy by reflection on their religious commitments. Religion creates a need for philosophy, just because religion makes broad philosophical claims about what exists (metaphysics), how the world began (cosmology), how we should live (ethics), the origin of justice and injustice in human history (social philosophy), and even about what kind of beings we humans are and what the purpose of our lives may be (philosophical anthropology). In a word, the philosophy of religion gives strong intellectual food and drink to any human being who has ever been raised in a religion and felt the presence (or the absence) of God in his life.

The philosophy of religion is concerned with three general topics, each of which require description (what is the nature of the thing?), analysis (how does it relate to other things like it?), and argument (what evidence do we have for the truth of a doctrine?).

- The *theistic* questions: What is the nature of God, as supposed by the Western religious tradition? What evidence, if any, is there to support claims that such a being in fact exists?

- The *religious* question: What forms have religious practices taken in the West? What are their functions? What is their value to society?

- The question of *faith:* What kind of experience is religious experience? What is its function in the life of an individual? What are the sources of faith, and how is it justified, if at all?

This chapter will confine itself to an exploration of the first group of questions. Its discussions will remain within the orbit and the experience of the three historical Western religions, Judaism, Christianity, and Islam. These religions trace their history to the story of Abraham in the Bible, whom God called upon for a very special task: the work of overcoming the separation between God and humankind caused by the Fall of Adam and Eve in the Garden of Eden. All of subsequent history—the covenant with the Jewish people and the giving of the Law to Moses, the lives and writings of the Jewish prophets, the birth, life, and death of Christ, and the giving of the Koran to Mohammed—has been understood by Jews, Christians, and Moslems respectively as stages in this great process of reconciliation and redemption.

The chapter will consider the following themes:

- Defining the Concept of God
- Arguments for God's Existence
- An Argument against God's Existence: The Argument from Evil
- God and Linguistic Philosophy

DEFINING THE CONCEPT OF GOD

The Uniqueness of God

Several characteristics of God are common to the beliefs of Jews, Christians, and Muslims. First, God is thought to be unique. The belief that there is only one God is called monotheism. "There is no God but God," begins a statement of the Muslim creed. There are, of course, beings worthy of reverence—angels, perhaps, or saints, as in the Catholic tradition, or messengers of God, the prophets, as in the Jewish and Muslim tradition. Yet no being is worthy of worship but God. **Idolatry** is precisely worshiping something less than the divine, as we say a person may make a god of money, or of his fatherland. Monotheism makes of God a kind of cosmic orphan; he has servants, perhaps, but no relatives or equals.

> **IDOLATRY:** Idolatry occurs in monotheistic religions when a person worships something less than God. A key case of this in the Bible occurs when Aaron allows the Jewish people to create a golden calf for worship while Moses was on Sinai, receiving the Commandments from God. The practice perhaps derives from the need of simple people to have some physical object before them that represents the divine for them to worship. But God is not an idol and cannot be represented physically. To confuse God, who stands over all things as their creator, with some item of his creation, is to engage in idolatry.

God's Omnipotence

In addition, God is said to be omnipotent, having all power. This notion, if correct, generates further characteristics of the monotheistic God: that **he** is eternal, absolute, omniscient, and possesses sovereignty over the world. What does it mean to say about a being that it is all-powerful? The simple answer is that this being can do anything at all. But such a notion has serious problems and is possibly incoherent. For example, one might challenge the notion of a God that can do anything at all by asking whether God can make "$2+2 = 5$." If he can do anything, then surely he can do that! No doubt there have been philosophers and theologians who have accepted this inference. Descartes, for example, extended God's power even over the rules of mathematics. Yet it is impossible for a human being to conceive what it would be like for "2+2 = 5" to be true. Would God change the meanings of the terms *2, 4, or =*? Anyone could do that! Or would he change the way in which these terms imply that "2+2 = 4" is a true sentence in arithmetic, that is, change their nature? If so, we are being asked to believe something that we cannot make sense of. As a result, most theologians have concluded that God's omnipotence does not imply that God can do things that, like "2+2 = 5," are logically impossible; others argue that God's power must reach beyond what is humanly conceivable.

GOD AS "HE": In all of sacred Scripture—the Torah, the Gospels, the Koran—God is spoken of as male. He is given characteristics that patriarchal society associates with the male sex: he is creator, father, punisher; he is active rather than passive. Modern monotheism conceives of God as being above maleness and femaleness, while continuing to speak of God as a he. Of course most languages are gendered and have no pronoun to refer to persons or person-like beings (dogs and cats and angels, perhaps), except in terms of *he* and *she*. It is not to the point of philosophy to become involved in what is a theological debate about how worshipers should conceive of God as a person, but it is clear that God must be thought of as a being that transcends human sexuality.

Because we human beings experience time as a kind of constraint, it is natural for us to attribute to God some kind of power over time. Every child understands when told that she has to wait a few more days for Christmas to be here; could God also be forced to wait for some event across the passage of the minutes and the hours, and in this way be dependent upon something over which he has no control? Again, we human beings know future things only imperfectly, upon the basis of evidence that may be convincing but not entirely certain. Our actions may therefore fall short of what they were intended to accomplish. For example, one may take steps to protect a friend from some anticipated harm, but the real danger to the friend may come from some other direction that we did not anticipate. Does God depend upon evidence of some kind for his knowledge of the world?

God's Eternity

The notion that God is omnipotent appears to imply that God is not subject to such temporal and evidential constraints and limitations. Consequently, most Jews, Christians, and Muslims hold that God is either eternal, outside of time entirely, or is everlasting, without beginning or end. They generally hold also that He is **omniscient**, knowing all things past, present, and future, for the power of an agent is limited by the knowledge of what he is acting upon. God's omnipotence therefore implies his omniscience. But do his omnipotence and omniscience imply that he is directly aware of, or already present to, all future events? Theologians who affirm God's eternity assert just that. God knows, for example, whether some human being will be saved or damned. He knows even before that person is born what she will grow up to be, and that she will die on a certain date. In this view, God does not predict these things, he knows them directly, for he apprehends all things from beyond time, from eternity. Now we cannot form a clear picture of eternity, although great art or music or even dreams can give us intimations of it. Some thinkers have held that the notion of eternity is incoherent. What would it be like, they ask, for there to be an awareness of some object that did not include its standing in some temporal relation of before and after to itself? The concept also raises the crucial question of whether a person's life and death are entirely determined. If God knows when Mary is a child that she will choose to marry John at age twenty, then in a certain sense, one that requires a great deal of analysis, she will have to make that choice—otherwise God's knowledge that she would so choose would not be knowledge at all.

OMNISCIENCE: Does God know all true propositions? That is, does He know all matters of fact, say, the truth or the falsity of the proposition, "Jones has 274,742 hairs on his head"? Or does God know the essential structure of the world, that is, the sum total of conceptual structures through which things are cognized (something like Plato's realm of Forms)? Or does He simply know every physical law that determines the behavior of objects on the microscopic level, and the position and velocity of every particle? Does God have a standpoint on the world; does God see everything that happens in the world from some privileged position? If God is outside of space and time, is he able to take in everything that happens in the world simultaneously? Is God everywhere, always, by our spacio-temporal reckoning? These questions all represent metaphysical puzzles that bear upon our understanding of the concept of God and the ultimate nature of the world.

The notion that God is everlasting avoids these problems by asserting that God is indeed in time, although without beginning or end. On this view, God is sovereign over the world and can influence the course of events, but he cannot know in any detail just what will happen in the future. The notion coheres with the belief that God is the **creator** of the world, for to create is to aim at some ends in or by means of the world. God must then be active in the changing events of the world in order to achieve those ends. God's everlasting nature also makes God independent of time, at least in the sense that there was and will be no time at which God did not exist. God is not merely immortal, as were the Greek gods, who were born, or came to be. God never came to be and will never cease to be, but time passes for God, just as it does for us. This view may be thought to challenge God's absolute omnipotence, unless one shares the view that knowledge of the future is as much a logical impossibility as is the notion of a square circle, or the truth of "2+2 = 5."

> **GOD AS CREATOR:** The Scriptures do not give believers much infor-
> mation as to what God does with his existence. There are descrip-
> tions of God in the Old Testament walking with Adam and Eve in
> Eden, and, notably, presiding over a court of angels in the Book of
> Job. But all Jews, Christians, and Moslems agree that God's central
> activity with respect to humankind is his creation of the world. God
> is not part of the world, as were the Greek and Hindu gods, who
> exist in a realm of their own within the world (on Mount Olympus,
> in the case of the Greek gods), and who are born, but who never
> die. They may have a role in the shaping of the physical world, but
> the physical world was there for them when they came along. The
> monotheistic idea is that God created the world out of nothing and
> gave it its shape and content. God is also not identical with the
> world in some way, as pantheism teaches; he stands beyond it as its
> creator: God is the great artist or artificer, and the world is his prod-
> uct. He also does not suffuse the world, as the water suffuses the
> sponge, as panentheism teaches. God is active or immanent in the
> world but is not physically present in it as energy or substance.

God As a Person

A further essential moral characteristic of the monotheistic God is his personhood. Crudely stated, God is not a force of nature, nor is he nature's laws and energy; he is a conscious being with thought and feeling, who can be spoken with in prayer, and who has designs for individual human beings and for human history. God is an infinite Person, analogous to human personhood, but infinitely transcendent of it. Now although the Greek and Roman gods were anthropomorphic, that is, had humanlike form, and although even in the Jewish Bible God is initially described as having human form—He "speaks" with Adam and Eve in Eden—the Judeo-Christian-Islamic tradition eventually came to see God as completely immaterial or spiritual in nature. But how can we hope to understand a thing that is in its nature so completely discontinuous with our own experience, our own life? It is difficult to imagine an action that has no material basis. God's creation of the world out of no preexisting matter or energy, by an act of disembodied will alone ("God said, 'Let there be light!' and there was light"), appears therefore to be an article of mere faith without understanding. But a tradition that reaches back to at least the medieval philosopher Saint Thomas Aquinas says that we can achieve partial understanding of God's moral nature by analogy with what we can know and experience.

The Catholic theologian Friedrich von Hügel (1852–1925) suggested a downward analogy to help us understand God as a person. A dog possesses what most dog lovers would call a personality distinct from every other dog. But this simple canine life can be called personal only by analogy with human personhood. The dog partakes of our inward life only slightly—he can, for example, respond a bit to our shifting moods, and sense our sympathy and goodness or our hostility, just as a human being can capture a sense of the spirit of God only slightly and by dim analogy with the spirit of a human being. The Greeks believed that the highest values are those of truth, beauty, and goodness. No animal can grasp the notion of a true or false proposition, a good or wicked human action, or a beautiful or ugly thing. Love and hate are also functions of the human spirit, and, perhaps, no animal loves or hates. Now God is thought by the Western religions to be essentially spirit, while we human beings are only partially spiritual; we are an amalgam of animal life and divine spirit. By analogy, then, we can try to imagine God as nonliving or nonbiologically embodied spirit who creates and knows the world in acts of loving its truth, beauty, and goodness. Such an argument from analogy would not satisfy persons who demand physical explanations of events as the only possible rational explanations of them, but, to faith, it opens a door to understanding God's nature, however limited, as with all analogies, it may be.

God's Moral Nature

The attempt of monotheism to describe God's moral nature is of interest to philosophers, for it relates to philosophy's concern with ethics. Whether the origin of moral law is divine reason or divine will, God's laws must be straightforward and clear, both to God and to the saved and the damned, as it was to Adam and Eve. For if a sinner is consigned justly to an eternity of hellfire, his guilt must be perfectly clear, and a human lifetime must be clearly identifiable as having been or not been in conformity with divine reason or will. God's judgment cannot be arbitrary, any more than a human judge's ought to be. Yet there is an important internal challenge to the notion of God as a moral person. It concerns God's capacity for certain kinds of moral action. If God can do anything that is logically possible, then can He tell lies, or annihilate Himself? Either act would be simple enough for a human being to perform; is God not capable of willing such things to happen? More generally, could God change the moral law itself, that is, could he make it morally right, or just, or obligatory, to enslave other people, to molest small children, or to rob the poor of whatever they have? Theologians who accept this implication of God's omnipotence argue for a position called voluntarism. This is the view that God's power embraces the moral law itself; the only reason why it is wrong for a person to enslave other persons is that God has forbidden it. This doctrine coheres well with the story of Adam and Eve in Genesis: It was wrong for Eve and then Adam to eat the fruit of the forbidden tree simply because they disobeyed the will of God.

The Euthyphro Question

A significant problem faced by voluntarist theologians, or by any believers taking that view, was first identified by Plato. A passage in one of Plato's dialogues formulates what has been called the *Euthyphro question*. Euthyphro, a young friend of Socrates, is bringing charges of murder against his own father in the death of a servant. Socrates is amazed by the young man's confidence that he is doing the right thing in this matter, but Euthyphro reassures Socrates that what he is doing is a pious or holy act on his part, and that he knows the nature of piety well enough to make that claim. When Socrates asks Euthyphro to explain the nature of piety to him, he receives as one of several answers the definition: "Piety is that thing [presumably some kinds of human action] that pleases all of the gods." But Socrates has a serious problem with this notion and he responds to it with what has become a famous philosophical puzzle: He asks Euthyphro whether something is pious because the gods are pleased by it, or whether the gods find it pleasing because it is pious.

The point of this odd question is hard to grasp, yet once grasped, its force is considerable. Socrates is questioning whether the gods' pleasure—their will, as it were—is what makes a thing good. If that is the case, then if the gods were to find the murder of one man by another pleasant, then that act of murder would be good. It does not help to object that the gods would not take pleasure in murder because murder is wrong, for if we define what is right and wrong in terms of the gods' pleasures, we cannot then say that a thing is wrong independently of their pleasure. Whatever pleases the gods would be good only for that reason; no moral reason could constrain the gods to find anything pleasant, for nothing is moral unless they find it pleasant. Socrates seems to believe—although as usual he commits himself to very little in these discussions, confining himself simply to asking questions and following up the implications of the answers he receives—that there must be a nature of piety, or of right and wrong, that is independent of the laws or the lawmakers, divine or otherwise. If a thing has that nature, then it is pious.

Consider the matter this way: Suppose Socrates and Euthyphro are learning the game of baseball by watching it played. They are wondering why, when the pitcher throws the ball and the batter does not swing, the umpire sometimes calls the pitch a strike, and sometimes a ball. Euthyphro thinks he knows the answer. A strike, he says, is a pitch that is pleasing to the umpire! Now if that is true, then the umpire makes up the rules of the game as he goes along. If he has that power, there is no way of criticizing him if he calls a ball pitched two feet over the batter's head a strike. But no, says Socrates, it must be that the umpire is trying to conform his judgment to some rule, and we are trying to find out what that rule is. What is a strike? Of course, the umpire likes to see the game played well, and he may be pleased when a pitch is thrown right across the plate and the batter is unable to "pull the trigger" and swing at it. But the umpire's likes and dislikes do not make a pitch a strike or a ball. The umpire can be wrong! If Euthyphro and Socrates studied the game of baseball some more, they would find the rule they are looking for: a pitch is a strike if it is across the plate and between the letters and the knees. Perhaps, therefore, it would be better to ask what moral qualities in human actions are pleasing to God, rather than to assume that the fact he finds them pleasing is the reason they possess moral qualities.

Most believers are made uncomfortable by the voluntarist belief that goodness and wickedness depend upon God's will alone. God is not a cosmic dictator whose will persons must obey if they are to avoid hellfire, even if what they are told to do by God does not appear to them to be good. Yet believers are also troubled by the notion that there is a moral law above even God: How could God be constrained by anything not to lie, or cheat, or to strike people dead just because he was annoyed with them? Perhaps one possible solution to this problem may be found in a notion borrowed from Jean-Jacques Rousseau. Moral wickedness, he thought, comes from human weakness. The reason a man can be tempted to lie or steal is his own insecurity; he does not have everything he wants or needs and must struggle to get those things. God, of course, has no weaknesses. he cannot be harmed, and he would therefore have no reason to desire or to do anything that was not rational or moral. God wills what is good because it is good, but he is not constrained by any moral law that hangs over him, for *constraint* means having to do what one does not want to do, and God never has reason to want what is wrong.

God's Purposes

No doubt members of the monotheistic religions do not claim to know all of God's purposes and the means he chooses to achieve them, but all believe that he created the world in order to have human companions for all eternity in a place he is preparing for those who are elected to join him. How one becomes elected is also in dispute, but the two questions of God's purposes and the conditions of a human being's election are interrelated. An answer depends upon readings of the various books that have scriptural status for each of the historical religions. All believe that humankind has been placed by God before some sort of test. They maintain that we must somehow make ourselves worthy of enjoying the eternal presence of God after this life is done. The contemporary Christian philosopher John Hick (1922–) has referred to the created world as a place of "soul making," one designed not for the sake of temporary happiness here, but full of challenges and heartaches and conflicts to which people must respond freely in a worthy way. For, Hick and others have argued, we would never develop such virtues as compassion if the world contained no suffering; we wold never develop a constant faith in God if suffering and despair did not make us recognize our need for God. God as a person speaks to the deepest part of our own person, challenging us to live for the sake of Him and for eternity, rather than for the changing and temporary things of this world.

Divine Love

The clearest analogy between the divine life and the life of persons, believers maintain, is found in the act of love. Love in human beings takes at least two forms. One is appropriate to our animal nature and is called erotic love, the lust to possess the objects of our desire, and the joy in their possession. The other form is appropriate to our spiritual nature, which all religions wish to foster. This is charitable love, or *agape*, the loving concern we may feel for the well-being of others. God's charity extends to all things in the universe; His loving concern embraces all things and offers them understanding and mercy. Charity, concern, and mercy are all functions of the human person as spirit. By analogy, God is infinite compassion, charity, and loving concern for each item of his creation.

Members of the monotheistic religions may approach the presence of God directly, though again dimly, in prayer, or in the study of the holy books or scriptures favored by their particular religion. Others seek to penetrate the veil between the finite and the infinite in ecstatic mystical experience. Or again, a believer may claim to sense God's presence to us in the order of the created universe itself. The English poet William Wordsworth (1770–1850) expressed this sentiment beautifully in his "Lines Composed a Few Miles above Tintern Abbey":

> . . . And I have felt
> A presence that disturbs me with the joy
> Of elevated thought; a sense sublime
> Of something far more deeply interfused
> Whose dwelling is the light of setting suns,
> And the round ocean and the living air,
> And the blue sky, and in the mind of man:
> A motion and a spirit, that impels
> All thinking things, all objects of all thought,
> And rolls through all things. . . .

Similarly a person may feel the presence of his friend's inward life in words and gestures, and in his own emotional responses to them.

ARGUMENTS FOR GOD'S EXISTENCE

As God's nature seems to extend so far beyond our own, it would not seem possible that we could know of His existence by some rational argument or inquiry, the way we may come to know of the existence of atoms or galaxies or stars, or of microscopic organisms. Such direct knowledge of God appears to be impossible, just because God is believed to transcend the world as its creator: he is not in the world the way atoms or galaxies are. How could we ever hope to discover God by exploring the world? Yet, if a religious believer can offer no reasons at all for her belief, she is in a very embarrassing position. Why select some beliefs to maintain, unless one also has reason to believe that they are true? One response to that question is that her faith has positive value for her life; it gives her hope, the courage to go on, the sense that all is not for nothing, that life makes sense in the end. But although these considerations may serve as a motive for believing, they are not reasons for asserting that the belief is true. Moreover, many different beliefs may improve, in some measure, the life of those who maintain them, assuming that we are able to measure the nature and the degree of the improvement. But should a person be concerned more with her happiness than with the truth of her beliefs? Believers should be willing to test their beliefs for their truth or falsity in the crucible of philosophical analysis and argument.

Benedict Spinoza. © *Thoemmes.*

Now many well-reasoned arguments have been put forward as offering sufficient reason for a rational person to accept the proposition "God exists" as true, where the term "God" refers to a being possessing the characteristics analyzed earlier. Three of these classic arguments for God's existence will be considered briefly: The Ontological Argument, the Cosmological Argument, and a version of the Cosmological Argument known as the Teleological Argument or the Argument from Design.

The Ontological Argument

The Ontological Argument is traced historically to the *Proslogium,* a work by the medieval theologian and Archbishop of Canterbury, Saint Anselm (c. 1033–1109). His argument takes two forms, and a further form of it was developed by René Descartes and **Benedict Spinoza**. The argument is purely logical or a priori in that it refers to no facts about the world but rather to some inherent necessities in our thinking about the world.

BENEDICT SPINOZA (1632–1677): Spinoza was born in Amsterdam to Jewish parents who fled persecution in Portugal. Because of the unorthodoxy of his religious beliefs, he was condemned and excommunicated by the Jewish community in Amsterdam, and he separated himself from the people of Israel. He lived a life of great independence, refusing to adhere to any religion but his own, and even refusing an offer of a professorship out of fear that he would eventually be condemned by the authorities for his beliefs. He supported himself as a lens grinder while writing his two most important works, the *Theological-Political Treatise* and the *Ethics*. The *Treatise* caused great controversy when it appeared in 1670, and Spinoza decided therefore not to publish the *Ethics* during his lifetime. The work, now considered to be one of the great monuments of Western philosophy, appeared in 1667.

Anselm's first step was to express the idea of God in the definition, "By God, we mean a being greater than which nothing can be thought." Two things must be noted about this definition. By "greater," Anselm is speaking qualitatively, not quantitatively. God is not infinitely large, or having infinite quantities of power or energy; he is perfectly good, perfectly knowing, independent of and sovereign over all other things. He is the most awesome or perfect being that a human being can think of. The first version of Anselm's argument adds one further premiss: it is better to exist in reality, or external to the mind of some person, than to exist only in the mind, for to live in the mind alone is a limitation of existence. A Hamlet who existed in reality would be greater than a Hamlet who existed only in the mind of Shakespeare and his readers. From these premisses, the conclusion that God exists in reality follows necessarily: A being greater than which nothing can be conceived must exist in reality, for if it did not (by the second premiss), then it would not be a being greater than which nothing can be conceived. One could easily conceive of a greater, namely, one that existed. A person who denies the existence of God contradicts himself.

Anselm seems to have been prompted to develop the idea of this argument in a new direction by a critic named Gaunilo, who pointed out that Anselm's argument could be used to prove the existence of the greatest conceivable anything. Imagine an island greater (more beautiful, having a more pleasant climate) than which no island could be conceived. Must such an island exist? Anselm responded that his argument applies only to God as the being greater than which nothing can be conceived, because only such a being must be conceived as possessing all possible perfections, including the perfections of existence and necessity. God therefore not only exists, he exists necessarily. The island greater than which none can be conceived, by contrast, need not possess all perfections, only those appropriate to an island. God alone exists necessarily; necessary existence is essential to his perfection as a being greater than which nothing can be thought.

Both Descartes and Spinoza gave an important role to the Ontological Argument in their systems of philosophy. Spinoza's statement of it in the *Ethics* is quite complex, for it depends upon a previously stated axiom and a previously derived theorem, but it is formidable and grand: "Proposition XI. God or substance consisting of infinite attributes, each one of which expresses eternal and infinite essence, necessarily exists." An element absent from Anselm's two versions of the argument may be noted here, that of an attribute. An attribute, or what Aristotle called a category, predicates of a subject some essence or nature, as when we say, "Socrates is mortal." The attribute of mortality is predicated of

Socrates; it is claimed that Socrates belongs to the class of things that are mortal. Now the Ontological Argument predicates of God all possible attributes to an infinite degree. As existence is an attribute, God must necessarily posses that attribute, that is, he must exist, otherwise he would not possess infinite attributes. To claim otherwise would be to contradict oneself.

Critical attacks upon the Ontological Argument have taken three forms. The first asks whether we can be certain that the argument's definition of God is a coherent one. We cannot know, for example, whether the idea of "infinite goodness" is a possible attribute of anything, just because the human mind cannot grasp a qualitative infinity in itself. We may perceive degrees of goodness in things, but we cannot inspect directly infinite goodness. Perhaps infinite goodness is not the concept of a possible thing, as the notion of a square circle does not designate a possible thing. Second, the notion of necessary existence, which figures in Anselm's second version of the argument, is said to be logically odd. We may correctly speak of logical necessity, as when we say that "if a = b and b = c, then a = c" is a necessary truth. Such necessity is a property of statements. But what does it mean to say that a thing exists necessarily? Presumably it means that a thing must exist, that it cannot help but exist. Yet the force of this "must" seems quite unclear. Third, to argue that we cannot conceive of God's not existing (for his existence follows necessarily from our concept of his nature) does not demonstrate that God exists in fact. Our inability to conceive of God's nonexistence may be a contingent fact of human thought. We cannot conceive of a mountain without conceiving of a valley, but it might be that neither mountains nor valleys exist in fact.

Immanuel Kant provided what most thinkers today consider to be the decisive objection to the Ontological Argument. He denied that existence is an attribute. Attributes, he believed, are qualities of the things to which they are attributed. Existence is not such a quality. We add nothing to our description of a thing when we say that it exists. A hundred existing dollars on one's pocket, he famously said, have the same qualities as a hundred imaginary dollars. The difference between the two consists in their effects in the world, not in their quality as a hundred dollars. If this is so, then ascribing existence to God does not increase our idea of his perfection. As a test for this notion, consider that existence does not come in degrees: one object may be heavier, greener, or more beautiful than another, but one thing cannot exist more than another; a thing either exists or it does not. The Ontological Argument fails, Kant argued, because it holds incorrectly that existence is a predicate like any other quality. There can be no logical relationship between the qualities of a thing and its existence.

The Cosmological Argument and the Teleological Argument are both a posteriori arguments. They do not claim that God's existence follows from self-evident principles alone, but also from unchallengeable facts about the world. They claim, very simply put, that given certain self-evident or a priori principles, certain facts about the world that we know a posteriori to be true would be incomprehensible if there is no God.

The Cosmological Argument

The fact referred to by the Cosmological Argument is the existence of the world itself as a collection of changing, contingent things. The cup on the table need not be there (it does not exist necessarily), and at one time it was not there. Its presence there requires some kind of causal explanation referring to the past events that caused it to be what and where it is. Someone must have made it; someone or something must have put it there, for it is self-evident (a priori) that every event, such as the cup's being on the table, must have a cause. It cannot have produced itself, for out of nothing comes nothing; the cup cannot have sprung into existence or, at the very least, it cannot be sensibly or rationally asserted to have done so. Since every item in the world is contingent in that way, we can render each item intelligible only by tracing it to some cause. But to do so for each item in the world would require tracing events back to infinity, and our accounting would never reach an end. The very effort to account for a world without a beginning appears to imply that a real infinity of events has already taken place. But that is clearly impossible; the notion of a real numerical infinity is incoherent. Therefore there must exist a necessary being that is self-created or the cause of itself, in whom all explanations of contingent existence and all change terminates. This would be God, the "unmoved mover," who exists before all time, or eternally, and in whom all things find their ultimate origin.

Similar reasoning can be applied to the world as a whole. If a person thinks of the world as contingent, or not carrying in itself the necessity of its existence, then it must be traceable to something that does exist necessarily. If, however, a person conceives of the world as having existed from all eternity, or at least as never created, then that person might dispense with God, but he would still have the task of making intelligible the notion of infinite time or an uncreated world. At least some writers, relying upon implications of modern physics and cosmogony, have argued that the second notion is a coherent one. According to this thinking, time is not an invariant subsisting reality, but a measure that emerged from observations of events. Events themselves cannot therefore be enumerated; there is no question of counting, even in our imagination, an infinite number of discrete events that took place in past time. No doubt this account grants that the existence of the world is unintelligible, a mere brute fact, but one might argue that postulating the existence of a necessary existing creative deity as the ground or origin of the world does nothing to relieve this lack of intelligibility. The notion of self-created being, though an awesome notion, is hardly an intelligible one. When the theist responds triumphantly to the atheist's or skeptic's admission that we do not know how the world came about, "I know—God created the world!" has she rendered the world a jot more intelligible? Not unless she can explicate God's true nature and his creative power (how did he do it?), and that no religious believer claims to be able to do.

The Teleological Argument

The facts invoked by the Teleological Argument concern the apparent order and purposiveness of things in nature. Living things, especially, manifest means-ends relationships that are similar in some respects to those created by human ingenuity in pursuit of some ends. A simple item like a pen possesses an arrangement of metal, plastic, ink, and a spring, all designed to fit into a person's hand and allow her to trace easily lines on paper. The design, of course, was provided by a human designer, or a succession of them, who created the pen in just that way as a means to achieve the end of writing. Similarly, the human arm, which also contains a variety of organized elements—flesh, bone, blood, nerves—seems designed to achieve a wide range of human ends. It is a means to such ends as eating, fighting, or hitchhiking. However, the arm was designed by no human designer, nor could any human today create such a thing. It must therefore have been created by a being capable of designing the arm and creating it according to the design. This superhuman designer the argument identifies as God.

Stated in this fashion, the Teleological Argument is one from analogy: As the pen, insofar as it exhibits elements of design or means-ends relationships, must be traced to a human designer, so must the arm, insofar as it displays similar design elements, be traced to a divine designer. Some forms of the argument rely upon a self-evident or a priori proposition known as the design axiom: "Orderly processes and structures (as, for example, the organization of means to achieve ends) always require intelligence for their design and execution." If we grant that the world contains examples of order and structure, and that this axiom is true, then we must concede the existence of some intelligence that designed and executed the elements of order and process in it. St. Thomas Aquinas wrote that the aim and energy of the archer brings the arrow to its designated end. Since no human provides the aim and the energy that brings the acorn to its designated end as an oak tree, a supernatural source of the acorn's direction toward an end must be invoked. "And this all men call God," he wrote.

David Hume is credited with the first serious critical analysis of the Teleological Argument. He attacks the premiss that the world contains examples of order and structure similar to those found in a manmade structure. The analogy between, say, the human arm and a watch or a pen is very slight. The aim or purpose of a watch is to tell time; the watch serves the purposes for which it was fashioned. But what is the end or aim of the arm? The list of ends given a moment ago—to eat, to fight, or to hitchhike—are ends for which we use the arm, but what were the ends for which the arm-maker fashioned the arm? Of course we do not know. The arm serves our ends, that is clear, but what ends beyond our own are served by it? Moreover, the claim that the world as a whole is designed requires the claimant to specify the ends for which is was designed. From a different point of view than our own, Hume notes, the world might appear to be a chaotic place whose structures serve no rational purpose at all. If the response is that the world serves the ends of the being who designed it, then the question is begged, for the argument is supposed to give us reasons for believing that such a designer exists. Further, Hume points out, a person may have seen a watch being designed and made, but we have never seen a world being made. How can we tell what is involved in the creation of a world? What kind of intelligence, if any, was required to create it?

Even if the Teleological Argument's conclusion that the world must have been fashioned by an intelligent designer is accepted, Hume argued further, we cannot identify that designer with the monotheistic God. First, and most importantly, the world we inhabit is finite. How can we infer the existence of an infinite creator from that of a finite world? A creator must possess only enough power to produce what it creates, as a beaver dam requires only the power of beavers to create, not the power of the forces that produced the Hoover Dam. Second, referring to the analogy with the watch: The watchmaker who created the watch currently on someone's wrist may now be dead. Perhaps the creator of the structures and the processes in the world is now dead: the argument alone cannot exclude that possibility. Again, there may have been a committee of watchmakers that made the watch; many gods may have worked on the creation of the world. Or again the watchmaker may have been an apprentice, for some of its processes do not work perfectly, and neither do some of those in the world. In sum, argued Hume, how can the bare requirement that structure and process require intelligence assure us that the intelligent designer was one in number, presently alive, and infinitely powerful and competent?

Another objection to the Teleological Argument that also derives from Hume, but which has recently been reformulated, is the anthropological principle. This is the consideration that any observer of any universe would have to conclude that the universe—or at least those parts of it that he is aware of—is designed. If the elements of design favorable to a life capable of making observations were not present, then there could be no such observation. It is said, for example, that the earth is at the optimum distance from the sun for the evolution of higher forms of life. A mere few thousand miles closer to or further from the sun and conditions would not have allowed for the appearance of creatures like ourselves. Similarly, a single living cell presents a complexity that is hard to attribute to the evolutionary processes alone that were first identified by Charles Darwin and postulated as his Theory of Evolution. Now according to the anthropological principle, such observations as these are precisely what an intelligent observer must encounter in her environment, for otherwise there would be no observer and no encounter. Whatever forces, or chance events, or intelligent choices of a divine mind may have been the origin of all the structure and processes we observe, we should not be surprised by them, for they are the conditions of their being observed at all.

A final objection applies to both the Cosmological Argument and the Teleological Argument, though not to the Ontological Argument. Some observers have claimed to find circularity in these two arguments, at least in the form presented here, and perhaps in any possible form they may be given. They both claim that there are some facts about the world that are unintelligible unless God exists. The Cosmological Argument says that change and contingency are unintelligible without God, and the Teleological Argument claims that structure and process are unintelligible unless God exists. Now what is intended by the antithetical terms intelligible/unintelligible? If by *intelligible* one means that an event is intelligible only if we can explain that thing with reference to the aims and purposes of some rational agent such as God, and it is merely a brute fact and unintelligible if we cannot, then the argument assumes what it is supposed to prove, namely that the world must be intelligible in just that way, that it must have been created by God. But why, the objection runs, must we make the assumption that the world must be intelligible in just that way? Perhaps the only thing we can say about the world is that it is a brute fact, that it exists and perhaps always did. If a person accepts that the world must be created and cannot be unintelligible, then he accepts God's existence; but the existence of God was what the argument was supposed to give evidence of. The atheist simply denies the claim that the world is intelligible because it is created by an intelligible God.

AN ARGUMENT AGAINST GOD'S EXISTENCE: THE ARGUMENT FROM EVIL

Hume added an objection to the Teleological Argument that has become part of a modern effort to disprove the existence of God. It takes the form of a moral, not an empirical or scientific objection to the idea that God created the world. Hume carried in a new direction the idea that some facts about this world are unintelligible unless they are the creation of the monotheistic God. There is, he noted, a great deal of evil in this world. Must we not conclude that the world was created by an evil God who takes pleasure in watching our torment? This line of reasoning is called the Argument from Evil for the Nonexistence of God. Its premises can be drawn out as follows:

God is conceived of by Jews, Christians, and Moslems at least as all good and as all-powerful, and as the creator of the world. A creator who was good would abhor evil, and, if he was powerful enough, he would banish evil from the world. A creator who was all-powerful could banish evil from his creation, and, if he was all good, he would desire to banish evil. Now evil exists in this world. It may take two forms: moral evil, as when one person murders another, and natural evil, as when innocent people suffer from plague or drought or earthquake. But then either the creator of the world lacks the power to banish evil, or he lacks the desire to do so. It follows that the Creator of the world is either not all-powerful or not all good. Therefore the monotheistic God does not exist.

The response to this argument may take two forms. The first attempts to justify evil as part of God's creation; it tries to make clear God's ways in the world. This effort was given the name **theodicy** by Leibniz in a book by that title, but it refers also to earlier efforts to solve the problem of evil, at least from a Christian point of view. A theodicy may simply deny the existence of evil: We call things evil because we are not able to see either the entire universe or all of God's purposes. Leibniz believed that God created the best of all possible worlds in the sense of the most complete world, one in which the greatest number of the diverse compossible goods were achieved. All of the things that seem evil to us contribute, in some measure, to the perfection of the whole world. Given the existence and nature of the monotheistic God, Leibniz's conclusion seems reasonable; a good God, like a good person, would not allow evil to happen unless it was productive of higher good. The question that remains is whether we have evidence that this world is a perfect world in Leibniz's sense.

THEODICY: Theodicy is a term sometimes called the "attempt to justify God's ways to man." It is in fact not a justification of God's actions—a blasphemous attempt to speak for God—but an analysis of the logical difficulties generated by the problem of evil. Theodicy has advanced several theories for dealing with this muddle. One is to deny the existence of evil. Augustine believed the world to be perfect at creation, but that there was a falling-away from that perfection by the acts of the Fallen Angels and of Adam and Eve. Another is to argue that evil has the positive function of insuring humankind's distance from God as a condition of our freedom. If the world were perfect, and God were obviously present in it, how could we act so as to make ourselves worthy of heaven or hell? Some moderns have developed as a theodicy the consequences of the notion that God is not all-powerful or not all good.

In the matter of moral evil, the options for the believer seem reasonably clear. If Cain slays Abel, this is a crime on Cain's soul, and not a fault built into the world that God created, as plagues and earthquakes might seem. No doubt God could have created men and women with a clear understanding of right and wrong, and a glowing desire always to do the right thing, from the moment of their birth. Humans could have been created as angels. But God was desirous that persons should make themselves worthy of salvation by their own actions, and thus he gave them freedom and moral responsibility, a capacity for love and hate, and desires for both good and evil. Each person, in this Christian view, is also given enough grace from God to hear the world of God and to save herself, if she freely chooses the path of faith and righteousness. Yet a person can also turn her back upon God and pursue her own purposes. The evil she may cause to others by her sinfulness is necessitated by the greater good produced by her possession of moral responsibility; humans must not be automatons or slaves. Some philosophers and theologians have asked whether God could have created a world in which people possessed moral responsibility, but in which all persons freely chose to do the right thing, or where there was the possibility of sin and moral evil, but where these were never in fact chosen. Current debate has not reached closure on this complex issue. The problem of free will, which is also a matter of current debate, will be taken up in the next chapter.

Other authors have attempted to strengthen the Argument from Evil, notably the great Russian novelist Fyodor Dostoevsky (1821–1881). In some passages in the form of a dialogue from *The Brothers Karamazov,* two brothers, Ivan and Alyosha, discuss the existence of God. Alyosha is a believer and Ivan a skeptic. Ivan does not appear to deny God's existence; rather he is indicting God with indifference to human suffering, and he is rejecting the world God created for containing what he holds to be irredeemable evil. No doubt, if a man is unjustly murdered, Ivan concedes, the murderer is responsible for the suffering of his victim, and the victim may in some sense have deserved his fate: he too, like his murderer, is a sinner. Yet what of the cases—and Ivan produces newspaper clippings documenting many such cases—in which the victims are small children who were tormented, tortured, or murdered? How could the suffering of these sinless infants possibly be justified in terms of the higher ends that God is pursuing in this world? The child, one may think, will wake up from her suffering in the next world and be happy. Yet how can God's granting her salvation atone for the terrible screams of agony he permitted people to cause her here on earth? Ivan's question to Alyosha can be expressed in this fashion: If you were God and planning to create the world, and you knew it would be the best of all possible worlds, and the righteous would, at the end, rise up to life eternal, but you knew too that this great and glorious world would necessarily contain the torture of children, and their unmerited suffering—would you agree to create such a world? Or would you instead say no, the whole damned world is not worth the screams of one child? And Alyosha agrees that he would not. Better that a world such as this one not exist at all! "I would not consent to create such a world," he says, simply.

Dostoevsky's argument attempts to undercut the arguments of theodicy sketched above. It relies on the idea that the ends (the highest possible harmony and the salvation of the righteous) cannot justify the means (the suffering of the innocent), because the horror of the means taints the ends with the evil of unredeemable wrong. It puts the stain of that evil upon God's creation and makes it impossible to worship its creator. To deny that the suffering is really evil because its effects are good is to trivialize the suffering. When the evil done by men is suffered by innocent children forced to bear some of the burden of God's great experiment with humankind, the experiment itself becomes evil. It does not blame God for the evil freely done by one person to another but asserts that God must bear some of the responsibility for such actions insofar as he created the stage upon which those actions are carried out. St. Augustine's claim that all physical suffering derives from the ancient sin of Adam and Eve and the sins of their progeny, is, Ivan says, a belief "not of this world."

GOD AND LINGUISTIC PHILOSOPHY

Much work in the philosophy of religion in the English-speaking world has concerned the meaning of religious language. When a believer utters such propositions as "God exists," or "God loves us," what does she mean? The phrases seem like straightforward claims and are grammatically similar to such expressions as "Cats have fur," or "John loves Mary." Why should expressions referring to God be problematic if these latter expressions are not? The only problem would seem to be whether the propositions "God exists" or "God loves us" are in fact true. But they are problematic, and in an interesting way.

Take the sentence, "John loves Mary." How may one decide whether it is true or false? Some ways are obvious. One could ask John and Mary, or one could watch how John treats Mary when they are together; one could ask John's friends and relatives, or read his letters to her, and so on. Two things must be distinguished: the truth or falsity of the statement, and its meaning. When we began to verify the statement, we assumed we knew what "John loves Mary" means. We know who John and Mary are, and we think we know what the term *love* means. Of course we cannot draw a sharp line about the term *love,* and define it in a way that would correctly apply to all forms of love. Yet it would not conform to normal usage of the term if a person said, "John loves Mary" when he knew that John beat her, or treated her contemptuously, or was obviously interested in another woman. Since we think we know what love means—what kinds of behavior are compatible with a loving relationship between two persons—we know what to look for when we are asked whether in fact John loves Mary.

But what of "God loves us?" First there is the question of meaning: Is the love of God for a human being the same kind of thing as the love of one person for another? Of course we do not mean that God's love is erotic, like that between a man and a woman. But is it like that of a parent for a child? In the Judeo-Christian-Islamic religions, God is often spoken of as a father, and believers are frequently called the children of God. Let us therefore assume that parental love is the kind of love that is spoken of when one says, "God loves you." We know what kinds of behavior on the part of the parent are compatible with the claim that he loves his child: caring concern for the child's well-being, desire to help the child develop into an adult, readiness to make sacrifices for the child, and the like; and what kinds are incompatible: indifference, absence, cruelty, and the like. What events could confirm the statement, "God loves us?" The speaker of that phrase will usually refer to such happy events as the survival of some person from a terrible disease, especially when physicians had given up all hope for the patient, as confirming evidence. This is the miracle and manifestation of divine love, she will say. But then the death of a man sick with that same disease should be confirming evidence for the claim, "God hated that man."

This conflict puts us into an evidential and logical difficulty. If the survival of the first patient was thought to give partial warrant for the claim, "God loves us," then the death of the other patient must partly warrant its denial. We say "partial," for the judgment that John loves Mary requires a great deal of observation of John's behavior before we accept the proposition that he loves her as being sufficiently warranted. And we may believe that John loves Mary even if we have some disconfirming evidence, some sign that he does not love her. No love-relation runs smoothly, but we would still attribute love for Mary to John if there is a great deal of positive evidence in its favor. Must the religious believer accept the death of some patient as offering evidence for the proposition, "God hates him?" If he grants that it serves as evidence that God does not love all of us, then he will be faced with an enormous body of similar disconfirming evidence. God lets many good people suffer and die who pray to Him for help. In fact, if "God loves us" is interpreted the same way as "John loves Mary," then we would have to admit that we have ample reasons for rejecting the claim that God loves you, or me, or anyone except a handful of persons who get through life happily and without suffering.

What if the person who believes that "God loves you" is true refuses to accept the death of a patient, or any of the other horrors suffered by people, as disconfirming the proposition? She may say that God's love is mysterious, not like human love at all, or a love manifest only in the next world. This strategy, however, requires that we not make any specific claims about God's love at all. We cannot claim that the patient who miraculously survives a disease is a recipient of God's love, for we have conceded that God's love may be quite different from our own, and we do not understand it at all. If human suffering cannot disconfirm divine love, then human happiness cannot confirm it. Even worse, if nothing can confirm or disconfirm the proposition, and if God's love is so mysterious that we do not know when we have a case of it or not, then we do not know what we are claiming when we say, "God loves us." Put another way: What difference does it make whether God loves us, if we cannot say what that love implies concerning God's behavior towards us? It makes a great deal of difference to Mary if she learns that John loves her, for she would then know, in some measure, what to expect and what not to expect from him, and she may be delighted or appalled by the prospect. But if a person is given no information about the nature of God's love for him, and if that love is compatible with both the realization of his highest hopes and his worst fears, then it offers him no comfort at all. This kind of analysis—which, in the twentieth century has also been applied to the claims, "God exists," and "God does not exist"—is an application of the epistemological principle called the Verifiability Criterion of Meaningfulness, discussed earlier. It attempts to show, as in this instance, that the statements "God loves you," or "God does not exist" are neither true nor false, for their content is unspecified. If we do not specify what kind of evidence would count for or against the truth of the statement, then that statement is meaningless: As Wittgenstein famously said, "That about which we cannot speak, we should be silent."

Much contemporary philosophy of religion is an attempt to respond to criticisms of this linguistic kind, which dismisses "God talk" as arising out of a misuse of language, a refusal to adhere to criteria of meaningfulness and truth that we otherwise invoke in making claims about things in this world: that John loves Mary, for example. Some defenders of the rationality of religious belief have conceded that no one argument for God's existence is sufficient to justify belief, but they maintain nevertheless that the force of the entire body of positive argument is sufficient to do so, or at least enable a believer to turn back the criticism that she is being irrational or delusional in her faith. Others have argued that a belief in God—and an acceptance of the "God-talk" it generates—is a different kind of belief and discourse than that typical of the sciences, but valid in its domain. Faith, in the view of these observers, depends on a kind of insight or vision that is different from, though just as much self-confirming and basic as, the self-evident and basic evidentiary considerations that scientists take as the starting point of their inquiries.

Problems generated within the philosophy of religion cut to the very nature of the entire philosophical enterprise and raise questions of truth, meaning, and value that open new lines of inquiry in metaphysics, epistemology, logic, and language, and, of course, pose the deepest moral questions of all: What is the human being and what is the significance of human life? The final chapter will explore questions prompted by scientific discoveries in the past century and a half about humankind and its nature in the hope of finding new insight into these perennial issues of philosophy.

CHAPTER 9

Science and Human Nature

This chapter will consider the following concepts and problems:

- The Problem of Human Nature
- The Scientific Approach to Human Nature
- A Humanist Approach to Human Nature: Existentialism

THE PROBLEM OF HUMAN NATURE

A familiar story deserves retelling. At Plato's Academy, the philosophers had decided upon a definition of the essence of the human being. "Man," they said, "is a rational animal." This definition seems quite right, at least at first sight. Human beings belong to the category of animals (we are not plants, or stones, or gods), and what distinguishes us from the other animals is our ability to reason. But then one of the philosophers noted the case of an idiot. He is surely human, but he is not rational. The philosophers thought a bit more, and a new definition was suggested: "Man is a featherless biped." This seems correct: humans are the only creatures that walk on two legs and lack feathers. But a member of the school of cynics, who reviled all philosophy as artificial and use-less ruminations, heard of this definition and threw a plucked chicken over the walls of the Academy. And all the philosophers were reduced again to confusion.

The confusion continues to this day. Writing at the beginning of the just-passed century, the philosopher Max Scheler noted that not since the ancient world has the question of the nature of the human being been subject to so much rethinking and profound questioning as in the modern world. Over the centuries, the human being had been conceived variously as the Child of God, the Tool-maker, the Speaker of Language, the Tormented Ego, or simply as the Naked

Ape. Can we hope to understand the world we inhabit if we do not understand ourselves? As Scheler wrote, "Never and at no time have human beings had less secure and universally accepted knowledge about their nature, their origin, and their purpose than today; never did they have reason to view themselves as problematic, as a question mark, than today. And this situation . . . has its main cause precisely in the unprecedented growth of the special sciences of man: physical, chemical, physiological, anatomical, psychological, developmental, anthropological, prehistorical, ethnological, sociological and historical." The more we know about ourselves, the less we understand ourselves.

Evolution and Human Nature

What specifically gave rise to all this new intellectual turmoil? Who threw the plucked chicken over our academy wall, forcing us to rethink what we had long taken for granted, that the human is essentially a rational animal? There were many new discoveries that shook the foundations of human self-understanding. But, without doubt, the watershed event in our thinking about human nature was the announcement in 1859 of the Theory of Evolution. Our picture of the essence of the human being was slowly redrawn after that year, when Charles Darwin's *On the Evolution of Species* appeared.

Before 1859, most educated Europeans accepted a picture of the human being that had been pieced together from Greek philosophy and Christian doctrine. After God had created the earth, the sky, and the oceans as a stage upon which his great purpose could be carried out, he made first a man from the clay of the earth and then a woman from one rib of the man. The animals and the plants had been created a bit earlier, God having called them forth from the earth. In man and woman he had breathed human life, an event that later came to be understood as bestowing upon us of the power of speech. Later, the soul came to be understood as the source of human rationality and spirit, which makes the human being the image of God, immortal, and **different in kind** from the animals.

DIFFERENCE IN KIND: This phrase signifies a kind of *irreducibility* of one thing to another, or the impossibility of understanding one thing in terms of another. In the premodern world, the earth and the heavens, for example, were thought to be different in kind. Aristotle had argued that the substance of which the celestial objects, the planets and the stars, were made were different in kind from the substances found on earth. The movements of the stars also were different from terrestrial movement; the stars all moved in perfectly circular orbits, while circular motion was not natural on earth. These beliefs were to be challenged in the seventeenth century by Newton, who showed that both the fall of an apple and the movement of the earth around the sun can be explained by a single set of formulas derived from the theory of universal gravity. The theory of evolution similarly challenges the notion that the life and

Charles Darwin. © *Library of Congress.*

behavior of human beings are different in kind and not continuous with that of the higher animals.

Darwin's theory and the development of it since his day paints a decidedly different picture. According to evolutionary theory, humankind is continuous in nature with all other living beings. Life began when simple material elements in the primordial oceans developed the capacity, by means of innumerable chance events, to form complex molecules that could replicate themselves, assimilate new elements to themselves, and protect themselves from destruction by other molecules. Those elements able to do these three things best would, by the nature of the case, survive and proliferate, while less competent forms of emergent life would not. From billions of chance events, biological mechanisms originated that could be turned to different ends as modules of new species that emerged, lived, and became extinct. With this simple schema—greater or less competence in reproduction and survival due to small variations in kind, and greater or less adaptation to a changing environment—evolutionary theory attempts to account for the great proliferation of life forms on this earth and their tendency toward increased complexity of adaptations across time. These mechanisms and modules, whatever they were, offered to their possessors, the living organisms, both opportunities and limitations. They made some forms of behavior possible and excluded others—just as a bird enjoys the freedom of the air but lacks the freedom of the oceans. The human brain, the most complex thing we know of in the universe, is the product of a long process of natural selection. Human creatures today dominate the earth, Darwinians believe, not because we possess God-given souls and are the subjects of divine supervision and providence, but because the brain is the most efficient mechanism for survival that the process of evolution has as yet "tossed up," so to speak, as life goes about, in mechanical fashion, its experiments with life-forms and their chemical components.

The Conflict between Science and Religion

A key difference between the religious and the scientific understanding of the human being is the insistence of most Western religions upon the spiritual and moral qualities of persons, whose behavior, unlike all other living things, must be understood under the categories of right and wrong, sacred and profane, saved and damned. Science, in contrast, understands the human being as one would any object of scientific inquiry, as an item that can be explained and perhaps controlled by means of physical laws. In the decades following Darwin, several new sciences arose, as Scheler noted, that took some aspect of human behavior as their object. The first laboratory for experimental psychology at a university was established in 1879 in Leipzig by Wilhelm Wundt. Franz Boas was made the first professor of anthropology at Columbia University in 1899. Economics was given its modern foundation by Karl Marx in his *Das Kapital,* the first volume of which appeared in 1867. Sociology was first taught as a distinct academic discipline by Emile Durkheim in the 1880s. Francis Lieber became the first professor of political science in America in 1857. The human being came to be treated in the sciences externally, as an object for observation, experimentation, and explanation. Naturally, each science presents a somewhat different picture of the human being and raises a different set of philosophical questions about us. *Scientific* and *humanistic* approaches to understanding the human being can be distinguished, so this chapter will be divided accordingly.

THE SCIENTIFIC APPROACH TO HUMAN NATURE

A theory, on a standard account of science, must meet at least three requirements. First, it must contain some general statements that describe relationships among phenomena or mechanisms within phenomena, in terms of which an event or a series of events can be explained. These general statements account for the known facts. Second, the account must lead us to expect as yet unobserved phenomena. It must suggest new avenues for future research. Third, it must be falsifiable, that is, it must be possible to state some observable conditions which, if they are met, would force the alteration or abandonment of the theory. In short, the theory must explain something about the world, must suggest new ways of exploring phenomena, and must tell us what it would be like for its explanations to be wrong.

Science today searches for theories whose laws give coherence to a large body of phenomena and enable researchers to explain and understand them. It insists upon the falsifiability of its propositions and upon the careful observation and measurement of events. The theories discussed in this section contain general statements abut some or all aspects of human nature. They propose some general principles or set of principles that explain human behavior and render it intelligible. They account for the known facts and are intended by their authors to be falsifiable in principle: they must be tested by reference to the facts of observation. Of course, there is debate as to whether, for a given theory, these conditions are always met. The theory of evolution, for example, gives coherence to an enormous body of observational data concerning the fossil record, DNA similarities in populations of morphologically different plants and animals, and even the structure of mammalian embryos. It is nonetheless difficult to say whether the theory is capable of disconfirmation, that is, whether it is possible to specify conditions that, if obtained, would show the general postulates of evolutionary theory to be false. It is also uncertain just what the theory proposes concerning human nature. Since the human animal is different in many significant features from all other living things, and since also the course of human biological and social evolution is still unknown in all but its broad outlines, it is difficult to derive from the theory an account of what aspects of human behavior are the result of evolutionary mechanisms and what aspects are the products of social conditioning. Like evolutionism, each theory considered here has its limitations, and yet each demonstrates the complexity of human nature.

Psychoanalysis

Sigmund Freud (1856–1939) is known for his development of psychoanalysis, which is a technique for relieving anxieties and neuroses by leading patients to the suppressed memories of events that prompt them. But Freud theorized also about the larger questions of human behavior. Some of the questions that troubled him were quite general: How can we account for the human personality, that is, the set of characteristics that make one consistent in one's selfhood and distinct from all other persons? Why do neuroses arise in otherwise normal people? Is there a consistent structure to the human psyche? Others were quite specific: Why is it that most people believe in God, despite a lack of evidence for God's existence? What is the psychology of preliterate peoples? What kinds of conflicts arise in the minds of children?

The answers to these questions that Freud pursued, proposed, and developed during his long lifetime relate to a few key ideas to which he held consistently. The first is his theory of psychosexual development, through which all people pass as they grow from infancy to adulthood. The stages of this development are well known: The first he called the oral stage, before the infant is weaned; the second the anal stage, which takes place during toilet training, from about two to three years of age; the third is the phallic stage, when the small child becomes interested in his penis (or, according to Freud, her lack of one); the fourth is the stage of latency, from about six years of age to puberty, when no sexual interest is recorded; the fifth and final stage is the genital, when the adolescent passes from puberty to adult sexuality. During this development, the elements of psychic life unfold and give rise to conflicts in each stage that affect

Sigmund Freud. © *Library of Congress.*

the adult personality. If these conflicts are not resolved, they can go underground to haunt the preconscious mind and become dimly visible in dreams, in slips of the tongue, or in adult neuroses.

The development of the human psyche occurs, in general, in a region of the person to which conscious awareness has no access. Consciousness takes up only a very small region of the psyche. The *id,* or it, is the deepest structure of the psyche. It is the source of libidinal energy, which is channeled to conscious behavior through various censoring devices that prevent the individual from understanding the true source of her behavior. The *ego,* or I, represents for Freud the reality principle; it is the part of conscious life that attempts to satisfy libidinal cravings in ways that permit the individual's survival. The *superego* constrains the ego to behave not according to its own partly conscious impulses, even those compatible with its survival, but according to the social mores and taboos of the individual's community, which have been foisted upon him by his social upbringing. The superego puts a public face upon the ego and gives it standing within its community.

Freud once wrote that if a person could see himself for what he really was, behind the veil of the mental censor that prevents the deepest feelings and desires from entering into the light of consciousness, the result would be psychological catastrophe: madness or suicide. It is therefore not surprising that Freud thought the passage from infancy through childhood to maturity would be a rocky one. The growing personality's sexuality or id-being thrusts itself up from the unconsciousness and must be repressed if the individual is to meet the demands of his parents and teachers, to live a civilized life, or just to survive. The classic conflict in this process of psychosexual growth towards adult sexuality is the Oedipal conflict, which takes place during the phallic phase. The small boy desires fervently to have his mother all to himself, and to get rid of his father ("No man weeps sincerely at his own father's funeral," wrote Freud). He does not know this clearly, but he senses that his father and mother have a secret relationship from which he is excluded: The mother gets some kind of satisfaction from the father that the boy cannot imitate, and she keeps the boy from her bedroom door. The child senses that the parents can read the forbidden desires in his mind, and he fears the father, who towers over him, at times threateningly, like a giant. His darkest fear is that his father will punish his wicked thought by castrating him, by taking away his penis, which gives a newly discovered but forbidden pleasure to him. At the same time, the boy knows the father is good and loving to him, also. Freud drew these conclusions, and the theoretical structures that give them coherence, from extensive clinical experience with patients, some of whom were children.

Freud believed that these childhood conflicts are more traumatic in some people than in others, and this fact can be used to explain the different behavior people exhibit as adults. The Oedipal conflict can also make comprehensible the practice of ancestor worship among precivilized tribes, or the belief in monotheism typical of the Western world. In the case of the latter, the Oedipal conflict mirrors, in some measure, the monotheistic belief in God as the Father; we worship him to atone for our wicked childhood desires about our real father. God threatens us with hellfire for our sins, which he alone can measure (he, too, reads our minds), and at the same time he offers us a paradise similar to what little boys enjoy when they lie securely in their mother's arms.

Freudianism is not a comprehensive theory of the human being, in that it does not attempt to explain all features of human existence in detail, but it does see all of civilization as resting upon a consciousness that emerges from, and is determined by, a deep submerged animal nature that we cannot bear to look at directly. Can this hypothesis of an unconscious mind, whose mechanisms generate at least some features of human behavior, be tested? Is it falsifiable? Freud believed that the sources of our conscious life are not immediately accessible to us, but that a special scientific standpoint can be attained from which we are able to get a glimpse of the true nature of consciousness and the mechanisms that produce our conscious life. For Freud, that standpoint is provided by psychoanalysis. Freudian psychoanalysis, which is the practical application of his theory of the psychic life, has not had great success in curing neuroses, and this suggests that there may be something wrong with the theory of the mechanisms that purport to explain their dynamics. Still, the notion that selfhood, personality, and even the choice of a spouse or a career are caused by submerged desires and feelings over which we have no control has affected enormously how we perceive these phenomena. Moreover, the notion that human culture is a mechanism designed to shield us from the desires of our animal nature is a troubling one. Freud's influence was felt for decades in Western art, poetry, and music, when they depicted a fragmented and sick human being out of touch with the wellsprings of his own life.

Behaviorism

B. F. Skinner (1904–1990) was the greatest American psychologist of the twentieth century. During his long tenure at Harvard, he supplied the theory of human behavior and its philosophical underpinnings that are now accepted in general outline by most academically trained psychologists in the United States. Skinner devised the concept of *operant conditioning* and applied it to laboratory research on pigeons and rats. A rat in a "Skinner box" was trained to run through a series of complex behaviors by controlling the box's responses to the rat's "operations" on the box in its efforts to satisfy its basic needs. For example, a rat will first respond to negative stimuli such as pain or hunger by random actions. When a specific action results in a desired effect—the reduction of pain or the presentation of food—the rat will repeat that action until it is satisfied. The effective action is one chosen by the human experimenter, perhaps by pushing a green lever chosen from several levers of different colors. The satisfaction of the need reinforces positively the push-the-green-lever behavior of the rat. It now runs through the behavioral routine of pushing the green lever when it is hungry. It has learned a *stimulus-response mechanism* taught to it by the environment: it now knows what to do when it is hungry.

The theoretical principles of operant conditioning—stimulus-response mechanisms, positive and negative reinforcement, and **behavioral** routines—and its experimental exploration seem straightforwardly scientific. Its hypotheses about learning mechanisms in rats appear to be falsifiable. If a rat in some experiment refused to change its behavior as predicted even after many trials, the experimenter would have reason to believe that something was wrong with her hypothesis. Now Skinner generalizes his theory and extends it to human beings, and here his account of human behavior becomes philosophically challenging. All human behavior can be reduced to atomic stimulus-response mechanisms, Skinner claims, which could be correlated with states of the brain. His rejection of the ideas of an unconscious mind and notion of purposive behavior is known as **noncognitivism**. Language learning, sexual behavior, dispositions to act in certain ways that determine what we call personality, are all acquired by the human organism as it operates upon the environment to achieve the ends it naturally desires: survival, recognition by others, and an enhanced capacity to act. If we study human learning in detail, Skinner believed, psychologists will eventually be able to control human behavior by controlling the environment in which people live. People can be taught to be happy, or to be nonaggressive, or—anything at all. Human beings, like rats, are extremely malleable; we are, like rats, respondent organisms.

COGNITIVISM AND BEHAVIORISM: These two concepts were for a long time considered to be irreconcilable positions in psychology. Cognitivism is the common-sense view that human behavior can only be understood by reference to events going on in the mind. We can only understand, for example, why a person is walking across the street if we understand such things as the aims or purposes in crossing the street, and these aims and purposes are men-

B.F. Skinner. © *AP / Wide World Photos.*

tal events. Behaviorism denies the necessity of referring to the mind—a "black box," as Skinner once called it. For him, it was sufficient to understand the stimulus-response mechanism behind the action, perhaps in this case that the person crossing the street has learned to walk in that direction by the satisfactions she received upon the other side of the street. However implausible such an account may seem, Skinner's point is to keep psychology an *empirical* science. States of mind are not empirical events; they are knowable only to the person whose states they are. Since Skinner denies that there is any difference in kind between the behavior of a human being and that of a rat, he—and other behaviorists—saw no need to have such states enter their equations. It is enough to observe the behavior of persons and correlate them with the basic needs that prompt them to understand that behavior fully.

In *Walden II* (1948), Skinner described the conversations of visitors and citizens of an imaginary commune, where behavioral principles are applied to the members by a self-appointed psychologist-king speaking in Skinner's voice. The communards are taught to want no more from life than they can reasonably expect to obtain. Private ownership of property, even of one's own children, is abolished. Citizens have plenty of free time to do what they want, hence they feel free, but the free-time occupations available to them—for example, the pursuit of science—are limited to those that develop a sense of belonging to the community and that foster its values. No one desires to do anything antisocial, so well have their responses been shaped by the conditions in their carefully constructed environment. They seem not to possess a sense of moral responsibility for what they do, for no one is inclined to do anything that is not in the interest of the community. Freedom, and the dignity that supposedly rests upon moral responsibility, are mere chimeras in any case, Skinner believes. To be free is simply to be able to do what you want, not to determine your wants. Determining what people will want is the function of the community as educator. If someone goes beyond the permissible in Walden II, he is not punished, for he has been improperly taught; the training cadre simply "reprogram" his stimulus-response mechanisms so that his rebellious behavior will not appear again. Skinner's purpose in this book is not simply to make a philosophical point. He believes that unless we learn the sources of aggressive and antisocial behavior and use that knowledge to make people less aggressive and antisocial, the world is doomed. We will either kill ourselves in war, or lay waste to the environment.

Unlike Freud, who attempted to control human behavior only by alleviating symptoms arising from conflicts between innate psychic structures and contingent social arrangements, Skinner wishes to produce radical behavioral change in humankind. By reorganizing the social structure, as in the imaginary commune Walden II, he will produce psychologically engineered human beings among whom class struggle or neurosis will be unknown. Oddly, Skinner believes that the sources of human behavior are transparent, and not hidden in economic structures or in the unconscious mind. The engineered citizens of Walden II will be aware of the forces that made them what they are, but they will be so programmed that the details of their manipulation by the leaders of the commune will not interest them. Their curiosity will be concerned with their daily activities. Their happiness and satisfaction reinforces their willingness to comply with the simple rules of the commune. Many observers criticized Skinner's plans as a social hell worse than a concentration camp, where the only differences are that people live comfortably and do not know they are in one. Skinner replied to such criticism that happiness for all is possible only in a psychologically engineered society. The alternative is the enslavement of the many to the few, with the social and economic chaos such enslavement produces.

The Problem of Free Will

Skinner's beliefs about the malleability of human behavior rest in part upon his solution to a metaphysical problem known as *free will and determinism.* This notion has enjoyed a long history, beginning with Aristotle, and Skinner is a modern proponent of the determinist position. The word *freedom* is ambiguous. It refers to what can be called freedom from constraint, as when a person is free to do what she wishes to do. She may have been sitting for a long time and desires to stand up. She is free to do so if nothing constrains her to keep seated, as, obviously, chains or paralysis, or simply the fear of offending others at a solemn church ceremony. Persons have more or less freedom from constraint; in general, we say that a person is less free when he is in jail than when he has an open calendar on a Sunday afternoon.

The kind of freedom involved in the controversy over free will and determinism is quite different. Its nature appears in the reasons that appear to support determinism. It is self-evident that any event has a cause. Nothing can "cause itself." An item for which we could not trace the causes, even in principle, would be simply incomprehensible. Scientists attempt to account for all the events and processes they encounter in nature in terms of their causes and the natural or scientific laws that determine them. If it is not possible at the present time to trace the causes of some known phenomenon, a scientist will always assume that future research will discover those causes. Without this assumption and expectation, there would be no reason to begin a scientific inquiry.

A determinist, such as Skinner, now generalizes on this position in two ways. First, he draws the metaphysical conclusion that the universe is determined in all its details by antecedent events and causal laws. Just as an examination of a clock enables us to predict that it will strike noon at twelve o'clock tomorrow, so too a mind that knew all causal laws and the present distribution of mass and energy in the universe could predict precisely what will happen tomorrow, or a hundred years from now. We say a mind with such information could do that; obviously, there exists no such mind, but if we deny that such prediction is impossible in principle, we seem to commit ourselves to the mysterious view that some events, at least, are random, exist without ground, or have escaped causal determination.

The second generalization that Skinner and others make leads to behaviorism; they apply the determinist thesis to human behavior. Just as every event is determined by causes, so too are human actions determined by causes, and scientific inquiry can, at least in principle, discover those causes. No doubt, most of us would grant that social, genetic, and psychological factors may influence the behavior of persons. If we learn that a young felon has been raised on the streets, taught criminal behavior, and had the milk of human kindness beaten out of him by adults when he was a child, we would be less inclined to blame him for his actions. "As the twig is bent, so grows the tree" is a saying that applies to human children as much as to twigs. Human behavior, like the behavior of animals, plants, or atoms, the determinist asserts, is determined in its last detail by prior events according to natural law. We humans, like all living things, are respondent organisms and cannot help but act as we do. Note that determinism does not imply constraint. John is not forced to marry Mary; he marries her because he wants to. But his wants have been shaped by social or genetic forces over which he has no control.

If the behaviorist is right, then human beings lack a certain capacity that most of us assume we have: the power to originate actions that cannot be explained by anything other than our own choice. It is this power that is asserted by free-will theorists, or *libertarians*. Free will is the power to act upon a choice that is not determined by prior causes over which the individual has no control. The nature of this power is unclear, and most determinists consider the notion to be vacuous. The key to libertarianism is its belief in the human power to control one's wants and desires as well as one's actions. One can originate actions that are inexplicable except by one's conscious choice, and that choice can be explained only by itself.

Self-determination does not imply that our behavior is random or inexplicable; the way we seek an explanation of the behavior of a person is to ask her why she behaved the way she did. No doubt, the behaviorist would respond to this account that the very occurrence of all the agent's thought can be explained by antecedent causes. Even the disposition to reflect rationally on what one should do is as much reducible to a learned stimulus-response mechanism as is the behavior of the rat in the maze. For both cases, science can determine their causal conditions.

Genetics and Human Nature

A kindergarten teacher once asked the children, "What do zebras have that no other animal has?" One child responded, "Little zebras!" This obvious fact—so obvious that the teacher would never expect it as an answer—that big zebras have little zebras and not little giraffes or rabbits or something entirely unpredictable each time it gives birth—was not understood in the slightest until about fifty years ago. But the rise of genetics as a special science, after the epochal discovery in 1953 of the double helix of DNA by James Watson and Francis Crick, has influenced our thinking, not only about zebras, but about the nature of the human animal. Perhaps, instead of our being a respondent organism, as the psychologist Skinner argued, we are essentially a genetic mechanism of some sort. Our behavior might be explained not by our learning environments, but by the study of the biological structures hard-wired into us by evolution. Two representatives of this view are the American Edward O. Wilson, author of *Sociobiology* (1975), and the Oxford biologist Richard Dawkins, author of *The Selfish Gene* (1976). They have caused considerable controversy among the general public and professional biologists.

Geneticists, evolutionary biologists, students of social evolution, and other scientists working in the broad fields of human biology have tied the nature of the human being to the genetic mechanisms that make possible and limit our linguistic behavior, our emotions, our aggressiveness, even our peculiar sexual posture. Remarkable discoveries have been made that appear to demonstrate the genetic origin of many behaviors that seem, at first sight, to be personal, idiosyncratic, or psychological in origin. Studies of identical twins separated from birth show a large number of behavioral similarities that, geneticists argue, cannot be explained by psychological shaping, just because these genetically identical children were raised in entirely different circumstances. Such evidence appears to undercut the contentions of behaviorists, like Skinner, that all our behavior is socially learned and that people are genetically indistinct from each other. The sociobiologist and geneticist Dawkins is as sweeping in his claims for the reducibility of human behavior to genetic structures as Skinner was for behaviorism. In *The Selfish Gene,* Dawkins writes: "The ancient replicators [the earliest self-replicating molecules] . . . did not die out. . . . Now they swarm in huge colonies, safe inside gigantic lumbering robots, sealed off from the outside world, communicating with it by tortuous indirect routs, manipulating it by remote control. They are in you and in me; they created us, body and mind; and their preservation is the ultimate rationale for our existence. They have come a long way, those replicators. Now they go by the name of genes and we are their survival machines."

This is an awesome claim and a surprising one too, although it is an extension of Darwinianism. It claims that we are the products of unsupervised and purposeless chance events in changing environmental conditions. The process of evolution was directed only by the principles of the struggle for survival and adaptation. Metaphors are out of place here. There is no *experiment* going on, for an experiment requires an experimenter, and there is none. Nor is there a *struggle* for survival, for there is no *striving to survive* or *will to power* in the genetic structures. Given a set of initial environmental conditions and their nonrandom change over time, a genetic structure or a population of similar simple organisms either survives or becomes extinct. There are no hard feelings in this struggle indeed, Dawkins notes, no feelings at all. Even different nonliving things display greater or less adaptation to their environment, which gives them differential survival capacities. A pyramid will fare better in an earthquake than a Greek temple. Even a population of similar organisms displays considerable variety. The human genome allows for variations among the human organisms constructed according to its chemical instructions. Dawkins says that these structures account for differences in our bodies and our minds. Although the meaning he gives to the notion of mind is somewhat unclear, he appears to include in the concept such features of our behavior as our speech, our loves and hates, our preferences among styles of art, expressions of feeling, or the differences in our dreams, aspirations, and secret desires—all capacities and behavioral routines the possession of which has given humankind great flexibility and made it possible for humankind to dominate this planet, at least for the past two million years. Humankind's success assures the stability of the human genome itself.

This dispute between psychologists (psychoanalytic, cognitivist, and behaviorist) and geneticists is called the *nature/nurture* conflict. It has large social and political implications that have spilled over to the public and has informed discussions between social liberals and social conservatives. If human behavior is entirely a function of the genes, then the genetic material an individual is born with defines his or her fate, as it were. Since we possess no means for altering the genetic materials of persons already born, we are unable to deal with antisocial behavior determined by those materials. Moreover, the prospect of scientists attempting to deal with social problems by the genetic manipulation of zygotes or the alteration of the human genome suggests the creation of a future dystopia on the model of *Brave New World*. The view of psychologists seems much more inviting. Although Skinner's vision of a future society in *Walden II* is hardly an inspiring fate for humankind, it does hold open the prospect of manipulating human beings in a humane and benevolent manner so as to eliminate antisocial or dysfunctional behavior. Indeed, all social programs that aim at solutions to such social problems as poverty, illiteracy, drug addiction, and crime assume such behaviors to arise from psychological conditioning that is alterable by liberal political action, and not from invariant genetic material. If it turns out that male sexism or xenophobic racism or the urge to war are determined genetically, then new forms of nonaggressive education, sensitivity and diversity training, and even the shaping of social attitudes in infancy are doomed to failure. From the standpoint of evolutionary biology, only if socially unapproved behavior leads in general to the early death or the incapacity to reproduce of the individuals who exhibited them will the genetic structures that produced them disappear from the human genome—if even then.

Clearly, the dispute between nature theorists and nurture theorists has not been resolved. This fact raises an interesting question: Why has it not? Both sides to the dispute believe that a science of human nature is possible; both sides hold, in general, to the metaphysics of universal determinism. Yet our ability to predict and control human behavior seems as rudimentary today as it was before the advent of the human sciences. We are not even able to predict the gross outlines of human behavior, say, in economics and politics: How long will the recession last? For whom will the people vote in the next election—to say nothing about predicting with any accuracy whether any one of a group of children will grow into a criminal one day (assuming, in all these cases, that the environing circumstances remain stable). Social programs for the poor, new educational methods for slow learners, the rehabilitation of criminals, even psychoanalysis as a cure for neurosis seem not to possess the effectiveness that their proponents had claimed for them. Psychologists and geneticists alike have been accused of pseudoscience, that is, of making theoretical claims and devising explanatory hypotheses that seem not to be falsifiable. Skinner's hypothesis in *Walden II* that certain exercises among kindergarten children will prompt self-discipline, or Dawkin's hypothesis that specific genetic mechanisms result in a mind or a personality of a certain kind, are not properly testable, perhaps because we cannot isolate the causal factors in each claim. Perhaps, too, the problem lies in scientists' inability to develop universal measurements or unambiguous descriptions of human behavior, the way physicists can describe and measure precisely defined events in their laboratories: weights, wavelengths, mass, and the like. Can human behavior be described and measured so objectively and unambiguously by human scientists?

Neurophysiology and the Philosophy of Mind

Other human sciences have tried a different route than those described thus far. One is the route of neurophysiology, the science of the human brain. Most scientists are naturalists; they adhere to a materialist metaphysics that denies the independent existence of nonphysical things such as ideas, minds, or souls. Mind, in this view, is an **epiphenomenon** of the brain. Other theorists assert that what we call mind is identical with the brain, perhaps in the sense that the mind simply is what the brain does. If this is so, the failure of such human sciences as dialectical materialism, psychoanalysis, behaviorism, or genetics to explain human behavior sufficiently can be attributed to their approaching human behavior macroscopically, at a great distance from its real sources in the brain. The study of the brain and how it functions proceeds microscopically, by inquiring into distinct brain states and how they intersect causally. Skinner expresses its purposes forcefully in *Science and Human Behavior:*

> Eventually a science of the nervous system based upon direct observation rather than inference will describe the neural states and events which immediately precede instances of behavior. We shall know the precise neurological conditions which immediately precede, say, the response, "No, thank you." These events in turn will be found to be preceded by other neurological events, and these in turn by others. This series will lead us back to events outside the nervous system and, eventually, outside the organism.

EPIPHENOMENALISM: Epiphenomenalism is a form of metaphysical dualism. Mind and matter both exist. However, the distinguishing feature of epiphenomenalism is its claim that mental events are produced by physical events in the brain, but they cannot have any influence on the brain themselves. Thus a human being thinks, but thought has no influence upon action; humans are entirely physical systems. The idea, which has recently received a great deal of attention in the philosophy of mind, is often traced to T. H. Huxley, who is said to have noted that the mind contributes nothing to the behavior of an organism, just as the whistle given off by a locomotive contributes nothing to the operation of the steam engine.

One event that supports hopes for a neurophysiologically based human science is the advent of the digital computer as a model of human thought. Can computers think? No doubt much in this question rides on the meaning of the world "think." If we can be shown that computers can think as measured by some criterion, such as a **Turing test,** we might be willing to accept the idea, however initially strange it may seem. But if such a computer could be devised, then we would have a strong basis for Skinners's claim that there is a direct correlation between mental states and ideas and the states and electrochemical actions of the brain. For the "thinking" of the computer can be fully known, and its states and processes can be directly correlated with its various inputs and outputs. If the computer's hardware structure, its inputs, and its routines (software) determine its outputs completely, then, analogously, the human "outputs" we call behavior must correlate with, or be reducible to, the electrochemical activities in our brains. Similar functions in a machine or in a person (thinking) must be based in similar processes (information processing by a computer/brain).

THE TURING TEST: One effort to define the term *thinking* in a way that might apply to a thinking machine based upon today's computers was undertaken by Allan Turing (1912–1954). Imagine a human being seated before a computer into which he is invited to write questions of his own devising. In some cases, the answers that appear on his screen are the responses of a human being seated at a terminal in another room; in other cases the answers are devised

> by a computer. When the human questioner is no longer able to distinguish between the human being's answers and those of the computer, then, Turing suggested, we would have a machine that thinks. To date (2004) no machine has been devised that has passed the Turing test.

The hope of interpreting the activity of the brain on the model of the computer has also been supported by discoveries about the structure and the processes of the brain itself. No doubt our present ignorance of how those activities give rise to what we call mental events, such as assertions of belief, memories of a past vacation, or the planning of some future undertaking, is still very deep. Yet we know now what parts of the brain are used for certain types of behavior, such as the use of language, the calling-up of mental images, or the hearing and recognizing of distant sounds. Such knowledge convinces most observers that whatever thinking is, and however it may be in fact produced in the mind, it cannot be independent of a material substance such as a brain, any more than the computer software can run apart from the computer's hardware. The idea of metaphysical dualism, or the essential independence of bodies and minds, which leaves open the religious concepts of reincarnation or life after death, is considered by most observers today as founded in no known facts.

However, philosophers still argue about how the facts are to be interpreted. The mind-brain identity thesis assumes that if two things that seem different are really identical, then it should be possible to speak of both of them in a uniform way. Specifically, it should be possible to translate mind-talk into brain-talk once we master and track the brain events to which mental events are thought to be equivalent. Instead of saying, "John believes that Mary will agree to his proposal," we will speak of the neural firings that are equivalent to that belief-event in John's mind. Statements in the brain-language will be dauntingly complex, but no one will be required to "speak" such a language. The important thing is that the mental events be translatable into brain events without remainder, that is, without any loss of content. When this becomes possible, we will be able to eliminate, in principle, mind-talk entirely. One important representative of this view is Paul Churchland (1942–). He believes that we will eventually be able to eliminate what he calls the language of "folk psychology," which refers to mental states (which, to Churchland's mind, do not exist) in favor of a language that refers to the events in the brain alone. An interesting feature of Churchland's position is that, against Skinner, he does not expect a one-to-one correspondence between the brain-state and mental-state languages, as one would normally expect when one is translating a description of a thing in one language to that in another. However, Churchland believes that the reason for this incapacity is that the mental-state language is fundamentally flawed.

When we use the term *mental states* to describe the contents of the mind, we are simply mistaken about the nature of those contents. Churchland makes this point by analogy with the language of astronomy before and after Copernicus.

Before Copernicus, we would speak of the stars "wheeling about" the axis of the North Star, and of all the heavenly bodies revolving around our planet Earth. Such talk gave rise to theoretical questions about whether the stars are fixed to crystalline spheres, just as questions about John's belief concerning Mary gives rise to questions about how an immaterial mind causes physical states in the body, or whether the mental state of "being in love" is located in the mind or in the soul. Questions about crystalline spheres and souls are pseudoquestions that arise out of our ignorance of the facts. Of course, we could translate talk about whirling orbs into mathematical talk about the earth's movements around the sun and within the galaxy. This correct theoretical and mathematical account would correlate with the pre-Copernican account and describe the facts in a new way, and it allows us to eliminate talk about crystalline spheres entirely. When we eliminate the old pre-Copernican language in favor of the modern language, we get the facts right about the movement of the stars and are able to explain how the pre-Copernican language arose at all. So too, Churchland believes, will the language of a "matured neuroscience" eliminate talk of ideas and minds and souls.

Jerry A. Fodor's (1935–) thesis concerning the nature and activity of mind is called *functionalism*. It is more liberal in its willingness to grant possible legitimacy to talk of mental states, brain states, artificial intelligences, or even of the states of intelligent alien visitors or disembodied spirits. For Fodor, the "hardware" or the places of thinking do not matter as much as the "software" or functions that constitute thinking. Thinking is a system of functions that could, in principle at least, be realized in any number of material places. The important thing is that the processing of data take place according to a regular pattern of causal relations between inputs, the states they cause in the mental mechanism (the brain in the case of a human being), the routines they give rise to, and the eventual outputs they produce. Skinner's noncognitivism, which denies that mental events play a role in determining behavior, is attacked by Fodor. One cannot grasp the meaning of behavior, he argues, without grasping events in the mind, for they also play a role in the production of behavior by processing the input. Human beings, at least, monitor their own inputs, and this internal monitoring may affect the eventual responses or outputs.

Some observers think that the materialist or physicalist account of the human being as an embodied processor of data leaves out an essential aspect of the human way of existing that is suggested by the notion of monitoring one's inputs. That aspect is called *intentionality*. A human being, unlike a computer, which merely processes inputs according to the program embodied in its software, is aware of the events taking place within himself. Consciousness goes out like a ray toward an object so that the conscious mind knows what it is conscious of: John's beliefs about Mary are known to John as his own, even while he is thinking of Mary. It is at least conceivable that a machine could pass the Turing test without ever knowing that it was doing it, even though it might affirm that it knows what it is doing. For it may not be able to intend—grasp, get a bead on—what it is doing when it affirms that it knows.

The philosopher best known for raising objections to all forms of the philosophy of the human being that seek to reduce our mental life to behavior, to brain states, or to software functions is John Searle (1932–). In his celebrated "Chinese room experiment," Searle asks us to imagine a person placed in a room where he has the task of translating, say, Russian into Chinese, when he has no knowledge of either language. When certain Russian characters are input to him, he looks them up in a special dictionary of syntax that contains complex instructions in English for dealing with those characters. He is told to replace always a certain sequence of Russian characters with a specific sequence of Chinese characters. He then outputs the corresponding Chinese characters. The result is a fluent and correct translation of a Russian text into Chinese. Would we say under those circumstances, Searle asks rhetorically, that the person doing this work knew Russian and Chinese? Of course not; he knows what he is doing, of course (for he is human), and how to do it correctly (for he is, let us imagine, as efficient as any computer in following instructions), but he cannot intend—grasp, get a bead on—the meanings of the text he has translated or the medium of their expression, namely Russian and Chinese. The human mind, in Searle's view, is not captured by the analogy with a computer, which only manipulates symbols. It does not refer those symbols to what they designate, as the notion of "cup" designates the cup on the table. The notion designates the cup as existing beyond the mind as the thing that is intended when a person grasps the object on the table as a cup.

REFERENCE AND MEANING: The dispute between Searle and functionalists such as Fodor can be expressed in terms of language. The theory of language distinguishes between *semantics* and *syntax*. Semantics is the study of how language can be used to *refer* to objects beyond language, typically, to objects in the world, to mental states, or to objects of the imagination. This semantical function of language is usually thought to involve intentionality, or the state of consciousness *of* something or other. The term *syntax* refers to the *structure* of language, the way it typically organizes symbols to create meaningful speech. A computer is entirely syntactical in its operations; it organizes data according to its program to create its outputs. Can an adequate description of the human mind dispense with semantics? After all, a computer does, and it still produces intelligible outputs. This is an important question for such functionalists as Fodor. Searle, of course, answers the question negatively: It is only because human beings are able to intend objects and create symbols to refer to those objects that we have human thought.

Is it possible to produce a computer that simulates human thinking (as a successful Turing machine would do), and also has a mind, in Searle's sense of one that intends the objects designated by its symbols? Well, of course, we do not know. Yet, it is surprising, given our admitted ignorance of how the human mind works at all, let alone how it produces consciousness and self-consciousness, that so many philosophers and AI engineers assume that it is only a matter of time be-

fore one is produced. This conviction may be based upon a metaphysical prejudice: The brain, it is assumed, must work by processing data. But any data processing can be emulated by a digital computer of sufficient complexity and
sophistication. Therefore, such a computer will be achieved *some day*. No doubt
the motive behind the assumption is the same as in all science since Thales: We
must assume that human behavior is determined by underlying rational principles, and that human reason, given enough time and effort, is capable of grasping
those principles. Otherwise the human being will not be an ordered and beautiful
whole, as the ancient thinkers believed the cosmos to be, but a chaos of unrelated
and unintelligible mental and physical events.

Determinism is an expression of that anxiety one feels before the
unimaginable complexity of things (the cosmos, the human mind) and the desire
to find order. However, many thinkers even today have indeed denied the ultimate rationality of human life, whatever the scientific orderliness of the cosmos
we inhabit. Indeed, some say there is no human nature; we are not bound by nature, we are always at work in a unique situation. We can describe the parameters of human existence, but not how we must exist. Some of these thinkers
embrace this chaos that is human life, some run from it, but all of them believe
that chaos and unintelligibility are inexpungeable from human life. They have
gone, some willingly, some not, under the title of *Existentialism.*

A HUMANIST APPROACH TO HUMAN NATURE: EXISTENTIALISM

The European tradition in twentieth-century philosophy has concerned
itself in great measure with the phenomenology of human existence. As phenomenology, it is less analytical and more descriptive than is the analysis of
language. Phenomenology is no less rigorous than linguistic analysis, but because it attempts to uncover and describe the experience of the essences or
meanings that underlie all language, its results are essentially less clear and
more controversial. The subliminal awareness of the meanings that underlie
the use of language is not a phenomenon within the public arena, as language
is. Phenomenology must rely upon intuition and introspection to uncover those
meanings and exhibit to others what the phenomenologist intends among the
meaning-structures towards which the ray of her consciousness is directed.
These meaning-structures are thought to be the source of all language. Further,
the kind of phenomenological research pursued by existentialists is quite rec-
ondite: they seek the meaning-structures that permeate subliminally the peculiarly human way of existing in the world.

The Continental tradition tends also to have less concern for theories of
ethics (with Max Scheler as a notable exception) than the English-speaking tradition. It holds that establishing moral rules and projecting a vision of human virtue,
as did the Enlightenment Project and the ancient moralists respectively, are irrelevant to the freedom and dignity of the individual. It is concerned with morals to
establish the conditions of human authenticity, which it understands as the choice

of a course of action or a form of life that grows out of one's deepest impulses, rather than one resting upon external rules or moral models. Such freedom to choose may be more worthy of human dignity than submission to rules, models, or even to God, but it has led to charges of arbitrariness and irrationality in what it praises in human beings. Existentialism is especially libertarian in its conception of the human will, and it argues vigorously against determinism and for the freedom and responsibility of persons. It is not concerned with harvesting what is of philosophical importance from the methods and the theories of science, for scientific knowledge is not directly relevant to questions of human existence. Existentialism has been jokingly called the "nonconformism to which nonconformists conform," but the jest is mistaken. The existentialist tradition takes unique and idiosyncratic forms in each of its members. For that reason, the existentialist picture of the human being will be presented in terms of several themes and theses that appear in the works of most twentieth-century existentialists.

The Absurdity of Human Existence

Nietzsche's famous pronouncement of the death of God in the 1880s was understood by many thinkers who experienced the warfare and chaos of the first half of the last century as God's abandonment of humankind. The absence of God generated moral confusion. Existentialists often quote a character in Dostoevsky's *The Brothers Karamazov* (whose influence upon Existentialism is considerable), "If God does not exist, then anything is allowed!" Western civilization had relied upon its One God to provide a moral center to the universe; if that moral center vanishes, then there is only the varying moral judgment of men and women to reckon with. To Friedrich Nietzsche, a precursor of Existentialism, it appeared that if there are no gods in heaven, then we must become like gods on earth. He once remarked, "There are no gods. For if there were, how could I possibly stand not being one?" If there is none, then we have only ourselves as a measure of value and meaning.

Few Existentialists wished to take up Nietzsche's challenge to become like supermen; even fewer aspired to be great criminals, thinking that everything was allowed them. Yet the idea that there are no external standards for judging human behavior, that we are alone, and the world has no meaning in itself was embraced by most existentialists. Albert Camus (1913–1960) said that life is absurd: It is an assemblage of brute facts through which humankind must make its way as best it can. In his essay, *The Myth of Sisyphus* (1942), Camus gave fresh meaning to the ancient tale of Sisyphus, the man whom the gods, as punishment for his crimes, condemned to roll a rock up a hill, then to let it roll back down, only to have to push it up again, and this for all eternity. Sisyphus is like us absurd men, Camus asserts; all of us work from sun to sun, eat, sleep, live, and achieve nothing final; we only keep life going. Unlike Sisyphus, each of us and everyone we love will die, and eventually no trace of us will remain on this planet. Whatever good we do during our lifetimes will finally be absorbed into the totality of things, and be indistinguishable from all else. The issue is not that life is meaningless, but that it is contingent, or without a necessary and sufficient ground or purpose. There is no foundation of human existence—no ultimate reason why people exist, no compelling reason why people should do one thing or the other, and no highest purpose to which human life contributes. Individuals are "condemned to be free" without excuses or guarantees, forced to solve alone or with others the riddle of what to live for.

In his novel *The Plague* (1947), Camus's Dr. Rieux, who is struggling to save people dying of the plague and risking his own life to do so, is asked by a friend whether he believes in God. Rieux answers that he does not. His questioner is incredulous: then why do you struggle against death, when you know that you will lose? This man you save from the plague today will die anyway, if not tomorrow, then sometime later. In your philosophy there is no afterlife for him, nor is there reward for you. How absurd that you struggle! Rieux can respond only that he struggles against the world such as it is, against human misery, suffering, and death. Elsewhere, Camus asks: Why not simply commit suicide? Now if a person cannot answer this question, then she does not know why she is living; she lives like the birds and the beasts. Persons need meaning to go on living, yet there is none to be found in this godless world—except the meanings we give to ourselves and the values we choose to pursue upon a horizon of absurdity.

THE PLAGUE: Camus's novel is one of the greatest Existentialist works. Men and women are placed in a situation of crisis—their city is placed under quarantine during a plague (which, for Camus, symbolized especially, but not exclusively, the German occupation of France, 1940–1945), and persons are randomly picked out by the plague for suffering and death. The meaning and value of life is always in question. Some choose to opt out; they try to escape the city, refusing any solidarity with their fellow inhabitants. One, the priest, Paneloux, at first preaches that the plague is a punishment and a warning from God, and, when he sees a child die in slow agony, he does not lose his faith, but chooses instead to take part in the suffering of his flock. Another, Tarrou, is troubled by the fact that one cannot rebel against injustice without creating injustice oneself. There is a limit beyond which one must not go in one's own free choices of oneself and one's philosophy, Camus argues, and that is the limit posed by the absolute value of the human person.

Consciousness

Jean-Paul Sartre (1905–1980) provided a large body of philosophical theory for an assault on such questions as Camus is asking. *Being and Nothingness* (1943) provides us with a phenomenology of human existence upon which the human situation can be grasped and assessed. Humankind experiences itself as abandoned but free. Our deepest aspirations are doomed to failure, yet we are not without resources. There may be no values except those we create though our actions, but it is still possible to live authentically. It is the peculiar nature of human consciousness (the phenomenology of mind Sartre produced from his struggles with Husserl and Freud) that distinguishes us from all other things, makes possible our singular awareness of ourselves and our situation, and allows us to respond to it.

JEAN-PAUL SARTRE: Sartre was born in Paris in 1905. He studied at the Ecole Normale Supérieure in Paris, and later in Germany, where he came under the influence of Heidegger. Sartre was mobilized in 1939, and when the Germans invaded France in 1940, he was taken as a prisoner of war. He returned to teaching in Paris after the armistice but was active in the resistance movement. His most important work, *Being and Nothingness,* appeared in 1943 during the German occupation. In the years following the war, Sartre became something of a cult figure and spokesman of Existentialism. His novels and plays were read and seen by a broad public. He was strongly committed to the political left and worked with the Communist Party of France until the Soviet invasion of Hungary in 1956. He was awarded the Nobel Prize in Literature in 1964, but he rejected the honor for personal and political reasons. Sartre worked for many years with his companion, Simone de Beauvoir (1908–1986), the philosopher and feminist noted especially for *The Second Sex.* Scholars dispute which of the two thinkers originated the doctrines associated with their work. Sartre died in 1980.

A person becomes conscious of the dog sitting nearby; the dog arises up out of the field of the person's vision and is focused upon or thematized: Ah yes, the dog. Thus far, the human observer has not distinguished herself from the animals, for the dog also is conscious of her presence. But then we notice two features of human consciousness that appear to be lacking in the dog: Humans use language to designate the dog—to grasp what we see *as* a dog—and we are always able to refer to ourselves as the ones who are aware of the dog. How is this possible?

The question of the origin or genesis of self-consciousness in the evolving human species is much disputed. It is uncertain whether or how being self-conscious gave early human populations a selective advantage in the universal struggle for survival. But we can say something of the conditions of self-consciousness. One such condition, analyzed by both Martin Heidegger and Sartre, is the peculiar awareness of time that we humans possess. It was noted earlier that some one of modern humankind's forebears discovered the future when she realized that a stick or a stone she had picked up as a temporary tool was worth keeping for tomorrow—for future use. To do that, she had to be able to visualize that object in its potential future use, that is, to grasp the idea of using it at a time that was not present. It is doubtful that animals are capable of such a visualization; the squirrel's gathering and storing of acorns for the winter seems to be driven entirely by instinct and not by self-conscious planning. Consider also that human language requires as a condition of its possibility just this

Jean-Paul Sartre. © *Library of Congress.*

ability to exist mentally in past and future times. To recognize the dog as a dog is to pull the notion of *dog* out of the toolbox of the mind. We have encountered dogs in the past and have saved up from those encounters a token that we can use for designating the same kind of animal in future encounters, or to describe possible (nonpresent) encounters with one. Time-consciousness unlocks our mental toolbox and prepares us for receiving the linguistic tokens by which we remember past and prepare for future experience.

This rather metaphorical and fanciful account of Heidegger on being and time provides some clue to Sartre's characteristic picture of human consciousness. In this picture, the human being liberates itself from the static existence that characterizes animals or objects by means of consciousness of the future, but in that very act becomes deeply problematic to itself. "[Human] consciousness," Sartre writes, "is a being such that in its being, its being is in question insofar as this being implies a being other than itself." This cryptic statement requires some analysis.

Sartre distinguishes between two realms of being, being for-itself and being in-itself. Being in-itself is being that is nonconscious and exists phenomenally for us as an object. Plants, animals, or stones exist in themselves in that they are not able to make themselves an object for themselves; simply stated, they do not know that they exist. The term *for-itself* refers to human beings or any other possible beings who, Sartre says, "nihilate" being in-itself by relating themselves to it. The human being wins her freedom by negating the world around her; she recognizes herself as not-an-object. The for-itself then stands forth in a world that, in itself, has no language and no meaning; the for-itself gives meaning to things by naming them, separating them off, or distinguishing one thing from another thing, and using them as items in its own projects. Thanks to consciousness, what was merely being as such becomes meaningful as an object to the for-itself. The for-itself brings meaning into existence.

Freedom

Now the for-itself, while encountering objects in the world, also encounters himself and others like him. Yet when a person becomes an object to himself, when he says, "I am," his existence slips away from him. He is forced to understand himself as not entirely present to himself, for he now grasps himself as a thing with a future—a thing that is not yet made. For that reason we can neither make a static object out of ourselves, nor can we make others into an object for us. A human being is essentially unobjectifiable, for it exists in the execution of its life, as it projects itself forward in time towards a future that is not yet made, while also recalling its own past life and *its* projects. The for-itself is free, indeed it is *condemned* to be free. This impossibility of objectifying the human being, for example, by making it an object for scientific study, is characteristic of Existentialism. It is a denial of the scientific objectification of persons and their reduction to a number by the political masters of the established technology. Sartre denies that human beings can be effectively studied, in Skinnerian fashion, as respondent organisms whose behavior is entirely determined by past events.

To this end, Sartre writes in *Being and Nothingness:*

> We have shown that freedom is actually one with the being of the For-itself; human reality is free to the exact extent that it has to be its own nothingness. It has to be this nothingness, as we have seen, in multiple dimensions: first by temporalizing itself—i.e., by being always at a distance from itself, which means that it can never let itself be determined by its past to perform this or that particular act; second by rising up as consciousness of something and (of) itself—i.e., by being presence to itself and not simply self, which implies that nothing exists in consciousness which is not consciousness of existing and that consequently nothing external to consciousness can motivate it; and finally, by being transcendence—i.e., not something which would first be in order subsequently to put itself into relation with this or that end, but on the contrary, a being which is originally a project—i.e., which is defined by its end.

This remarkable summation of the nature of the For-itself asserts that freedom to become what one is not now is an essential characteristic of the human way of existing. Nothing external to consciousness can determine consciousness, says Sartre, for consciousness is a presence to oneself as existing; nothing exists in consciousness that is not present to it. An object, of course, is simply what it is; it is not a presence to itself, at a distance from itself, or a transcendence of itself. Yet a person, paradoxically, can never *be* simply what he *is*. For *negativities* permeate the three dimensions of human existence.

First, a person is *not himself;* he is always at a distance from himself, for he exists simultaneously in past, present, and future. He can grasp himself only by referring to a future that defines his present activity, and to a past that has meaning for him in the present. An animal does not engage in activities, although it may appear to us as if it does. But consider a person engaged in the activity of waiting for a bus. The person would not know (not "grasp in conscious awareness") what she was doing standing there if she did not know how the bus trip fits into some future project (going to work that day, perhaps), did not remember the past events and projects that led to this moment, and could not grasp the nexus of human practices that included working for a living, traveling on public transportation, and the time of day.

Second, self-awareness requires us to distinguish the self from what it is not, that is, the world that it has as its object. Being in-itself is *closed upon itself;* no such dualism of self and world rises up in it. In every human person there is an inner space created by his reflexivity. Simply put, a person is present to himself and perceives himself as distinct from what he is not.

Third, Sartre claims that the for-itself is a *transcendence,* that is, a human being is not what it is but is what it chooses to become. This is Sartre's famous doctrine that, in the case of being for-itself, "existence precedes essence." What a person becomes is neither determined by prior causes—genes, or external psychological factors—nor by some God to whose plan her life must conform, but rather by the free choices she makes in the pursuit of her self-chosen ends.

"Existence Precedes Essence"

In an often-discussed passage in the essay, "Existentialism is a Humanism" (1946), Sartre tells the story of a young man faced with a moral decision of some importance. He wishes to attempt an escape from Nazi-controlled France in order to join General De Gaulle's Free French forces that were collecting in England to prepare the eventual liberation of their homeland. But he is also concerned about the welfare of his mother, whose other son had been killed in the German invasion, and whose husband, she thinks, has become a Nazi collaborator. Should the young man stay home and take care of his mother, or should he go off to liberate France and avenge his brother? Sartre argues that no moral theory could have anything of value to say to this young man. Universal moral laws cannot apply to a situation as unique as this one; moreover, duties to one's fatherland and to one's immediate loved ones are in unresolvable conflict. The only recourse for the young man is to look deeply inside himself and choose the course of action to which he is most profoundly impelled. The young man must create his values by choosing one course of action over the other. This advice illustrates Sartre's belief that values do not exist in themselves; they exist phenomenally only when they are embraced by a human being in his pursuit of some end. If the young man chooses to stay home with his mother, then his mother becomes valuable for him. Sartre's advice illustrates also what has been condemned as the irrationalism of Existentialism, for it celebrates choices made not on the basis of careful thought and the weighing of objective values prior to our choices, but upon one's deepest impulses. And the story illustrates, finally, how a human life becomes meaningful in contrast with the meaninglessness of being in-itself. A further example will make this contrast clearer.

A man uses a pen to write a letter. The pen has a clear meaning and value for him. It is made according to an engineer's design and was shaped to fit the human hand. It was given a mechanism that causes ink to flow onto paper, and its purpose for the maker is profit. Its essence—manufacture, structure, purpose— clearly precedes its existence. But now think about the person who is using the pen. He is conscious of himself working on a project, the completion of the letter, and the further projects its will serve. He has come out of a past in which this project of writing took shape for him. But how is it that he has this project? Of course, he decided to set aside some time and desired to make this communication to some other person. The pen's essence was determined by someone else; who determined the letter-writer to decide to set aside time to fulfill just this task? At this point, all recourse to further "reasons" stops: Even if it could be shown that some prior cause impelled him to write, we would still not have his reasons why he wrote; the reasons can only emerge from his choices of projects that are meaningful to him. If we should ask him the further "Why?"—why does he have these projects rather than others—he would feel the ground slipping out from under his feet. The only thing he could say is, "I have chosen thus." Similarly, the young man cannot find anything that necessitates his fighting or staying home with his mother, or justify whatever choice he eventually makes. He chooses the path he will take without any assurance that it is the right one.

Dread, the Other, and Bad Faith

For Sartre, the fact that the meaning of a human life is without external and universal foundation is a source of dread. And this dread, or anguish, is not occasioned by some specific fear—not, for example, by one thinking that one ought to be doing something else at this time, or even that one ought to be a farmer, or active in workers' or consumers' or ecological movements, rather than what one is currently doing. Dread is produced by the thought of one's contingency and one's freedom: there is no other reason for one's choice except that one has chosen it. Moreover, we exist with others; one engages oneself in a project with all other persons, and one is responsible for that project before all others. Dread takes several forms, all of which emerge from this freedom and responsibility of the for-itself.

Sartre's literary works show a constant concern for those special situations—such as Sartre's own, in which he chose to risk his life in the resistance against the German occupation of France—in which human freedom asserts itself. We are never more free, said Sartre, than when we are placed in a situation in which the necessity of a life-or-death choice forces us to encounter the ultimate groundlessness of our existence. Normally, our dread of freedom impels us to escape our freedom, to convince ourselves that we cannot help but do what we now are doing. The sensation of being merely an instrument in a design that has been imposed upon us by fate, or by God, or by other persons makes life easier to bear, for it relieves us of our freedom. But when we are forced to choose between our own life and that of a friend, between facing the possibility of torture or hiding in safety, we see in all clarity that we human beings alone can and must choose. Yet nothing forces us to make the decision one way or the other. A man says the insurmountable fear of pain made him choose to run away. But who is responsible, Sartre may ask, for making the fear or the pain insurmountable, if not that person himself? A man says he ran away because he is a coward. But cowardice is not a mental property or Platonic essence that inhabits consciousness and makes people do things; that man chose to be a coward, to project himself forward in time as a person who always runs away.

But aren't at least some of our choices determined by factors beyond our control? A person is either born male or female. Does not one's sex determine to some extent the nature of one's projects, or one's choices? One is stricken with a disease; one is born blind; one is thrown in jail; one is born very rich or very poor. These are all things that Sartre calls elements of our *facticity*. This facticity does not determine the meaning of our projects. A person is born in fact a male, but chooses himself as a female. He cross-dresses, works at female occupations, perhaps becomes transsexual. Another man cannot afford to take a trip abroad. His choice of himself as desiring to travel, and not the fact of his poverty or the distance of the places he wishes to visit, erects barriers around him. Things that are meaningless in themselves—the Atlantic Ocean, for example—become a barrier to the poor American who wishes to travel to Europe, but not to another American, rich or poor, who does not choose himself as a European traveler. Our projects create the very meaning of the facts around us.

The denial of freedom, the refusal of a person to accept that her choices have created herself, or the denial of facticity (that is, the refusal to accept that she always finds herself in a situation to which she must respond), is called by Sartre *bad faith*. A woman may indeed try to rid herself of her freedom by becoming a mere object for another person and allow that person's image of her to determine who she is and what she must do. Conversely, she may try to capture the freedom of other persons and tell them who they are, imagining her control over them to be total. But her control of another person can never be total, for a human being cannot be an object, an in-itself. The willing acceptance of the groundlessness of our freedom, and of our responsibility to others, Sartre calls the *authentic life*. The authentic man or woman freely commits himself or herself to self-chosen projects.

Yet the human being is doomed not only to death and nothingness, but to the incompleteness and even to the incoherence of its deepest impulses. People long for a completeness that is denied to them. Characters in novels complete their stories; a human being never does. This *inability to become an object* is the deepest source of anguish. A person chooses both to be entirely free, to be his own possibilities, and at the same time chooses to escape those possibilities and become an object. All people aspire to be a for-itself and an in-itself at the same time. The absurdity of human existence consists in this discrepancy between our aspirations and our possibilities. In effect, we wish to be God, says Sartre, in a telling passage in *Being and Nothingness:* a being that *is* all of its possibilities. But this is impossible; we cannot rid ourselves of the worm of nothingness, of unrealized possibility at the core of our being: *man is a useless passion.* To be human is to be endless possibility. No definition can ever encompass it, as the Greeks tried to do; no science can ever objectify it. We are what we will become.

POSTSCRIPT

It is disconcerting to learn that two of the seminal minds in twentieth-century Continental philosophy had highly questionable political commitments. Martin Heidegger was for a time committed to the Nazi party in his native Germany and began some of his lectures with "Heil Hitler." Sartre was a Communist in France even during Stalin's reign in the Soviet Union, and, in a late interview, said he believed that the Maoist model of socialism, which had cost a large but unknown number of Chinese lives, was the only thing that could save France. It may be that the long history of warfare, exploitation, and hatred in Europe during the first half of the century led its intellectuals to flirt with dangerous ideas and overlook the injustices that had already been committed in the names of those ideas. And the day may come when observers will look back in disbelief at the thinkers of the late twentieth century in the English-speaking lands who attempted to give a purely physicalist explanation of human behavior in psychological, genetic, or neurophysiological terms, denying the freedom of human beings and the existence and value of the human spirit. Those future observers may well wonder whether such mechanical or chemical explanations of human behavior do not do as much damage to the human being's love of freedom, hope for autonomy, and ambition to make human life more worth living, than the experiments with Nazism and Communism of their European kinsmen. Yet, as is evident in this study of the basics of philosophy, philosophers are concerned far more for the truth as they are best able to perceive and express it than they are for any damage the truth might do. We should all wish to be so honest and, perhaps, so courageous.

Timeline

The reader should take this and all timelines simply as guides. The classifications are the creations of historians and may not reflect the self-understanding of the persons classified. For example, while Seneca would no doubt have considered himself a Stoic, Descartes would not have called himself a *rationalist* philosopher, and, among the Existentialists, only Sartre, it seems, was willing to accept this term as a classification of his thought.

Year	Periods and Schools	Philosophers Active
800 B.C.E.	Before Philosophy	Homer, Greek poet (9th/8th (?) century)
700		Hesiod, Greek poet (8th (?) century)
600	Pre-Socratic Philosophers	Thales of Miletus, Ionia, Greece (c. 585); Pythagoras of Samos, Aegean Island (c. 582?–500?); Parmenides of Elea, Greek colony in southern Italy; Heraclitus of Ephesus, Ionia (540?–475?); Empedocles of Agrigentium, Greek colony in Sicily (490?–430)

Timeline

Year	Periods and Schools	Philosophers Active
500	Greek defeat of Persia, 479; Sophists, teachers in Athens	Democritus of Abdera, Thrace (c. 460–371); Protagoras of Abdera (c. 481–c. 411), Sophist philosopher active in Athens
	Golden Age of Greek Philosophy	Socrates of Athens, (469–399); Plato of Athens (427–347)
400	Academy founded in Athens by Plato, 388–387	Diogenes of Sinope (Asia Minor) (412?–323), Cynic philosopher
	Lyceum founded in Athens by Aristotle, 335 Death of Alexander the Great, 323; beginning of Hellenistic era	Aristotle of Macedonia (384–322)
		Epicurus of Samos (341–270)
	Epicurus founds Epicurean school in Athens, 306	Zeno of Citium (fl. late 4th–early 3rd century)
	Zeno founds Stoic school in Athens, 301	
300		
200	Greece submits to Rome, 149–46	
	Greco-Roman period	
100	Closing of the Academy and Lyceum in Athens (c) 43; Beginning of Roman Empire, 27	Cicero, Roman orator (106–43); Lucretius, epicurean philosopher in Rome (c. 97–c. 55)
1 C.E.	Augustus, Emperor of Rome, 27 B.C.E–14 C.E.	Seneca, Stoic philosopher in Rome (c. 4 B.C.E.–65 C. E.)
	Philosophical schools founded in Alexandria, now in Egypt	Epictetus (c. 55–c. 135), Stoic philosopher
	Stoic school founded in Nicopolis by Epictetus, 93–94	
100	Reign of Marcus Aurelius, 161–180	Marcus Aurelius, Stoic philosopher (121–180)
200		Sextus Empiricus, Skeptic philosopher and Greek physician, early 3rd century

Year	Periods and Schools	Philosophers Active
200		Diogenes Laërtius, historian of Greek philosophy
		Plotinus (205–270) founded in Rome a school of Neo-Platonism.
300	The Emperor Constantine converts to Christianity, 312–313	St. Augustine, first great Christian philosopher, Bishop of Hippo in North Africa (354–430)
400	Decline of Roman Empire	Boethius, Roman philosopher (480–524?)
500	Early Middle Ages	
600		
700		
800	Charlemagne, King of the Franks, becomes Holy Roman Emperor in 800	Eriugina (c. 825–c. 870), Irish philosopher active in Europe
900		Saint Anselm
1000		(c.1033–1109), Italian, Archbishop of Canterbury
1100	University of Paris officially recognized	Peter Abelard, (1079–1142), French teacher and monk
1200	Beginning of Scholasticism High Middle Ages	St. Thomas Aquinas (c. 1225–1274), Italian, active in Paris; Duns Scotus (1266–1308), Scottish philosopher
1300		William of Ockham (1280–1349)
1400	Early Renaissance	M. Ficinio (1433–1499), Italian Platonist philosopher; Giovanni Pico della Mirandola (1463–1494), Italian philosopher
1500	Scientific Revolution Nicholas Copernicus (1473–1543), Polish astronomer	Francis Bacon (1561–1626), English philosopher of science
1600	Age of Genius: the Rationalist philosophers on the Continent and the Empiricist philosophers in Great Britain Isaac Newton (1642–1727), *Principia Mathematica*, 1687	Galileo (1564–1642), Italian scientist; Thomas Hobbes (1588–1679) English philosopher; René Descartes (1596–1650), French philosopher; Benedict Spinoza (1632–1677), Dutch philosopher;

Timeline

Year	Periods and Schools	Philosophers Active
1600		John Locke (1632–1704), English philosopher; Gottfried Wilhelm Leibniz (1646–1716), German philosopher
1700	Age of Enlightenment	George Berkeley (1685–1753), Irish philosopher; David Hume (1711–1776), Scottish philosopher; Adam Smith (1723–1790), Scottish economist; François Marie Arouet, known as Voltaire (1694–1778); Etienne Bonnot de Condillac (1715–1780); Jean d'Alembert (1717–1783); Charles-Louis de Sconday, Baron de Montesquieu (1689–1755); Denis Diderot (1713–1784); the Marquis de Condorcet (1743–1794); Baron d'Holbach (1723–1789), French essayists and men of letters; Jean-Jacques Rousseau (1712–1778), Swiss/French philosopher and man of letters; Immanuel Kant (1724–1804), German philosopher
	French Revolution, 1789	
1800	Absolute Idealism in Germany	Johann Gottlieb Fichte (1762–1814); Georg Wilhelm Friedrich Hegel (1770–1831); Friedrich Wilhelm Joseph Schelling (1775–1854), German philosophers
	New Social and Political Philosophies	Jeremy Bentham (1748–1832), English philosopher; Karl Marx (1818–1883), German economist and social philosopher; John Stuart Mill (1806–1873), English philosopher;

Year	**Periods and Schools**	**Philosophers Active**
1800		Søren Kierkegaard (1813–1855), Danish theologian and philosopher
	Pragmatism in the United States	C.S. Peirce (1839–1914); William James (1842–1910); John Dewey (1859–1952); American philosophers
1900	Phenomenology	Edmund Husserl (1859–1938); Max Scheler (1872–1928); Martin Heidegger (1889–1976), German philosophers
	Logical Positivism/Logical Analysis	Gottlob Frege (1848–1925), German logician; Bertrand Russell (1872–1970), English philosopher; Moritz Schlick (1882–1936), Austrian philosopher; Alfred Tarski (1902–1983), philosopher in Poland and the USA; Rudolf Carnap (1891–1970) and Carl Hempel (1905–1997), philosophers in Germany and the USA; Willard van Ormand Quine (1908–2000), American philosopher
	Existentialism	Gabriel Marcel (1889–1973), Jean-Paul Sartre (1905–1980), Simone de Beauvoir (1905–1986), French philosophers; Albert Camus (1913–1960), philosopher in Algeria and France; Paul Tillich (1886–1965), theologian and philosopher in Germany and the USA; Martin Buber (1878–1965), scholar and philosopher in Germany and Israel

Timeline

Year	Periods and Schools	Philosophers Active
1900	Marxism	Max Horkheimer (1895–1973) and Theodor Adorno (1903–1969), German social philosophers; Herbert Marcuse (1898–1979), social philosopher in Germany and the USA; Jürgen Habermas (1929–), German sociologist and philosopher
	Linguistic Analysis	Ludwig Wittgenstein (1889–1951), philosopher in Austria and England; John Wisdom (1904–1993), Gilbert Ryle, (1900–1976), J. L. Austin, (1911–1960), English philosophers
	Moral and Social Philosophy	John Mackie (1917–1981), Australian philosopher; Alasdair MacIntyre (1929–), philosopher in Britain and the USA; John Rawls (1921–2002), Robert Nozick (1938–2002), American philosophers

Bibliography

REFERENCE WORKS: DICTIONARIES, ENCYCLOPEDIAS, AND GENERAL HISTORIES

(Introductory works are starred*)

Audi, Richard. *Cambridge Dictionary of Philosophy.* Cambridge: Cambridge University Press, 1993.

Bullock, Allan, and Oliver Stalybrass. *The Harper Dictionary of Modern Thought.* New York: Harper & Row, 1977.

Copleston, Frederick S. J. *A History of Philosophy,* 8 vol. Westminster, Md.: The Newman Press, 1946–80.

DeGeorge, Richard T. *A Guide to Philosophical Bibliography and Research.* New York: Meridith, 1971.

*Durant, William J. *The Story of Philosophy.* New York: Simon & Schuster, 1933.

Edwards, Paul. *The Encyclopedia of Philosophy,* 8 vol. New York: Macmillan, 1967.

Frost, S. E., Jr. *Basic Teachings of the Great Philosophers,* rev. ed. Garden City, N.Y.: Doubleday & Co., 1962.

Guthrie, W.K.C. *A History of Greek Philosophy.* Cambridge: Cambridge University Press, 1963.

*Harré, Rom. *One Thousand Years of Philosophy.* Cambridge, Mass.: Blackwell, 2000.

Hospers, John. *An Introduction to Philosophical Analysis,* 2nd ed. Englewood Cliffs, N.J.: Prentice-Hall, 1967.

Jaspers, Karl. *The Great Philosophers,* 2 vol. New York: Harcourt, 1962.

Kiernan, T. P. *Who's Who in the History of Philosophy.* New York: The Philosophical Library, 1965.

*Kolenda, Konstantin. *Philosophy's Journey: A Historical Introduction.* Reading, Maine: Addison-Wesley, 1974.

*Lamprecht, Sterling P. *Our Philosophical Traditions: A Brief History of Philosophy in Western Civilization.* New York: Appleton-Century Crofts, Inc., 1955.

Magill, Frank N., and staff. *Masterpieces of World Philosophy in Summary Form.* New York: Harper & Row, 1961. One volume in a series.

Bibliography

Martin, Robert M. *The Philosopher's Dictionary,* 3rd edition. Guelph, Ont.: Broadview Press, 2002.

Mauntner, Thomas, ed. *A Dictionary of Philosophy.* Cambridge, Mass.: Blackwell, 1996.

O'Connor, D. J. *A Critical History of Philosophy.* New York: Free Press, 1964.

The Oxford Companion to Philosophy. Oxford: Oxford University Press, 1995.

Randall, John H. *The Career of Philosophy,* 2 vols. New York: Columbia University Press, 1962–65.

Reese, W. L., ed. *Dictionary of Philosophy and Religion.* Princeton, N.J.: Humanities Press, 1980.

*Stumpf, Samuel E. *Socrates to Sartre: A History of Philosophy,* 2nd ed. New York: McGraw-Hill, 1975.

Thomas, Henry. *Biographical Encyclopedia of Philosophy.* Garden City, N.Y.: Doubleday, 1965.

*Toulmin, Stephen. *Knowing and Acting: An Invitation to Philosophy.* New York: Macmillan, 1976.

GENERAL INTRODUCTIONS TO PHILOSOPHY

Copi, Irving. *Introduction to Logic.* New York: Macmillan, 1994.

Danto, Arthur C. *What Philosophy Is: A Guide to the Elements.* New York: Harper & Row, 1968.

*Facione, Peter A. *The Student's Guide to Philosophy.* Mountain View, Calif.: Mayfield Press, 1988.

Hospers, John. *An Introduction to Philosophical Analysis*, 2nd edition. Englewood Cliffs, N.J.: Prentice-Hall, 1967.

*Woodhouse, Mark B. *A Preface to Philosophy.* Belmont, Calif.: Wadsworth, 1980.

PRIMARY SOURCES: READILY AVAILABLE EDITIONS IN ENGLISH OF WORKS BY THE PHILOSOPHERS MENTIONED IN THE TEXT

Adorno, Theodor, and Max Horkheimer. *Dialectics of Enlightenment.* London: Vesto, 1979.

Anselm of Canterbury. *The Major Works.* Oxford: Oxford University Press, 1998.

Aristotle. *The Complete Works of Aristotle,* ed. Jonathan Barnes. Princeton, N.J.: Princeton University Press, 1984.

Augustine, Saint. "The City of God." In *The Basic Writings of Saint Augustine.* New York: Random House, 1958.

Barnes, Jonathan, ed. *Early Greek Philosophy.* New York: Penguin, 1987. A collection of the fragments of the pre-Socratic philosophers.

Bentham, Jeremy. *An Introduction to the Principles of Morals and Legislation.* Garden City, N.Y.: Doubleday Anchor, 1973.

Berkeley, George. *Three Dialogues Between Hylas and Philonous.* Oxford: Oxford University Press, 1998.

———. *A Treatise Concerning the Principles of Human Knowledge.* Oxford: Oxford University Press, 1998.

Buber, Martin. *I and Thou,* 2nd ed. New York: Charles Scribner's Sons, 1958.

Descartes, René. *Selected Philosophical Writings*. Cambridge: Cambridge University Press, 1988.

Dilthey, Wilhelm. *Selected Works,* Vols. I, III, V. Princeton, N.J.: Princeton University Press, 1991–1996.

Dostoevsky, Fyodor. *The Brothers Karamazov,* trans. R. Pevear and L. Volokhonsky. San Francisco: North Point Press, 1990.

Feuerbach, Ludwig. *The Fiery Brook: Selected Writings of Ludwig Feuerbach.* New York: Anchor Press, 1972.

Foucault, Michel. *The Order of Things: An Archaeology of the Human Sciences.* London: Tavistock, 1970.

Freud, Sigmund. *The Future of an Illusion.* New York: Random House, 1960.

Gadamer, Hans-Georg. *Truth and Method.* New York: Seabury Press, 1975.

Habermas, Jürgen. *Theory and Practice.* Boston: Beacon Press, 1973.

Hegel, G.W.F. *Hegel's Philosophy of Right.* Oxford: Oxford University Press, 1942.

———. *Phenomenology of Spirit.* Oxford: Oxford University Press, 1979.

Heidegger, Martin. *Basic Writings of Heidegger,* 2nd ed. New York: Harper & Row, 1977.

Hobbes, Thomas. *The Leviathan.* Oxford: Oxford University Press, 1946.

*Hume, David. *An Enquiry Concerning Human Understanding,* ed. Tom L. Beauchamp. Oxford, Oxford University Press, 1999.

Husserl, Edmund. *The Essential Husserl*, ed. Donn Welton. Bloomington: Indiana University Press, 1999.

Inwood, Brad, and L. P. Gerson. *Hellenistic Philosophy,* 2nd ed. Indianapolis: Hackett, 1997. A collection of the writings of the Stoics, Epicureans, and Skeptics.

James, William. *The Writings of William James,* ed. John McDermott. New York: Random House, 1967.

Kant, Immanuel. *The Critique of Pure Reason.* Cambridge: Cambridge University Press, 1999.

———. *Critique of Practical Reason and Other Writings in Moral Philosophy.* Chicago: University of Chicago Press, 1949. Includes the complete *Groundwork of the Metaphysic of Morals.*

Kierkegaard, Søren. *A Kierkegaard Anthology.* New York: Modern Library, 1959.

———. *Concluding Unscientific Postscript*, eds. H. V. Hong and E. H. Hong. Princeton, N.J.: Princeton University Press, 1992.

———. *Either/Or,* eds. H. V. Hong and E. H. Hong. Princeton, N.J.: Princeton University Press, 1987.

Leibniz, Gottfried Wilhelm. *Philosophical Essays.* Indianapolis, Ind.: Hackett, 1989.

———. *Discourse on Metaphysics.* New York: Open Court, 1976.

Locke, John. *Two Treatises of Government.* Cambridge: Cambridge University Press, 1988.

———. *An Essay Concerning Human Understanding.* Oxford: The Clarendon Press, 1976.

MacIntyre, Alasdair. *After Virtue.* Notre Dame, Ind.: Notre Dame University Press, 1981.

Marcuse, Herbert. *One Dimensional Man.* Boston: Beacon Press, 1964.

Marx, Karl. *Selected Writing,* ed. D. McLellan. Oxford: Oxford University Press, 1978.

*Mill, John Stuart. *On Liberty.* Indianapolis, Ind.: Bobbs-Merrill, 1956.

Montesquieu, Charles Louis de Secondat. *The Spirit of Laws.* Berkeley: University of California Press, 1977.

The New English Bible with the Apocrypha. Oxford University Press, Cambridge University Press, 1970.

Nietzsche, Friedrich. *Basic Writings,* ed. Walter Kaufmann. New York: Modern Library, 1968.

Nozick, Robert. *Anarchy, State and Utopia.* New York: Basic Books, 1974.

*Plato. *The Collected Dialogues of Plato,* eds. E. Hamilton and H. Cairns. Princeton, N.J.: Princeton University Press, 1961. Also: *Plato: Complete Works,* ed. John Cooper. Indianapolis, Ind.: Hackett, 1997.

Putnam, Hilary. *Reason, Truth, and History.* Cambridge: Cambridge University Press, 1981.

Quine, Willard van Orman. *From a Logical Point of View.* New York: Harper's, 1961.

Rawls, John. *A Theory of Justice.* Cambridge, Mass.: Harvard University Press, 1971.

Rorty, Richard. *Philosophy and the Mirror of Nature.* Princeton, N.J.: Princeton University Press, 1981.

Rousseau, Jean-Jacques. *Basic Political Writings.* Indianapolis, Ind.: Hackett, 1987.

*Russell, Bertrand. *The Problems of Philosophy.* Oxford: Oxford University Press, 1912.

Ryle, Gilbert. *The Concept of Mind.* Chicago: University of Chicago Press, 1984.

Sartre, Jean-Paul. *Being and Nothingness.* New York: Philosophical Library, 1956.

Scheler, Max. *Formalism in Ethics and Non-Formal Ethics of Values: A New Attempt Toward the Foundation of an Ethical Personalism.* Evanston, Ill.: Northwestern University Press, 1973.

Skinner, B. F. *Science and Human Nature.* New York: The Free Press, 1965.

Spinoza, Benedict. *Ethics.* New York: Free Press, 1974.

Strawson, P. F. *Individuals.* London: Methuen, 1959.

Thomas Aquinas, Saint. *Basic Writings of Saint Thomas Aquinas.* New York: Random House, 1945.

Wittgenstein, Ludwig. *Philosophical Investigations.* Oxford: Blackwell, 1953.

———. *Tractatus Logico-Philosophicus.* London: Routledge, 1961.

SECONDARY WORKS ON PHILOSOPHY

Metaphysics and Epistemology

*Audi, Robert. *Epistemology.* New York: Routledge, 1998.

Ayer, A. J. *Language, Truth and Logic.* New York: Dover, 1946.

———. *The Problem of Knowledge.* London: Macmillan, 1956.

Banger, Laurence. *The Structure of Empirical Knowledge.* Cambridge, Mass.: Harvard University Press, 1985.

Chisholm, Roderick. *Theory of Knowledge,* 3rd ed. Englewood Cliffs, N.J.: Prentice-Hall, 1988.

Collingwood, R. *An Essay on Metaphysics.* Oxford, Clarendon Press, 1940.

*Dancy, J. *Introduction to Contemporary Epistemology.* Oxford: Blackwell, 1989.

Grayling, A. C. *The Refutation of Skepticism.* London: Duckworth, 1985.

Levin, Michael E. *Metaphysics and the Mind-Body Problem.* Oxford: Clarendon Press, 1979.

*Pears, D. F., ed. *The Nature of Metaphysics.* London: Macmillan, 1957.

Popkin, R. *The History of Scepticism.* Berkeley: University of California Press, 1979.

*Schaffer, Jerome A. *The Philosophy of Mind.* Englewood Cliffs, N.J.: Prentice-Hall, 1968.

Sprague, Elmer. *Metaphysical Thinking.* New York: Oxford University Press, 1978.

*Taylor, Richard. *Metaphysics.* Englewood Cliffs, N.J.: Prentice-Hall, 1963.

Van Inwagen, Peter. *Metaphysics.* Boulder, Colo.: Westview Press, 1993.

Ethics

Baier, Kurt. *The Moral Point of View,* 4th ed. New York: Cornell University Press, 1992.

Baylis, Charles A. *Ethics.* New York: Henry Holt, 1958.

Brandt, Richard B. *Ethical Theory.* Englewood Cliffs, N.J.: Prentice-Hall, 1955.

*Brinton, Crane C. *A History of Western Morals.* New York: Harcourt, 1959.

*Cahn, Edmund. *The Moral Decision: Right and Wrong in the Light of American Law.* Bloomington: Indiana University Press, 1955.

Edwards, Paul. *The Logic of Moral Discourse.* New York; The Free Press, 1955.

Foot, P. *Virtues and Vices and Other Essays on Moral Philosophy.* Oxford: Blackwell, 1978.

*Frankena, William. *Ethics.* Englewood Cliffs, N.J.: Prentice-Hall, 1959.

Garner, Richard, and B. Rosen. *Moral Philosophy.* New York: Macmillan, 1967.

Hare, R. M. *The Language of Morals.* New York: Oxford University Press, 1950.

Hospers, John. *Human Conduct.* New York, Harcourt, 1972.

*MacIntyre, Alasdair. *A Short History of Ethics.* New York: Macmillan, 1966.

Mackie, J. L. *Ethics: Inventing Right and Wrong.* Harmondsworth: Penguin, 1977.

*Montefiore, Alan A. *A Modern Introduction to Moral Philosophy.* New York: Routledge and Kegan Paul, 1967.

Mothershead, John L. Jr., *Ethics.* New York: Henry Holt, 1955.

Nowell-Smith, P. *Ethics.* London: Penguin Books, 1954.

Parfit, Derek. *Reasons and Persons.* Oxford: Clarendon, 1984.

Ross, W. D. *The Right and the Good.* Oxford: The Clarendon Press, 1930.

Scanlon, Thomas. *What We Owe to Each Other.* Cambridge, Mass.: Harvard University Press, 1998.

*Singer, Peter. *Practical Ethics.* New York: Cambridge University Press, 1979.

Swabey, William C. *Ethical Theory: From Hobbes to Kant.* New York: Citadel, 1961.

*Wall, George. *Introduction to Ethics.* Columbus, Ohio: Chas. E. Merrill, 1974.

Warnock, Mary. *Ethics Since 1900.* London: Oxford University Press, 1958.

Williams, Bernard. *Ethics and the Limits of Philosophy.* Cambridge, Mass.: Harvard University Press, 1985.

Social and Political Philosophy

Barker, Ernest. *Principles of Social and Political Theory.* London: Oxford University Press, 1951.

Dworkin, Ronald. *Taking Rights Seriously.* Cambridge, Mass.: Harvard University Press, 1977.

Feinberg, Joel. *Social Philosophy.* Englewood Cliffs, N.J.: Prentice Hall, 1973.

Hart, H.L.A. *Law, Liberty, and Morality.* New York: Vintage Books, 1963.

Hook, Sidney. *From Hegel to Marx.* Ann Arbor: University of Michigan Press, 1962.

Mabbott, J. D. *The State and the Citizen.* London: Hutchinson, 1948.

Mappes, Thomas A. *Social Ethics: Morality of Public Policy.* New York: McGraw-Hill, 1977.

Bibliography

Plamenatz, John. *Man and Society.* London: Longman, 1992.

Popper, Karl. *The Open Society and Its Enemies,* 5th edition. London: Taylor and Francis Books, 2002.

Robson, John M. *Improvement of Mankind: The Social and Political Thought of John Stuart Mill.* Toronto: University of Toronto Press, 1968.

*Thomas, Geoffrey. *Introduction to Political Philosophy.* London: Duckworth, 1999.

The Philosophy of Religion

*Capitan, William H. *Philosophy of Religion.* Indianapolis, Ind.: Bobbs-Merrill, 1972.

Collins, James. *God in Modern Philosophy.* Chicago: Regnery, 1967.

Ducasse, C. J. *A Philosophical Scrutiny of Religion.* New York: Ronald Press, 1953.

*Hick, John. *Faith and Knowledge,* 2nd ed. Ithaca, N.Y.: Cornell University Press, 1966.

———. *The Philosophy of Religion.* Englewood Cliffs, N.J.: Prentice-Hall, 1963.

Marton, M. *Atheism.* Philadelphia: Temple University Press, 1990.

*Matson, Wallace I. *The Existence of God.* Ithaca, N.Y.: Cornell University Press, 1965.

*Nielsen, Kai. *An Introduction to the Philosophy of Religion.* New York: St. Martin's, 1982.

*Russell, Bertrand. *Mysticism and Logic.* Garden City, N.Y.: Doubleday Anchor, n.d. Contains the essay, "A Free Man's Worship."

Smith, John E. *The Philosophy of Religion.* New York: Macmillan, 1965.

*Swinburne, R. *The Existence of God.* Oxford: Clarendon, 1979.

Unamuno, Miguel de. *The Tragic Sense of Life.* New York: Dover, 1954.

Science and Human Nature

Barnes, Hazel. *An Existentialist Ethic.* Chicago: University of Chicago Press, 1978.

*Barrett, William C. *Irrational Man.* Garden City, N.Y.: Doubleday, 1958.

*Camus, Albert. *The Myth of Sisyphus.* New York: Knopf, 1955.

Churchland, Paul M. *Matter and Consciousness: A Contemporary Introduction to the Philosophy of Mind.* Cambridge, Mass.: MIT Press, 1988.

*Dawkins, Richard. *The Selfish Gene.* New York: Oxford University Press, 1976.

Fodor, Jerry A. *The Modularity of Mind.* Cambridge, Mass.: MIT Press, 1983.

*Freud, Sigmund. *New Introductory Lectures on Psychoanalysis.* New York: Norton, 1964.

*Gregory, R. I. *The Oxford Companion to the Mind.* Oxford: Oxford University Press, 1983.

Grene, Marjorie. *Introduction to Existentialism.* Chicago: University of Chicago Press, 1970.

*Herschel, Abraham J. *Who Is Man?* Stanford, Calif.: Stanford University Press, 1965.

*Kaufmann, Walter, ed. *Existentialism from Dostoevsky to Sartre.* New York: Meridian Books, 1956.

*Nielsen, Harry A., ed. *The Visages of Adam: Philosophical Readings on the Nature of Man.* Notre Dame, Ind.: Notre Dame University Press, 1968.

May, Rollo. *Existence: Studies in Existentialist Psychoanalysis.* New York: Basic Books, 1958.

Olsen, Robert G. *An Introduction to Existentialism.* New York: Dover, 1962.

Scheler, Max. *Man's Place in Nature*, ed. Hans Meyerhoff. New York: Noonday Press, 1961.

Searle, John. *Mind, Brains, and Science.* Cambridge: Harvard University Press, 1984.

Solomon, Robert, ed. *Existentialism.* New York: Modern Library, 1974.

*Stevenson, Leslie. *Seven Theories of Human Nature.* New York: Oxford University Press, 1979.

Watson, Gary, ed. *Free Will.* Oxford: Clarendon Press, 1982.

Index

Abelard, P., 44
Absurdity, 267, 274
Adam, 42, 47, 186, 231, 242, 243
Adorno, Theodor, 215–16; identitarianism, 215; negative dialectics, 215
Agape, 233–34
Ambiguity, 24, 167, 256, 260
Analytic/synthetic statements, 119
Anarchism, 175, 193, 194, 221
Anaximander, 33
Anaximenes, 33
Anselm, Saint, 235–36, 237
Anthropological principle, 240
A priori/a posteriori, 119–20, 178, 235, 237
Aquinas, Saint Thomas, 41, 89, 112, 115, 187–89, 230, 239; moderate realism, 112; phantasmagoria, 112. Works: *Summa contra Gentiles,* 44; *Summa Theologica,* 44
Argument from Design (Teleological Argument), 235
Argument from Evil, 241–43
Arguments, 14–27
Aristotle, 35, 36–37, 39, 41, 42, 44, 49, 52, 64, 69, 70, 71, 72, 90, 99, 103, 108, 110, 111, 115, 132, 139, 153, 170, 177, 182–83, 188, 194, 248; categories, 15, 236–37; *eudaimonia,* 141, 142, 184; evolution, 83–84; First Philosophy, 74; form and matter, 83; Golden Mean, 142; metaphysics, 79–84; Potency and Act, 82, 84, 100; the State and the Individual,

184–86; theories of virtue, 141–44; Theory of the Four Causes, 81–82. Works: *Nicomachean Ethics,* 184–85; *The Organon,* 15; *Politics,* 184, 185
Armageddon, 42, 43
Athens, 7, 36, 38, 41, 73, 74, 181
Atomism, 127
Augustine, Saint, 41, 42, 111, 186–87, 188, 189, 242, 243. Works: *The City of God,* 43; *Confessions,* 186
Austin, J. L., 63, 280
Ayer, A. J., 127

Bacon, Francis, 54, 84, 85. Works: *Novum Organum,* 54–55
Bakunin, M. A., 221
de Beauvoir, Simone, 64; and Jean-Paul Sartre, 268. Works: *The Second Sex,* 268
Beethoven, Ludwig van, 57, 164
Behaviorism, 254, 257, 258, 260, 264
Being, 76, 77, 79, 85, 107, 209; as Being, 69, 95
Benefits and Burdens, 212
Benjamin, Walter, 213
Bentham, Jeremy, 149–53, 155, 156, 157, 158, 165, 210. Works: *Introduction to the Principles of Morals and Legislation,* 150
Berdyayev, Nicolai A., 64
Berkeley, George, 55, 88–89, 91, 92, 113; *Three Dialogues Between Hylas and Philonous,* 88

Index

Berlin, Isaiah, 202
Blanshard, Brand, 64
Bloch, Ernst, 213
Boas, Franz, 250
Bradley, F. H., 98
Buber, Martin, 64
Buddhism, 104; Zen, 102

Camus, Albert, 64, 266–67. Works: *The Myth of Sisyphus*, 266; *The Plague*, 267
Capitalism, 46–48, 56, 61, 65, 165, 189, 206, 207, 208, 209, 213, 214
Carnap, Rudolf, 18, 63
Casuistry, 134
Catholicism, 44, 48, 51, 63, 134, 227, 230
Causality, 7, 19, 49, 50, 80, 81, 91, 92, 116–17, 256, 257, 263
Christian philosophy, 38, 41, 42, 60, 65, 84, 107, 165, 187, 188, 196, 209, 248
Church Fathers, 38
Churchland, Paul, 262–63
Cicero, 209
Civil Society, 42, 140, 179, 187, 190, 191, 198, 200, 201, 204, 205, 207, 220
Classes, 14
Clinias, 144–45, 166
Clocks, 49–50
Columbus, Christopher, 46
Common Law, 191–92
Communism, 182, 203, 215, 268, 274
de Condillac, Etienne Bonnot, Baron de Montesquieu, 55
de Condorcet, Marquis, 55
Confucianism, 104
Confucius, 145
Conservatism, 217, 218
Constitution of the United States, 148, 178
Contingency, 267
Contract Theory, 173, 199, 218–20
Copernicus, 27, 93, 262–63
Corpus Juris Civilis, 38
Cosmological Argument, 235, 238–39, 240–41
Cosmology, 33, 36, 39, 69–72, 78, 226
Covenant, 192, 195
Creationism, 45, 229, 241
Crick, Francis, 258
Critical Theory, 213–17, 218
Croce, Benedetto, 98
Cynicism/cynics, 39, 143

D'Alembert, Jean, 55
Dante Alighieri, 49

Darwin, Charles, 132, 240, 248–50; *On the Origin of Species,* 248
Dawkins, R., 258–59, 260; *The Selfish Gene,* 258
Death, 97, 266, 273
Declaration of Independence, U.S., 143, 196
Deduction, 15, 53
Deism, 196–97
Della Mirandola, Pico, 45
Delphic Oracle, 8, 74
Democracy, 7, 56, 166, 169, 183, 192, 223
Democritus of Abdera, 88
Deontology, 148, 157–58, 160, 171
Derrida, Jacques, 65, 100
Descartes, 4–5, 52, 60, 63, 85–87, 89, 90, 93, 112–15, 118, 120, 125, 228, 236. Works: *Discourse on Method,* 53, 85; *Meditations on First Philosophy,* 53, 85, 189
Descriptive Ethics, 138
Dewey, John, 62, 63, 129, 130
D'Holbach, Baron, 35
Dialectic, 77
Dialectical Materialism, 208
Diderot, Denis, 51, 52, 55
Difference in Kind, 248
Dilthey, Wilhelm, 122, 123
Diogenes of Sinope, 143
Distributive Justice, 179, 185, 212–13, 217, 222
Dostoevsky, Fyodor, 243, 266
Dualism, Metaphysical, 87, 107, 262
Duns Scotus, 45
Durkheim, Emile, 250

Education, 8, 9, 11, 56, 181, 184, 211
Einstein, Albert, 60, 131, 132
Empedocles, 34, 79
Empiricism, 52, 54, 55, 58, 84, 86, 93, 112, 114, 118, 127, 178, 185, 255
Engels, Friedrich, 47, 204, 208, 209
Enlightenment, The, 50–53, 55, 122, 128, 197, 216
Entitlement, 194, 221–23
Epictetus, 40
Epicureanism, 39, 41
Epicurus, 39
Epiphenomenalism, 261
Epistemology, 60, 75, 95, 105, 177
Equality, 212, 217, 219
Eriugena, 43
Essence, 3, 77, 83, 115, 122, 125, 273
Eternity, 229, 233
Ethical Emotivism, 165

Ethics, 5, 28, 53, 60, 135, 226; feminist, 169–72
Ethnocentrism, 100
"Euthyphro Question," 231–33
Eve, 42, 186, 231, 242, 243. *See also* Adam
Evolution, Theory of, 59, 83, 132, 133, 240, 251, 259
Existentialism, 64, 247, 265, 266, 272

Faith, 177, 224, 226, 230, 231, 246
Fascism, 61
Feudalism, 45–46
Feuerbach, Ludwig, 209
Feyerabend, Paul, 123
Fichte, Johann Gottlieb, 57, 95, 121
Ficinio, Marsilio, 45
Fodor, Jerry A., 263, 264; and functionalism, 263
Foucault, Michel, 65, 101
Frankfurt School, 213–16
Free will and determinism, problem of, 138, 242, 256–58, 260, 265, 266
Freedom, 135, 136, 172, 185, 192, 197, 199, 200, 202, 210, 216, 255, 289, 272–73, 274; negative and positive freedom, 202, 210
Frege, Gottlob, 63, 124
Freud, Sigmund, 133, 251–53, 256, 268; Oedipal conflict, 253; theory of psychosexual development, 253

Gadamer, Hans-Georg, 123, 124
Galileo Galilei, 48, 49, 92, 95, 114, 189, 199
Gaunilo, 236
Gender, 170
Genetics, 136, 258, 259, 260; DNA, 73, 251, 258
Geometry, 77, 78
German Idealism, 57
Gert, Bernard, 168, 169, 173; *Morality, Its Nature and Justification,* 168
Gibbon, Edward, 187; *The Decline and Fall of the Roman Empire,* 187
Gilligan, Carol, 171
God, 50, 52, 53, 56, 92, 95, 102, 137, 205, 246, 266, 267, 271, 273; arguments against, 241–43; Aristotle's, 84; City of, 186; in the contemporary world, 60; as creator, 230; in Deism, 197; divine love, 233–34; eternity of, 228–29; existence of, 110, 130; as the Father, 253; laws of, 188, 189; as male, 228; Mind of, 111, 112, 113; moral nature of, 163, 231; omnipotence of, 227–28; as a person,

230–31; and philosophy, 42–45, 177, 225–27, 243–46; proof of, 87; purposes of, 233; uniqueness of, 227; Will of, 6, 178, 193, 203
Goethe, J. W. von, 57, 93
Good Life, The, 7, 39, 42, 60, 166, 185, 212
Gorgias, 105–6, 108
Gospels, 161, 228
Greatest Happiness Principle, 150–51

Habermas, Jürgen, 213, 216–17, 218, 280; discourse ethics, 216–17; *Theory of Communicative Action,* 216–17
Hamilton, William, 58
Hamlet, 236
Hedonism, 39, 150, 156
Hegel, Georg Wilhelm Friedrich, 57, 60, 64, 69, 95–97, 101–2, 121, 124, 126, 203, 204, 207, 209, 215; Absolute Idea, 62, 96, 98, 101, 121, 207; dialectical method, 96–97, 207, 214; *Phenomenology of Spirit,* 96
Heidegger, Martin, 64, 102, 268, 269, 274; *Being and Time,* 102
Hempel, Carl, 63
Heraclitus, 34, 79
Herder, Johann Gottfried, 55
Hermeneutics, 122, 128, 165
Hick, John, 233
Hinduism, 104, 110, 230
Historicism, 121
History, 124, 177, 193, 205, 208, 220
Hobbes, Thomas, 55, 189–95, 198, 200, 218, 220; *Leviathan,* 189, 190, 191
Horkheimer, Max, 213, 215
Hügel, Friedrich von, 230
Hume, David, 55, 91, 92, 115–17, 119, 120, 124, 173–74, 239–40, 241. Works: *Dialogues on Natural Religion,* 55; *An Enquiry concerning Human Understanding,* 55; *An Enquiry concerning the Principles of Morals,* 55; *History of England,* 55; *Treatise on Human Nature,* 55
Husserl, Edmund, 64, 102, 124, 125, 268; *Logical Investigations,* 102
Huxley, T. H., 261
Hypothetical statements, 18, 19

Idealism, Metaphysical, 87, 88, 177
Idolatry, 227
Illusions, 75, 77, 93, 100
Immortality, 52, 88, 262
Incest, 133

Index

Incommensurability, 65, 128, 165
Induction, 15, 21, 117, 132
Industrial Revolution, 56–57
Innate ideas, 113–14, 118
Intentionality, 263
Islam, 84, 225, 226, 227, 228, 230, 241, 245

James, William, 62, 129, 130, 131; "Hunter and Squirrel," 130; *Varieties of Religious Experience,* 129
Jaspers, Karl, 64
Jesus, 38, 60, 158, 161, 186; *Sermon on the Mount,* 124
Judaism, 38, 42, 84, 101, 139, 140, 147, 148, 165, 225, 226, 227, 228, 230, 241, 245
Justice, 31, 76, 140, 143, 155–56, 177, 180, 182, 186, 193, 195, 210, 216, 217, 219, 222

Kant, Immanuel, 51, 93, 95, 96, 100, 102, 118, 119, 121, 124, 148, 158–61, 164, 165, 172, 174, 217, 237; antinomies of pure reason, 95; categorical/hypothetical imperative, 161–63, 166; disinterested rational spectator, 159, 169; good will, 159–60, 163–64; transcendental unity of apperception, 120; unity/plurality, 120. Works: *Critique of Pure Reason,* 55, 94, 95, 118, 120; *Fundamental Principles of the Metaphysic of Morals,* 158
Kierkegaard, Søren, 58, 59; *Concluding Unscientific Postscript,* 58
Kropotkin, P. A., 221
Kuhn, Thomas, 123

Law, 38, 92, 178, 185, 188, 193, 197, 198, 200, 211
Leeuwenhoek, A. van, 49
Legalism, 148, 187
Leibniz, Gottfried Wilhelm, 53–54, 119, 240, 241–42. Works: *Discourse on Metaphysics,* 53; *Monadology,* 53; *Theodicy,* 53, 242
Leucippus, 88
Liberalism, 177, 179, 210, 217, 222
Lieber, Francis, 250
Linguistic Philosophy, 27, 128, 227, 243, 265
Locke, John, 55, 89, 90, 91, 115, 148, 193–95, 197, 200, 208, 218, 220, 221, 228; *tabula rasa,* 89, 114. Works: *An Essay concerning Human*

Understanding, 114, 199; *Treatises of Civil Government,* 194–96
Logic, 11, 13, 53, 63, 96, 120, 166
Logos, 34
Love, 34, 49, 78, 134, 233–23, 242, 244–45
Lyotard, Jean François, 65; *The Postmodern Condition,* 65

MacIntyre, Alasdair, 165–67, 280; *After Virtue,* 165; "Enlightenment project," 165, 167, 265
Mackie, J. L., 138; *Ethics: Inventing Right and Wrong,* 138
Marcel, Gabriel, 64
Marcus Aurelius, 40; *Meditations,* 41
Marcuse, Herbert, 213
Marx, Karl, 57, 89, 101, 204–10, 213, 178; alienation, 204, 207, 209; business cycles, 208–9, 214; class struggle, 207, 208, 265. Works: *Communist Manifesto,* 47, 204, 207, 209; *Das Kapital,* 57, 204, 208, 214, 250; *Economic and Political Manuscripts of 1844,* 206; *The German Ideology,* 57, 210; *The Poverty of Philosophy,* 207; *Theses on Feuerbach,* 208
Marxism, 63, 65, 122, 179
Material implication, 18, 120
Materialism, metaphysical, 87, 88, 107, 260, 263
Merleau-Ponty, Maurice, 124
Metaphysics, 54, 59, 60, 69, 93, 98, 103, 128, 131, 138, 185, 226, 229, 257, 260, 265
Metascience, 5
Michelangelo, 81, 83
Milesian philosophy, 33, 113
Mill, John Stuart, 7, 58, 149, 153–54, 156, 158, 163, 166, 210–13, 218; *act utilitarianism,* 156; *On Liberty,* 155, 211; *rule utilitarianism,* 153–56
Mimesis, 78
Mind-Body Problem, 86, 113, 262
Modus Ponens, 20, 22, 25
Mohammed, 226
Monarchy, 188, 189, 192
Monotheism, 227, 228, 230, 240, 242, 266
Montesquieu, Charles-Louis de Sconday, Baron de, 55, 196
Moore, G. E., 125, 126, 128
Morality, 5, 39, 55, 133, 134
Moral Law, 92, 137, 146, 148, 157, 162, 163, 202, 231, 271
Moral Relativism, 138

Moral responsibility, 136, 139, 187, 174, 242; obligation, 175
Moses, 157, 158
Motivationalism, 146–47, 157, 161
Myth, 32–33, 148

Nagel, Thomas, 29
Napoleon, 61
Natural Law, 38, 148, 156, 178, 189, 191, 192, 193, 195, 197
Nazism, 102, 203, 213, 271, 274
Necessary existence, 237, 238
Necessary and sufficient conditions, 80
Neo-Platonism, 38
Neurophysiology, 260–65
Newton, Isaac, 48, 53, 92, 95, 115, 118, 123, 248; *Principia Mathematica* (Mathematical Principles of Natural Philosophy), 50
Nietzsche, Friedrich, 59, 65, 98, 101, 156; Death of God, 59, 61, 266; transvaluation of all values, 101; superman, 59, 102; will to power, 101, 259. Works: *Beyond Good and Evil,* 59, 100; *The Genealogy of Morals,* 101; *Thus Spoke Zarathustra,* 59
Nominalism, 100, 112
Noncognitivism, 263
Normative ethics, 133, 134
Nozick, Robert, 218, 221–23, 280; *Anarchy, State and Utopia*, 218, 221–23; distribution pattern, 223; Lockean Proviso, 222

Obligation, 146, 175
Ockham, William of, 45, 112; Ockham's Razor, 45
Oligarchy, 192
Omnipotence, 227–28, 231
Omniscience, 227, 228–29
Ontological Argument, 235–37
Ontology, 92, 93
Ortega y Gasset, José, 62

Paideia, 9
Pantheism, 230
Parliament, 192
Parmenides 34, 75, 82, 93, 106, 107
Peirce, Charles Sanders, 62, 129
Perception, 75, 90, 91, 94, 107, 109, 113, 114, 118, 120, 126, 137
Phenomenology, 96, 102, 124, 265, 268
Philosophical anthropology, 226
Philosophy, nature of, 3, 4, 5, 6, 31, 48, 78, 103, 177, 189, 208, 225, 265

Philosophy of religion, 60, 177, 225–40
Picasso, Pablo, 60
Planck, Max, 60
Plato, 6, 11, 35, 36, 37, 39, 41, 43, 52, 60, 64, 70, 79, 80, 81, 83, 84, 89, 103, 108, 110, 139, 144, 173, 175, 177, 182, 183, 185, 208, 231; academy, 36, 79, 247; allegory of the cave, 9–11, 77; Demiurge, 78; Euthyphro question, 6, 231; forms, 36, 38, 76, 77, 78, 79, 88, 92, 95, 110, 111, 112, 115, 131, 139, 140, 143, 180, 185, 229; Gorgias, 105; guardians, 181, 182, 184; Laches, 76, 77; Philosopher-kings, 181, 182, 183, 184. Works: *Apology,* 74; *Dialogues,* 76; *Euthydemus,* 144; *Laws,* 36; *Meno,* 113; *Republic,* 10, 36, 77, 140, 179, 181, 182, 184; *Statesman,* 36; *Theaetetus,* 27; *Timaeus,* 36, 78
Plausibility, 23, 26
Plotinus, 38
Polemarchus, 179
Polis, 9, 38, 142, 143, 180, 181, 184
Positivism, 127
Postmodernism, 65
Pragmatism, 62, 128–30, 215
Pre-Socratic Philosophy, 71, 73, 75
Precising definitions, 24
Primary and secondary qualities, 113–15
Prime matter, 80
Principle of sufficient reason, 53–54, 267
Prometheus, 32
Protagoras, 35, 108
Proudhon, Pierre Joseph, 221
Psychoanalysis, 251, 260
Psychology, 171, 190, 191, 251, 254, 255, 259, 260
Putnam, Hilary, 63, 129
Pythagoras, 3, 4

Quine, Willard van Orman, 63, 129

Radicalism, 177
Raphael de Sanza, 36–37, 131, 132
Rationalism, 52, 84, 86, 93, 112–14
Rawls, John, 218–20, 280; original position, 220; *Theory of Justice,* 218, 223
Realism, epistemological, 126, 177
Reason, 13, 118
Reference and meaning, 264, 126
Reincarnation, 42, 262
Rembrandt Harmensz van Rijn, 154
Renaissance, 45, 49, 60
Rights, 178, 192, 193, 196, 200

Index

Roman Empire, 37, 38, 40, 41, 42, 43, 101, 186, 197
Romanticism, 121, 197, 201, 209
Rorty, Richard, 65, 129, 131; *Philosophy and the Mirror of Nature,* 130
Roscelinus, 112
Rousseau, Jean-Jacques, 197–204, 207, 208, 233; "Forced to Be Free," 202, 210; General Will, 197, 200, 201, 202, 203. Works: *Autobiography,* 197; *Confessions,* 198; *Discourses on the Sciences and the Arts,* 198; *Discourse upon the Origin and the Foundation of Inequality among Men,* 198; *Julie, ou La Nouvelle Héloise,* 198; *Social Contract,* 198
Rule-based ethics, 145
Russell, Bertrand, 18, 61, 125–27
Russian Revolution, 61, 64
Ryle, Gilbert, 63

Santayana, George, 71
Sartre, Jean Paul, 64, 267–74; authenticity, 265, 273; bad faith, 272–74; being-for-itself, 271, 274; being-in-itself, 269, 271, 273, 274; dread, 272; existence precedes essence, 271; facticity, 273. Works: *Being and Nothingness,* 64, 267, 268, 270, 274; "Existentialism is a Humanism," 271
Scanlon, Thomas, 166, 172, 173, 174; *What We Owe to Each Other,* 167, 173
Scheler, Max, 64, 102, 122–25, 247–48, 250, 265
Schelling, Friedrich Wilhelm Joseph, 57, 95, 121
Schiller, Johann Christoph Friedrich von, 57
Schlick, Moritz, 127
Scholasticism, 44
Schönberg, Arnold, 60
Science, nature of, 5, 13, 37, 48, 50, 54–55, 73, 83, 92, 122, 125, 128, 132, 214, 226, 250, 260, 265
Scientific Revolution, 49, 102–3
Searle, John, 264; "Chinese room experiment," 264
Seneca, Lucius Annaeus, 40
Sense-data, 120, 127
Sentential variable, 20
Sextus Empiricus, 108, 115
Shakespeare, William, 154
Simonides, 179
Sin, 205, 242

Skepticism, 39, 93, 105, 116, 122, 137, 238
Skinner, B. F., 254–60, 261, 262, 263, 270; stimulus-response mechanisms, 255. Works: *Science and Human Behavior,* 261; *Walden II,* 255, 256, 259, 260
Slavery, 97, 202
Smith, Adam, 55
Social Contract, 202, 203, 207
Sociology of knowledge, 122
Socrates, 6, 7, 10, 33, 36, 59, 60, 71, 73, 74, 76, 77, 144, 145, 166, 175, 179, 189, 181, 182, 231–32
Solidarity, 200, 261, 205
Sophism and sophists, 4, 35, 36, 144, 179, 181
Soul, 9, 120, 140, 143
Space and time, 119, 228–29, 238; consciousness of, 269
Spencer, Herbert, 58, 141, 142
Spinoza, Benedict, 53, 125, 235–36
Stalin, Joseph, 61
State of nature, 39, 40, 41, 194, 198
Stoicism, 39–41
Strawson, Peter, 64
Syllogism, 16, 20
Synthetic statements, 119

Tarski, Alfred, 18, 63
Taylor, Charles, 169; *Philosophical Arguments,* 169
Teleological Argument, 235, 239–40
Teleological ethics, 163, 171
Teleology, 81, 84, 141, 142
Ten Commandments, 5, 52, 139, 148, 186
Thales, 33, 34, 48, 70, 71, 72, 106, 107, 265, 273
Theodicy, 241–42, 243
Thought-experiments, 131, 168, 218
Thrasymachus, 179, 180
Tillich, Paul, 64
Timocracy, 185
Torah, 228
"Tree in the Forest," 108
Trolley experiment, 168
Trust, 28, 29, 134, 173
Truth, 17, 23, 25, 26, 35, 52, 76, 87, 104, 106, 126, 234, 244
Truth-functional logic, 16–17
Truth-table, 17, 20
Turing, Allan, 261
Turing Test, 261, 263, 264
Tyranny, 180, 184, 203

Ulpian, 38
Use and mention, 28
Utilitarianism, 149, 150, 152–57, 210, 212, 215, 219
Utopianism, 179

Vagueness, 24, 28
Verdi, Giuseppe, 135
Verifiability criterion of meaningfulness, 127, 245
Vienna circle, 127
Virtue, 134, 139, 140, 142, 144, 145, 164, 170, 181, 182, 184, 185, 188
Voltaire, François-Marie Arouet, 51, 55, 197
Voluntarism, 45, 232

Warrant, 21, 24–27
Watson, James, 258
Weiss, Paul, 64

Whewell, William, 58
Whitehead, Alfred North, 61, 63; *Process and Reality,* 63–64
Williams, Bernard, 166, 174; *Ethics and the Limits of Philosophy,* 166
Wilson, Edward O., 258
Wisdom, John, 63, 280
Wittgenstein, Ludwig, 27, 63, 126, 127, 245. Works: *Philosophical Investigations,* 63, 128; *Tractatus Logico-Philosophicus,* 127, 128
Wordsworth, William, 234
World War I, 61, 81, 213
World War II, 61, 165, 213, 215
Wundt, Wilhelm, 250

Young Hegelians, 57

Zeus, 32

About the Author

EUGENE KELLY is Professor of Philosophy, New York Institute of Technology. He is the former chairman of the Long Island Philosophical Society and a co-editor of the American Philosophical Association's Newsletter, Teaching Philosophy. He is the author of *Structure and Diversity* (1997).